P9-CDJ-248

Linda gave to me
Sept. 22nd @
Quilts for valuer
cca p̄ here garage
sale - she encouraging
me to Quilt

THE Quilters' COMPANION

Everything You Need to Know to Make Beautiful Quilts

Mimi Dietrich
Donna Thomas
Joan Hanson
Jeana Kimball
with Roxanne Carter and Roxi Eppler

MISSION STATEMENT

WE ARE DEDICATED TO PROVIDING QUALITY PRODUCTS THAT ENCOURAGE CREATIVITY AND PROMOTE SELF-ESTEEM IN OUR CUSTOMERS AND OUR EMPLOYEES.

WE STRIVE TO MAKE A DIFFERENCE IN THE LIVES WE TOUCH

That Patchwork Place is an employee-owned, financially secure company.

The Quilters' Companion: Everything You Need to Know to Make Beautiful Quilts ©
© 1994 by That Patchwork Place
PO Box 118, Bothell, WA 98041-0118 USA

Printed in the United States of America
99 98 97 96 95 94   6 5 4 3 2 1

No part of this product may be reproduced in any form, unless otherwise stated, in which case reproduction is limited to the use of the purchaser. The written instructions, photographs, designs, projects, and patterns are intended for the personal use of the retail purchaser and are under federal copyright laws; they are not to be reproduced by any electronic, mechanical, or other means, including informational storage or retrieval systems, for commercial use.

The information in this book is presented in good faith, but no warranty is given nor results guaranteed. Since That Patchwork Place, Inc., has no control over choice of materials or procedures, the company assumes no responsibility for the use of this information.

Library of Congress Cataloging-in-Publication Data

The quilter's companion: everything you need to know to
    make beautiful quilts / Mimi Dietrich . . . [et al.].
        p.   cm.
        ISBN 1-56477-040-0:
        1. Quilting. 2. Patchwork. 3. Appliqué.   I. Dietrich,
Mimi.
    TT835.Q5359 1994
    746.9'7—dc20   93–45437
                                            CIP

CREDITS

Editor-in-Chief . . . . Barbara Weiland
Technical Editor . . . . Ursula Reikes
Managing Editor . . . . Greg Sharp
Copy Editor . . . . Liz McGehee
Proofreader . . . . Tina Cook
Text and Cover Design . . . . Judy Petry
Typesetting . . . . Laura Jensen
Photography . . . . Brent Kane
Illustration and
Graphics . . . . Stephanie Benson
            Linda & Chris Gentry of Artworks
                        Karin LaFramboise
                        Joanne Lauterjung
                        Nicki Salvin-Wight
                        André Samson
                        Laurel Strand

CONTENTS

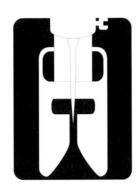

SHORTCUTS

A PERFECT MATCH

THE ART OF APPLIQUÉ

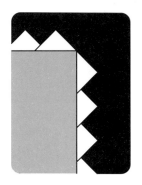

SENSATIONAL SETTINGS

LOVING STITCHES

HAPPY ENDINGS

PREFACE

My interest in quiltmaking was sparked in the early 1970s, while I was the editor at a New York City publishing house. At that time, I was working on a book of patterns that were being adapted for contemporary needlework from designs found in vintage magazines, such as *Godey's Lady's Book* and *The Delineator*. While the book was to feature patterns for several forms of needlework, I was particularly drawn to the quilt patterns that figured prominently in the stitchery repertoire of Victorian women and to those that turned up in magazines of the 1930s when quiltmaking experienced its first modern revival. As a result of this new interest, I decided to include several quilts in *Needlework Nostalgia,* along with patterns suitable for a variety of other forms of needlework.

Of course, that meant it was necessary to create quilts for the photographs in the book. As I searched the stacks in the library for information on quiltmaking, it became apparent that instruction books for quilting and patchwork were all but nonexistent. At best, I could find a few basic instructions buried in short chapters on other techniques. Undaunted by the lack of instructions, I made the quilts anyway, relying on my sewing skills. Since I was a proficient home sewer, it was easy for me to cut and machine stitch simple quilt designs. The quiltmaking directions I included in *Needlework Nostalgia* were adequate but did not add substantially to the printed body of knowledge about quiltmaking.

Needlework Nostalgia was published in 1976—the year that quilt historians recognize as the beginning of the current revival. Since then,

quiltmaking has seen many changes, and there has been a proliferation of quilt pattern books that include basic quiltmaking techniques. Books on revolutionary quiltmaking methods are also available, but until now, it has been difficult to find everything you wanted to know about quiltmaking in one basic reference.

To fill that need, we created *The Quilters' Companion,* a compilation of quiltmaking techniques from some of the leading authorities in the field. In this unique volume, you will find everything you need to know about rotary cutting and machine piecing or appliquéing the blocks for your quilt, followed by directions for planning a setting for your quilt and adding borders, hand quilting it, and finishing the edges. Each subject is treated in depth in a separate chapter with its own expanded table of contents. The chapters, each one a small book in itself, are organized in the order you would follow to make a quilt, from cutting to finishing. As a bonus, several quilt patterns are included so you can practice the techniques you learn as you read. And to make it easy to find everything, we've included a comprehensive index at the back of the book.

I know that you will turn to *The Quilters' Companion* again and again as you explore the wonderful world of quiltmaking. You'll find the answers to your questions and the directions you need to make each of your quiltmaking projects an enriching and exciting experience.

Barbara Weiland
Editor

QUILTMAKING TERMS

There are many more elements besides quilt blocks that make up a quilt. Since these terms will be used throughout this book, it is important to become familiar with them by studying the illustration and definitions that follow. Alternate names for terms are given in parentheses.

Common Quilt Terms

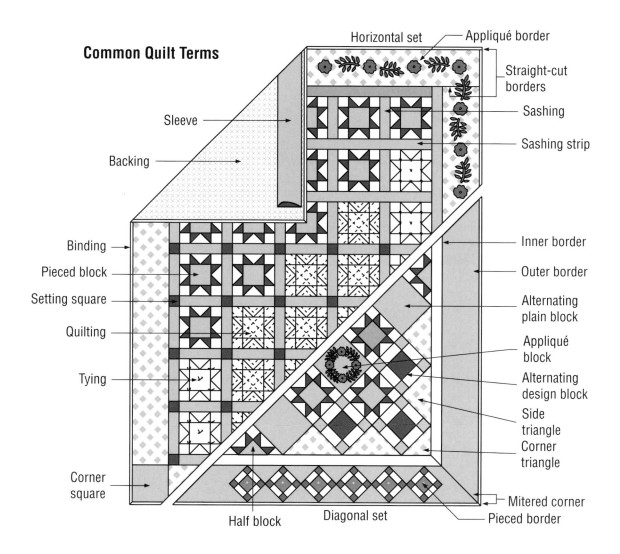

Alternating Plain Block. A block made out of one whole piece of fabric that is placed between stitched blocks. It is often embellished with an elaborate quilting pattern.

Alternating Design Block. A pieced or appliquéd block that is placed between the main stitched blocks. They usually "join up" with the main blocks to move the design across the quilt.

Appliqué Block. A design made up of small (usually curved) pieces that are stitched by hand or machine onto a larger background block that forms a unit of the quilt top.

Appliqué Border. A design made up of small (usually curved) pieces that are stitched by hand or machine onto long strips that form the border of the quilt.

Backing (lining). A large piece of fabric that covers the back of a quilt. It may have to be seamed together from more than one piece of fabric for a large quilt.

Batting. A layer inside the quilt, sandwiched between the quilt top and the quilt backing. It is usually a fluffy polyester, cotton, wool, or silk (or some combination thereof) that adds warmth and texture to the quilt.

Binding. A fabric strip, cut on either the straight of grain or the bias, that is stitched to the edge of a quilt to cover the raw edges.

Block. Usually a square or rectangular design unit that is pieced or appliquéd. Typically, quilt tops are made by repeating one or more quilt block designs in a pleasing arrangement.

Border. The area surrounding the main body of the quilt top. It acts like the frame on a picture to enhance the design. It may be a pieced or appliquéd design, or it may be made of one or more strips of fabric of varying widths.

Corner Square. A square of fabric sometimes used to join adjacent border strips.

Cornerstone (corner post, setting square, sashing square). A square of fabric at the intersection of two sashings. It may be one piece of fabric, or pieced or appliquéd.

Corner Setting Triangle. A quarter-square triangle used to fill in the four corners of a diagonally set quilt before the borders (if any) are added.

Diagonal Set (on-point set). A design arranged so the blocks are pieced together in diagonal rows, with side and corner triangles added to complete the rows.

Half Block. Half of a design unit used to fill in at the side, top, or bottom of a diagonally set quilt to create a straight edge.

Horizontal Set (straight set). A design arranged so that the blocks and other components are oriented horizontally and vertically.

Mitered Corner (set-in corner). A point where three seams intersect at an angle to form a "Y."

Pieced Block. Small pieces of fabric in various shapes stitched together by hand or machine to form a larger design.

Pieced Border. A design made up of small shapes stitched together into long strips that form the border of the quilt.

Quilt Top. The upper layer of a quilt that is usually appliquéd or pieced to form the overall design. It can be made up of any combination of blocks, sashing, setting squares, and borders.

Sashing Strip (lattice strip). A strip of fabric sewn between two rows of blocks.

Sashing (lattice). Strips of fabric sewn between blocks.

Side Setting Triangle (edge triangle). A half-square triangle used to fill in at the side, top, or bottom of a diagonally set quilt to create a straight edge. These should be cut so the straight grain of the fabric is on the long side of the triangle to add stability to the quilt and prevent stretching along the edges.

Sleeve (rod pocket). A tube attached to the backing at the top edge of a quilt so that a hanging rod or dowel can be inserted.

Straight-Cut Border. A border that is applied to the quilt top in two steps. First, border strips are stitched to two opposite sides (usually the longest sides). Then the remaining borders are stitched to the quilt and already-attached borders. The two sets of borders butt into each other rather than meeting at an angle, as in a mitered corner.

General Information

Fabric for Quilts

A love of color and design in fabric is the common denominator that draws people from all walks of life to quiltmaking. Most quiltmakers prefer to use 100% cotton fabrics for their quilts, because it is durable and it has the wonderful ability to adhere to itself, preventing slippage and puckering while you sew. Fabrics made of synthetic and synthetic/natural fiber blends are often quite slippery and are more difficult to handle. Cotton fabrics do not fray as easily as other fabric types and they are easier to press. That makes it easy to match seam intersections as you assemble the blocks and sew them together into a finished quilt top.

Fabric Preparation

To prepare fabrics for quiltmaking, the generally accepted rule is to prewash washable fabrics to preshrink them and to make sure that the dyes will not run in the finished quilt. However, there are many schools of thought about prewashing fabrics. Use the following information to help you decide how to prepare your fabrics.

- Cottons and cotton blends usually shrink at different rates. If you are mixing them in a quilt, it is best to prewash all of them.
- Cottons of different weights and weaves also shrink at different rates. Prewash all fabrics when mixing different weights, even those of the same fiber content.
- If one of the fabrics you are using has been prewashed, it is best to wash them all.
- Specialty fabrics, such as silk or metallics, may require dry cleaning. Since the entire quilt will require dry cleaning, it is not necessary to prewash the other fabrics—unless you really want to.

To test fabrics for bleeding:

If you decide to prewash your fabric, it is extremely important to test it for bleeding. When fabrics have excess dye, the dye runs or bleeds in the wash water. Some fabrics, especially dark- or bright-colored ones, continue to bleed through several washings. Vinegar and salt baths, commonly suggested as remedies, are only temporary preventative solutions.

To test fabric for running or bleeding:
1. Cut a 6" swatch of fabric and drop it into a jar of boiling water. Wait twenty minutes.
2. If the water is clear after twenty minutes, the fabric is safe to use in your quilt. If the water changes color, do further testing.
3. Empty the jar, retain the swatch, and repeat the process until the water no longer changes color. This will help you determine whether you need to wash the yardage more than once to remove excess dye.
4. Wash the fabrics that require it; rinse several times to ensure that the excess dye is gone. If the fabric continues to bleed after several baths, consider using a different fabric in your quilt.

To prewash quilt fabrics:
1. Wash fabrics in lukewarm water. Extremely hot or cold water damages natural fabrics.
2. Use a very mild detergent or substitute Orvis washing paste, which is recommended by quilt conservators, or plain, sudsy ammonia. Ammonia is mild, inexpensive, and environmentally safe. Use ¼ cup in the washer or 1 tablespoon in an average-sized sink of warm water.
3. Fluff dry or hang the fabric over a line until it is damp dry.
4. Fold fabric in half with selvages matching and press. If the fabric is slippery or difficult to handle, apply a bit of spray sizing.
5. Store in a dry place, away from direct sunlight.

After selecting the quilt you want to make and preparing the fabrics you will use, it's time to cut the pieces. If you prefer rotary cutting and strip piecing, turn to "Shortcuts," beginning on page 9. If you prefer to cut the pieces using templates, turn to "A Perfect Match," beginning on page 63.

Shortcuts

A CONCISE GUIDE TO ROTARY CUTTING

CONTENTS

INTRODUCTION

It is human nature to constantly seek out new ways and new tools to accomplish a task. It is this quality in man that took us from caves into organized agriculture and society and on into our modern world. Of course, on a much humbler level, it has resulted in a revolution in the world of quiltmaking. Innovations along the way, such as marked sewing lines, layered cutting, plastic for templates, and a myriad of "tricks-of-the-trade," have made the job easier.

Several years ago, some ingenious mind devised the idea of quick piecing. Sewing strips of fabric together first and cutting them into segments saves time and avoids the tedious marking and cutting required when you use traditional templates to cut the many pieces required for a patchwork quilt. Someone also thought of using an office paper cutter to quickly cut quantities of strips. The idea was hot; quilters began seeing tremendous possibilities, and they set their minds to work. What followed was an avalanche of ideas and techniques for quick-piecing quilts. Somewhere in the midst of this, tools for accurate quick cutting—the rotary cutter and ruler—emerged. Consequently, they became the perfect companions for quick piecing.

There are some who dismiss these modern techniques because they feel they take away from the primary pleasures of quiltmaking. This may be true for some, but generally, there is a place for both the old and new in our lives. Even though I do most of my piecing by machine, I still need the quiet, retrospective time spent hand piecing and hand quilting, so there is always a "by-hand" project in my quilt basket. On the other hand, sometimes I can't wait to see an idea come together, and other times rotary cutting and fast piecing are the only techniques that provide accuracy needed to make certain quilts, such as the tiny miniature quilts I dearly love to make.

The Shortcuts section of this book includes these basic quick-cutting techniques and a number of techniques that expand the basics. They are intended not only to inform you but also to get your mental juices flowing with other possibilities. As you explore these methods, you most likely will discover some shortcuts of your own.

If on the other hand, you prefer using templates for hand or machine piecing, turn to the next chapter, "A Perfect Match," beginning on page 63.

Donna Lynn Thomas

GENERAL INFORMATION

One of the first things you'll notice about rotary cutting is the absence of a marked sewing line on the fabric. Seam allowances (the traditional ¼" on each side) are included in the dimensions of the pieces. Be sure to remember this when working with patterns geared specifically for rotary cutting. It is even more important to remember to add the seam allowances to your figuring when preparing to adapt your own patterns for rotary cutting. Included here is all the information you need to properly figure what size to cut your pieces to obtain the desired finished size.

Generally, the use of a rotary cutter eliminates the need to use hard templates, although you will find that there are instances where you do use paper cutting guides attached to the ruler to accurately quick-cut shapes with odd sizes or angles. Once you make your cutting guide, the method is quick and accurate compared to individual hand marking.

With the discussion of each geometric shape, you will find a sample block using that shape and also an icon identifying that shape. Icons  provide a quick visual means of identifying what needs to be cut for a particular pattern without lengthy descriptions. They are like a quilter's shorthand. Icons in this book help show you how to adapt several block patterns for rotary cutting.

Icon

All the accurate cutting methods in the world won't mean a thing if your sewing is not accurate. Be careful to stitch accurate ¼"-wide seams. A first step is to check the accuracy of your machine's ¼" guide by doing a strip test. Cut three 1½" x 3" strips and seam them together side by side. When sewn, the center strip should measure exactly 1". If not, try shifting your machine needle one notch to the right, or

mark a new guide on the throat plate of your machine with masking tape.

1. Align the ¼" mark on a piece of graph paper just to the left of the needle. Put the unthreaded needle into the paper just to the right of the ¼" grid line so the needle is included in the ¼" area.

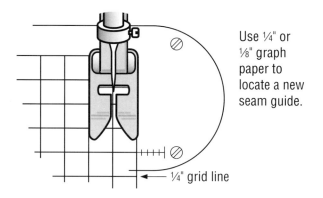

Use ¼" or ⅛" graph paper to locate a new seam guide.

¼" grid line

2. Place masking tape on the throat plate along the right edge of the graph paper. Adjust the guide so that it runs straight down from the needle and is not angled to either left or right. Remove the graph paper.

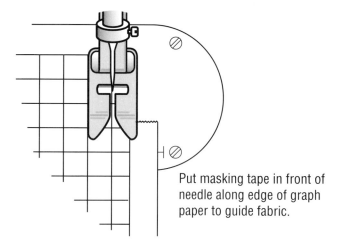

Put masking tape in front of needle along edge of graph paper to guide fabric.

Cut a new set of strips and try the strip test again with the new guide. Keep adjusting and testing the guide until you can produce a perfect 1" strip every time. Once you have the proper mark, build up several layers of tape or place a piece of adhesive-backed moleskin on the right side of this mark to better guide the fabric edge.

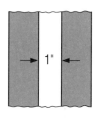

After you sew the three 1½" strips together side by side, center strip should measure a perfect 1" from seam to seam.

Equipment

SEWING MACHINE

Obviously, the most important piece of equipment for machine piecing is your sewing machine. It does not need to be a fancy machine; all that's really necessary is a machine that stitches forward and backward with a fine-quality straight stitch. Like any piece of equipment, it is important to maintain it properly. You should be familiar with its parts and operation, so take the time to read your owner's manual if you haven't done so already. You will be surprised at what you can learn from it.

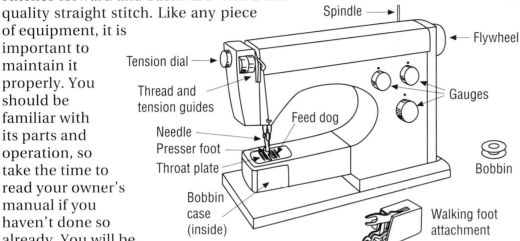

Spindle

Flywheel

Tension dial

Thread and tension guides

Feed dog

Needle

Presser foot

Throat plate

Gauges

Bobbin

Bobbin case (inside)

Walking foot attachment

In addition to a yearly professional service, which should be a regular part of the maintenance, clean and oil your machine regularly, following the directions in the manual. Generally, this involves a simple cleaning under the throat plate and in the bobbin housing to remove lint buildup. Oiling methods vary from brand to brand, so check your manual. If you clean the machine every time you begin a new quilt, you and your machine will spend many happy years together. Your local dealer can answer any specific questions you may have concerning your machine and its care and operation. If he can't help, write to the manufacturer.

ROTARY CUTTING TOOLS
Rotary Cutters

A rotary cutter is a round-bladed cutting instrument attached to a handle. It looks like a pizza cutter with a protective shield that is either manually or automatically released, depending on the model. Rotary cutters come in large and small sizes. Many quiltmakers prefer the larger blade as it stays sharp longer, but when working with miniature or small quilts, the small cutter is eaiser to use.

Be sure to keep several replacement blades on hand. Periodically, the blade will become dull or nicked and must be replaced. It is also necessary to clean the lint from between the blade and the front sheath. To do this, dismantle the cutter, carefully wiping the blade clean with a soft, clean cloth, and add a very small drop of sewing machine oil to the blade where it lies under the front sheath. You may find that your cutter feels like it has a new blade after this simple cleaning process.

Rotary blades are extremely sharp cutting instruments and must therefore be treated with great care to avoid accidents. Keep these tools well out of the reach of children—they can easily scver tiny fingers. Before using a cutter with a manual safety shield, make a practice of tightening the back screw so that the safety shield cannot be easily pushed back from the blade with simple pressure on the cutter. *Make it a habit to engage the manual safety mechanism at the completion of every single cutting stroke.*

Even though the automatic safety shield is designed to "remember" for us, cutters with the manual safety shield may actually be safer. The automatics have a spring mechanism that automatically covers the blade when not in use and easily retracts when pressure is applied for cutting. In addition to the obvious dangers in the hands of children, these mechanisms retract when dropped on adult feet or hands. Also, the automatic spring sometimes impedes cutting when working with several layers of fabric.

Another important safety precaution is to *always cut away from your body.* One slip or overly powerful stroke toward yourself could result in a painful cut.

Rotary Mats

You must have a rotary mat to use with your rotary cutter. If you try to cut fabric on anything but a mat specifically made for rotary cutters, you will immediately ruin both your blade and the cutting surface.

Mats are available in a variety of sizes. It is nice to have a large one for your cutting surface and a smaller, more portable one if you plan to take classes or take work with you when you travel. Always store your mats flat and keep them away from extreme temperatures that can warp them irreparably. Keep hot items such as irons, coffee pots, and mugs away from the mats.

Rotary Rulers

A good rotary ruler is an invaluable tool and a necessity for rotary cutting.

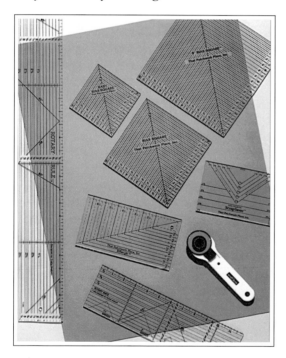

Rotary rulers are made of clear, hard acrylic that is ⅛" thick. They come in all shapes and sizes with an assortment of markings. A ruler with ⅛" markings is absolutely essential. These marks should appear on every inch line both horizontally and vertically. A ruler with 30°, 45°, and 60° lines is also essential. Of course, the corner of the ruler is the 90° guide.

A 24"-long ruler is useful when cutting large shapes and when cutting strips from fabric folded selvage to selvage. These rulers are usually 6" wide, which is helpful when cutting wide strips.

A 3" x 18" or 6" x 12" ruler is a nice size for most work as long as fabric is folded twice—selvage to selvage and then again to selvages.

It's also a good idea to keep a 1" x 6" ruler by your sewing machine to check for accuracy as you work. This ruler is definitely a must when working with small quilts or small pieces. One 15" x 15" is useful for cutting large squares.

You will also need the Bias Square®. It comes in three sizes—4" x 4" in linear; and 6" x 6" and 8" x 8" in either linear or metric versions—and has ⅛" markings with a 45°-angle line running diagonally, corner to corner. Its main use is for cutting presewn bias squares, but it serves many other useful purposes as you will learn later.

Until the Bias Square was introduced several years ago, the most advanced way to preassemble bias squares was to draw grid lines on two layers of fabric, sew the layers together on the lines, and then cut the grids apart. Unfortunately, this method has too many variables that increase the chances of inaccuracy with each step. The new bias-square method and the Bias Square, developed by Nancy J. Martin, enable quilters to construct highly accurate bias squares. The degree of accuracy is considerably greater and more easily attained with this new method, so it is the recommended method in this book for constructing bias squares.

Last, but not least, if you plan on using pieced rectangles in any of your quilts, consider purchasing Mary Hickey's BiRangle™ ruler. Her method for strip piecing and cutting presewn, pieced rectangles (pages 35–38) is a tremendous addition to any quilter's inventory of techniques.

BASIC SUPPLIES

Many books and patterns are available today with instructions specifically geared toward rotary cutting. Listed below are the supplies and equipment you will need to adapt your own pattern ideas to rotary-cutting specifications.

Graph paper. Every design begins with a drawing, whether full-size or to scale. It is important to have accurate ⅛"-or ¼"-grid graph paper on hand for your drawings. Some people like paper with the inch lines highlighted, but it is not necessary.

Lead Pencil. I prefer a fine-point mechanical pencil, but a well-sharpened, #2 lead pencil works equally well.

Eraser. Be sure to use a good-quality eraser for mistakes. An engineer's eraser does not damage the paper as easily as a basic school eraser does.

Tracing paper. Use for making paper cutting guides that you will tape to your rotary ruler for cutting certain shapes (pages 22–24).

Transparent tape. Use removable tape to avoid tearing your tracing paper.

Drafting ruler. A 3" x 18" rotary ruler is nice for drafting, not only because it has all the necessary markings but also because its angle markings are helpful in drafting diamonds, triangles, and other geometric shapes.

Scissors. Use a pair of sharp utility scissors to cut out paper cutting guides.

Iron and Ironing Board. A steam iron is ideal. Set on the cotton setting.

GETTING READY

Fabric and Grain Line

Each type of fabric grain has its own special properties. When fabric is woven on a loom, long warp yarns are attached to the front bar of the loom. If ten yards of fabric are desired, then the warp yarns are cut ten yards long, plus enough extra yardage to roll the ends tightly onto the bar on the opposite end of the loom. There are as many yarns lined up across the front bar as are needed to make the fabric as wide as desired. When the fabric is finished, these warp yarns are referred to as the lengthwise grain of the fabric.

Once the warp yarns are secured to the loom, yarns are wound on a shuttle and woven back and forth from side to side through the warp yarns. These new side-to-side weft yarns are referred to as the crosswise grain of the finished fabric. The process, though simplified, is the same process used in modern, mechanized fabric production.

Lengthwise grain has little or no give because the warp yarns are tightly secured at both ends during the weaving process. The lack of give means that edges cut parallel to this grain will not stretch very much.

Crosswise grain has a slight amount of give, since the weft yarns are not secured to anything except the warp yarns when woven from side to side. Even so, the yarn itself will only give so far, depending on its quality. Edges cut parallel to the crosswise grain can stretch slightly if roughly handled. *Cutting on either the lengthwise or crosswise grain is considered "cutting on grain,"* unless a pattern specifically instructs you to cut on one type of grain instead of the other.

Bias is anything other than lengthwise or crosswise grain, although true bias is defined as the direction running at a 45° angle to the two straight grains. Think of the lengthwise and crosswise grains as forming a square. Bias runs from corner to corner across the diagonal of the square. It has a generous amount of give when pulled since there are no diagonal yarns restraining it. Be careful when handling edges cut parallel to the bias. They are easily distorted and stretched, and become wavy if pulled and overhandled.

When making quilts, try to cut shapes as close to straight of grain (S-O-G) as possible. It's difficult to rotary cut strips that are true straight of grain, so you can settle for "close" grain with satisfactory results. Due to quirks of mass production, few fabrics are printed on grain, and many are stretched off grain when rolled onto bolts. A piece of fabric that is badly off grain can sometimes be straightened by holding opposite diagonal corners and pulling gently.

Cut all squares, strips, and rectangles on grain. Some shapes, such as triangles, cannot have all edges cut on grain. Therefore, it is a good idea to look at the position of the shape in the pattern and consider a few guidelines when deciding which edges should be cut on grain.

1. Place all edges on the perimeter of a quilt block on grain so the block does not stretch out of shape.
2. Whenever possible, without violating rule 1, sew a bias edge to a straight edge to stabilize the seam.

PREPARING THE FABRIC EDGES FOR CUTTING

Lay the freshly pressed fabric on the rotary mat with the fold toward you, the raw edges to the left (reverse if left-handed), and the selvages at the top of the mat. (See top right.)

Place the edge of your rotary ruler inside the raw edge of the fabric. To make a cut at a right angle to the fold, lay an edge of the Bias Square along the fold and adjust the straight ruler so that it is flush with the Bias Square. Now, push the Bias Square out of the way. Retract the rotary cutter's safety mechanism, place the blade next to the ruler's edge, and begin to cut slowly away from yourself with firm, downward pressure. (See photo at bottom right.) Hold the ruler absolutely still with firm, downward pressure, spreading fingers wide so the ruler doesn't shift. Some quilters anchor their ruler by placing their outer fingers or the palm of their hand on the

table to the left of the ruler.

As the blade rolls along the ruler's edge, you may need to slowly and carefully "walk" your hand up the ruler. Do not shift the ruler out of line. Cut completely past the selvages and engage the safety mechanism again before putting the cutter back on the table. This newly cut edge is now your straight-of-grain cutting edge.

Now you are ready to rotary cut the pieces of your quilt!

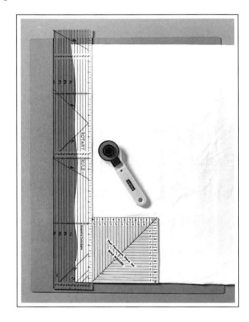

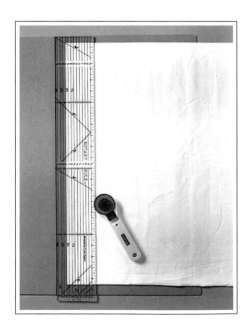

SIMPLE CUTTING

Strips

Almost all rotary cutting begins with strips of fabric that are then cut into other shapes, such as squares, triangles, rectangles, and diamonds. Strips are cut with the straight-of-grain cut edge on the left. (Reverse these directions if you are left-handed.) The rest of the fabric lies to the right.

Let's say you want to cut a 3"-wide strip. First, align the 3" line inside the right edge of your ruler with the prepared left edge of the fabric (page 16). In addition, place one of the ruler's horizontal lines even with the bottom edge of the fabric. If the cut is not at a right angle to the fold, you will end up with a "bent" strip. *Always cut strips ½" wider than the desired finished size to allow for ¼"-wide seams.* It is very important to remove the selvages from all strips before continuing so they are not accidentally included in any cut pieces or seam allowances.

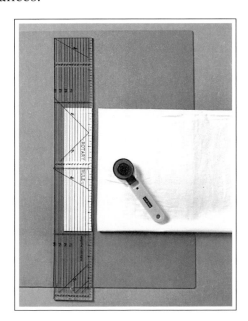

To cut a strip a particular length, line up the ruler to the proper length from the bottom at the same time you line up the width lines. After completing the upward cut, make a quick slice across the top of the ruler to cut a strip of the specified length. In this case, do not extend your upward cut all the way past the selvages of the fabric. However, it is usually faster to cut the strip all the way across the fabric width and then crosscut the desired length, saving excess pieces for other projects. This may not be advisable if you are short on fabric or if your quilt plan directs you to cut in a specific manner.

Squares

It is easy to cut squares from strips. If you need 2" squares for a Ninepatch block, for example, cut a 2"-wide strip. Then, turn the short end of the strip so it is facing left, and start cutting 2" squares from the left to the right.

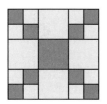

Ninepatch

Simple square: ☐

Be sure to align a horizontal line of the ruler or Bias Square across the bottom of the strip each time you prepare to cut. *Always cut squares from strips that are ½" wider than the desired finished size to account for the ¼"-wide seams required for piecing.*

The Bias Square is an excellent tool for cutting one or two squares. Lay the Bias Square at the lower left of the prepared fabric corner, with the appropriate marks on the fabric edges. Make a neat slice across the strip to yield the square.

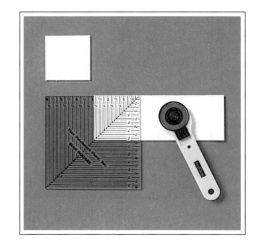

Right Triangles

There are two ways to cut right triangles for blocks, such as the Color Wheel block shown here.

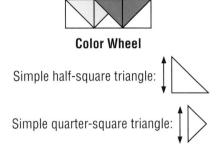

Color Wheel

Simple half-square triangle:

Simple quarter-square triangle:

To determine the method to use, choose the edge on which the straight of grain should be placed. Both methods begin with a square that is then cut into either two or four triangles.

HALF-SQUARE TRIANGLES

To cut a half-square triangle, cut a square in half on the diagonal. This yields two identical triangles with the straight of grain on the edges adjacent to the right-angle corner.

To compute the size square to cut, first determine the finished size of the short edge of the triangle. Add $\frac{7}{8}$" to this figure and cut a square this size. Then, cut the square in half on the diagonal as shown in the photo, above right. Once all the seams are sewn, it will be the correct size.

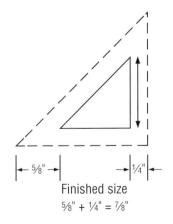

$\mapsto$ $\frac{5}{8}$" $\mapsto$ $\mapsto$ $\frac{1}{4}$" $\mapsto$

Finished size

$\frac{5}{8}$" + $\frac{1}{4}$" = $\frac{7}{8}$"

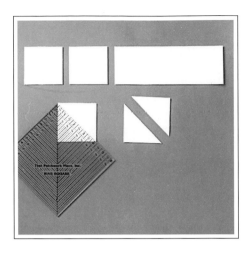

Half-square triangles are often used for the corner triangles of a quilt block or quilt top.

QUARTER-SQUARE TRIANGLES

To create this type of triangle, cut a square in half on the diagonal in both directions. A triangle cut in this fashion has the straight of grain on its long side.

To compute the size square needed for this method, determine the *finished size of the long side* of the triangle. To this figure, add $1\frac{1}{4}$" and cut a square that size. Now, cut the square in half on both diagonals.

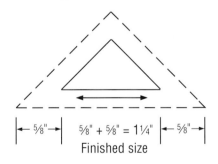

$\mapsto \frac{5}{8}" \mapsto$ $\frac{5}{8}" + \frac{5}{8}" = 1\frac{1}{4}"$ $\mapsto \frac{5}{8}" \mapsto$

Finished size

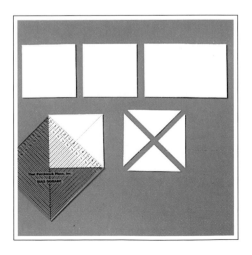

Quarter-square triangles are often used for the side triangles of a quilt block or quilt top. In many cases, the long edge is not an easily measured distance, but the short edge is the same size as the block piece next to it.

There are two ways to handle the situation. One is to overestimate the finished size of the long edge of the triangles, set them in, and then cut them to size after the quilt top or block is assembled. The second is to use half-square triangles instead, since these triangles are cut the finished length of the short side. Unfortunately, the bias is also on the long edge of these half-square triangles. Instead, you can cut the squares on point so the short edges are on the bias and the diagonal is on the straight of grain. When you cut a square like this in half, the triangles have the long edge on grain and the short edge is of a specific size.

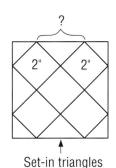

Set-in triangles

As an example, let's say you want to produce set-in triangles that are 2" long on the short edges and have the straight grain on the long edge. You will need to cut squares that measure 2⅞" (2" + ⅞" for half-square triangles). Cut these using the Bias Square. Lay the Bias Square on the fabric with its diagonal line on grain so that the point where the 2⅞" line meets the Bias Square's diagonal line lies within the fabric boundaries. Cut the top two edges, turn the piece around, align the 2⅞" marks with the cut edges, and cut the remaining two sides. Cut square in half diagonally.

Bars and Rectangles

Cut bars and rectangles, such as those in the Puss in the Corner block shown here, in a similar fashion to squares.

Puss in the Corner

Simple rectangle:

Cut strips ½" wider than the finished width of the shape and turn them sideways. Then cut bars or rectangles (finished length plus ½") from the strips.

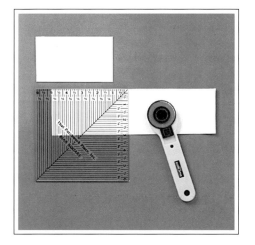

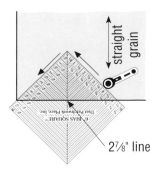

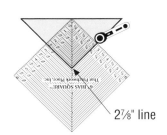

straight grain

2⅞" line   2⅞" line

Half Rectangles

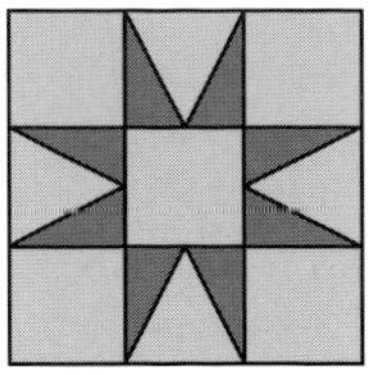

Simple half-rectangle: 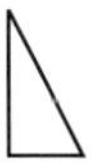

Star

Half rectangles, like those in the Star block, are cut from rectangles that are ⅝" larger than the desired finished width and 1¼" longer than the finished length. For instance, if you want two finished half rectangles, each 2" x 4", cut a full rectangle 2⅝" x 5¼" and then cut it in half on the diagonal. When all seams are sewn, the finished half rectangle will be the desired finished size.

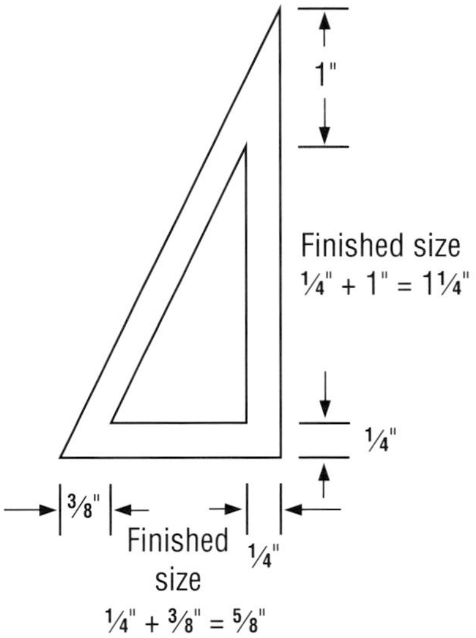
1"
Finished size
¼" + 1" = 1¼"
¼"
⅜"
Finished size
¼"
¼" + ⅜" = ⅝"

Equilateral Triangles

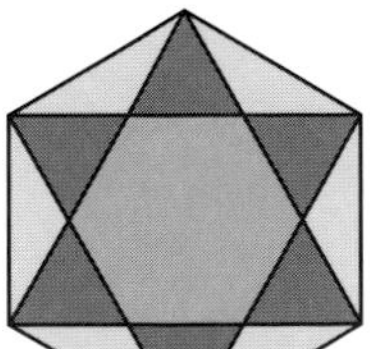

Simple equilateral triangle: 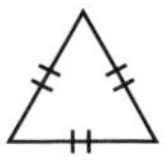

Colorado Star

Equilateral triangles, such as those in the Colorado Star block, are triangles that measure the same length on each of the three legs. The angle at each corner is 60°. Cut these triangles from fabric strips, using the 60° line on a rotary ruler.

Cut straight-of-grain strips that are ¾" wider than the finished height of the triangles. Add ⅞" to the finished length of the triangle leg. See triangle illustration below. On the raw edge of the strip, make marks this distance for as many triangles as you need.

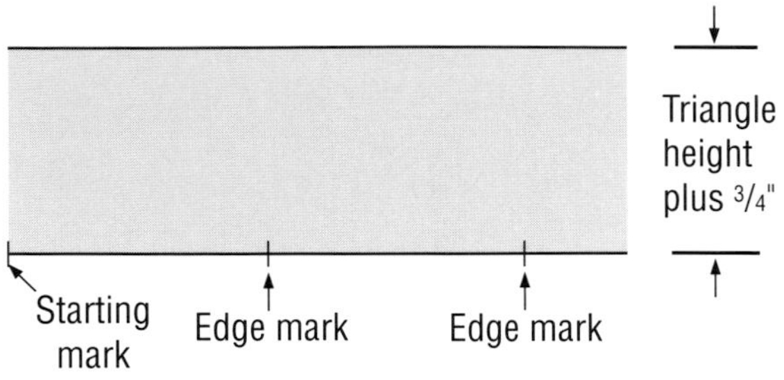
Triangle height plus ¾"
Starting mark
Edge mark
Edge mark

Make marks along strip edge ⅞" larger than finished size of triangle leg.

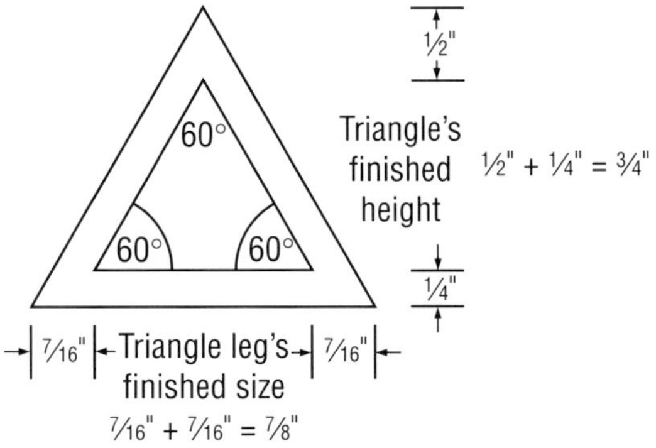
½"
60°
60°
60°
Triangle's finished height
½" + ¼" = ¾"
¼"
7/16"
Triangle leg's finished size
7/16"
7/16" + 7/16" = ⅞"

Align the 60° line of the ruler with the raw edge of the strip so that the straight edge of the ruler intersects the first leg mark on the edge. Make a cut from raw edge to raw edge.

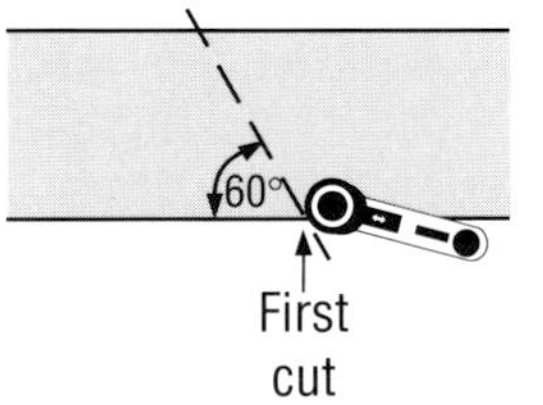
60°
First cut

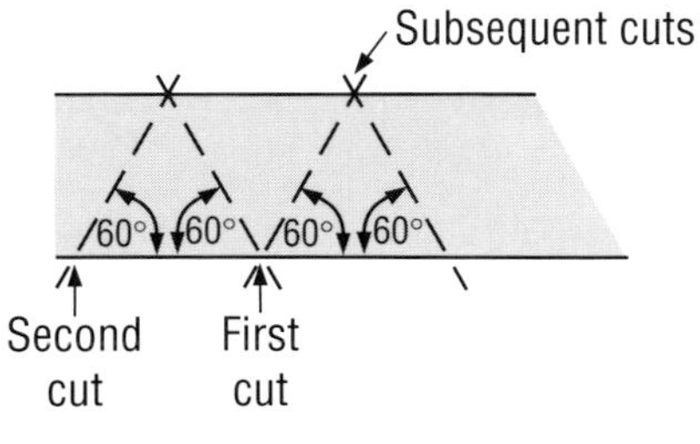
Subsequent cuts
60°
60°
60°
60°
Second cut
First cut

Rotate your ruler to the opposite side of the strip and continue cutting as many triangles as you need.

Diamonds

Full-size diamonds, such as those in the LeMoyne Star block, come in three basic, easy-to-cut sizes: 30°, 45°, and 60° diamonds.

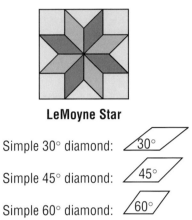

LeMoyne Star

Simple 30° diamond:
Simple 45° diamond:
Simple 60° diamond:

The degree indicates the angle of the narrow points. All three are easy to cut from straight-of-grain strips in the same basic way shown for equilateral triangles on page 20.

True diamonds are squares tilted at an angle. All four sides (legs) measure the same length. In all cases, determine the strip width by adding ½" to the height of the diamond. To cut diamonds from strips of fabric, measure a certain distance along the edge of the strip (as indicated below) and then cut at an angle to create the diamond. The amount to add to the finished size of the diamond leg, so you know where to mark the strip, varies with each type of diamond.

30° diamond: Add 1" to the finished leg size. Mark this distance along the raw edge of the strip and cut diamonds by aligning the 30° ruler line with the strip edge.

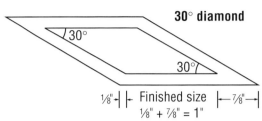

30° diamond

30°
30°
⅛"⊢ Finished size ⊢⅞"→
⅛" + ⅞" = 1"

45° diamond: Add ¾" to the finished leg size, mark the strip, and cut, using the 45° ruler line.

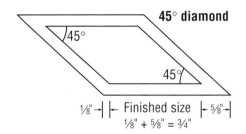

45° diamond

45°
45°
⅛"→⊢ Finished size ⊢⅝"→
⅛" + ⅝" = ¾"

60° diamond: Add ⅝" to the finished leg size, mark the strip, and cut, using the 60° ruler line.

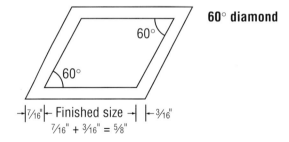

60° diamond

60°
60°
→⁷⁄₁₆"⊢ Finished size →⊢³⁄₁₆"
⁷⁄₁₆" + ³⁄₁₆" = ⅝"

CUTTING GUIDES

Although one of the basic concepts behind rotary cutting is to avoid the use of templates and hand marking, there are always exceptions. Some shapes, such as triangles with very sharp angles, are too difficult to measure easily for rotary cutting. There are also situations in pattern drafting where $\frac{1}{16}$" rather than $\frac{1}{8}$" increments must be used. To handle both of these situations, you can combine the use of paper cutting guides with the rotary cutter. You can also use cutting guides to modify a shape.

Making Cutting Guides

There are two ways to make and use cutting guides: paper cutting guides and hard templates.

PAPER CUTTING GUIDES

In this method, you make a cutting guide of the desired shape from tracing paper with seam allowances included. You then tape the guide to the rotary ruler, aligning a straight edge with the edge of the ruler as shown in the illustration on page 23.

If the shape has parallel edges, you can cut fabric strips the width of the guide. Using a cutting guide as a means of measuring strip width is an extremely valuable technique, especially when dealing with widths that are difficult to measure.

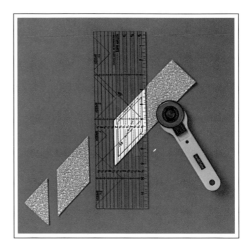

Cut shape from strips.

HARD TEMPLATES

This method is similar to using traditional templates until it comes to cutting. You prepare standard plastic or cardboard templates with seam allowances included. You mark the shape on one layer of fabric, then cut with the rotary cutter, using the rotary ruler as the cutting guide. You can speed up the process by marking once, then layering four to six pieces of fabric underneath the marked layer and cutting through all layers at once.

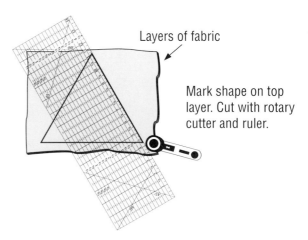

Layers of fabric

Mark shape on top layer. Cut with rotary cutter and ruler.

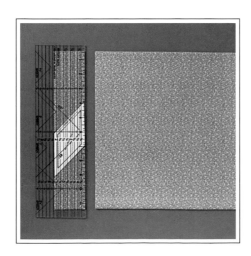

Cut strips of correct width.

Be careful of mirror-image shapes. You must cut these from fabric that is layered with all right sides facing the same direction—right sides up OR right sides down. If you wish to cut an equal number of both images, alternate the fabric directions in the layering.

Mirror-image shapes are not interchangeable.

Modifying Shapes

It is easy to make some shapes, such as octagons and trapezoids, by altering other simple shapes, such as triangles and squares. To create an octagon, such as the one used in the Snowball block below right, remove the four corners of a square. A trapezoid, such as the one used in the Castles in the Air block shown below, is a right triangle with its right-angle corner removed; create it by using a paper template as a cutting guide to modify the parent shape.

TRAPEZOIDS

Castles in the Air

Simple trapezoid:

1. Draft the trapezoid and parent right triangle. Cut a parent half-square triangle from a fabric square that is ⅞" larger than the finished size of the drafted triangle. See cutting "Half-Square Triangles," page 18.

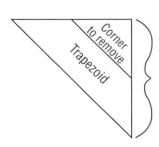

Corner to remove

Trapezoid

To produce the parent half-square triangle, cut a square finished size + ⅞". Cut it in half to yield two half-square triangles.

2. Add seam allowances to the drawing of the trapezoid. Make a paper-template guide this size, tape it to the ruler, and use it as a guide to remove the corner of the right triangle.

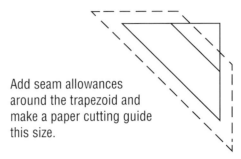

Add seam allowances around the trapezoid and make a paper cutting guide this size.

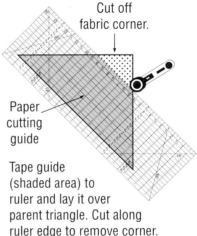

Cut off fabric corner.

Paper cutting guide

Tape guide (shaded area) to ruler and lay it over parent triangle. Cut along ruler edge to remove corner.

OCTAGONS

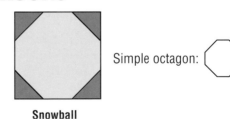

Simple octagon:

Snowball

1. Draft the octagon and parent square.
2. Add seam allowances to the square and cut a fabric square this size.

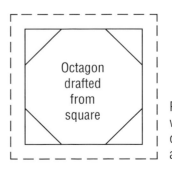

Octagon drafted from square

Parent square is width of finished octagon + seam allowances.

3. Add seam allowances to the octagon and make a paper cutting guide from it. Tape the guide to the ruler and use it to remove the corners of the parent square, creating an octagon.

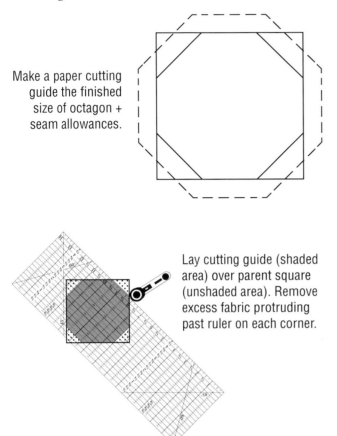

Make a paper cutting guide the finished size of octagon + seam allowances.

Lay cutting guide (shaded area) over parent square (unshaded area). Remove excess fabric protruding past ruler on each corner.

Design Considerations

Another use of hard templates in rotary cutting is for design considerations. There are times when you may wish to position a particular part of a fabric design on one or more of the pattern pieces. The best way to do this is with the use of see-through plastic templates so that you can manually mark each piece and cut from the desired area. Templates include seam allowances; trace around them on the fabric before cutting with the rotary cutter.

Look at the LeMoyne Star table pad on page 62. Each diamond was cut from the same repeat of border design so that after piecing was completed, the print created a secondary design.

NUBBING POINTS FOR SEWING

When stitching different shapes together, a point of fabric often extends beyond the outer edges of the pieces. Nubbing the points removes this excess to make it easier to match the pieces for accurate stitching.

In many situations, it is best to make paper templates with seam allowances included and sewing lines drawn. Then lay the paper pieces together as if they are to be sewn, match sewing lines, and trim the excess paper beyond the seam allowances. Use the trimmed paper pieces as guides to nub the points on fabric pieces.

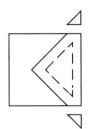

Align sewing lines of paper cutting guides and remove excess points. Use to nub all corresponding fabric pieces for easy matching when sewing.

You can nub some shapes, such as half-square and quarter-square triangles, without templates, by using simple addition.

Half-Square Triangles

Add ½" to the finished dimension of the triangle's short side. (If this measurement is an odd size, use the paper-template method described above to determine where to nub the points.) Lay the Bias Square along the raw edges of the triangle and cut off the excess points extending beyond both side edges.

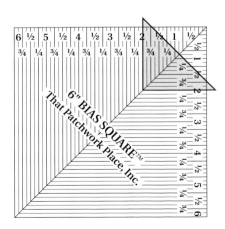

Quarter-Square Triangles

You need two measurements to nub these triangles since they are nubbed perpendicular to the long edge. Both measurements are based on the finished size of this long edge. (If the long edge is an odd size, use the paper-template method described at left.) If you can measure the long edge, add ⅞" to the finished size and measure this distance from the left corner toward the right. Remove the excess fabric to the right of the cutting guide.

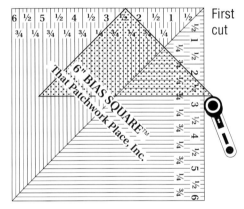

First cut

Finished size + ⅞"

Now add ½" to the finished size, turn the triangle over, and measure from the nubbed edge to the right; remove excess fabric to the right of the cutting guide.

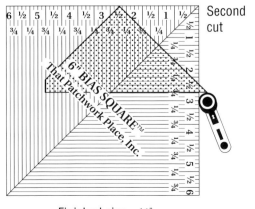

Second cut

Finished size + ½"

STRAIGHT-OF-GRAIN STRIP PIECING

So far we have discussed the use of the rotary cutter to quickly cut simple shapes that are then matched and sewn together. The only real variation on traditional techniques is in how the shapes are cut. Fortunately, rotary cutting can take us beyond fast cutting into the world of quick piecing by combining cutting techniques with the sewing machine. These techniques involve using both straight-of-grain and bias strip piecing and the myriad manipulations that can occur as a result.

Basic Concept

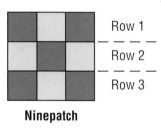

Ninepatch

Strip piecing:

Cutting squares and sewing them together is the traditional way to assemble the simple Ninepatch block. Whether cutting is done with scissors or a rotary cutter, the basic construction process is the same. Many complex patterns can only be assembled in this simple, straightforward fashion, but a multitude of designs, including the humble Ninepatch, can be quickly assembled in large quantities, using innovative methods.

If you break the Ninepatch block into rows, you can see that there are two types of rows. Rather than cut individual squares, you can cut strips, sew the strips side by side, then cut segments (presewn rows) from this new strip unit. Sew two types of strip units—one for each type of row—and speed the piecing process by doing all the "block" sewing at one time without stopping and matching before each seam.

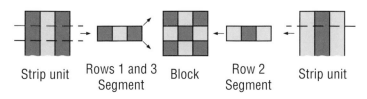

Strip unit   Rows 1 and 3 Segment   Block   Row 2 Segment   Strip unit

Since the resulting squares should be on the straight of grain, cut the strips on grain, perpendicular to the fold of the fabric.

Cutting Strips and Assembling Strip Units

Begin by preparing your fabric for cutting as outlined in "Getting Ready," pages 15–16. Since the resulting squares should be cut on grain, cut the strips on grain too. Follow the instructions for cutting "Strips," page 17.

1. Cut strips the required finished width of the square plus ½" to allow for the ¼"-wide seam allowance on either side of the strip. To determine the length of strip to cut, multiply the number of segments to be cut by the width of each segment with seam allowances included. Add a few inches to this length to allow for human error.

2. Assemble the strip unit by sewing the strips together, side by side, using accurate ¼"-wide seam allowances.

3. Press the seams. (See instructions for using pressing plans on pages 69–70.)

4. To cut segments, turn strip unit sideways so that one short end can be "trued up." Lay a horizontal ruler line on one of the seam lines near the short edge of the strip unit. If the seams are straight, they will align with a ruler line.

Keeping everything in line, move ruler up to the edge of the strip unit and cut off any unevenness at the edge. Even if the edges are straight, it's a good idea to trim the ends  to give a clean cut and eliminate any rough starts on the seams. This true edge is the guide you need to cut segments at right angles to the seam.

5. Cut segments according to your quilt pattern directions. Begin with the freshly cut end of the strip unit and measure in the required distance for the segment. Never make a 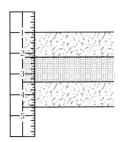 segment cut without also placing a horizontal ruler line along one of the interior seam lines. The cut must be at right angles to the seams. Ideally, the upper and lower raw edges also align, but, if necessary, you can make adjustments to these when the final seams are sewn. An interior seam is already locked in and will appear slanted if the cut is not made at right angles to it.

> **Tip**
> If, at any time, the short edge and interior seams no longer form a right angle, true up the edge again. This happens periodically and shouldn't cause concern. It is due to the minuscule amount of ruler slippage that occurs with each cut. Of course, the more carefully you cut, the less frequently you will have to recut the edges.

6. Now sew the segments together to form a Ninepatch block. If the various strip-unit seams are always pressed toward the darker fabric, the seams where the rows meet face opposite directions. These are called opposing seam allowances and are highly desirable since they butt next to each other and form a tight intersection that will match perfectly when sewn. Pressing seams so they butt at intersections is important to keep in mind when planning the pressing pattern for your blocks. See pages 69–70 for more information on planning the pressing.

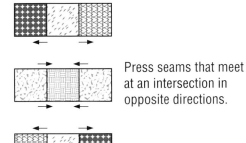

Press seams that meet at an intersection in opposite directions.

As you look at quilt designs, you will find many opportunities to use strip piecing in place of traditional piecing.

BIAS STRIP PIECING

Basic Concept

The most common use of bias strip piecing is to quick-cut pieced bias squares. A bias square is a square composed of two right triangles joined on the long side. This particular triangle combination is used extensively in both traditional and contemporary quilt patterns. The Variable Star shown here is one such design.

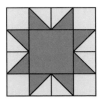

Variable Star

Bias square:

In most situations, the outside edges of a bias square should be cut on the straight of grain (S-O-G) to avoid stretching. This means that the seam running across the diagonal of the square is on the bias.

S-O-G

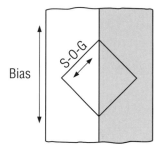

S-O-G

Strips are cut on straight of grain. Squares are cut with edges on bias.

If you sew two strips of fabric together as shown in "Straight-of-Grain Strip Piecing" (pages 26–27), you can cut squares on point from the strips to yield presewn bias squares.

If you cut the strips on grain, the resulting squares have the bias on the four outer edges and the straight of grain on the diagonal seam. This is not desirable. However, if you cut the strips on the bias, the resulting squares have their outer edges on the straight of grain.

Bias

Strips are cut on bias grain. Squares are cut with edges on straight of grain.

Bias strips are cut and sewn together; bias squares are then cut diagonally from the bias strip unit. This basic idea is the key to the bias-square system. You should know the answers to a few questions, however, before proceeding. For instance: How do you cut bias strips? What size strips do you cut? How do you cut squares from the bias strip units?

The following sections will help answer these and other questions you may have.

Cutting Bias Strips

If a square is cut with the straight of grain on the outer edges, then strips cut from the diagonal will have bias edges. Begin by making a center diagonal cut through a fabric square. Using the long center edge as the cutting guide, cut bias strips from each large triangle.

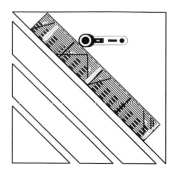

A complete square is unnecessary as long as the two edges of one corner are cut at a right angle. Measure the distance (x) along the selvage side. Measure this same distance along the lower edge. Make the first bias cut from point to point. Cut bias strips parallel to this bias edge.

To save time, cut the bias strips for the two fabrics that will be sewn together for the bias squares at the same time. Steam press them together, *right sides facing up* (so they adhere slightly when steamed).

1. Make the first bias cut from the upper left corner to a point on the lower edge that measures the same height as the selvage edge. Cut bias strips from this first cut edge. Full bias strips are the ones that run from one side to the other. Their short edges are parallel to each other.

2. The corner piece created by the first bias cut can also be cut into bias strips. A second corner piece is left on the right edge of the fabric after all the full bias strips are cut. The bias strips cut from these corner pieces are called corner bias strips and corner bias triangles. The corner pieces can be cut into bias strips or reserved for other purposes.

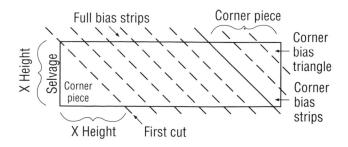

Assembling Bias Strip Units

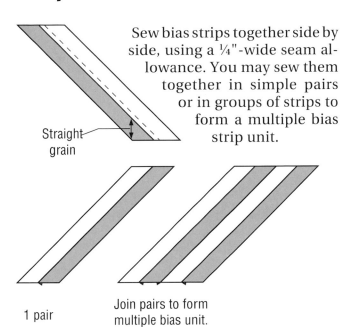

Sew bias strips together side by side, using a ¼"-wide seam allowance. You may sew them together in simple pairs or in groups of strips to form a multiple bias strip unit.

Straight grain

1 pair

Join pairs to form multiple bias unit.

Determining Strip Width

There are two ways to determine bias strip width. The first method is a general rule, which is always sufficient but often overly generous; thus, it requires more fabric. The general rule states that, *when sewing only two bias strips together, cut the strips the width of the unfinished bias square.* For instance, if you are sewing simple bias-strip pairs together and cutting a 3" unfinished bias square (2½" finished), then cut the bias strips 3" wide.

When sewing multiple bias strips together, cut the bias strips ¼" wider than the unfinished bias square to account for the extra seam. For instance, to cut a 3" unfinished bias square from a multiple bias strip unit, cut bias strips 3¼" wide.

When using this method to calculate strip width, strips may be wider than really needed, especially for larger bias squares, but they are never smaller. Normally, this is not a concern, but if you have a limited amount of fabric, you may want to know precisely how wide the strips need to be. Strip widths for common bias-square units are shown in the chart above right. For sizes not given in the chart, draw the bias-square triangle with seam allowances included and mea-

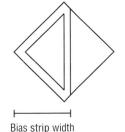

Bias strip width

sure the distance from the outer corner to the diagonal. Round this figure up to the nearest ⅛". For example, if a triangle measures 3 1/16", round it up to 3⅛" and cut bias strips 3⅛" wide.

CUT SIZE OF BIAS SQUARE	BIAS STRIP WIDTH*
1½"	1⅜"
1¾"	1½"
2"	1¾"
2¼"	1⅞"
2½"	2⅛"
2¾"	2¼"
3"	2½"
3½"	2¾"

*Add ¼" to strip widths for assembling multiple bias strip units.

Cutting Bias Squares

After cutting and sewing bias strips together, cut bias squares from the bias strip unit, using the Bias Square. The ⅛" markings on two sides make it possible to cut many different sizes. For odd-sized bias squares, tape a paper cutting guide (pages 22–24) to the corner of the Bias Square. Use the diagonal line that bisects the ruler to establish your cutting line.

1. Place the Bias Square over the lower end of the bias strip unit, with the diagonal line on top of the seam and the dimension of the template or desired markings on the ruler just inside the lower raw edges of the strip.

2. Cut the two top edges of the square, from raw edge to raw edge. Set the resulting piece aside. Continue to cut as many pieces from the strip unit as possible, making sure that the markings are always within the strip-unit boundaries and not extending past the lower point.

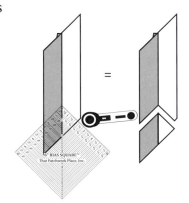

3. Turn each cut piece 180° so the two lower raw edges are up; trim raw edges to size with Bias Square.

When cutting bias squares from multiple bias strip units, use the same procedure, being careful to always cut from the bottom edge across the bias strip unit before cutting farther up the strip unit. Move systematically from either left to right or right to left, cutting bottom edge first.

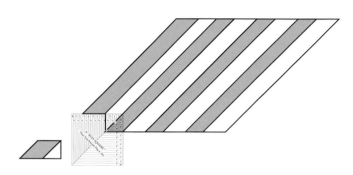

As you cut bias squares from bias strip units, you will notice that edge triangles are left over along the outer edges of the strips. You will also notice that fewer edge triangles are produced when you cut from multiple bias strip units than from simple bias strip units. If these edge triangles are large enough, you can use them in patterns that require only a few triangles.

RESIZING EDGE TRIANGLES

Before using edge triangles, they must be resized. The diagonal edge may also need adjustment.

1. Use the corner of your Bias Square to check and square off the corner of the triangle.

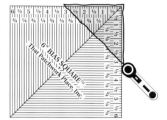

Square off the corner of edge triangle.

2. Nub the triangle points.

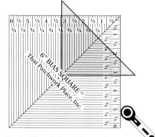

Nub the triangle points.

3. Align the 45° line on your Bias Square with one of the triangle's short sides. Adjust the ¼" line so it runs from inside point to inside point on the nubbed long edge of the triangle. Trim away all excess.

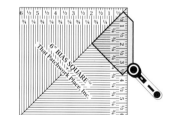

Trim excess.

CREATING SCRAP QUILTS

You can create scrappy quilts using strip-piecing techniques. Cut strips from a wide variety of fabrics, substituting dark and light fabrics for the same positions instead of one or two specific prints. Seam strips together and cut the desired segments or bias squares from them.

I used this technique to make the scrappy Puss in the Corner blocks found in the Woodland Tree quilt top shown on page 59.

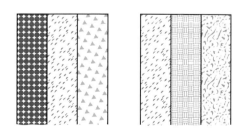

Scrappy straight-of-grain strip units

You can assemble bias strip units in the same fashion to create scrappy bias squares. Sew a wide variety of light and dark bias strips together and cut bias squares from this multiple bias strip unit. An example that includes this technique is the First Star quilt on page 59.

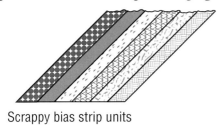

Scrappy bias strip units

You can use the ScrapSaver™, a rotary cutting guide designed by Judy Hopkins, to quickly resize edge triangles that result from cutting bias squares. This tool makes it easy to quick-cut half-square triangles from scraps without tedious calculations or the need for templates. Complete directions accompany this tool.

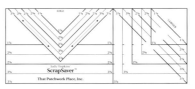

ScrapSaver™

OTHER USES FOR STRIP PIECING

You can use straight-of-grain and bias strip piecing methods to create shortcuts for many presewn shapes. Following are some examples.

Side-by-Sides

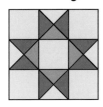

Ohio Star

Side-by-Side:

Side-by-side triangles consist of two quarter-square triangles that are joined to each other on one of their short legs rather than along the diagonal. The Ohio Star block contains side-by-side triangles.

Note that in a block such as the Ohio Star, the long edges of the four triangles making up the square are on the straight of grain as indicated by the arrows.

Each side-by-side is made up of two quarter-square triangles.

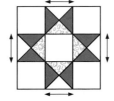

Long edges of the four triangles should be on the straight of grain.

The quick method for constructing side-by-sides is a variation on bias-square construction. If you cut a bias square in half on the diagonal, you end up with two sets of side-by-side triangles. Each set is the mirror image of its mate.

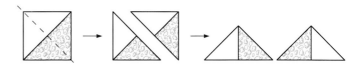

Before you start cutting, you need to know:
1. The desired finished size of the *long edge* of the quarter-square triangle;
2. The size of the bias square you need to cut to yield the correct size of the side-by-side unit;
3. The width of the bias strip you need to cut to make the bias strip unit.

Draft the pattern on graph paper and measure the long edge of the quarter-square triangle found in the side-by-side unit.

Think of the side-by-side unit as if it were a half-square triangle that you will cut from a square. If you are making half-square triangles (page 18), you may remember that the magic number to add to the finished size of the triangle is ⅞". The same number applies to cutting bias squares large enough to produce side-by-sides. Add ⅞" to desired finished size of the long edge of one of the quarter-square triangles in the side-by-side unit; cut bias squares that size from the bias strip unit.

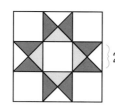

Measure long edge of quarter-square-triangle. Add ⅞" to determine size of bias square. In this example, a 2⅞" (2" +⅞") bias square is needed.

2" Finished size of long edge of quarter-square triangle

Cut bias strips for this size bias square, following the same procedures as outlined in "Cutting Bias Strips"on page 28. Assemble a bias strip unit and cut bias squares from it as described in "Cutting Bias Squares" on pages 29–30.

For example, to produce side-by-side units that will be 2" finished size on the long edge:
1. Cut 2⅞" bias squares (2" + ⅞"= 2⅞") from a bias strip-pieced unit. For the precise bias-strip-width measurement required, draw the side-by-side triangle with seam allowances included. Measure from the center ¼" seam to the corner point with seam allowances in-cluded. Round up and add another ¼" if you are going to sew a mul-tiple bias strip unit.

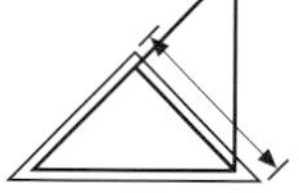

Measure this distance for bias strip width. (Add ¼" for multiple bias strip unit.)

2. Cut the bias squares in half on unseamed diagonal.

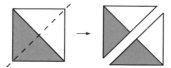

If you need the long edges of the quarter-square triangles to be on the bias in the side-by-sides, cut straight-of-grain strips instead of bias strips. The rest of the process remains the same.

Striped Squares

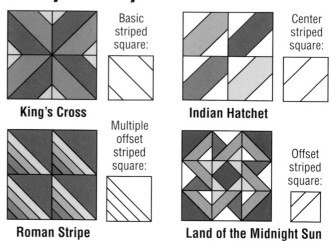

Basic striped square:

King's Cross

Center striped square:

Indian Hatchet

Multiple offset striped square:

Roman Stripe

Offset striped square:

Land of the Midnight Sun

Striped squares have stripes running through the diagonal of the block. They can have three or more stripes running through the block or they can be offset to one side as in Roman Stripe. The rules for assembly are the same for each of the striped squares shown here, wheth-er there is one stripe or many stripes.

Cut striped squares from strip units just like bias squares. Depending on where you wish to place the straight of grain in the finished unit, cut the strips either on grain or on the bias. In most instances, you will need to cut bias strips. Cut each strip the desired finished width. It is best if the center stripes are an easily mea-sured width (with no size increment less than ⅛"), but the outer stripes forming the corners can be odd widths that are rounded up to the nearest ⅛".
1. Draft the block with measurable center stripes.
2. Add ½" to the finished width of each center stripe and cut strips this width.
3. Measure the corner stripes from the inner seam to the corner point, rounding up to the nearest ⅛", and add ⅝" to this figure. Cut strips this size for the outer strips only.

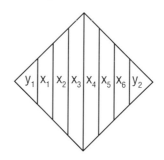

Number and width of center stripes can vary. (Here they are x_1-x_6.) They are cut ½" wider than desired finished width. Outer strips (y_1, y_2) are rounded up to nearest ⅛" and cut ⅝" larger.

SC-68

4. Cut and assemble the strip unit as you would normally.

5. Cut squares from the strip-pieced unit, making them ½" larger than the desired finished size, just as with any simple square.

   If your block has a stripe centered over the diagonal of the square as in the center striped square, you will need a diagonal guide for centering your cutting guide on the strip unit. Create one by either pressing a crease or drawing a line through the middle of the center strip with a wash-out chalk pencil or wheel. Align the diagonal line on your cutting guide or Bias Square with the line on your strip unit and cut squares, following the instructions for "Cutting Bias Squares" on pages 29–30.

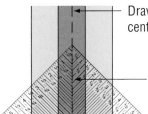

Draw or press line through center stripe in strip unit.

Align diagonal line of cutting guide or Bias Square® over line marked through stripe.

Multiple strip units can also be constructed by reversing the order of the strips in the strip unit and sewing many strips together. Be sure to add another ¼" to the width of the outer strips in the simple strip unit before building multiple strip units, to account for the extra seam where the reverse begins.

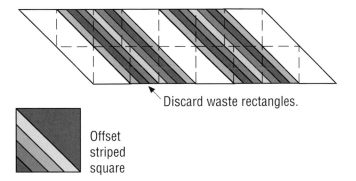

Discard waste rectangles.

Offset striped square

Striped Half-Square Triangles

If you cut striped squares in half perpendicular to the seams, you have two half-square triangles like those in the blocks, above right.

Basic-striped half-square triangle:

All Dressed Up

Offset-striped half-square triangle:

Dutch Windmill

Center-striped half-square triangle:

Sparkler

Assemble strip units exactly as you would for striped squares, but cut the outer strips ⅞" wider than the finished width. Cut the squares from the strip unit, cutting them ⅞" larger than the finished short edge of the triangle. The two triangles from each square are mirror images of each other and, thus, they are not always interchangeable.

Center-Striped, Half-Square Triangles. The strip-unit assembly is slightly different when you decide to cut a center-striped square in half through the center stripe instead of perpendicular to the stripes. This cut produces stripes parallel to the long edge of the triangles as shown in the Castles in the Air block, below.

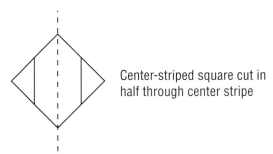

Center-striped square cut in half through center stripe

When planning the strip unit for this type of triangle, cut the center stripe 1" wider than the desired finished size to accommodate the two seams that will eventually be sewn on either side of the cut. If you wish to produce a triangle like the one in Castles in the Air, first measure finished width of the two stripes. As an example, let's say the large stripe measures 1" wide when finished. The corner stripe measures 1⅛" when finished.

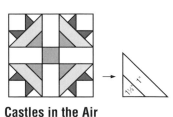

Castles in the Air

Since the center strip in the square will be cut in half to create a 1"-wide stripe in each of the two triangles, it must be cut twice as wide (2") plus extra for seam allowances. To this figure, add ½" for the seam on either side of the strip in the strip unit and another ½" for the seams that will be sewn later on either side of the cut, through the center of the strip unit. The total to add to the doubled finished size then is 1", so you will cut strips 3" wide. Cut the corner stripes ⅝" wider than the finished size, as usual. Add another ¼" for multiple bias strip units.

Assemble the strip unit and cut the squares as you would for any striped triangle. Then, cut the squares in half through the center stripe.

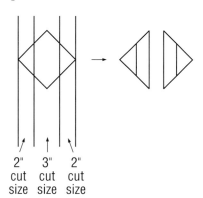

2" cut size 3" cut size 2" cut size

Side-Striped, Half-Square Triangles. The last type of pieced triangle has stripes running parallel to one of the short sides of the triangle.

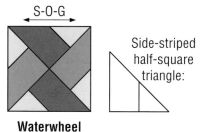

S-O-G

Side-striped half-square triangle:

Waterwheel

It can be cut from another type of striped square. The two triangles produced are opposites in color placement just as in side-by-sides. First, cut strips to form the strip unit, then cut squares from the strip unit. Finally, cut squares in half on the diagonal to produce triangles.

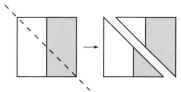

Cut the strips for the outer edges of the strip unit ⅞" wider than the desired finished size to accommodate the seam allowance and corner.

If there are only two strips, cut both of them ⅞" wider. Cut center strips ½" wider than the desired finished size.

+⅞" +⅞"

With a two-strip unit, cut both strips ⅞" wider.

+⅞" +½" +⅞"

In strip units with more than two strips, outer strips are cut ⅞" wider than finished size. Inner strip(s) are cut ½" wider than finished size.

Cut squares from the strip-pieced unit, cutting them 1¼" wider than the finished size of the triangle's short edge. Then cut squares in half to yield two triangles.

Cut a square from the strip unit that is 1¼" larger than the triangle's short leg.

Short leg + 1¼"

One additional step is required to trim the triangles to the desired size. To be able to use both triangles, trim the short leg of the triangle opposite the corner triangle to the finished size plus ¼".

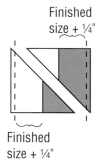

Finished size + ¼"

Trim outer strips in each triangle to finished size + ¼".

Finished size + ¼"

You might wonder why the triangle was not cut narrower in the beginning. On closer examination, you will realize that if this had been done, the second triangle created would not have a corner triangle of the desired size. You add the ⅞" to accommodate the triangles produced at each side of the square when it is cut.

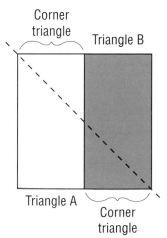

Corner triangle Triangle B

Triangle A Corner triangle

To create proper-size corner triangle from each of two triangles (A and B), EACH strip must be ⅞" larger than desired finished size.

Strip-Pieced Rectangles

Crazy Ann

Pieced rectangle:

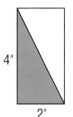

Pieced rectangle

Generally, a rectangle is an elongated square that is twice as long as it is wide, for example, 1" x 2", 2" x 4", or 3" x 6". Just as with squares, the sides should be cut on the straight of grain. This means that the diagonal seam in a pieced rectangle composed of two triangles is on the bias. In the case of a rectangle, it is not a true 45° bias. I call this bias angle "off bias." Pieced rectangles appear in the Crazy Ann block, above left.

Pieced rectangles are made up of two elongated triangles. They can be strip pieced in a fashion similar to bias squares. Mary Hickey developed a wonderful system for strip piecing these bias rectangles, using the BiRangle cutting guide. This method is featured in her book *Angle Antics*.

To cut strips for pieced rectangles, begin by preparing the fabric edges for cutting as outlined on page 16. Then complete the following steps.

1. Layer together one piece each of the two fabrics that make up the rectangle. Place them right sides up, with the selvages to the left and right as shown for Unit A pieced rectangles. Place fabrics right sides down for Unit B pieced rectangles. Half-yard pieces are a good size to use, because you can cut sufficiently long strips.

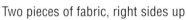

Two pieces of fabric, right sides up

If you need both mirror-image versions of the pieced rectangle, as in the Fifty-four Forty or Fight block above right, layer the fabric right sides up and then fold so all four selvages are together. With fabric layered in this manner, you will be cutting an equal number of mirror-image strips, that is, an equal number face up and face down.

Fifty-four-Forty or Fight

Mirror-image
strip-pieced rectangles

- To cut strip-pieced rectangles like Unit A, cut strips with both fabrics face up.
- To cut strip-pieced rectangles like Unit B, cut strips with both fabrics face down.
- To cut both types at once, position both fabrics face up and then fold in half, selvages to selvages.

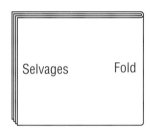

Two pieces of fabric, right sides up, and then folded in half, selvage to selvage

2. If you don't have a BiRangle, make an oversized half-rectangle template, about 4" x 8". Use a hard template material, such as cardboard or plastic. Align the right-angle corner of the template with the lower-left corner of the prepared fabric. Lay your rotary ruler next to the diagonal edge of the template and move them together to the right, keeping the template even with the cut edge until the ruler intersects the upper left-hand corner of the fabric.

Note: If you are using a ½-yard piece of fabric, you will probably need a 24"-long ruler.

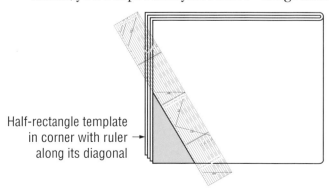

Half-rectangle template
in corner with ruler →
along its diagonal

Keeping the ruler in place, remove the template guide and cut away the corner of fabric to the left of the ruler. Use this diagonal cut as the starting point for cutting strips. By using the diagonal of the rectangle as the bias guide, you will produce strips at the correct angle to yield rectangles with their edges cut on the straight of grain.

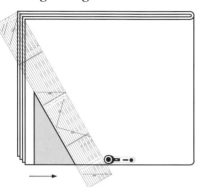

Move template and ruler together to right until ruler intersects upper-left corner of fabric. Cut along edge of ruler.

You can also use a BiRangle ruler to determine the correct angle of the strips. Place the ruler on the edge of the fabrics with the long side on the selvages.

Place a large cutting ruler on the diagonal line of the BiRangle.

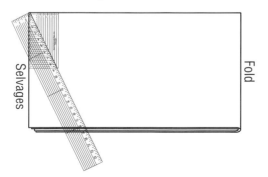

Carefully slide BiRangle out of the way. Cut along the ruler's edge. Use diagonal cut as the starting point for cutting the strips.

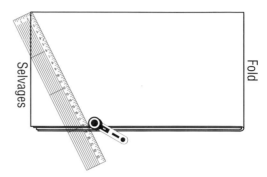

3. Cut off-bias strips the required width. For simple pairs of strips, add ¾" to the finished width of the pieced rectangle and cut off-bias strips this width. For example, if you want a pieced rectangle with a finished width of 2", cut off-bias strips 2¾" wide.

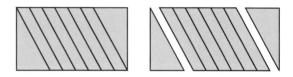

If you are sewing multiple pairs of strips together, add an additional ¼" for the extra seams. For example, cut off-bias strips 3" wide if you want a pieced rectangle with a finished width of 2" (2" + ¾" + ¼" = 3"). Use the chart to determine the cut width of diagonal strips for multiple strip units.

| STRIP WIDTHS FOR MULTIPLE STRIP UNITS | | CUT WIDTH OF DIAGONAL STRIP |
FINISHED RECTANGLE SHORT SIDE	LONG SIDE	
¾"	1½"	1¾"
1"	2"	2"
1¼"	2½"	2¼"
1½"	3"	2½"
1¾"	3½"	2¾"
2"	4"	3"
2¼"	4½"	3¼"
2½"	5"	3½"
2¾"	5½"	3¾"
3"	6"	4"
3¼"	6½"	4¼"
3½"	7"	4½"

4. If you layered fabric to produce two types of rectangles, separate the strips into piles according to whether they were face up or face down in the fabric layers. Sew the strips from each pile into pairs or multiple strip units.

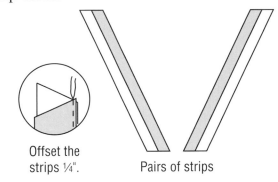

Offset the
strips ¼".

Pairs of strips

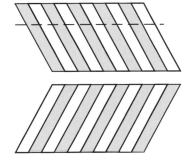

Arrange into
multiple strip units.

5. To cut bias rectangles from simple pairs of strips, use the BiRangle ruler and Mary Hickey's bias-rectangle technique. If the BiRangle is not available in your local quilt shop, you can make a clear plastic cutting guide to tape to your rotary ruler as shown in the tip box on page 38.

   Align the diagonal line of either the BiRangle ruler or the cutting guide with the seam of the strips as shown in the diagram. Beginning at the top of the strips, cut the first two sides of the rectangle.

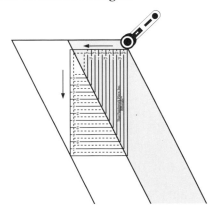

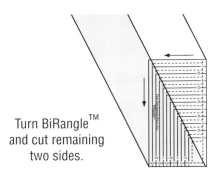

Turn BiRangle™
and cut remaining
two sides.

6. Turn the strip unit so the cut edge is toward you, realign the diagonal line, and cut the remaining two sides of the rectangle. Continue to cut as many pieced rectangles as you need.

> *Tip* To cut rectangles from pieced strips slanting to the right, I find it easiest to turn the strips over, face down, and cut from the wrong side of the fabric. These strips yield rectangles that are mirror images of the strips slanted to the left. Keep this in mind when planning your fabric-strip color arrangements.

7. Before cutting rectangles from multiple strip units, trim the top edge of the unit first. Position the diagonal line of the BiRangle or cutting guide on a center seam line near the top of the unit. Place a ruler flush with the top edge of the BiRangle and trim the edge even across the top of the strip unit.

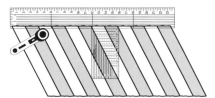

Use BiRangle™ as a guide to trim top.

8. Add ½" to the finished length of the pieced rectangle and cut segments parallel to the trimmed edge. Before cutting each segment,

check the angle of the upper edge and correct if necessary by repeating step 7.

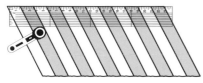

Cut segments parallel to top.

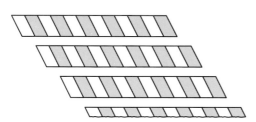

9. Sew segments end to end to create longer segments and to avoid wasting the triangle at the end of a segment. Be careful not to stretch the bias edges as you sew the ends together.

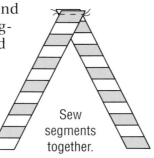

Sew segments together.

10. Place the diagonal line of the BiRangle or cutting guide on the seam line and cut the first two sides across the row of strips. Turn the segments around 180° and cut the remaining two sides of the rectangle.

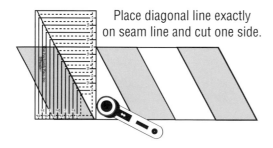

Place diagonal line exactly on seam line and cut one side.

Turn fabrics and cut other side.

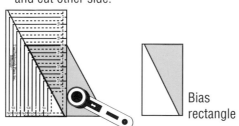

Bias rectangle

To make a cutting guide for bias rectangles:

1. Draw a pieced bias rectangle in the finished size on a piece of paper.
2. Draw a diagonal line from corner to corner.
3. Add a ¼"-wide seam allowance to each side of the rectangle. Note that the diagonal line on the completed template intersects the opposite corners of what will be the size of the finished rectangle but not the corners at the outer edge of the template. Cut out the bias rectangle template you have created.

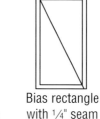
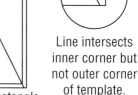

Line intersects inner corner but not outer corner of template.

Finished size bias rectangle

Bias rectangle with ¼" seam allowances added

4. Tape the plastic template to the corner of your rotary ruler and use it in place of the BiRangle, following the rotary-cutting directions given for the quilt you are making.

You will need to make a new template for each size bias rectangle required for the quilt you are making.

Strip-Pieced Diamonds

It is possible to strip piece any type of diamond. The most commonly used diamonds in quiltmaking are 30°, 45°, or 60° diamonds. Remember that true diamonds have four legs that all measure the same length. The slenderest of these diamonds is the 30° diamond. It has a 30° angle at its narrow points. It requires twelve of these to complete a circle. It takes eight 45° diamonds or six 60° diamonds to make a circle.

Half-length pieced diamonds appear in the Star of the East block and half-width pieced diamonds are used in the King's Star block.

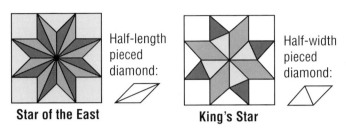

Star of the East   Half-length pieced diamond:

King's Star   Half-width pieced diamond:

Simple Strip-Pieced Half Diamonds. You can cut each of the common diamonds from strip-pieced units to make either half-length or half-width diamonds.

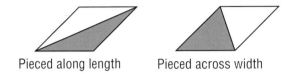

Pieced along length   Pieced across width

1. Draft the half diamond needed. Add seam allowances and make a paper cutting guide this size. Measure the width of the half diamond from center seam to opposite angle, including the seam allowances.

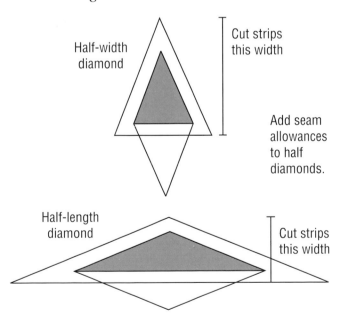

Half-width diamond — Cut strips this width — Add seam allowances to half diamonds.

Half-length diamond — Cut strips this width

2. Cut straight-of-grain fabric strips this width and seam them, right sides together, on *both* raw edges. Tape the paper guide to your rotary ruler with one of the exterior legs of the diamond aligned with the edge of the ruler.

Align the center of the diamond with the raw edge of the fabric strips and make a cut.

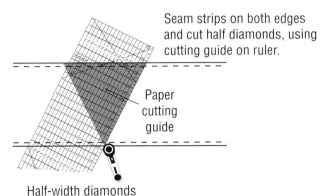

Seam strips on both edges and cut half diamonds, using cutting guide on ruler.

Paper cutting guide

Half-width diamonds

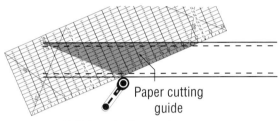

Paper cutting guide

Half-length diamonds

3. Turn the cut piece over and align the cutting guide over first cut edge. Trim the second side. Continue in this manner, cutting as many diamonds as you need. Remove the few stitches at the points and press the diamonds open.

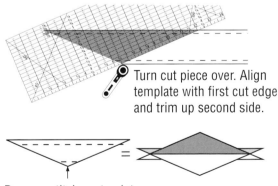

Turn cut piece over. Align template with first cut edge and trim up second side.

Remove stitches at point and press diamond open.

String-Pieced Half Diamonds. Using the same principles as above, substitute one multi-pieced strip for a plain strip in the strip unit to make string-pieced half diamonds like those in the Fiesta block.

String-pieced diamond:

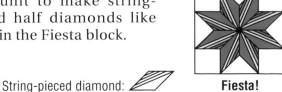

Fiesta!

Diamonds cut from this strip piecing are solid on one half and string-pieced on the other half.

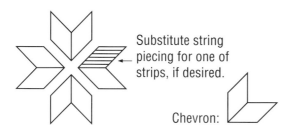

Use strip piecing in place of plain strip on one side.

Chevrons. Create pieced full diamonds (chevrons) by cutting simple, full-sized diamonds as described on page 21, using pairs of strips sewn together on one raw edge. Join pairs of chevrons to form a star.

Substitute string piecing for one of strips, if desired.

Chevron:

1. Draft the single diamond.
2. Cut strips the width of the diamond, plus seam allowances.
3. Seam strips into pairs along one edge but *do not press*.
4. Following the instructions for simple diamonds on page 21, measure and cut the desired-size diamond (30°, 45°, or 60°) from the strip unit, using either the ruler angle markings or a paper cutting guide.

For a more elaborate chevron or diamond pair, string-piece one of the strips in the strip unit.

Diamonds within Diamonds. This unit is commonly used to make Lone Star or Virginia Star diamonds. The concept is the same as that of basic strip piecing for a simple Ninepatch block, only it is done at an angle.

Diamonds within diamonds:

Virginia Star

1. Draft the diamond. Think of it as a square on a slant.
2. Divide it into an equal number of segments across and down; for example, three across and three down or four across and four down. Draw the inner lines parallel to the outer diamond legs.
3. Decide on the fabrics for each segment and each color.
4. Measure the width of the small diamonds and add seam allowances to this dimension. Cut straight-of-grain strips this width to form a strip unit for each row.

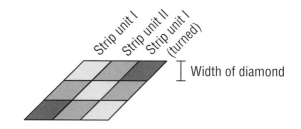

Strip unit I Strip unit II Strip unit I (turned)

Width of diamond

5. Cut segments (finished size plus seam allowances) from each strip unit at an angle, matching the type of diamond being made. For instance, to make a 60° diamond, cut the segments at a 60° angle, using the 60° line on your ruler. It's a good idea to align the degree line on the ruler with one of the inside seams, rather than with the fabric edge. Sew the cut segments together to form the completed diamond.

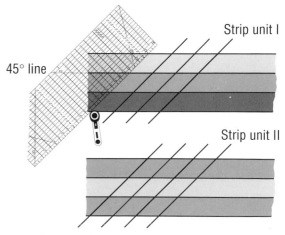

Strip unit I

45° line

Strip unit II

Cut strips the width of small diamond + seam allowances. Make first cut at proper angle, using ruler markings, in this case, 45°. Then, cut segments from strip units the width of small diamond + seam allowances.

ANALYZING BLOCKS FOR ROTARY CUTTING

Now that you have the basics of rotary cutting in mind, you can adapt other patterns to rotary cutting. Many books and patterns are written specifically for rotary techniques. Others have been adapted to rotary cutting, but it is helpful to know how to do it for your own designs. Here are a few examples of specific blocks that have been adapted to rotary cutting, step by step, to demonstrate the thinking behind the method. As you can see, each has two options for cutting the blocks. The option you choose depends on the number of blocks you want or your own personal preference.

Sister's Choice (10" block)

Block description: This is a 10" square, consisting of 5 patches of equal sizes across and down. Thus, each finished patch measures 2" square.

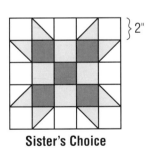

Sister's Choice

OPTION I: SIMPLE CUTTING

Shapes needed:

1. Cut simple 2½" squares (2" finished size plus ½" for seam allowances).
2. Cut half-square triangles from 2⅞" squares (2" finished size plus ⅞").

OPTION II: STRAIGHT-OF-GRAIN AND BIAS STRIP PIECING

Shapes needed:

1. Use straight-of-grain strip piecing to assemble the Ninepatch unit in the center of the block. Cut strips 2½" wide (2" finished size plus ½" for seam allowances). See "Straight-of-Grain Strip Piecing" on pages 26–27.
2. Cut eight single 2½" squares for the corner squares and sides.
3. Cut bias-square units instead of half-square triangles. Cut bias strips 2½" wide for simple strip units or 2¾" wide for multiple bias strip units. See "Bias Strip Piecing" on pages 27–30.

Crazy Ann (10" block)

Block description: This 10" block has 4" pieced corner squares of two sizes of half-square triangles and a 2" square. The center sashings are 2" x 4" pieced rectangles with a 2" center square.

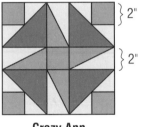

Crazy Ann

OPTION I: SIMPLE CUTTING

Shapes needed:

1. Use simple cutting techniques to cut four 2½" corner squares and one 2½" center sashing square.
2. Use simple cutting techniques to cut the 4" half-square triangles from 4⅞" squares (4" + ⅞"). Cut the 2" half-square triangles from 2⅞" squares (2" + ⅞"). See "Half-Square Triangles" on page 18.
3. Cut 2" x 4" half rectangles from 2⅝" x 5¼" rectangles. See "Half Rectangles" on page 20.

OPTION II: STRIP PIECING

Shapes needed:

1. Use simple cutting techniques to cut eight 2½" corner squares and one 2½" center sashing square.
2. Cut eight 2½" bias squares. Use 2½"-wide bias strips for simple bias strip units or 2¾"-wide bias strips for multiple bias strip units. See "Bias Strip Piecing" on pages 27–30.
3. Cut pieced rectangles from 2½"-wide off-bias strips, using the BiRangle ruler or a cutting guide. See "Strip-Pieced Rectangles" on pages 35–38.

Star of the East (10 ¼" block)

Block description: This block has eight 45° pieced diamonds with 3" corner squares. The diamond legs are 3" long.

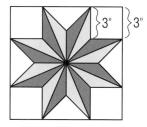

Star of the East

OPTION I: SIMPLE CUTTING

Shapes needed:

1. Cut 3½" corner squares, using simple cutting techniques.
2. Cut the set-in triangles as quarter-square triangles so that the long edges are on the straight of grain. Measure the long edge. In this case, it is 4¼", but if it is an odd size, round it up to the nearest ⅛". Cut a square 1¼" larger than the long edge. In this case, 4¼" + 1¼" = 5½". Cut one square for every four triangles needed. Trim the outer edge to size after it is sewn in place. See "Quarter-Square Triangles" on pages 18–19.

3. Cut the half diamonds from straight-of-grain strips of fabric that are the width of the half diamond, including its seam allowances. Make a paper cutting guide of the half diamond and cut as many half diamonds as you need from the fabric strips. See "Paper Cutting Guides" on page 22.

OPTION II: STRIP PIECING

Shapes needed: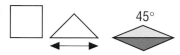

1. Same as Option I.
2. Same as Option I.
3. Cut simple strip-pieced half diamonds from seamed strips of fabric, using a half-diamond paper cutting guide. Cut the strips the width of 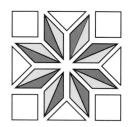 the half diamond, including seam allowances. Seam the strips together on both raw edges. Using a half-diamond paper cutting guide, cut the half diamonds from the seamed strips. See "Simple Strip-Pieced Half Diamonds" on page 39.

Castles in the Air (10" block)

Block description: When drafted, each pieced corner unit is 4" square and is composed of a square, two sizes of triangles, and a trapezoid. The four rectangles are 2"x4", and the center square is 2" square.

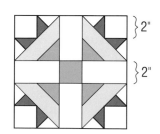

Castles in the Air

OPTION I: SIMPLE CUTTING

Shapes needed: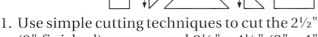

1. Use simple cutting techniques to cut the 2½" (2" finished) squares and 2½" x 4½" (2" x 4" finished) rectangles.
2. Cut the small triangles as quarter-square triangles so the straight grain is on the long edge. The long edge of this triangle is one-half the finished size of the pieced corner square (4") and thus, measures 2". To cut quarter-square triangles of this size from a square, add 1¼" and cut a square this size (3¼") for every four triangles needed. See "Quarter-Square Triangles" on pages 18–19.
3. Cut the larger triangles as half-square triangles since they require the straight of grain on the short edges. Cut them from squares ⅞" larger than the finished size of the short leg, which is also 2". Cut one 2⅞" square for every two triangles needed. See "Half-Square Triangles" on page 18.
4. To cut the trapezoids, use one of the following methods:
   a. Cut the trapezoids from bias strips of fabric ½" wider than the trapezoid, using a paper cutting guide. Be sure to use bias strips so the outer edges of the trapezoids are on the straight of grain. See "Paper Cutting Guides" on pages 22–23.

OR

   b. Cut the trapezoids by modifying right triangles. Cut two 4⅞" squares into four half-square triangles. Remove corners, using a paper cutting guide of the trapezoid that includes seam allowances. See "Modifying Shapes" on pages 23–24.

OPTION II: STRIP PIECING

Shapes needed:

1. Cut simple squares for the corner squares.

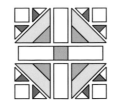

2. To make the center block sashings, use one of the following methods:
   a. Cut a simple 2½" square and four 2½" x 4½" rectangles for center block sashings.

OR

   b. Strip piece part of the center block sashing if there are a number of blocks to construct. Cut strips ½" wider than the finished width of the shapes, then seam and cut into segments ½" longer than the desired length. See "Straight-of-Grain Strip Piecing" on pages 26–27.
3. Cut side-by-sides from 2⅞" bias squares (2" finished size plus ⅞"). See "Side-by-Sides" on pages 31–32. Cut bias strips the width of the bias squares or ¼" wider for multiple strip units.
4. Cut the center-striped, half-square triangles from striped squares. Cut the corner bias strip ⅝" wider than the finished width of the triangle. Cut the center bias strip 1" wider than double the width of the trapezoid since this strip will be cut in half through its middle. Cut bias squares from the strip unit ⅞" wider than the finished size of the triangle's short edge (4" + ⅞" = 4⅞"). See "Center-Striped, Half-Square Triangles" on pages 33–34.

In Conclusion

If you set aside some time to practice the rotary-cutting techniques presented here, it will be easy to use them with your own creative ideas and applications. Make it a practice to look for rotary-cutting potential in every design you see, whether traditional or original, using the section on analyzing blocks to help you adapt it to rotary cutting. With a little imagination and experimentation, you're sure to discover some shortcuts of your own.

To practice the techniques presented here, make the Shortcuts Sampler quilt designed by Roxanne Carter. Roxanne used the blocks and cutting techniques featured in this section to create it so you could perfect your rotary cutting and strip-piecing skills while you make a beautiful quilt. Directions begin on the next page.

SHORTCUTS SAMPLER

Introduction

Learning new techniques is always fun, but it is even more exciting when you create a new project at the same time. When you make "Shortcuts Sampler," you will gain new skills while you put together a beautiful quilt.

The 12" blocks included in Shortcuts Sampler are easy to make, using all of Donna Thomas's great timesaving methods featured in this chapter. When you combine the twelve blocks with the lattice pieces, pieced cornerstones, and the border, you will have a quilt that measures 60" x 76". You can make a larger quilt by using some of the block patterns more than once and changing color placement so they look different. Study the quilt photos on page 61 to see what an intriguing difference color placement can make in the final appearance of each block and the entire quilt.

Fabric #1   Fabric #2   Fabric #3   Fabric #4   Fabric #5

If you want to set blocks diagonally as they wcrc in "Confetti Delight" on page 61, you will need to make two versions of one of the blocks. In "Confetti Delight," I made a second version of the Card Trick block on pages 48–49. I varied the color placement within this block from the traditional layout to create a block that looks very different from the first. See if you can find both Card Trick blocks in the quilt. The Rolling Stone block illustrations shown below also show how different color placement can change the look of a block.

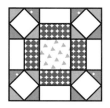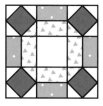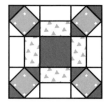

Note: Each sampler block appears on a grid in which one square is equal to 1". By examining the grid and counting the number of squares in a block, you can easily see its size. If you wish to make the sampler blocks in a different size, assign a different measurement to the grid squares. For example, if you prefer to make 6" finished blocks, each square would equal ½". For a 16" block, each square would equal 1¼".

To determine the cut size of squares and rectangles, simply add a total of ½" to both the width and height of the finished size. To determine the cut size of diamonds, triangles, trapezoids, chevrons, and hexagons, you must add different seam allowances. Refer to pages 31–40 for the correct seam allowances to add.

For your convenience, correct cutting measurements are included in directions for each 12" sampler block so you won't need to do any calculations when you make this quilt as shown. All seam allowances are ¼" wide. It is important to use an accurate ¼" stitching guide on your machine. See page 12 for directions on how to test your seam width for stitching accuracy before you begin to assemble your blocks.

The yardage requirements given are based on 44"-wide fabrics that have been prewashed and have a usable width of 42". You will cut many strips across the fabric width. Full strip lengths are given as 42". Because of varying fabric widths after preshrinking, your strips may be longer or shorter. In most cases you won't need the entire strip. You will have fabric left over to save for other quilts.

Roxanne Carter

Shortcuts Sampler Blocks

Color photo on page 61.
Finished Quilt Size: 60" x 76"
Finished Block Size: 12"

MATERIALS: 44"-WIDE FABRIC

Choose fabrics that you love and that work together. For easy identification, the quilt blocks shown here have been shaded to match the original "Shortcuts Sampler" shown at the top of page 61. I suggest you place tracing paper over each block and color it to match your fabric colors. You might want to make several tracings of each block so you can try a variety of color arrangements before selecting the one you will use for your quilt. Then use your colored tracing as a guide as you cut and piece each block.

Blocks and Background
1 yd. each of 4 different fabrics
1½ yds. background fabric
Sashing
1 yd. background or color used for center of strip-pieced lattice
1½ yds. dark fabric (a solid works best)
¼ yd. contrasting fabric for cornerstones
Border
2½ yds. light print or solid-colored fabric for borders cut along the lengthwise grain. (If you wish to cut the borders across the width of the fabric, you will need only 1 yard.)
Backing
3½ yds. fabric of your choice
Binding
¾ yd. fabric of your choice

ROLLING STONE

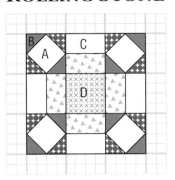

Rolling Stone Block

Make the Rolling Stone block to learn how to make a boxed square and how to strip piece the side units. See page 26.

Corner Units: Pieces A and B
1. Piece A: From Fabric #1, cut 4 squares, each 3⅜" x 3⅜".
2. Piece B: From Fabric #2 and Fabric #3, cut 4 squares, each 2⅞" x 2⅞", for a total of 8 squares. Stack the squares and cut once diagonally for 16 half-square triangles.

3. Sew 2 triangles (B) to opposite corners of a square (A). Repeat with the remaining 2 triangles for each block. Nub the corners of the triangles before stitching them to the squares. See page 25.

Make 4.

Side and Center Units: Pieces C and D
1. Piece C: From Fabric #1 and from Fabric #4, cut 1 strip each, 2½" x 22".
2. Place strips right sides together with raw edges even and stitch ¼" from one long edge. Press the seam toward the darker fabric. Cut the strip-pieced unit into 4 segments, each 4½" wide.

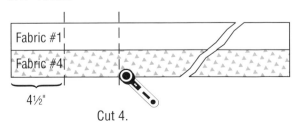

Cut 4.

3. Piece D: From Fabric #5, cut 1 square, 4½" x 4½".

Block Assembly

1. Arrange units as shown in piecing diagram.

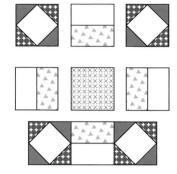

Piecing Diagram

2. Sew the units together in horizontal rows.
3. Sew rows together to complete the block.

SNOWBALL

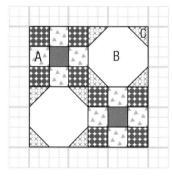

Snowball Block

Make the Snowball block to learn how to strip piece the Ninepatch unit and how to trim the corners from a large square to create the Snowball unit. See pages 23–24 and 26–27.

Ninepatch Unit: Piece A

1. From Fabric #2, cut 1 strip, 2½" x 12". From Fabric #3, cut 2 strips of the same size. From Fabric #4, cut 3 strips of the same size.
2. Sew the strip-pieced units as shown. From the first strip-pieced unit (Fabrics #3 and #4), cut 4 segments, each 2½" wide.

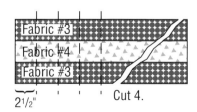

Cut 2 segments, each 2½" wide, from the second strip-pieced unit (Fabrics #2 and #4).

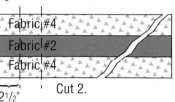

2½"   Cut 2.

3. Assemble 2 Ninepatch units as shown.

Ninepatch Unit
Make 2.

Snowball Unit: Pieces B and C

1. Piece B: From Fabric #1, cut 2 squares, each 6½" x 6½". Use Cutoff Template #1 on page 58 as a guide to trim off the 4 corners. See "Modifying Shapes" on pages 23–24 for information about making a paper cutting guide.

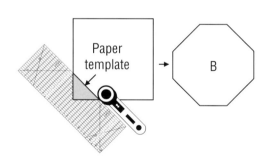

Paper template → B

2. Piece C: From Fabric #5, cut 4 squares, each 2⅞" x 2⅞". Layer the squares and cut once diagonally to make 8 half-square triangles.

3. Sew 4 triangles (C) to the trimmed edges of Piece B. Be sure to nub the corners of the triangles before stitching them to Piece B. See page 25.

Note: *Be sure to sew the triangles to the longer, bias edges of the Snowball. They will not fit the shorter, straight-of-grain edges.*

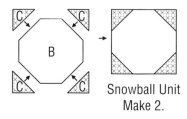

Snowball Unit
Make 2.

Block Assembly

1. Arrange the units as shown in the piecing diagram.

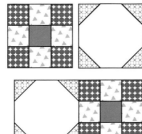

2. Sew the units together in rows.
3. Sew the rows together to complete the block.

Piecing Diagram

JENNY'S BLOCK

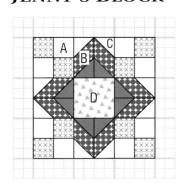

Jenny's Block

Make Jenny's block to learn how to make four-patch units for the corners and chevron units for the sides.

Four-Patch Units: Piece A

1. Cut 1 strip, 2½" x 22", from Fabric #1 and 1 strip from Fabric #5. (Use leftover strips from other blocks if available.)
2. With right sides together and raw edges even, stitch ¼" from one long edge. Press the seam toward the darker fabric.

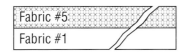

3. Cut the strip-pieced unit into 8 segments, each 2½" wide.

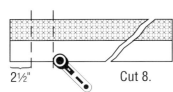

2½"   Cut 8.

4. Sew 2 segments together to form a four-patch unit as shown. Make 4 units for the block.

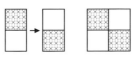

Four-Patch Unit
Make 4.

Chevron Side Units: Pieces B and C

1. Piece B: From Fabric #3, cut 1 strip, 2" x 42", for the chevrons. With the strip still folded in half as cut, use Chevron Template #2 on page 58 to cut a 45° angle. See page 22. With the strip still folded, cut 4 sets of chevron units. You will have mirror-image sets of chevron units, one for each side of the block.

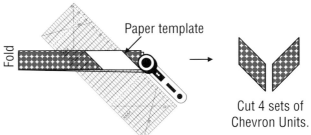

Paper template

Fold

Cut 4 sets of
Chevron Units.

2. Piece C: Cut 4 squares, each 2⅞" x 2⅞", from Fabric #1 and 4 from Fabric #2 for a total of 8 squares. Stack the squares and cut once diagonally to yield 16 half-square triangles.

3. Working in pairs, sew a triangle (C) of Fabric #2 to a long edge of each chevron unit (B) as shown. *The block will not fit together if you try to sew the triangle to the shorter end of the chevron unit. Measure them if you are uncertain.* Then sew a triangle (C) of Fabric #1 to the opposite long edge of each chevron unit C/B to create unit C/B/C.

Chevron Pair

4. Sew each chevron pair together as shown, carefully matching the seam lines where the chevrons meet.

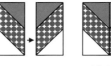

Make 4
Side Units.

Center Unit: Piece D

From Fabric #4, cut 1 square, 4½" x 4½".

Block Assembly

1. Arrange units as shown in the piecing diagram.

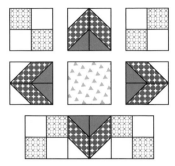

Piecing Diagram

2. Sew the units together in rows.
3. Sew the rows together to complete the block.

UNION SQUARE

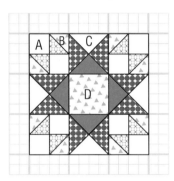

Union Square Block

Make the Union Square block to learn how to cut and sew half-square and quarter-square triangles. Refer to page 18 for more information.

Corner Units: Pieces A and B

1. Piece A: From Fabric #1, cut 8 squares, each 2½" x 2½".
2. Piece B: Cut 4 squares, each 2⅞" x 2⅞", from Fabric #4 and 4 from Fabric #5 for a total of 8 squares. Layer the squares and cut once diagonally to yield 16 half-square triangles for the corner units.
3. Sew 2 half-square triangles (B) together along the bias edges to form a half-square triangle unit. Make 8.

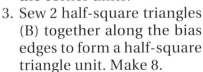

Make 8.

4. Sew a square (A) to a half-square triangle unit as shown. Make 8. Then sew 2 of these together to form a four-patch unit. Make 4.

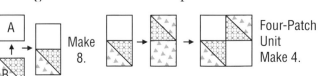

Make 8.

Four-Patch Unit Make 4.

Side Units: Piece C

1. Cut 1 square, 5¼" x 5¼", from Fabric #1 and 1 from Fabric #2. Cut 2 squares from Fabric #3 for a total of 4 squares. Stack squares and cut twice diagonally to yield 16 quarter-square triangles.

2. Sew the short sides of 2 triangles (C) together to form a triangle unit composed of quarter-square triangles. Make 4 triangle units from Fabrics #1 and #3, and 4 from Fabrics #2 and #3. Then sew 2 triangle units together to form the side unit. Make 4.

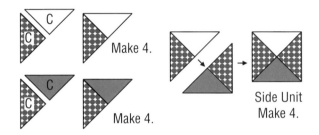

Make 4.

Make 4.

Side Unit Make 4.

Center Unit: Piece D

From Fabric #4, cut 1 square, 4½" x 4½".

Block Assembly

1. Arrange units as shown in the piecing diagram.
2. Sew the units together in horizontal rows.
3. Sew the rows together to complete the block.

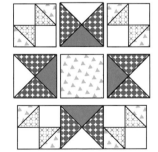

Piecing Diagram

CARD TRICK

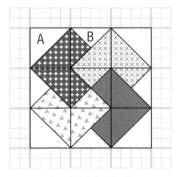

Card Trick Block

Make the Card Trick block to learn how to sew half-square triangles. Refer to page 18. Color placement is important. Cut all the pieces and lay out the block before you begin to sew the units together.

Corner Units: Piece A

1. From Fabric #1, cut 2 squares, each 4⅞" x 4⅞".
2. Stack the squares and cut once diagonally to yield 4 half-square triangles for the corners of the block.

Cards: Piece A

1. From each of the 4 remaining fabrics (#2, #3, #4, and #5), cut 1 square, 4⅞" x 4⅞".
2. Stack the squares and cut once diagonally as shown above to yield 2 half-square triangles of each color.
3. Sew 1 triangle (A) of each color to a triangle (A) of Fabric #1 to form 4 corner units. Press the seam toward the darker fabric in each unit. (You will have an extra triangle of each of the 4 card colors. Set them aside for the side units.)

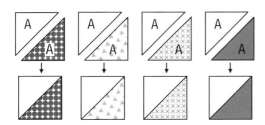

Side Units: Pieces A and B

1. From Fabric #1, cut 1 square, 5¼" x 5¼".
2. From each of the 4 remaining fabrics, cut 1 square, 5¼" x 5¼".
3. Stack the squares and cut twice diagonally to yield 4 quarter-square triangles (B) of each color. (Use only 1 of each color to make the side units and set aside 1 of each color for the center unit, below. Set extras aside for another project.)
4. Sew 1 triangle (B) of Fabric #1 to 1 triangle (B) of each card color. Sew together on the short side to make a side-by-side unit. You will have 4 finished units.

5. Sew each side-by-side unit to a triangle (A) left over from making corner units. Check color placement carefully before stitching.

Center Unit: Piece B

1. Using the triangles (B) left over from making the side units, sew 2 quarter-square triangles together to make a side-by-side unit. Color placement is very important in this step. Arrange the completed corner and side units to determine the placement of the quarter-square triangles for the center unit.
2. Sew the side-by-side units together for the center unit.

Center Unit

Block Assembly

1. Arrange the units as shown in the piecing diagram.
2. Sew units together in horizontal rows.
3. Sew rows together to complete the block.

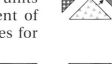

Piecing Diagram

EVENING STAR

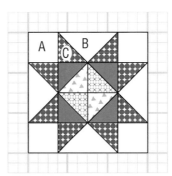

Evening Star Block

Make the Evening Star block to learn how to sew half-square triangles to quarter-square triangles for the Flying Geese side units.

Corner Units: Piece A

From Fabric #1, cut 4 squares, each 3½" x 3½".

Side Units: Pieces B and C

1. Piece B: From Fabric #1, cut 1 square, 7¼" x 7¼". Cut twice diagonally to yield 4 quarter-square triangles.

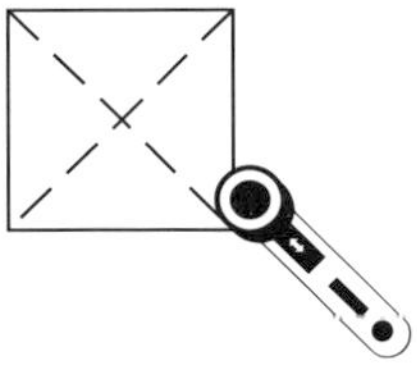

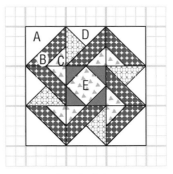

2. Piece C: From Fabric #3, cut 4 squares, each 3⅞" x 3⅞". Stack squares; cut once diagonally to yield 8 half-square triangles.

3. Sew 1 half-square triangle (C) to the short side of the quarter-square triangle (B), then sew another half-square triangle (C) to the other side of the pieced unit. Make 4.

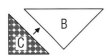

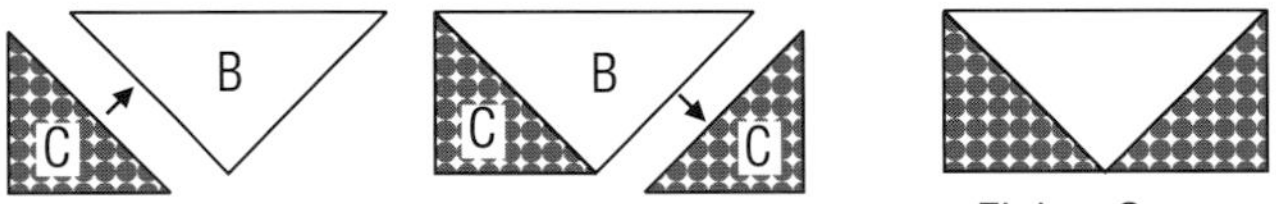

Flying Geese
Side Unit
Make 4.

Center Unit: Piece D

1. From Fabric #2, cut 2 squares, each 3⅞" x 3⅞". Cut 1 square, 3⅞" x 3⅞", from Fabric #4 and 1 from Fabric #5 for a total of 4 squares. Stack the squares and cut once diagonally to yield 8 half-square triangles.

2. Sew a triangle (D) of Fabric #2 to each of the triangles (D) of Fabrics #4 and #5.

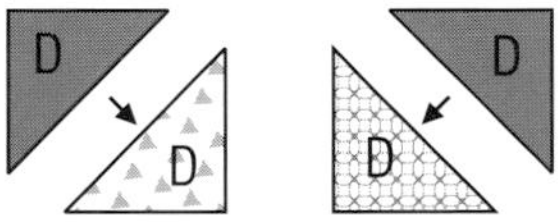

Make 2. Make 2.

Block Assembly

1. Arrange units as shown in the piecing diagram.

2. Sew the units together in horizontal rows.

3. Sew the rows together to complete the block.

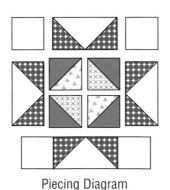

Piecing Diagram

LAND OF THE MIDNIGHT SUN

Land of the
Midnight Sun Block

Make the Land of the Midnight Sun block to learn how to modify a half-square triangle to make a trapezoid shape. Color placement is important. Cut all the pieces and lay out the block before you begin to sew.

Corner Units: Pieces A, B, and C

1. Piece A: From Fabric #1, cut 2 squares, each 4⅞" x 4⅞". Stack the squares and cut once diagonally to yield 4 half-square triangles.

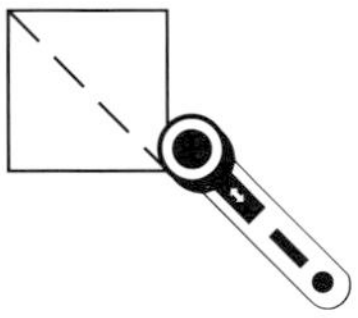

2. Piece B: From Fabric #3, cut 4 squares, each 4⅞" x 4⅞". Stack the squares and cut once diagonally to yield 8 half-square triangles. Use Cutoff Template #1 on page 58 to trim off the 90° corner on each one to make a trapezoid shape. See page 23. Set aside 4 trapezoids (B) for the side units.

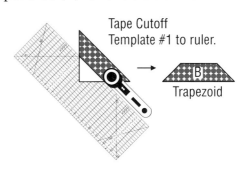

Tape Cutoff
Template #1 to ruler.

Trapezoid

3. Piece C: From Fabric #4, cut 4 squares, each 2⅞" x 2⅞". Cut once diagonally to yield 8 half-square triangles. Set aside 4 half-square triangles (C) for the side units.

4. Sew each of the 4 tri-angles (C) to a trap-ezoid (B). Press the seam toward darker fabric.

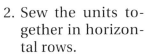

Make 4.

5. Sew a half-square triangle (A) to the pieced unit (B/C). Press the seam toward the darker fabric.

Side Units: Pieces B, C, and D

1. Piece B: Use the 4 trapezoids cut in step 2 of "Corner Units."
2. Piece C: Use the 4 half-square triangles cut in step 3 of "Corner Units."
3. Piece D: Cut 1 square, 5¼" x 5¼", from Fabric #1 and 1 from Fabric #5. Stack squares and cut twice diagonally to yield 8 quarter-square triangles.

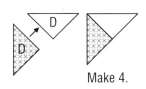

4. Sew triangles (D) to-gether on the short side. Press the seam toward darker fabric. Make 4.

Make 4.

5. Sew a triangle (C) to a trap-ezoid (B). Press the seam to-ward the darker fabric. Sew a triangle unit (D/D) to each pieced unit (C/B). Press the seam toward the trapezoid (B).

Boxed Square Center: Pieces C and E

1. Piece C: From Fabric #2, cut 2 squares, each 2⅞" x 2⅞". Stack the squares and cut once diagonally to yield 4 half-square triangles.
2. Piece E: From Fabric #4, cut 1 square, 3⅜" x 3⅜".
3. Nub the corners of the triangles. See page 25. Sew 2 triangles (C) to opposite corners of square (E). Press. Repeat with the remaining 2 tri-angles.

Block Assembly

1. Arrange units as shown in the piec-ing diagram.
2. Sew the units to-gether in horizon-tal rows.
3. Sew the rows to-gether to complete the block.

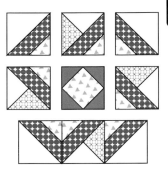

Piecing Diagram

CASTLES IN THE AIR

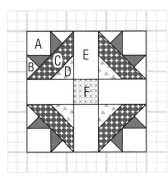

Castles in the Air Block

Make the Castles in the Air block to learn how to make a trapezoid from a half-square triangle.

Corner Units: Pieces A, B, C, and D

1. Piece A: From Fabric #1, cut 4 squares, each 2⅞" x 2⅞".
2. Piece B: From Fabric #1 and Fabric #2, cut 2 squares, each 3⅝" x 3⅝", for a total of 4 squares. Stack squares and cut twice diagonally to make 16 quarter-square triangles.

3. Sew 2 triangles (B) together on the short side. Make 2 mir-ror-image, side-by-side units for each corner unit.

Make 4.

4. For each corner unit, sew a side-by-side unit (B/B) to ad-jacent sides of a square (A). Make 4.

Measure long edge of quarter-square-triangle. Add ⅞" to determine size of bias square. In this example, a 2⅞" (2" +⅞") bias square is needed.

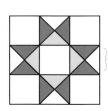

2" Finished size of long edge of quarter-square triangle

5. Piece C: From Fabric #3, cut 2 squares, each 5⅝" x 5⅝". Stack the squares and cut once diagonally to yield 4 half-square triangles. Use Cutoff Template #3 on page 58 to trim off the 90° corner, making a trapezoid shape.

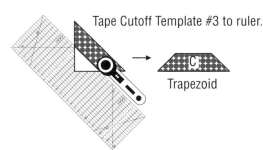

Tape Cutoff Template #3 to ruler.

Trapezoid

6. Piece D: From Fabric #4, cut 2 squares, each 3¼" x 3¼". Stack squares and cut once diagonally to yield 4 half-square triangles. Nub the corners of the triangles. See page 25.

7. Sew a triangle (D) to a trapezoid (C) to make a half-square unit. Press seam toward the trapezoid. Make 4.

8. Sew a half-square unit (C/D) to half-square unit (A/B) to complete the corner unit. Make 4.

Side Units: Piece E
1. From Fabric #1, cut 1 strip, 3" x 22".
2. Cut the strip into 4 segments, each 3" x 5¼".

Center Unit: Piece F
From Fabric #5, cut 1 square, 3" x 3".

Block Assembly
1. Arrange units as shown in the piecing diagram.
2. Sew the units together in horizontal rows.
3. Sew the rows together to complete the block.

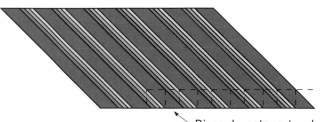

Discard waste rectangles.

ROMAN STRIPE

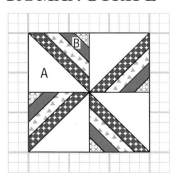

Roman Stripe Block

Make the Roman Stripe block to learn how to cut a half-square triangle unit from a strip-pieced unit.

Quarter Block: Pieces A and B
1. Piece A: From Fabric #1, cut 2 squares, each 6⅞" x 6⅞". Stack the squares and cut once diagonally to yield 4 half-square triangles.

2. Piece B: From each of Fabrics #2, #3, and #4, cut 1 strip, 1½" x 42". From Fabric #5, cut 1 strip, 2" x 42".
3. Sew the strips together in the order shown (3/4/2/5). Press all seams in one direction.

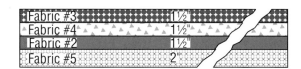

4. Using the half-square triangle (A) as a template, cut 4 triangles as shown, *so that Fabric #5 is always at the point of the triangle.* Save the extra triangles in between for another project.

Cut 4, using Piece A as a template.

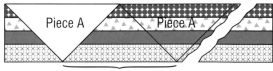

Not used

5. Sew the strip-pieced half-square triangle (B) to a triangle (A) to make a square. Make 4.

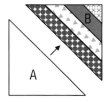

Make 4.

Block Assembly

1. Arrange squares as shown in the piecing diagram.
2. Sew the squares together in rows.
3. Sew the rows together to complete the block.

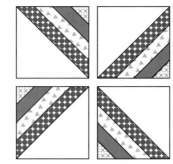

Piecing Diagram

FIFTY-FOUR FORTY OR FIGHT

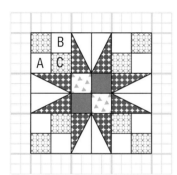

Fifty-four Forty or Fight Block

Make the Fifty-four Forty or Fight Block to learn how to cut and sew half rectangles. See page 20.

Corner Four Patch Units: Piece A

1. From each of Fabrics #1 and #5, cut 1 strip 2½" x 22".
2. With strips right sides together and raw edges even, stitch ¼" from one long edge. Crosscut 8 segments, each 2½" wide.

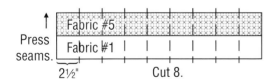

3. Sew 2 segments together as shown to make each four-patch unit. Make 4.

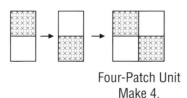

Four-Patch Unit
Make 4.

Half-Rectangle Side Units: Piece B

1. From each of Fabrics #1 and #3, cut 1 strip, 2¾" x 24".
2. Fold each strip in half crosswise *with wrong sides together.* Cut each one into 4 rectangles, each 2¾" x 5¼". Leave rectangles layered in sets of two.

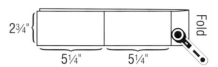

3. Cut each set of rectangles diagonally to make 2 half rectangles. Trim the points, using the Half Rectangle Template #4 on page 58. Transfer the dots on the paper template to the resulting half rectangles.

Trim, using Half Rectangle Template #4.

4. Sew 2 half rectangles together along the diagonal edge, matching the dots. Press the seam toward the darker fabric. Make 8.

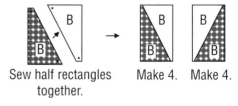

Sew half rectangles together.   Make 4.   Make 4.

5. Sew 2 half-rectangle units together to make the side unit. Make 4.

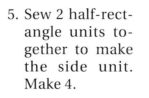

Side Unit
Make 4.

Center Four Patch Unit: Piece C

1. From each of Fabrics #2 and #4, cut 2 squares, each 2½" x 2½".
2. Sew squares together to form a four-patch unit.

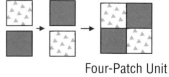

Four-Patch Unit
Make 1.

Block Assembly

1. Arrange units as shown in the piecing diagram.

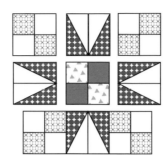

Piecing Diagram

2. Sew the units together in horizontal rows.
3. Sew rows together to complete the block.

MORNING STAR

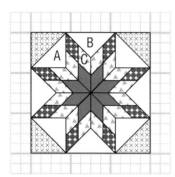

Morning Star Block

Make the Morning Star block to learn how to cut a pieced diamond from a strip-pieced unit. You will also learn how to construct an Eight-Pointed Star.

Refer to page 40, but note that the diamond shown there is made up of nine smaller diamonds. The diamond in this block is made up of four larger diamonds, but the technique is the same.

Corner Units: Piece A

1. From each of Fabrics #1 and #5, cut 2 squares, each 4⅜" x 4⅜", for a total of 4 squares.
2. Stack the squares and cut once diagonally to yield 8 half-square triangles.
3. Sew a triangle (A) of Fabric #1 to a triangle (A) of Fabric #5, stitching ¼" from the long edge. Press the seam toward darker fabric. Make 4.

Corner Unit
Make 4.

Side Units: Piece B

1. From Fabric #1, cut 1 square, 6¼" x 6¼".
2. Cut the square twice diagonally to yield 4 quarter-square triangles.

Diamond Units: Piece C

1. From each of Fabrics #2 and #3, cut 1 strip, 1¾" x 42". From Fabric #4, cut 2 strips, each 1¾" x 42".
2. Sew the Fabric #3 strip to a Fabric #4 strip to make Strip-Pieced Unit #1. Sew the remaining Fabric #4 strip to the Fabric #2 strip to make Strip-Pieced Unit #2.

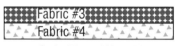

Strip-Pieced Unit #1

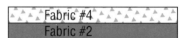

Strip-Pieced Unit #2

3. Place 1 strip-pieced unit above the other as shown to make sure you cut the correct angle on each strip. At one end of each strip-pieced unit, make a cut at a 45° angle to the long edge.

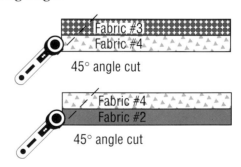

45° angle cut

45° angle cut

4. Cut each strip-pieced unit into 8 segments, each 1¾" wide, *making each cut parallel to the previous 45°-angle cut.* See page 40.

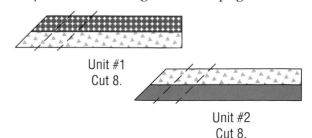

Unit #1
Cut 8.

Unit #2
Cut 8.

5. Sew a segment from each strip-pieced unit together to form a diamond. Make 8.

Make 8.

Block Assembly

1. Arrange units as shown in piecing diagram.
2. Follow the directions on page 56 for constructing an Eight-Pointed Star to assemble this block.

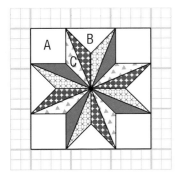

Piecing Diagram (See page 56.)

STAR OF THE EAST

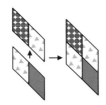

Star of the East Block

Make the Star of the East block to learn how to cut a half-length diamond from a strip-pieced unit. See pages 38–39 for more information.

Corner Units: Piece A

From Fabric #1, cut 4 squares, each 4" x 4".

Side Units: Piece B

1. From Fabric #1, cut 1 square, 6¼" x 6¼".
2. Cut the square twice diagonally to yield 4 quarter-square triangles.

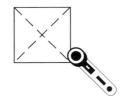

Half-Length Pieced Diamond Units: Piece C

1. From each of Fabrics #2, #3, #4, and #5, cut a strip, 2" x 42".
2. Sew the strip of Fabric #2 to the strip of Fabric #3, right sides together, stitching ¼" from *both* long edges. Repeat with the strips of Fabric #4 and #5.
3. Use the Strip Star Template #5 on page 58 to cut 4 triangles from each strip-pieced unit. See pages 38–39 for more information.

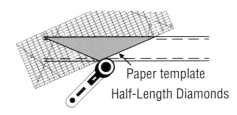

Paper template
Half-Length Diamonds

4. Carefully undo the stitching at the point of each piece, open out into a diamond, and press the seam open.

Half-Length
Pieced Diamond

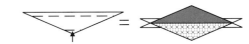

Remove stitches at point
and press diamond open.

Block Assembly

1. Arrange units as shown in piecing diagram.

Piecing Diagram (See page 56.)

2. Follow directions on page 56 for making an Eight-Pointed Star to assemble this block.

Constructing an Eight-Pointed (Le Moyne) Star

A simple way to construct a Le Moyne Star is to first attach the background pieces to the diamond-shaped star pieces, then sew the star pieces to each other. As you sew the pieces together, notice that seams must turn a corner where the background pieces meet the star pieces. To do this accurately, you must stop stitching *exactly* ¼" from the raw edge at the end of each seam where the pieces meet.

Note: Dots on illustrations indicate end points for stitching. Stitch in direction of arrows.

To make the diamond units, each made of 2 diamonds and 1 triangle:

1. Sew triangle to a diamond. Begin stitching *exactly* ¼" from the inner edge of the 2 pieces. Stitch all the way to the outer edge of the block.

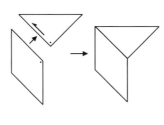

2. Sew a second diamond to the triangle, starting at the inner point *exactly* ¼" from the raw edges. Stitch to the outer edge of the block.

3. Match the points of the diamonds and sew them together. Press this seam to one side and press triangle seams toward the diamonds.

To add a square between 2 diamond units:

1. Sew a square to the diamond unit. Start sewing at the outer edge and end your stitching ¼" from the inner edge.

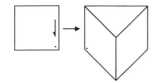

2. Sew the second diamond unit to the square. Begin stitching ¼" from the inner point and stitch to the outer edge.

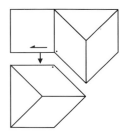

3. Match the points of diamonds and sew them together; press the seam in one direction. Press seams between the square and diamond units toward the diamonds.

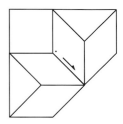

To join the 2 units with remaining squares:

1. Sew the edges of the diamond units to both edges of 1 square.

2. Repeat with the remaining square.

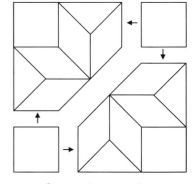

Sew center seam last.

To complete the block assembly:

1. Match the center points and pin.
2. Pull the corner squares out of the way and stitch the two halves of the block together through the center, from the inner point of one square to the inner point of the other square.

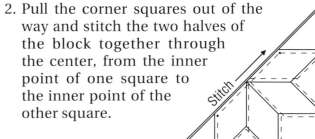

3. Press center seam to one side and press seams of the squares toward the diamonds.

Setting the Blocks

LATTICE

1. From the dark lattice fabric, cut 26 strips, each 1¼" x 42". From Fabric #1 (background fabric in blocks or other fabric of your choice), cut 13 strips, each 2½" x 42".

2. Make 13 strip-pieced lattice units as shown. Crosscut 31 segments, each 12½" wide, for lattice strips, and 40 segments, each 2½" wide, for the cornerstone units.

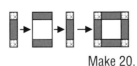

Make 13 units.

12½"
Cut 31 segments.   2½"
Cut 20 segments.

CORNERSTONES

1. Cut 4 strips, each 1¼" x 42", from the contrasting fabric for the cornerstones. Cut 2 strips, each 2½" x 42", from lattice fabric. Make 2 strip-pieced units as shown; crosscut 40 segments, each 1¼" wide.

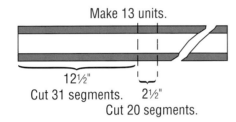

1¼"   Make 2 units.
Cut 40 segments.

2. Assemble corner-stones as shown, using the 1¼"-wide segments just cut and the 2½"-wide segments set aside earlier. Make 20.

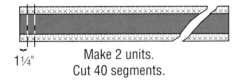

Make 20.

Quilt Top Assembly

1. Referring to the quilt plan on page 44, arrange the blocks in rows of 3 across and 4 down, with lattice strips between the blocks and at the outer edges of each row. Place blocks in an arrangement that pleases you. It is not necessary to place them in the same positions shown in the quilt plan.

2. Sew the blocks and lattice strips together in horizontal rows. Make 4 rows.

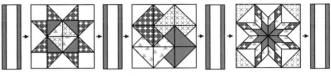

Make 4 rows.

3. Make 5 rows of alternating cornerstones and lattice strips, beginning and ending with a cornerstone in each row.

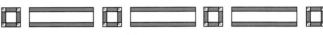

Make 5 rows.

4. Beginning and ending with a row of cornerstone/lattice, sew the blocks and lattice together in alternating rows.

Borders

1. From the border fabric, cut 2 strips, each 4½" x 60", for the top and bottom edges of the quilt top. Cut 2 strips, each 4½" x 76", for the sides. Sew the border strips to the quilt top with 4½" of each strip extending beyond the raw edges of the quilt at each end for mitering corners. Begin and end stitching exactly ¼" from the raw edge at each corner of quilt top.

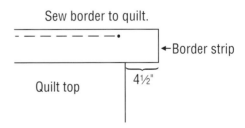

Sew border to quilt.

←Border strip

Quilt top   4½"

2. Miter border corners as shown on pages 206–8.

Quilt Finishing

1. Layer the completed quilt top with batting and backing; baste. See page 255.

2. Quilt as desired. Refer to "Loving Stitches," beginning on page 225.

3. Bind the edges. Refer to "Happy Endings," beginning on page 275.

TEMPLATES

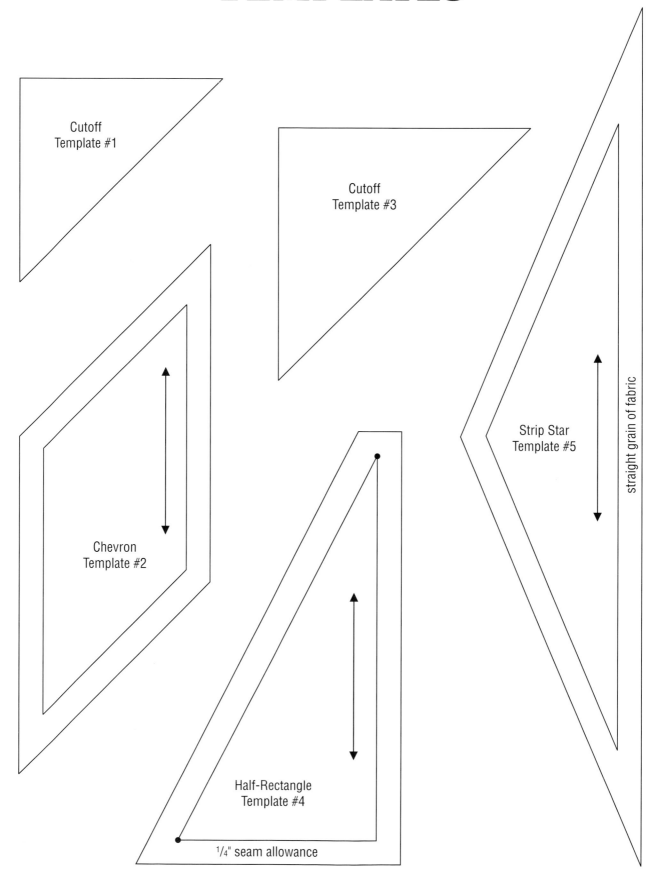

Cutoff
Template #1

Cutoff
Template #3

Chevron
Template #2

Strip Star
Template #5

straight grain of fabric

Half-Rectangle
Template #4

1/4" seam allowance

Shortcuts
GALLERY

The quilts shown here are examples of patterns that can be made easily and quickly using the techniques featured in this chapter.
Directions for full-size quilt patterns are not given unless otherwise noted, but block cutting and piecing information appears throughout the chapter.

Woodland Tree by Donna Lynn Thomas, 1990, Dorf-Guell, Germany, 36" x 36". Strip piecing and layered cutting of the tree triangles allowed Donna to complete this quilt top in five hours.

First Star by Donna Lynn Thomas, 1989, Frankfurt, Germany, 70" x 70". As quick as this piece was to make, yet another household move was quicker, preventing the project's intended completion as a shower curtain. It is constructed from bias squares, simple squares, and rectangles.

Snowball (right) by Nancy J. Martin, 1985, Woodinville, Washington, 40" x 58". The striking overall pattern is created by modifying squares into octagons to create Snowball blocks that are then alternated with scrappy, strip-pieced Ninepatch blocks. Quilted by Andrea Scadden. (Collection of That Patchwork Place, Inc., Bothell, Washington)

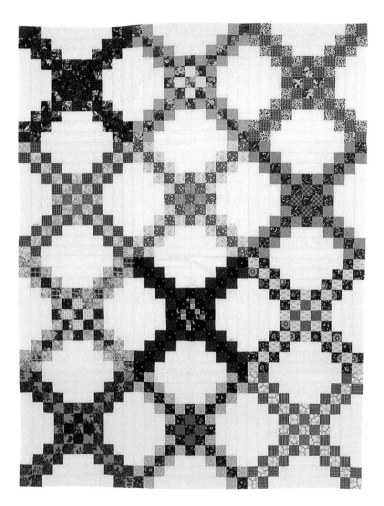

Friendship Quilt (above) by Donna Lynn Thomas, Joan Scone, and Kathy Meredith, 1988, Swarthmore, Pennsylvania, Chadds Ford, Pennsylvania, and Frankfurt, Germany, 54" x 76". This friendship quilt was inspired by an antique quilt seen in Sara Nephew's book My Mother's Quilts: Designs from the Thirties. *A medley of fabrics and strip-piecing techniques increased the joy of sharing with friends. (Collection of Donna Lynn Thomas)*

Goose in the Pond by Donna Lynn Thomas, 1989, Frankfurt, Germany, 60" x 75½". A traditional color combination and an intricate-looking design disguise a simple construction process. Bias squares and straight-of-grain strip piecing make this an easily assembled quilt to grace a young boy's bed.

Shortcuts Sampler *by Roxanne Carter, 1992, Mukilteo, Washington, 60" x 76". Roxanne made this quilt with pastel scraps as a teaching tool for her classes on rotary cutting. Making the individual blocks gives you the opportunity to try many of the strip-piecing and rotary-cutting methods in "Shortcuts." Directions for this quilt begin on page 44.*

Confetti Delight *by Roxanne Carter, 1993, Mukilteo, Washington, 81" x 81". The same Shortcuts Sampler blocks sparkle on a black background print in this variation of the original sampler quilt. Can you find the duplicate block required to turn this into a diagonally set quilt?*

Rosebud Sampler *by Roxanne Carter, 1992, Mukilteo, Washington, 60" x 76". Add one more fabric to the number required and the sampler blocks take on a new look.*

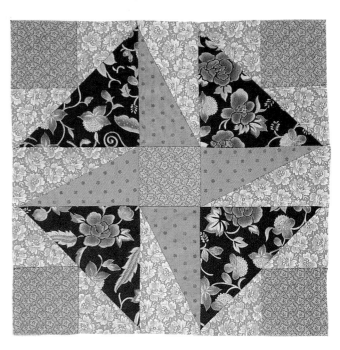

Star of the East *quilt block by Donna Lynn Thomas, 1991, Dorf-Guell, Germany, 10¼" x 10¼". This light and airy springtime block required only half the usual assembly time; the secret—strip-pieced half diamonds.*

Crazy Ann quilt block *by Donna Lynn Thomas, 1987, Brookhaven, Pennsylvania, 12" x 12". Someday, this pretty little block will be part of a sampler quilt but, for now, it is an excellent example of how to use strip-pieced rectangles.*

LeMoyne Star table pad *by Donna Lynn Thomas, 1988, Brookhaven, Pennsylvania, 15" x 15". The use of a repeat pattern in plain diamonds creates an exciting, overall secondary design. Each diamond was individually marked and cut with the rotary cutter to exactly repeat the design.*

Waterwheel *by Donna Lynn Thomas, 1987, Brookhaven, Pennsylvania, 26" x 26". Almost a charm quilt—can you find the three fabric repeats?—this inviting wall quilt is quick to make, using side-striped, half-square triangles.*

APerfect Match

A GUIDE TO PRECISE MACHINE PIECING

CONTENTS

INTRODUCTION

I was introduced to a needle at the tender age of four. My mother was a home-economics teacher, and she started me out on a pretty little cross-stitch heart project. In Brownies, she helped my troop with their sewing badges. Her special interest was in tailoring and garment construction. I remember many a night falling asleep to the whir of her machine as she worked on her latest project. It was only natural that my sisters and I were personally introduced to her sewing machine and the wonders of fabric. My mother has never made a quilt, and I stopped making clothes many years ago when I discovered quilts, but neither of us can imagine life without a sewing machine.

During my formative teen years, I adopted the prevailing philosophy—the Walden Pond idea of self-sufficiency and "make it from scratch." Even though I made my first crude quilt with my own sewing machine, I still felt it didn't count until I could make one by hand. I even thought that at some point, I should weave my own fabric for my quilts, just as I thought the pioneer women had done! Ah, the romance and misconceptions of youth! It didn't dawn on me that pioneer women were not so foolish as to cut up newly woven fabric into little pieces for the sake of making a pieced quilt, nor did they piece by hand for aesthetic reasons or by choice. Once the opportunity arose to get a quilt together quickly by machine in time for the harsh winters, they would ride long distances, if necessary, to get to the nearest sewing machine.

I continued to piece by machine but, a few years later, achieved my dream of making at least one quilt by hand. It is one of the few bed-sized quilts I've ever made, and it's made from the not-so-pretty fabrics found before the current quilt revival. But, it keeps my husband and me warm, and I treasure it. Being more practical than dreamy, I am convinced that machine piecing is more my speed, literally and figuratively. I have been happily whirring away ever since, enjoying the special challenges and amazing accuracy and precision that are possible with machine piecing.

In this chapter, I have included all the tips, techniques, and tidbits I have acquired from my teachers, beginning with my mother. I learned many other things through hours of quiet frustration, struggling alone with each new quilting challenge. I worked in a wonderful quilt shop for several years and taught quilting classes overseas for another few years. As a result, I have also learned from customers, other teachers, and from my students.

Whether by machine or by hand, a quilt must be stitched. This section of the book is about machine piecing. There are some differences in machine piecing when you work with pieces that have marked sewing lines and those without. The first method is traditional. You make templates the finished size of the shape and trace around the template onto fabric. The marks around the template define the finished size and are, therefore, the stitching line, *not* the cutting line. (Information on accurate template construction is included here.)

The second instance covers two different cutting techniques —using templates with ¼"-wide seam allowances included, or rotary cutting individually or from strip-pieced units. There are no marked sewing lines with these techniques, only raw edges. (Basic techniques for sewing rotary-cut pieces are discussed in detail in "Short-cuts," beginning on page 9.) As you read this section, you will find distinct references to one or the other of these two cutting techniques when it affects how to machine piece.

Six quilt patterns are included so you can practice the techniques in this chapter. *Both rotary-cutting and template-cutting directions are provided for three of the quilts so you may construct them using the method of your choice.*

Machine piecing can be extremely rewarding, not only because of its speed but because of the extreme accuracy possible. "A Perfect Match" shows you the stitching basics plus lots of "blue ribbon" stitching techniques and instructions on how to handle some special seams you will undoubtedly stitch across as you do more and more machine piecing. Master these skills and all your quilts will be a "perfect match!"

Donna Thomas

EQUIPMENT AND SUPPLIES

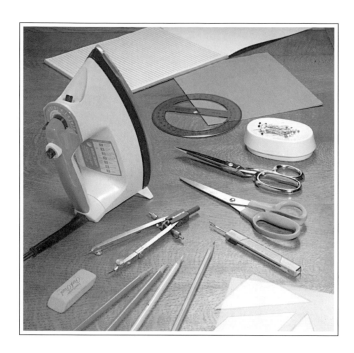

In addition to a sewing machine in good working order, you will need the following supplies.

Graph paper, ruler, pencil, and eraser. It is a good idea to check the accuracy of a pattern's templates before making your own. Draft the full-size block and then check this against the pattern. Investigate any differences to determine whether it's your error or the pattern. You can save a lot of fabric by taking this simple precaution. You may also need these items if you arc going to adapt template-cut patterns for rotary cutting.

Compass and protractor. These are two other useful tools to have on hand if you are drafting designs with curves and angles.

Template material. The best material is a translucent plastic, since it is easy to mark and cut. It also lasts longer than cardboard. In addition, you can see through it for correct positioning when you want to use a particular section of a print.

Utility scissors. Use these instead of your good fabric scissors to cut template plastic.

Lead and colored pencils. Keep pencils sharp for accurate marking. A good #2 lead pencil marks clearly on the majority of fabrics but on some fabrics, marking is more visible when done with a bright yellow, silver, or orange pencil. Hard, colored leads keep their points better, resulting in fine marking lines. Look for a basic set of good colored pencils at art or office-supply stores.

Fabric shears. Good, sharp shears are a must for accurately cutting fabric pieces, although you can also use rotary equipment to cut out marked pieces. See pages 13–14.

Sandpaper board. This is an invaluable tool for accurately marking fabric. Glue fine sandpaper to a hard surface, such as wood, cardboard, poster board, linoleum squares, or needlework mounting board. The sticky surface on a mounting board eliminates the need for more glue—just stick the sandpaper in place! An 8" x 10" board is portable and one that measures 16" x 20" is a handy size for the sewing room.

Pins. The best pins for cotton are silk pins. They are long, slender, and sharp, making it easy to pin very precisely at corners and intersections. Colored glass heads are not essential, but many quiltmakers prefer them for their visibility.

Seam ripper. This item is essential, not only for ripping stitching mistakes, but also for use as a "better finger." See "Blue Ribbon Stitching Techniques," beginning on page 73.

Ironing supplies. Good ironing supplies need not be fancy, just clean and in good working order. The ironing surface can be a traditional ironing board or just a simple terry cloth towel, placed on a heat-resistant surface. A steam iron that has a cotton setting is best. Keep the iron clean, following the manufacturer's instructions, and use distilled water in it, especially if you have hard water. Hard water leaves mineral deposits in your iron that will ruin it. These deposits may cause your iron to spit through the steam vents. Hard water also clogs the spray nozzle of an iron.

It is very nice to have a spray feature on your iron, although an ordinary spray bottle is a handy substitute. Do not use the same spray bottle for your fabrics that you use for any household chemicals. Use it only for water.

BEFORE YOU STITCH

Before you start sewing, there are a few minor details to take care of, such as cutting your quilt pieces, checking your seam guide, and deciding how you will press your seams. Let's review.

Cutting with Templates

No amount of accurate sewing can make up for inaccurate cutting. If you plan to rotary cut your quilt, see "Shortcuts," beginning on page 10. Cutting techniques are different when using templates, but care and accuracy are just as important. Because there are several steps, small inaccuracies with each step can compound the problem tremendously. Whether making templates with or without seam allowances included, begin with an accurate drawing of the pattern piece. Add seam allowances to all sides if you want seam allowances included in the cut piece and then transfer the pattern to plastic template material. Do this by marking the points and/or corners of the shape on the plastic first. Then use a straight edge to draw the lines in between.

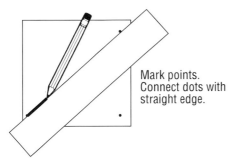

Mark points. Connect dots with straight edge.

It is also important to mark the fabric accurately with the templates. Place the templates face down on the wrong side of the fabric. Work on a sandpaper board as described on page 66. Fine sandpaper grips the fabric so it doesn't shift but is fine enough that the pencil lines will not "wobble" as you trace. Mark along the sides of the template with a sharp lead or colored pencil held at an angle. The angle keeps the point sharp so it moves over the fabric smoothly. A pencil held

upright while marking can hang up between the threads in the weave of the fabric, causing it to drag and to draw a distorted line. The point also wears down faster, which causes marking inaccuracies.

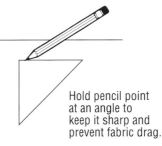

Hold pencil point at an angle to keep it sharp and prevent fabric drag.

For sharp points, do not trace around corners. Instead, extend the side lines past the corners, forming accurate cross hairs.

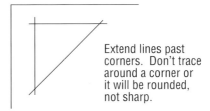

Extend lines past corners. Don't trace around a corner or it will be rounded, not sharp.

When cutting, cut right on the line, not to either side. If you prefer, use a rotary cutter to cut pieces with or without seam allowances. *When cutting pieces with only the sewing line marked, use the cutter in conjunction with a rotary ruler to add an accurate ¼"-wide seam allowance around each piece as you cut.* Otherwise, if using scissors, estimate the ¼"-wide seam allowance visually and cut approximately ¼" from the sewing line. It is easy to cut on the marked lines for pieces with seam allowances already included.

One other point to consider when cutting fabric is grain line. Be sure to review "Fabric and Grain Line" on pages 15–16. The same rules regarding grain line apply to cutting with templates.

Establishing an Accurate Seam Allowance

The standard seam allowance for quiltmaking is ¼" wide. There are three ways to add ¼"-wide seam allowances to all sides of each piece you cut for a quilt.

FINISHED-SIZE TEMPLATES

1. Trace the template onto template plastic or cardboard and mark the grain line.
2. Trace around the template on the wrong side of the fabric, leaving ½" between pieces as you position the template and mark the required number of pieces. *The marked line is the sewing line.*
3. Cut the pieces from the fabric, adding an approximate ¼" seam allowance all around.
4. *Align the sewing lines,* not the raw edges, and sew on the marked line. See page 71 for detailed directions.

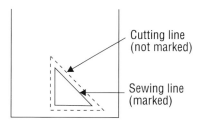

Template without seam allowances included.

Note: Before cutting, some people prefer to mark a cutting line ¼" away from the sewing line, and still others use the rotary cutter and ruler to cut ¼" away from the sewing line. No matter which way you choose to cut the pieces, *the critical aspect of this method is the accuracy of the sewing line, not the seam allowance.* (In reality, the seam allowance can be any width, from ¼" on up, as long as the sewing line is accurate and there is fabric to spare.) Since raw edges are not aligned in this method, the accuracy of the seam allowances is not important, and they can be trimmed to even widths later if necessary.

TEMPLATES WITH SEAM ALLOWANCES

With this method, there is no marked sewing line on which to sew, making it critical that you draft accurate templates and mark them carefully on the fabric. Accuracy is the key to a successful quilt top.

1. Draft templates with ¼"-wide seam allowances around all sides of each piece, being sure to mark grain-line arrows.
2. Trace around templates on the wrong side of the fabric. *The marked line is the cutting line;* thus, it is unnecessary to leave space between marked pieces. Cut out pieces on the line.

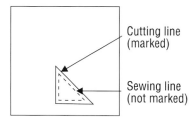

Template with seam allowances included.

3. To sew the pieces together, align raw edges and stitch ¼" from them, using an accurate ¼" guide on the machine's throat plate.

TEMPLATE-FREE® ROTARY CUTTING

With this method, you cut the required pieces from the fabric without templates. Instead, the pieces are cut as individual units, from strips or from strip-pieced units. The cut size includes ¼"-wide seam allowances added to the desired finished size of the piece.

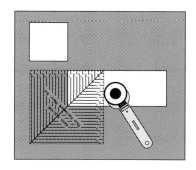

1. Cut the pieces or strips required.
2. To sew pieces together, align the raw edges and stitch, using a ¼"-wide seam allowance.

With this method, accurate cutting is important, along with adding the proper amount for seam allowances. For example, to create a finished 3" square, cut a 3½" square (3" + ½" for the two ¼"-wide seam allowances, one on each side of the square). For complete information on how to use the rotary cutter to cut just about any shape and strip unit, review the information in "Shortcuts," beginning on page 9.

Note: Both of the last two methods depend on accurate cutting for successful results, but it is of equal importance to have an accurate ¼" sewing guide. If the seam you sew is slightly wider than it should be, the seam will cut into the finished dimension of the fabric piece. If the seam is too narrow, the finished size of the piece will be too large. Either way, the quilt pieces will not fit together well, and the quilt block will not be the desired finished size. This will affect the size of everything else in the quilt, including any sashings, borders, or alternate blocks. As you can imagine, the problem becomes greater and greater with each seam sewn in the block—just like a runaway snowball.

> *Tip* Some sewing machines have a ¼" seam guide marked on the throat plate. On others that don't, many people assume that they can use the outer right-hand edge of the presser foot as the ¼" seam guide. However, it is best to check your presser foot or the ¼" marking on the throat plate for accuracy before you begin stitching your quilt pieces together. See page 12 for information on how to test your seam allowance and create an accurate seam guide.

Making a Pressing Plan

You may wonder why we are discussing pressing now before you sew a single stitch. The general rule for pressing patchwork seams is to press them toward the darker of the two fabrics. However, there are many exceptions to this rule. Plan your pressing before you begin so that 1) your completed block or quilt will lie flat and smooth; and 2) the seams butt at intersections when matching them for stitching.

For this reason, I recommend making a pressing plan before taking a single stitch. It eliminates guesswork! Be aware, though, that sometimes there is just no such thing as a perfect pressing plan where everything works out exactly. In such cases, the only solution is a best effort.

It is easy to make a pressing plan. Begin by making a scale drawing of your block(s) or quilt design. Include any pieced blocks, sashings, or borders that will butt against other pieced areas.

A simple example is the Ninepatch block. To successfully butt seams and evenly distribute them at the intersections, you must press the squares in one of two ways. The first way is to press all seams in rows 1 and 3 in one direction, and the seams in row 2 in the opposite direction. The second solution is to press all seams toward the dark squares since they alternate.

You can press the seams that join the rows of blocks in either direction, but it is also a good idea to plan this pressing so the direction alternates from row to row. That way, the intersecting seams will also butt together for accurately matched seam intersections.

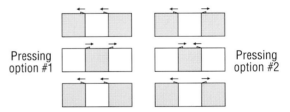

Pressing option #1   Pressing option #2

If the Ninepatch block will be next to another pieced block of a different design, be sure to consider the direction you will press the seams where the two blocks meet. Depending on the pressing needs of the adjoining block, you may end up favoring one way of pressing the Ninepatch over another.

The process is basically the same for any block. Figure the most logical plan for the block. If it sits alone, you're done, but if it sits next to other piecing, the pressing must be adjusted to fit the adjoining seams. Don't forget that there are four sides to the block. Unless the seams on each of the four sides are pressed exactly alike (as they usually are), then all four sides must be worked out individually.

There is a pressing plan with several of the quilts in this book. Take the time to study the plans and understand each one. Consider drawing the same blocks without the pressing arrows so you can try your own hand at planning. When you are finished, compare the two to see the differences. It could be that your plan works equally well, but seeing the different approaches is also good practice.

Pressing Seams

As simple as pressing may seem, there are a few things to remember when pressing seams. A properly pressed seam is clearly and crisply pressed to one side without any pleats or puckering on the right side. Here are a few tips that will help you.

1. *Press, don't iron.* Ironing is an aggressive back-and-forth motion that we use on clothing to remove wrinkles. This action can easily pull and distort the bias edges or seams in your piecing. An overly aggressive use of the iron can distort perfectly marked and sewn quilt pieces. You may notice this particularly after sewing two perfectly marked, cut, and sewn triangles together to make a square. Many times the finished unit is no longer square if you've ironed it.

   Pressing is the gentle lowering and lifting of the iron along the length of a seam without pushing back and forth along the seam, which can cause distortion. Let the heat, steam, and an occasional spritz of water press the fabric in the desired direction instead.

2. *Always press the line of stitches after sewing.* Use a shot of steam if your iron has this feature. This relaxes the thread, eases out any puckers from the stitching, and smooths out any fullness you may have eased in as you stitched. You'll be surprised at how smoothly

and nicely the seam will turn when you press it to one side.

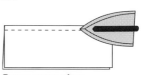

Press seam after sewing, before pressing one way or the other.

3. *Press from the right side.* Arrange the stitched fabric pieces with the open edges facing toward you and the seam away from you as shown. Now use the tip of the iron to gently open the unit, so the right sides are exposed. Gently press the top fabric away from you and over the seam allowance.

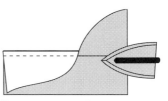

Press seam open by opening the pieces with the iron.

4. *Correct mistakes in pressing by returning the unit to its unpressed position and steaming the seam.* I call this unpressing a seam. A particularly crisp seam may need a spritz of water to relax the crease out of the fabric. Once you have steamed away the incorrect pressing, press in the new direction.

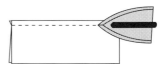

Press seam back to original unpressed position. Once unpressed, repress seam in a new direction.

STITCHING BASICS

Machine stitching is the process of joining two pieces of fabric with a straight running stitch. Let's examine the steps involved in basic stitching, step by step.

Matching the Pieces

With seam allowances included:

If you include the ¼"-wide seam allowances when you cut your pieces, using either templates or rotary cutting, carefully align the raw edges of the seam and stitch ¼" from the raw edges. Nub the corners of triangles, diamonds, and angles other than 90° that extend past the seam allowances before stitching to make it easier to align edges precisely. See "Nubbing Points for Sewing" on page 25.

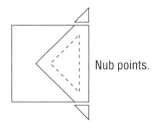
Nub points.

With marked stitching lines:

Use pins to align the marked stitching lines. Place the fabric pieces right sides together and use a pin to pierce the corner markings exactly at each end of the seam line of the top fabric. At the same time, run the pin exactly through the corner markings on the bottom piece. Secure the corners by running the pins through the fabric vertically.

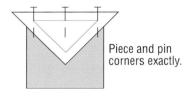
Piece and pin corners exactly.

Every inch or so, align the stitching line in the same fashion, using pins. Make sure each pin pierces both lines exactly, front and back. Vertical pins keep the fabric from shifting, just as horizontal pins do. Just the same, I like to run every other pin horizontally on the stitching line

so that I am sure the stitching lines are aligned along the length of the seam rather than only at pin points.

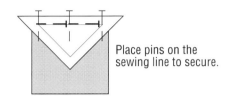
Place pins on the sewing line to secure.

Stitching

With a few exceptions, when you machine stitch quilt patches together, you usually stitch from raw edge to raw edge, and backstitching is unnecessary. This is because you will eventually sew across every seam as you sew the blocks together and finish the quilt top. Set the machine for a stitch length of 12–15 stitches per inch. This stitch length is short enough to hold the seams during the block and quilt construction.

In those cases where it is necessary to stitch from point to point rather than from the outer edge to the outer edge, backstitching *is* necessary. It is also important to begin and end stitching precisely at the point.

Backstitch at seam intersections when stitching point to point.

When backstitching is necessary, the tendency is to begin sewing exactly in the point, stitch a few stitches, then backstitch, and continue stitching. Unfortunately, when you use this method, you must guess how far to stitch backwards before you reach the corner, which is covered by the presser foot while backstitching. There is a solution for this situation.

1. Rather than starting in the corner, rotate the fabric so the seam allowance is to the *left* of the needle and begin stitching on the sewing line about ¾" in from the corner. Sew to and stop precisely at the point with the needle down in the fabric. (See the diagram at the top of the next page.)

2. Lift the presser foot and rotate the fabric back to its normal position with the seam allowance to the right of the needle.

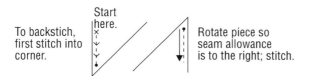

To backstich, first stitch into corner.

Start here.

Rotate piece so seam allowance is to the right; stitch.

3. Stitch along the remainder of the seam to the other point, where you can backstitch normally since you have full view of the point at all times. When stitching on a marked sewing line, be sure the needle is in the center position and pierces the stitching line. When stitching without a marked sewing line, run the matched raw edges of the seam along the ¼" seam guide on your machine's throat plate.

No matter which method you use, sew slowly and carefully. Remember, it's not a race. Fast stitching is usually sloppy stitching, resulting in inaccuracies that mean frustration later. Take the time to do it right at the start.

Tip Be careful not to tug or pull on the fabric as it feeds through the machine; guide it but don't exert any pressure on it, or you will discover that you have inadvertently distorted the final size of the pieces. Next to forceful pressing, this distortion is probably the most common cause of misshapen triangles and pieced squares that are not really square.

Matching Intersections

The easiest way to match the intersection of two seams is to press seam allowances in opposite directions. (Remember the "pressing plan.") This creates a ridge at each seam allowance. When you put the pieces together for stitching, you match intersecting seams by pushing the seam ridges tightly against each other. This technique is called butting the seams. You can pin these intersections if you feel more comfortable doing so.

When sewing rotary-cut quilt pieces together, align raw edges and butt the seams. Do the same for quilt pieces that are cut with templates that include seam allowances.

Butt straight seams.

Butt diagonal seams.

To sew pieces with marked sewing lines together, butt the seams as described above and match the sewing lines with pins as described earlier. Pin corners first, then butt the matching seams and pin them securely on either side of the intersection. Stitch the seam as you would normally, sewing slowly and carefully.

Trimming and Pressing

Press each seam immediately after sewing, trimming the seam allowance to an even width if necessary. Check to make sure the seam is accurately stitched before trimming or pressing.

Trimming is especially important for pieces that have marked sewing lines and were cut with approximate rather than exact ¼"-wide seam allowances. Trim seams to ¼" before you sew across them in the next step. Pieces that include seam allowances when they are cut usually don't require trimming.

Following a pressing plan, press all seams after sewing. See "Pressing Seams" on page 70.

Resizing

Sometimes, it is necessary to resize a pieced unit, even though you stitched and pressed with care. Measure each unit and compare to the required size. It is a good idea to discard or replace anything that is too small.

If units are too large and they were rotary cut or cut with templates that included the seam allowances, trim them back to size.

If finished-size templates were used to mark the pieces for cutting, mark a new accurate sewing line. Pieces in the interior of the quilt should measure the finished size, while pieces that are on the perimeter of the quilt should still have one ¼"-wide seam allowance along the outer edge. Keep this in mind when evaluating the unit.

BLUE RIBBON STITCHING TECHNIQUES

Stitching accuracy and attention to detail result in a beautiful quilt. There is no single magic trick that will ensure perfection. Taking the time to be careful and finish each step before continuing with the next increases piecing accuracy and eliminates the frustration of trying to sew pieces together that don't quite match up. Here are a few little tips and tricks to add to your sewing repertoire. They will make a difference in how quickly and accurately your quilts go together.

Scrap Lead-on/off

This is one of the niftiest little tricks for machine piecing I have ever learned.

1. Rather than starting your stitching out cold, begin by sewing across a folded, 1"- to 2"-wide strip of fabric that is the same weight as what you are sewing (quilt-weight cotton). Leave the needle down in the forward edge of the strip and do not lift the presser foot.
2. Clip the thread tails at the back of the strip and then position the seam you want to sew under the presser foot about ⅛" in front of scrap lead-on. You are now ready to sew the seam or chain of seams. (See "Chain Sewing" on page 74.)

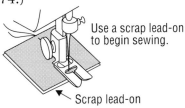

Use a scrap lead-on to begin sewing.

Scrap lead-on

3. When you have finished sewing the seam or chain of seams, don't remove your fabric right away. Instead, leave the needle down in the end of the last stitched seam and repeat the process in reverse by sewing across a second folded scrap (the scrap lead-off). Clip the stitched seam from the thread twist at the back of the scrap lead-off, which then becomes the scrap lead-on for the next seam or chain of seams. Use the scrap leads over and over until they are covered with stitching be-

fore replacing them. Save leftover lengths of fabric strips and keep them in a little basket by your sewing machine for this purpose.

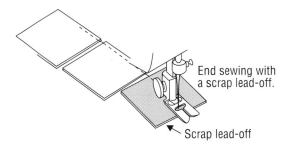

End sewing with a scrap lead-off.

Scrap lead-off

There are several advantages to this little trick. The most obvious is that you will no longer have thousands of thread tails all over your work area. The scrap lead-on also helps prevent the problem of the machine "eating" the fabric as you start a seam. With the scrap lead-on between the feed dog and presser foot, the machine seems to feed the fabric through more smoothly.

Finally, for those machines that tend to produce a few rough stitches as the stitching begins, the scrap lead-on absorbs these stitches, producing better stitch quality in the seam, where it counts.

The "Better Finger"

Sometimes your fingers are too big for the close work you do with machine piecing. Try using a seam ripper or other slender, pointed instrument as a "better finger" to guide the fabric pieces gently and accurately right up to the needle. Use it to hold intersections with pinpoint accuracy and to make minute adjustments easier than is possible with fingers. There is less likelihood of stretching the fabric while sewing when you use a seam ripper.

Use seam ripper to gently and lightly guide fabric while stitching.

Point-to-Point Sewing

When sewing a long seam that crosses over several other seams that require matching, butt and sew just to the first intersection and lock it in place with a stitch. Before continuing, butt the seams of the next intersection and use the seam ripper to hold it securely in place as it moves up to the needle. Use this point-to-point system for sewing all intersections along the entire length of the seam.

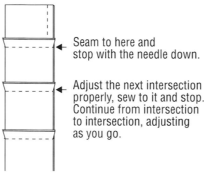

Seam to here and stop with the needle down.

Adjust the next intersection properly, sew to it and stop. Continue from intersection to intersection, adjusting as you go.

Whether butting simple or intricate seams, stitching to match at seam intersections is easier if the raw edges of the seam allowances on the top layer face the needle. Raw edges of the bottom-layer seam allowances should face away from the needle whenever possible. The tendency for the top layer of fabric to be pushed forward slightly ensures a tight intersection, since the top layer will be forced into the ridge of the bottom seam allowance.

Face top seam allowance toward the needle whenever possible.

Chain Sewing

Chain sewing is an assembly-line approach to stitching. The idea is to save time by sewing as many seams as possible, one right after the other, rather than stopping and starting after sewing each unit.

1. Begin a stretch of chain sewing with the scrap lead-on (page 73), followed by the first unit. Stop at the edge of the finished seam, but do not raise the needle, lift the presser foot, or remove the unit from the machine.

2. Prepare the next unit for sewing, lift presser foot slightly, and slip the unit underneath, leaving a small space between the stitched unit and the new unit. Lower the presser foot and continue sewing.

3. Continue sewing in this fashion with the remaining units, ending with a scrap lead-off.

4. Clip the chain of units from the lead-off, leaving the lead-off in the machine for your next stretch of sewing. You should now have a long "kite-tail" of stitched units connected by small chain twists of thread.

5. Clip the units apart and press them according to your pressing plan. With the scrap lead-off still in place to act as the next scrap lead-on, you are ready to sew the next batch of seams.

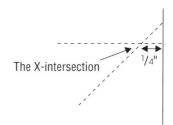

Chain sewing

Using the X

Unless you make patchwork blocks with only squares and rectangles, you will eventually come across a seam with a triangle or other point that you must sew across precisely. The last thing you want to do is to decapitate the point by sewing too far in from the raw edge or to allow it to float by sewing too close to the raw edge. If you have been careful up to now, the point where the seams intersect in an X configuration measures ¼" from the raw edge.

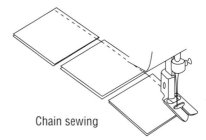

The X-intersection   ¼"

If not, adjust so that it does. The seam you sew now should intersect the X precisely ¼" from the raw edge. By sewing precisely across the point where the two seams intersect to form the X, you create an accurate point on the right side.

If you sew to the inside of the X intersection, you will lop off the point made at the intersection of the two pieces. If you sew closer to the raw edge, you will float the point. The X intersection is the precise location of the triangle or diamond point where you want to stitch. Use the X as your guide whenever crossing a seam that should form a precise point at the ¼"-seam mark.

Positioning Pins

Sometimes, there are instances where you must match two or more intersections at one point on a seam. At times like this, using the X is not enough.

1. Use a pin to precisely spear the points on each of the two seams being matched. Leave this positioning pin upright in the fabric; do not secure it in the layers as you would normally. Instead, place a pin on either side of the upright pin to secure the seam so it does not shift.

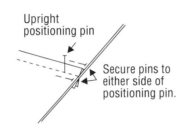

Upright positioning pin

Secure pins to either side of positioning pin.

2. Stitch toward the positioning pin, removing other pins as you reach them. Sew slowly and carefully up to the positioning pin and remove it just before stitching across the intersection.

Partial Basting

Partial basting is a very handy technique for situations where butting seams is not helpful. For example, it is especially useful when matching one set of seamed diamonds to another. Many star blocks have this feature. When you place these two units right sides together for stitching, the diagonal seams run in opposite directions from the seam, making alignment difficult.

You can use pins to match the seams at the ¼" seam, but with a heavily or closely pieced unit, this often results in too many pins for comfortable sewing. Also, too many pins can cause seam distortions as they tend to shift the fabric slightly when they are twisted and secured in the fabric layers. To solve the problem, spear each intersection with a positioning pin and then quickly secure it with a hand-basting stitch. Remove the

pins so that when you machine stitch, the units are very flat and without distortions. Remove the hand basting later.

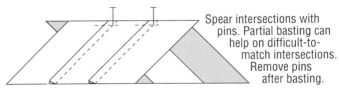

Spear intersections with pins. Partial basting can help on difficult-to-match intersections. Remove pins after basting.

Easing

Like it or not, due to stitching inaccuracies, there are times when it's necessary to ease in a little extra fullness in a seam. If there is a great deal of excess fabric on one seam, correct the source of the problem before continuing to piece. The result of easing in too much fullness is a heavily puckered seam, unsightly distortion, and continued problems with matching. Use easing for small discrepancies, not large problems.

To ease successfully, work with the excess fullness on the bottom layer. In the case of a very tiny excess on a short seam with butted intersections, pinning is unnecessary as long as you butt the seams and use the point of a seam ripper to hold all of the pieces in place while stitching. See the "Better Finger" on page 73. Otherwise, it is important to use pins to evenly distribute the excess along the length of a longer seam so there isn't any bunching at one particular point.

1. Begin by placing pins at the outer edges of the seam. Then place a pin in the middle of the seam, shifting half the excess to either side of the pin.
2. Place a pin in the middle of each half, again dividing the excess between the two halves.
3. Keep pinning and dividing the excess until it is evenly distributed and eased in with the pins. When pinning is complete, you should barely be able to tell there's any fullness.

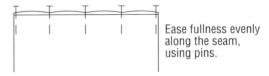

Ease fullness evenly along the seam, using pins.

4. Sew with the excess on the bottom so that the feed dog can "walk" the excess in. If you work with the full seam on top, the presser foot has a tendency to push the excess into pleats rather than ease it in.

SPECIAL SEAMS

Set-in Seams

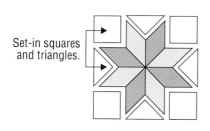

Set-in squares and triangles.

Set-in seams are required when the only way to add a piece to a block is by stitching the piece into a corner in two stages. Diamond blocks frequently have set-in squares and triangles. Stitch this type of seam from the inside corner to the outer edge.

1. Mark the ¼" seam intersections at the outer corners and inside corner. If you are working without a marked stitching line, use your ruler to measure and mark ¼" cross hairs at the seam intersections.

Because you will be marking a sewing line on your fabric that was cut without one, place the ¼" line of your ruler just outside the raw edge of your fabric. If you measure with the ruler line exactly on the fabric edge or just inside it, the pencil marks you make will be inside the finished area of your fabric piece, and the seam you take will be too wide.

2. Begin by pinning only one side of the seam, being very careful to pin and match the corners exactly. Fold any pressed seams out of the way of the sewing area; pin them out of the way, if necessary.

3. Stitch from the inside corner to the outer edge (arrow "a" in the illustration). Begin by backstitching in the corner as described in "Stitching" on pages 71–72.

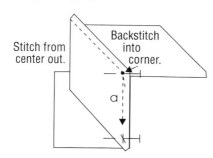

Stitch from center out.

Backstitch into corner.

a

If you are sewing all the way to the raw edge, backstitching is not necessary at the outer edge. If you are sewing exactly from point to point on the outer edge, finish with a backstitch in the outer point.

Now go back to the inside corner and pin the other side of the seam and sew from the inside corner to the outer edge. *Be careful not to catch any part of the other seam or seam allowance when stitching the second side.*

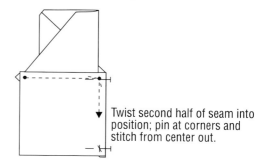

Twist second half of seam into position; pin at corners and stitch from center out.

You can use this method to set in squares, triangles, and all kinds of angled shapes.

Half Seams

One way to avoid set-in seams is to use half seams. Half seams are partially sewn seams that you use in situations where there is no clear-cut, patch-type assembly process. Usually this situation arises when seams build on each other in a circular fashion. Look at the exploded block for an example.

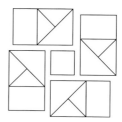

To avoid complicated piecing, partially sew the first seam so that you can sew the second in the normal way. Then sew each subsequent seam onto the previous seam.

If you examine this situation carefully, you will see that if you had completed the first seam, the last seam would have had a set-in corner.

With the first seam only half sewn, you can sew the last seam quickly and easily. After completing the last seam, complete the first seam. Backstitching is unnecessary as long as you stitch over the last bit of stitching where the first stitching ended.

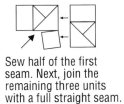

Sew half of the first seam. Next, join the remaining three units with a full straight seam.

Now sew second half of first seam to finish the block.

Diamonds and Other Central Intersections

Piecing an eight-pointed star is probably one of the most intimidating situations that a quilter faces. Stitching one accurately takes a bit of care and sometimes a little practice, but in the end, it really is a "toothless dragon."

There are several different methods for machine piecing stars, and one of the easiest for beginners mimics the hand-piecing method for piecing stars. The key is to sew from point to point and to press the seams in a circular fashion so they not only butt when stitching but also lie perfectly flat when completed. Add any squares, triangles, or other set-in shapes last. Let's use the traditional LeMoyne Star as an example for this technique.

Note: An alternate method for machine piecing an eight-pointed star appears on page 56.

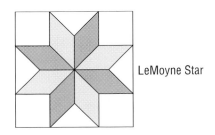

LeMoyne Star

1. If you are working without marked sewing lines, begin by marking the ¼" seam-allowance intersections at all four corners of each diamond. Use the same method as described

for "Set-in Seams" on page 76. This method is a little extra work but it is worth it.

Mark crosshairs at four corners on wrong side of all diamonds.

2. Arrange the pieces for the diamonds in the order you will assemble them.
3. Pin diamonds together in pairs. (You will assemble the diamond by first sewing quarter sections, then joining two quarters to make halves, and finally joining the halves.)

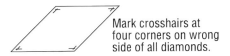

Pin diamonds into pairs. Sew from center out.

Pin points exactly and sew from center point out, backstitching at the center intersection as described in "Stitching" on pages 71–72.

4. Press seams consistently either clockwise or counterclockwise.

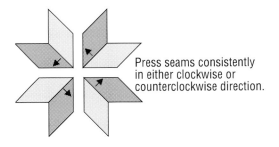

Press seams consistently in either clockwise or counterclockwise direction.

5. Join diamond pairs to form two star halves. The seams will butt nicely, making alignment easy. Sew from the center out, backstitching at the center intersection and pressing in a consistently circular fashion.

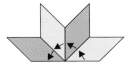

6. Pin the two star halves together, using a positioning pin or partial basting to secure center point. See "Blue Ribbon Stitching Techniques" on pages 73–75. The seams on each half should butt nicely, making matching easy. Pin the two outer points securely as well.

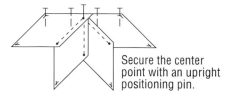

Secure the center point with an upright positioning pin.

7. Sew the final seam to join the two halves, stitching from one side to the other. Sew this seam from point to point as well. Even though you sew this seam completely through the center point, you can still press in a circular fashion. When the pressing is completed, you should have either a nice rosette formed by the seam allowances converging in the center or a pinwheel-type square, depending on whether you nubbed the diamond points or not. See "Nubbing Points for Sewing" on page 25.

Tip Check the center seam of each half before joining them. Make sure that the points that meet in the center of each star half are ¼" from the raw edge. If not, cut away any excess. If there is less than a ¼"-wide seam allowance from the edge to the point, figure out what you did wrong and fix it!

8. Set in any necessary pieces at this point, folllowing the directions for set-in seams on page 76. Press the set-in seams in the same clockwise or counterclockwise direction as you pressed the diamond seams.

Curved Seams

Curved seams are another type of seam that quilters tend to avoid. Happily, with a little bit of care, they are not that difficult at all. Every curved seam has two types of curves: convex and concave. My geometry teacher taught us how to remember which was which by describing the concave curve as the one you could walk into like a cave. Maybe that will help you remember, too.

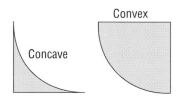

Convex

Concave

When matching these two curves to sew them together, you will notice that they are mirror images of each other and that the concave seam must be "stretched" to fit around the convex seam. To do this, clip periodically into the concave seam allowance. It is not necessary to clip the convex seam. Make clips no deeper than ⅛". It is better to *clip sparingly* first and make additional clips later, if necessary, to create a smooth seam.

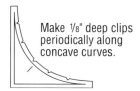

Make ⅛" deep clips periodically along concave curves.

Place pins in the outer raw edges to keep them from slipping out of position. Place a pin at the center of the seam, aligning the center guidelines that you marked from the templates.

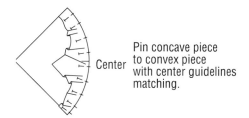

Center

Pin concave piece to convex piece with center guidelines matching.

If your templates do not have center guidelines, make a finished-size paper template and fold it in half to find the center of the seam. Use this guide to mark guidelines at the center of the seam edges. You can also fold the fabric piece in half and finger press a center guideline.

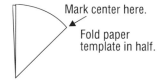

Mark center here.

Fold paper template in half.

If you are working with pieces that have marked stitching lines, finish pinning the rest of the seam as shown on page 71.

When working with pieces that do not have marked sewing lines, you do not need any more than three pins at the edges and center to sew a smooth and accurate seam. Sew slowly and carefully, aligning the raw edges as you go. It is OK to do more pinning to achieve the same results if necessary. Try a practice seam to determine what works best for you. You will need more pins for deep curves and fewer pins for gentle curves.

A curved seam lies smooth and flat, without pulls and puckers, if it is adequately clipped and pressed toward the concave piece. You may need to add a few extra clips to help it lie flat.

Mitered Seams

Mitered seams are diagonal seams stitched from an inner corner to an outer edge. A square-corner miter (90°) is the most common, although you can also miter strips at the corners of other angled shapes, such as hexagons, octagons, and diamonds. In any case, you must pin and stitch the fabric pieces in a mitered corner at an angle and the resulting piece must lie flat. Mitered borders are often used in quilts, as are mitered corners in some pieced block designs. You can miter corners, using either template-marked pieces or rotary-cut strips.

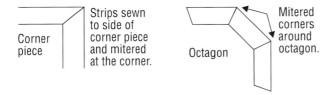

Corner piece / Strips sewn to side of corner piece and mitered at the corner.

Octagon / Mitered corners around octagon.

MITERING WITH TEMPLATES

If you are working with templates, mitering is relatively simple. The angle of the mitered seam is already determined for you in the drafted template. Careful matching and sewing will yield a perfectly mitered corner. The following steps make it easy.

1. If you are working with templates that include seam allowances, use your ruler to mark the intersecting ¼" seam lines at the corners of both strips and the corner piece.
2. Pin the side strips to be mitered to the sides of the corner piece, whether it is a square, hexa-

gon, or any other shape. Sew them to both sides of the corner piece exactly from point to point without stitching into the ¼" seam allowances.

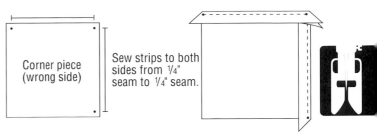

Corner piece (wrong side)

Sew strips to both sides from ¼" seam to ¼" seam.

The two stitching lines must meet exactly at the corner but must not overlap. *Do not press yet.*

3. Depending on the type of templates used, sew the angled corner seam by either aligning the stitching line or the raw edges. With the side strips right sides together, backstitch and sew exactly from the corner where the side strips meet to the outside corner. Check the accuracy and flatness of the seam before trimming and pressing the seam to one side. Be very careful when pressing the mitered seam as the grain is bias and is easily distorted.

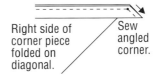

Right side of corner piece folded on diagonal.

Sew angled corner.

MITERING WITH ROTARY-CUT STRIPS

There are three requirements for mitering rotary-cut strips at a corner.

1. Cut the strips extra long to accommodate the miter. A few inches longer than the cut width of the strip is a safe bet. If several strips are to be mitered around a particular corner, seam them together first and miter all at once. In this case, the excess strip length must be greater than the combined width of the seamed strips. This is most often done as a border treatment on a finished block or a finished quilt.

Seam the strips for a multiple border together before attaching.

2. Sew the strips in place so the stitching does not extend into the ¼" seam allowance on either side of the corner, as described in "Mitering with Templates" on page 79. Mark the intersecting ¼" seam lines on the corner piece before attaching the strips. Center each strip along the edge of the seam and stitch from mark to mark. Do not press yet.

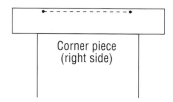

Corner piece
(right side)

3. Fold the corner piece diagonally from the corner, so that the fabric strips are on top of each other, right sides together, and the excess length extends straight out to the right. Align the excess so the strips line up exactly on top of each other. Secure with a pin if necessary.

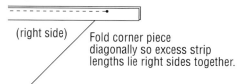

(right side)

Fold corner piece diagonally so excess strip lengths lie right sides together.

Since there are no templates used when rotary cutting strips, the correct mitering angle is not marked or cut when you cut the strips. That makes it necessary to mark the correct angle. For your convenience, several mitering guides appear on page 112. To use them, select the one for the angle you wish to miter and trace it onto a piece of template plastic. Be sure to include all markings. See "Making Your Own Mitering Guides," above right.

4. Place the angled corner of the correctly angled mitering guide at the point where the stitching stops at the corner. Draw a line along the mitered edge from the stitching at the corner to the opposite raw edge of the fabric strip.

5. Sew on the drawn line, matching any seams or fabric designs that meet at the seam.

Backstitch at the beginning and stitch exactly from the corner to the opposite raw edge.

6. Check the mitered seam for accuracy and flatness before trimming the excess to ¼" from the seam. Press in one direction, being careful not to stretch the bias.

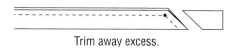

Trim away excess.

MAKING YOUR OWN MITERING GUIDES

To miter around a corner with an odd angle, you need to make your own mitering guide. This is really quite easy. You will need graph paper, pencil, and a protractor. A protractor is a circle or half circle with cross hairs in the center and degree lines on the outer edge. You use it to measure angles from any given point.

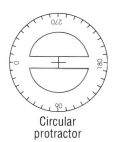

Circular protractor

To determine the angle of the corner that you are going to miter:

1. Pencil in the sewing lines on the wrong side of the fabric corner, ¼" from the raw edges.

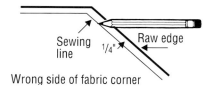

Sewing line 1/4" Raw edge

Wrong side of fabric corner

2. Place the cross hairs of the protractor on the intersection of the sewing lines at the corner, aligning the 0 cross hair with one of the sides.

3. Look at the other sewing line and find the number of degrees from 0 that the side measures. This is your corner angle.

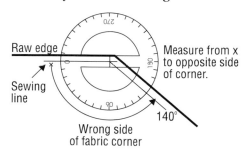

Raw edge

Measure from x to opposite side of corner.

Sewing line

140°

Wrong side of fabric corner

To determine the degree of the mitering angle:

1. Subtract the corner angle from 360°.
2. Divide the resulting number in half. This is the mitering angle. For example, for a corner angle that measures 140°, subtract this from 360 to get 220. Divide 220 in half to get 110. The mitering angle is 110°.

To turn the angle into a template-mitering guide:

1. Draw a 6" horizontal line on a piece of graph paper. Make a mark at the center of the line.

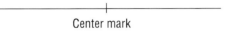

Center mark

2. Lay the cross hairs of the protractor on the horizontal line at the center point. Arrange it so the 0 mark is to the left on the line.
3. Measure in a counterclockwise direction the correct number of degrees from 0 (in the example, 110°). Make a mark on the paper at this degree position on the protractor. This is the mitering angle.

Measure from 0° counter-clockwise to the correct mitering angle and make a mark.

4. Draw a line from the center point to the degree mark. Make a template from the shaded area to use as your mitering guide, squaring off the other side.

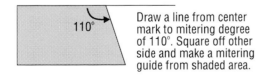

Draw a line from center mark to mitering degree of 110°. Square off other side and make a mitering guide from shaded area.

Foundation Piecing

Foundation piecing is the process of attaching fabric pieces to a larger foundation fabric. Pieces are placed face down onto the foundation fabric, stitched in place along one seam, and then flipped right side up and pressed. Designs suitable for foundation piecing have a central piece, which is sewn in place first, followed by the remaining pieces in progression.

Usually, the foundation block is marked with a particular design, such as a Pineapple or a Log Cabin block, although you can foundation piece free-form designs without a planned pattern. Many quilt artists find foundation piecing perfect for some of their innovative designs. The advantage of foundation piecing is its extreme accuracy.

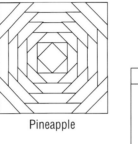

Pineapple

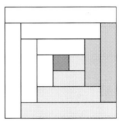

Log Cabin

The most commonly used types of foundation materials are muslin and tear-away interfacing. Muslin is a non-removable foundation. That means it becomes part of the quilt and often replaces the batting or backing (if the stitching on the back of the foundation is attractive). You can also finish the project in the traditional manner with a thin batting and backing and quilting or tying to hold all the layers together. Foundation piecing with muslin results in a quilted-in-the-ditch appearance to the block and is a wonderful way to create a quilted-look duvet without using batting.

If you do not want the added weight of muslin in the finished quilt, use tear-away interfacing for the foundation blocks. There are several brands available. Choose one that is easily marked with a pencil and is sturdy enough to provide a flat surface that won't shift while sewing. After completing all stitching, you will tear the interfacing away from the back of the block. You may also substitute paper for a foundation.

DIRECTIONS
Preparation for Foundation Piecing

1. Draw the design in the desired *finished size* on graph paper. (Finished size is indicated by dashed lines in drawing.)

2. Using a lead pencil in a different color, draw lines (solid lines in drawing) ¼" outside each seam line, beginning in the center and working out.

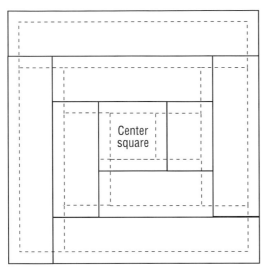

First draw the finished-size block. Next draw ¼" from the outside edges of each shape in a different color.

3. *Transfer the colored lines* to the foundation fabric by tracing directly onto the foundation or by using a hot-iron transfer pencil; follow the manufacturer's directions. *Do not transfer the original finished-size design.* Use a straight edge to trace the lines. Cut out the foundation block along outer traced lines.
4. Now you are ready to start sewing. Cut the fabric strips and center piece the finished width, plus ½" total for seam allowances.
5. If you cannot use the edge of your presser foot for an accurate ¼" seam guide, find another way to measure this distance. When stitching pieces to a foundation, you cannot see the throat plate. The best solution is to find a presser foot that measures an accurate ¼" from the needle to the right-hand edge of the right toe of the foot. This foot is now available for some machines.

If a presser foot is not available, the next best solution is to cut your strips wider to accommodate the larger seam your presser foot does sew and continue to use the foot edge as a guide. To find the actual width of the seam you get when using the edge of the foot as a guide, conduct a strip test as described in "Shortcuts" on page 12.

For instance, I have found most machines sew a strip test that leaves the center strip ⅞" wide instead of 1". This is a difference of ⅛"— a loss of 1⁄16" per seam on each side of the strip. *To allow for this difference with foundation piecing only*, cut your strips ⅛" larger than normal (for a total of ⅝" larger than the desired finished size of the strip to allow for seam allowances).

If your test indicates a different, smaller amount, add this amount to your strip cut size. For example, if your center strip measures ¾" when sewn, the difference from 1" is ¼". To accommodate this difference, cut your strips ¼" wider than you normally would. In this case, you would cut the strip 1¾" wide to end up with a finished width of 1".

Note: Do not try to accommodate for your presser-foot width in this fashion with regular machine piecing; it works only in very limited cases.

The center piece will be smaller than it really should be, but the outer strips of the block will reach the edge of the marks, meaning the final block will still be the proper size.

Sewing

Using a Log Cabin block as an example, here's how to foundation piece.

1. Begin in the center and place the center square in position. Secure it with a pin on each side or use a dab of glue stick underneath to hold it in place.
2. Place the first fabric strip (or cut piece) in place, face down on the center piece with raw edges aligned. Stitch it in place with the edge of your presser foot running along the marked line on the foundation. Backstitching is unnecessary.

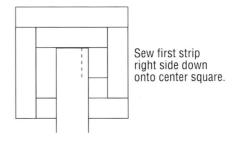

Sew first strip right side down onto center square.

3. Press the strip open and cut the strip end to match the marked line as shown.

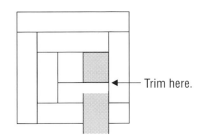

— Trim here.

4. Repeat the process for the second strip.

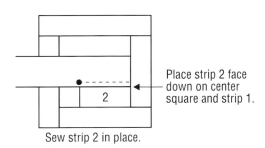

Place strip 2 face down on center square and strip 1.

Sew strip 2 in place.

5. Continue adding strips in a progressive order, working around the center out to the edge. Trim the edges of the outer strips to match the outer edge of the foundation. For maximum accuracy when using a tear-away foundation, leave it in place until you have joined all the blocks.

6. Baste the raw edges of the outer strips to the foundation so they don't shift when joining blocks.

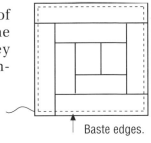

Baste edges.

7. To join the blocks, match the edges of the foundations; stitch.

Note: You have to make a choice here if your presser foot sews a seam wider than ¼". If you continue to use the edge of your presser foot as your guide, the outer strips will be the correct finished size, but the block will be slightly smaller than the planned finished size.

If your blocks will be set next to each other as in most Log Cabin and Pineapple designs, a consistently smaller block will not be a problem. If the finished block must be the exact planned size, use the ¼" guide you established on your throat plate for regular machine piecing as your guide. Your outer strips will be slightly larger than planned, but your block will be the proper finished size.

8. Stitch the completed blocks together. If you used tear-away interfacing (or paper) for the foundation block, remove it in the following manner. Begin in the center of each block and pull the foundation away from the seam. Use a seam ripper to get it started. It pulls away easily, but be gentle to avoid distorting any bias edges.

QUILT PATTERNS

Three of the patterns in this section ("Ohio Sparkler," page 85; "Evening Shades," page 94; and "Country Crossing," page 98) include directions for both template and rotary cutting. Choose the cutting method you prefer or wish to practice. Templates appear on pages 106–11. "Ferris Wheel," page 103, is rotary cut and strip pieced. No templates are given for this quilt.

To practice the foundation-piecing method described on page 81, make "Sweetheart," page 90. Template cutting directions only are

given for "Starpool," page 92, which features curved seams.

The dimensions for all sashing, border, and binding strips are given in cut sizes, which includes the necessary ¼"-wide seam allowances. Rotary-cutting dimensions are given for simple squares and rectangles that do not require templates.

Each quilt plan includes a block diagram as well as a pressing guide. Press seams in the direction indicated by the arrows in the pressing guide.

Ohio Sparkler

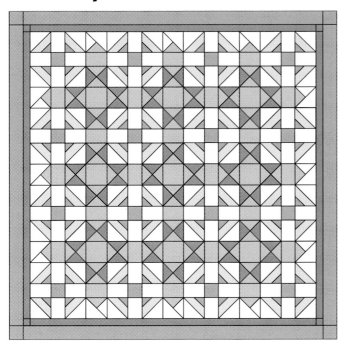

Color photo on page 116.
Finished Size: 47" x 47"
Finished Block Size: 8"

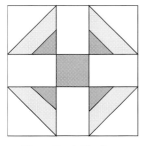

Churn Dash Block
Variation

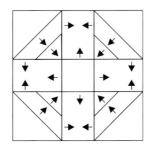

Pressing Plan

Template Method

MATERIALS: 44"-WIDE FABRIC

If you plan to rotary cut and strip piece this quilt, you will need additional yardage. See the Materials list on page 87.

½ yd. dark green for sashing and inner border
⅞ yd. medium green for sashing
½ yd. pale floral print for blocks and sashing
1 yd. dark red for blocks and outer border
⅜ yd. medium pink for blocks
½ yd. light peach for blocks
⅜ yd. for binding
3 yds. for backing

TEMPLATE CUTTING

Templates begin on page 106. If you prefer to rotary cut this quilt, see the directions that begin on page 87.

From the dark green, cut:
    72 Template 22 (T22) for pieced sashing
    4 Template 21 (T21) for inner border corner squares
    4 strips, each 1½" x 42", for inner border
From the medium green, cut:
    9 Template 15 (T15) for pieced sashing
    84 Template 22 (T22) for pieced sashing
    24 Template 14 (T14) for pieced sashing
From the pale floral, cut:
    76 Template 1 (T1) for blocks
    12 Template 22 (T22) for pieced sashing
From the dark red, cut:
    64 Template 5 (T5) for blocks
    20 Template 11 (T11) for block centers and outer border corner squares
    4 strips, each 2½" x 43½", for outer border*
From the medium pink, cut:
    64 Template 4 (T4) for blocks
From the light peach, cut:
    64 Template 14 (T14) for blocks
From the binding fabric, cut:
    5 strips, each 2" x 42"

*If your fabric has shrunk to less than 43½" wide, you will need to cut 6 strips in order to piece 4 border strips of the proper length.

DIRECTIONS

Churn Dash Blocks

1. Assemble 64 pieced squares as shown, using the dark red triangles (T5), medium pink trapezoids (T4), and pale floral triangles (T1).

2. Stitch a light peach rectangle (T14) to opposite sides of 16 of the dark red squares (T11).

3. Stitch a pieced square from step 1 to opposite sides of the 32 remaining peach rectangles (T14). Be careful to position the squares as shown in the diagram.

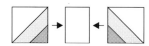

4. Assemble 16 Churn Dash blocks by joining the units created in steps 2 and 3.

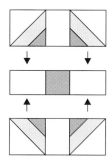

Sashing

1. Sew 72 dark green triangles (T22) and 72 medium green triangles (T22) together into 72 side-by-side triangle pairs. Press seams toward the dark green triangles. Then join the side-by-side triangle units together as shown to form 36 Ohio Star patches. Press center seams in either direction.

Assemble 72 triangle pairs.   Make 36.

2. To make 12 special Ohio Star patches for the sashing at the outer edges of the quilt, stitch 1 medium green triangle (T22) to 1 pale floral triangle (T22). Press seams toward the pale floral. Sew each of the 12 side-by-side triangle units to 1 pale floral triangle (T1) and press the seam toward the pale floral.

Make 12.

3. Assemble 12 sashing units from the special Ohio Star patches and 12 from the regular Ohio Star patches by joining them with medium green rectangles (T14). Press the seams in all 24 sashing units away from the green rectangles.

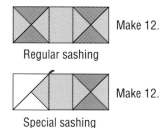

Make 12.
Regular sashing

Make 12.
Special sashing

Quilt Top Assembly

1. Assemble 2 rows, using Churn Dash blocks and the special sashing units. Assemble 2 rows, using Churn Dash blocks and regular sashing units. Press the sashing seams toward the Churn Dash blocks.

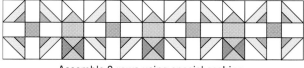

Assemble 2 rows using special sashing.

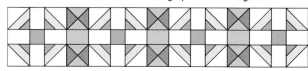

Assemble 2 rows using regular sashing.

2. Assemble 3 sashing rows by joining sashing units alternately with the medium green squares (T15). Press seams toward squares.

Assemble 3 rows.

3. Referring to the quilt plan, join the Churn Dash rows and sashing rows together to form the quilt top. Place the Churn Dash rows with the special Ohio Star patches at the top and bottom of the quilt, making sure the special patches are positioned along the outer edges.

4. Cut the dark green border strips for the inner border to fit the length and width of the quilt top, referring to the directions for borders with corner squares on page 206. Add the corner squares (T21) to the ends of the top and bottom strips. Press seams toward the borders.

   Sew the border strips to the sides of the quilt first, then add the top and bottom borders with corner squares. Press seams toward the borders.

5. Prepare and attach the dark red border strips and corner squares (T11) for the outer border in the same manner.

Quilt Finishing
1. Layer the quilt top with batting and backing; baste. See page 255.
2. Quilt as desired. Refer to "Loving Stitches," beginning on page 225.
3. Bind the edges. See "Happy Endings," beginning on page 275.

Rotary-Cutting Method

MATERIALS: 44"-WIDE FABRIC

¾ yd. dark green for sashing and inner border
⅞ yd. medium green for sashing
⅞ yd. pale floral print for blocks and sashing
1 yd. dark red for blocks and outer border
⅝ yd. medium pink for blocks
½ yd. light peach for blocks
⅜ yd. for binding
3 yds. for backing

ROTARY CUTTING
From the dark green, cut:
  1 piece, 9" x 42"
  1 piece, 9" x 20"
  4 strips, each 1½" x 42", for inner border
From the medium green, cut:
  1 piece, 9" x 42"

1 piece, 9" x 30"
3 strips, each 3½" x 42", for sashing; crosscut into 9 squares, each 3½" x 3½", and 24 bars, each 2½" x 3½"
From the pale floral, cut:
  3 pieces, each 9" x 42"
From the dark red, cut:
  2 pieces, each 9" x 42"
  1 strip, 2½" x 42"; crosscut into 2 strips, each 2½" x 21", for Strip Unit II
  5 strips, each 2½" x 42", for outer border
  1 strip, 2½" x 12"; crosscut into 4 squares, each 2½" x 2½", for corner squares of outer border
From the medium pink, cut:
  2 pieces, each 9" x 42"
From the light peach, cut:
  2 strips, each 3½" x 42"; crosscut into 4 strips, each 3½" x 21", for Strip Unit II
  2 strips, each 3½" x 42"; crosscut into 32 bars, each 2½" x 3½", for Churn Dash blocks

DIRECTIONS
Churn Dash Blocks
1. *Place the right side of the fabrics face up* on your cutting mat. Cut bias strips as shown on page 28.

From 9" x 42" and 9" x 20" pieces of dark green, cut:
  8 bias strips, each 3½" wide. (Cut bias strips from leftover corner pieces also.)
  4 squares, each 1½" x 1½", for corner squares of inner border
From 9" x 42" and 9" x 30" pieces of medium green, cut:
  10 bias strips, each 3½" wide. (Cut bias strips from leftover corner pieces also.)
From 9" x 42" pieces of pale floral, cut:
  16 bias strips, each 3⅛" wide
  2 bias strips, each 3½" wide
  6 squares, each 3⅞" x 3⅞"; crosscut in half on the diagonal to yield 12 half-square triangles (Cut squares from the leftover corner pieces.)
From 9" x 42" pieces of dark red, cut:
  20 bias strips, each 2⅛" wide
From 9" x 42" pieces of medium pink, cut:
  32 bias strips, each 1½" wide

2. Assemble 4 Strip Unit I as shown in the diagram; use 5 dark red (R) 2⅛"-wide bias strips, 4 pale floral (F) 3⅛"-wide bias strips, and 8 medium pink (P) 1½"-wide bias strips for each strip unit. Sew the strips together in the proper order and make sure the top edges are even as shown. Press seams away from the floral strips and toward the dark red strips.

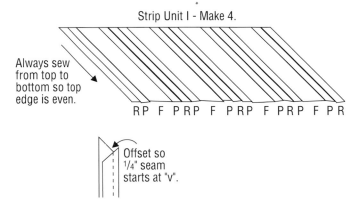

Strip Unit I - Make 4.

Always sew from top to bottom so top edge is even.

R P F P R P F P R P F P R P F P R

Offset so ¼" seam starts at "v".

3. Turn the strip unit so the even edge is facing you, and cut striped squares from this edge across the bottom. Cut a total of 64 striped squares, each 3½" x 3½", from the 4 strip units. Be careful to lay the diagonal line of the Bias Square ruler on the medium pink/ pale floral seam as this is the center seam of the square. You will have waste rectangles between each pair of cut squares.

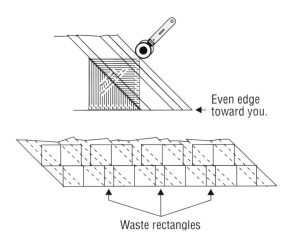

Even edge toward you.

Waste rectangles

4. Assemble 2 Strip Unit II as shown in diagram, using 2 light peach 3½" x 21" strips, and 1 dark red 2½" x 21" strip for each unit. Press seams toward peach strip. Cut a total of 16 segments, each 2½" wide, from strip units.

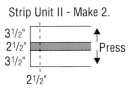

Strip Unit II - Make 2.

3½"
2½" Press
3½"

2½"

5. Sew a striped square to each side of a 2½" x 3½" peach bar. Be careful to position the squares as shown.

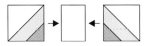

6. Assemble 16 Churn Dash blocks by joining the units created in steps 4 and 5.

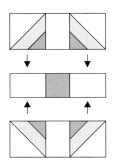

Sashing

1. Assemble 2 Strip Unit III as shown in the diagram, using 4 dark green 3½"-wide bias strips and 4 medium green 3½"-wide bias strips for each strip unit. Use corner bias strips and triangles at both ends. Press seams toward the dark green.

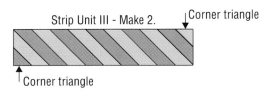

Strip Unit III - Make 2. Corner triangle

Corner triangle

2. Placing the Bias Square with its diagonal line on the seam, cut a total of 36 bias squares, each 3⅞" x 3⅞", from the strip sets; crosscut the bias squares in half on the diagonal to form 72 side-by-side triangles.

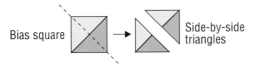

Bias square → Side-by-side triangles

3. Sew pairs of side-by-side triangles as shown to make 36 Ohio Star patches.

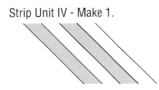

Assemble 72 triangle pairs.   Make 36.

4. Assemble Strip Unit IV as shown in the diagram, using the 2 remaining medium green 3½"-wide bias strips and the 2 pale floral 3½"-wide bias strips. Press seams toward the pale floral strips.

Strip Unit IV - Make 1.

5. Cut 6 bias squares, each 3⅞" x 3⅞", from Strip Unit IV; crosscut the bias squares in half on the diagonal to yield 12 side-by-side triangles. Sew each of the 12 side-by-side triangle units to 1 pale floral half-square triangle as shown to make 12 special Ohio Star patches.

Make 12.

6. Assemble 12 sashing units from the special Ohio Star patches and 12 from the regular Ohio Star patches by joining them with medium green 2½" x 3½" bars. Press the seams in all 24 sashing units away from the green bars.

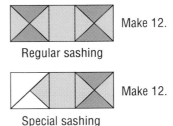

Make 12.
Regular sashing

Make 12.
Special sashing

7. Assemble the quilt top, referring to "Quilt Top Assembly" on pages 86–87 and ignoring template references.

8. Finish the quilt, referring to "Quilt Finishing" on page 87.

Sweetheart

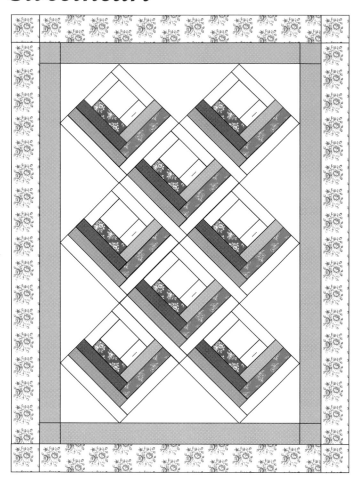

Color photo on page 115.
Finished Size: 29" x 39"
Finished Block Size: 7"

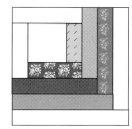

Log Cabin Heart Block

MATERIALS: 44"-WIDE FABRIC

⅛ yd. each of 6 different red prints for the "logs"
¾ yd. muslin print for blocks and setting tri-
    angles
1 yd. tear-away stabilizer (22" wide) for foun-
    dation blocks
¼ yd. red for inner border
½ yd. light floral for outer border
⅜ yd. for binding
1¼ yds. for backing

CUTTING

Templates begin on page 106.

Note: Because of the block assembly method
used for this quilt, be sure to make templates
that *include* ¼"-wide seam allowances. See
"Templates with Seam Allowances" on page 68.

**From each of the red prints for logs 1 and 2 in the
Log Cabin Heart block, cut:**
    1 strip, 1½" x 42"
From each of the remaining 4 red prints, cut:
    2 strips, each 1½" x 42", for logs 5, 6, 7, 8
From the muslin print, cut:
    6 strips, each 1½" x 42", for the light logs
    8 Template 11 (T11) for the square in the Log
        Cabin Heart block
    6 Template 20 (T20) for side setting triangles
    4 Template 3 (T3) for corner triangles
From the tear-away stabilizer, cut:
    8 squares, each 8" x 8"
From the red for inner border, cut:
    2 strips, each 2" x 31"
    2 strips, each 2" x 21"
    4 Template 2 (T2) for border corner squares
From the light floral, cut:
    4 Template 15 (T15) for the outer border
        corner squares
    2 strips, each 3½" x 25", for the outer top and
        bottom border
    2 strips, each 3½" x 35", for the outer side
        border
From the binding fabric, cut:
    4 strips, each 2" x 42"

DIRECTIONS

**Log Cabin
Heart Blocks**

1. Using a fine lead
   pencil, accurately
   draft the block
   foundation lines
   as shown at right
   onto graph paper;
   make the pencil
   lines dark enough
   to see easily.

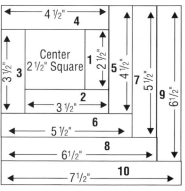

Foundation lines - ¼ scale. Redraw
onto graph paper. Draw all logs 1" wide
by the indicated length. The center
square is 2½" square.

2. Carefully trace foundation lines onto each 8" square of tear-away stabilizer, using the drafting on graph paper as a pattern underneath. Be sure to label each log position and color on the stabilizer.

3. Place a muslin square (T11) face up in the center square position. Use a dab of water-soluble glue stick to keep it from shifting.

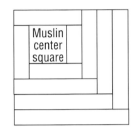

4. Lay the log 1 fabric strip face down on top of the center square and align the raw edge of the fabric strip with innermost traced line for log 1 on the stabilizer. Stitch ¼" from the line. Press the log 1 fabric strip so it is face up on the traced log 1 area. Trim the excess fabric strip even with the traced line for log 2. Use a few dabs of glue stick to hold the first log in place.

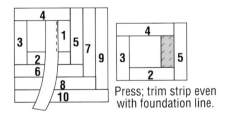

Press; trim strip even with foundation line.

5. Continue adding and stitching logs to the foundation square in the same manner, adding them in numerical order until the block is complete and looks like the Log Cabin Heart block shown on page 90. Trim the block (including the foundation stabilizer) even with the outside edge of the foundation lines. The block should measure 7½" x 7½".

6. Working from the wrong side, carefully pull the foundation away from the fabric block.

7. Make 7 more blocks in this fashion.

Quilt Top Assembly

1. Lay out the completed blocks and the muslin side triangles (T20), following the quilt plan. Sew them together in diagonal rows, pressing the seams in opposite directions, row to row.

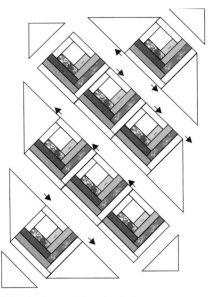

Join blocks and triangles to form rows. Press the seams in each row in opposite directions as indicated by the arrows.

2. Join the rows to form the quilt top and add the corner triangles (T3).

3. Square up the quilt by trimming the edges of the quilt top to ¼" from the block corners, making sure the corners are also square. See "Border Basics" on pages 204–8.

4. Cut the red border strips for the inner border to fit the length and width of the quilt top, referring to the directions for borders with corner squares on page 206. Add the corner squares (T2) to the ends of the top and bottom border strips. Press seams toward the borders.

   Sew the border strips to the sides of the quilt first, then add the top and bottom borders with corner squares. Press seams toward the borders.

5. Prepare and sew the light floral border strips and corner squares (T15) for the outer border in the same manner.

Quilt Finishing

1. Layer the quilt top with batting and backing; baste. See page 255.

2. Quilt as desired. Refer to "Loving Stitches," beginning on page 225.

3. Bind the edges. Refer to "Happy Endings," beginning on page 275.

Starpool

Color photos on page 114.
Finished Quilt Size: 28½" x 39¾"
Finished Block Size: 10¼"

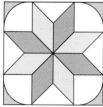

Starpool Block   Pressing Plan

MATERIALS: 44"-WIDE FABRIC

1 yd. teal print for block corners, sashing, inner
    border, and corner squares
¼ yd. black print for the stars
⅝ yd. medium pink print for the stars, outer
    border, and corner squares
½ yd. pale pink print for Star block background
⅜ yd. for binding
1¼ yds. for backing

CUTTING

Templates begin on page 106.

From the teal print, cut:
    24 Template 9 (T9) for the outer corners of
        the Starpool blocks
    4 Template 25 (T25) for the inner border
        corner squares
    3 strips, each 1½" x 10¾", for vertical sashing
    2 strips, each 1½" x 22", for horizontal sashing
    2 strips, each 3" x 34½", for side inner bor-
        ders
    2 strips, each 3" x 23½", for top and bottom
        inner borders
From the black print, cut:
    24 Template 6 (T6) for the stars
From the medium pink print, cut:
    24 Template 6 (T6) for the stars
    4 Template 21 (T21) for outer border corner
        squares
    2 strips, each 1½" x 39½", for outer side
        borders
    2 strips, each 1½" x 30½", for outer top and
        bottom borders
From the pale pink, cut:
    24 Template 8 (T8) for Star block background
    4 Template 7 (T7) for Star block background
From the binding fabric, cut:
    4 strips, each 2" x 42"

DIRECTIONS

Starpool Blocks

1. Mark ¼" sewing-line intersections at corners of each piece. Mark center slash marks
   on the curved pieces. See "Diamonds and
   Other Central Intersections" on pages 77–78.
2. Lay out diamond pieces (T6) on a flat work
   surface, forming stars of alternating pink
   and black diamonds.
   Join diamonds into
   pairs as shown, re-
   membering to pin and
   sew exactly from cor-
   ner to corner (not raw
   edge to raw edge). Do
   not allow stitching to
   extend past the ¼"
   marks at the seam in-
   tersections.

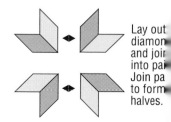

Lay out
diamon[ds]
and joi[n]
into pa[irs.]
Join pa[irs]
to form
halves.

3. Measure the seam allowance at the intersection where the diamond points meet. If it is not ¼" wide, trim it. Use positioning pins to secure the center of the intersection when joining. If sewn carefully and pressed according to the plan, the center intersection should butt nicely, making alignment relatively easy. Join the halves to form the star.

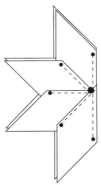

Trim seam allowance to ¼" from center star point if necessary.

4. Clip the curve on the T9 units, making ⅛"-deep clips about every ¼" to ⅜" apart. Pin the outside corners first, then match and pin the center slashes. Pin the rest of the curve. Stitch. Make a total of 16 pieced squares. On the wrong side of each one, mark the ¼" seam intersection at the corners of the pink piece as shown.

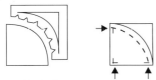

Mark ¼" seam marks on wrong side of squares.

5. Set the pieced squares into the corners of the stars, being careful to pin and match the inside corners properly. See "Set-in Seams" on page 76.

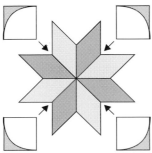

6. Set in pale pink triangles (T7) on the four sides of each star. Be sure to mark the ¼" seam-line intersections on the wrong side of each triangle before stitching.

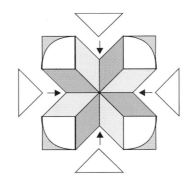

Quilt Top Assembly

1. Join the completed stars into 3 rows of 2 blocks each, with a 1½" x 10¾" teal sashing strip between each pair. Press seams toward the sashing strips.

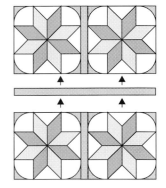

2. Join the rows, using the 1½" x 22" teal sashing strips between the rows. Press seams toward sashing.

3. Cut the 3"-wide teal border strips for the inner border to fit the length and width of the quilt top, referring to the directions for borders with corner squares on page 206. Add the corner squares (T25) to the ends of the top and bottom strips. Press seams toward borders.

   Sew the border strips to the sides of the quilt first, then add the top and bottom borders with corner squares. Press seams toward the borders.

4. Prepare and attach the medium pink border strips and corner squares for the outer border in the same manner.

Quilt Finishing

1. Layer the quilt top with batting and backing; baste. See page 255.

2. Quilt as desired. Refer to "Loving Stitches," beginning on page 225.

3. Bind the edges. Refer to "Happy Endings," beginning on page 275.

Evening Shades

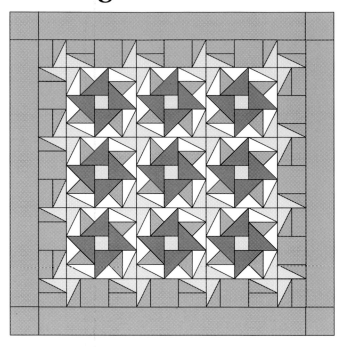

Color photo on page 113.
Finished Quilt Size: 45" x 45"
Finished Block Size: 10"

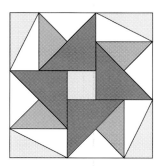

Evening Shades Block

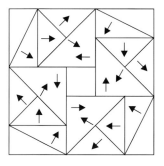

Pressing Plan

MATERIALS: 44"-WIDE FABRIC

If you plan to rotary cut and strip piece this quilt, you will need additional yardage. See the Materials list on page 96.

½ yd. purple print for blocks
½ yd. medium mauve for blocks
½ yd. green check for blocks and pieced inner border
½ yd. light mauve print for blocks
1¼ yds. deep purple floral print for pieced inner border and outer border
½ yd. for binding
3 yds. for backing

TEMPLATE CUTTING

Templates begin on page 106. If you prefer to rotary cut this quilt, see the directions that begin on page 96.

From the purple print, cut:
  36 Template 13 (T13) for blocks
From the medium mauve, cut:
  36 Template 12 (T12) for blocks
From the green check, cut:
  64 Template 23 (T23) for blocks and pieced inner border
  9 Template 11 (T11) for block centers
From the light mauve, cut:
  36 Template 12 (T12) for block background
  36 Template 23 (T23) for block background
From the deep purple floral, cut:
  28 Template 23 (T23) for the pieced inner border (triangles)
  12 Template 18 (T18) for the pieced border (squares)
  16 Template 10 (T10) for the pieced border (rectangles)
  4 Template 19 (T19) for the outer border corner squares
  4 strips, each 4" x 43", for the outer border
From the binding fabric, cut:
  5 strips, each 2" x 42"

DIRECTIONS

Blocks

1. Sew each of the 36 medium mauve triangles (T12) to a light mauve triangle (T12).

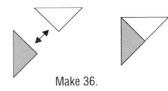

Make 36.

2. Sew each side-by-side triangle pair to a purple triangle (T13).

Make 36.

3. Sew each of 36 light mauve half rectangles (T23) to a green half rectangle (T23) for the blocks. Join the remaining 28 green half rectangles with the 28 deep purple floral half rectangles and set aside for pieced border.

Make 36.   Make 28.

4. Stitch each green/light mauve rectangle to the side of a square made in step 2. Refer to diagram below for color placement.

5. Join one of the units created in step 4 to a green center square (T11), using a half seam. See "Half Seams" on pages 76–77.

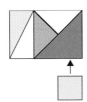

6. Complete the block, following the diagram and adding the triangle/rectangle units one at a time to each side of the center square.

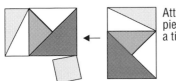

Attach rest of pieced units one at a time to each side.

7. Finish the last half of the first seam to complete each block.

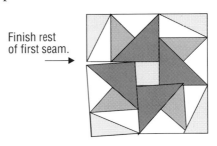

Finish rest of first seam.

Quilt Top Assembly

1. Join the completed blocks, side by side, in a 3 x 3 setting.
2. Referring to the diagram at right, make 2 inner border strips from the deep purple floral squares (T18) and rectangles (T10) and the deep purple floral/green pieced rectangles set aside earlier. Press the seams so that they will butt correctly with the seams in the quilt top. Sew these border strips to opposite sides of the quilt top.
3. Assemble the top and bottom borders in the same manner, following the diagram below and using the remaining squares, rectangles, and pieced rectangles. Press so the seams will butt correctly with the seams at the top and bottom edges of the quilt top. Attach to the top and bottom of the quilt top.

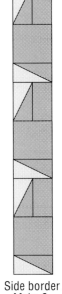

Side border Make 2.

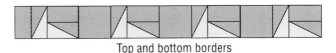

Top and bottom borders

4. Cut the deep purple floral border strips for the outer border to fit the length and width of the quilt top, referring to the directions for borders with corner squares on page 206. Add the corner squares (T19) to the ends of the top and bottom strips. Press the seams toward the borders.

Sew the border strips to the sides of the quilt first, then add the top and bottom borders with corner squares. Press seams toward the borders.

Quilt Finishing

1. Layer the quilt top with batting and backing; baste. See page 255.
2. Quilt as desired. Refer to "Loving Stitches," beginning on page 225.
3. Bind the edges. Refer to "Happy Endings," beginning on page 275.

Rotary-Cutting Method

MATERIALS: 44"-WIDE FABRIC

½ yd. medium mauve for blocks
½ yd. purple print for blocks
½ yd. light mauve print for blocks
⅞ yd. green check for blocks and pieced inner border
1½ yds. deep purple floral print for pieced inner border and outer border
½ yd. for binding
3 yds. for backing

ROTARY CUTTING

From the purple print, cut:
 3 strips, each 4⅞" x 42"; crosscut into 18 squares, each 4⅞" x 4⅞"

From the medium mauve, cut:
 2 strips, each 5¼" x 42"; crosscut into 9 squares, each 5¼" x 5¼"

From the green check, cut:
 2 pieces, each 11" x 42", for pieced rectangles
 9 squares, each 2½" x 2½" (Cut these squares from the leftover corners after making the pieced rectangles, step 4 on page 97.)

From the light mauve, cut:
 1 piece, 11" x 40", for pieced rectangles
 1 strip, 5¼" x 42"; crosscut into 8 squares, each 5¼" x 5¼". Cut a 9th square, 5¼" x 5¼",
from a leftover corner of the 11" piece after making the pieced rectangles.

From the deep purple floral, cut:
 1 piece, 11" x 32", for pieced rectangles
 4 squares, each 4" x 4", for the outer border corner squares (Cut squares from leftover corners after making the pieced rectangles.)
 2 strips, each 4½" x 42"; crosscut into 12 squares, each 4½" x 4½", for pieced border
 1 strip, 4½" x 42"; crosscut into 16 rectangles, each 2½" x 4½", for the pieced border
 4 strips, each 4" x 43", for outer border*

*If your fabric is less than 43" wide after preshrinking, cut 6 strips and piece the borders as needed to fit the quilt top.

DIRECTIONS

1. Cut the 5¼" medium mauve and light mauve squares twice diagonally to yield 36 quarter-square triangles of each color. Sew a medium mauve quarter-square triangle to a light mauve quarter-square triangle as shown.

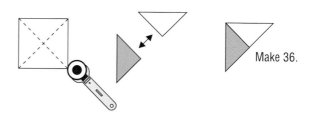

Make 36.

2. Cut 4⅞" purple print squares once diagonally to yield 36 half-square triangles. Sew a pair of side-by-side triangles to a purple half-square triangle as shown.

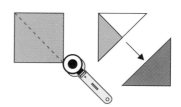

Make 36.

3. Place the wrong side of each fabric listed below face up on your cutting mat. Cut off-bias strips for pieced rectangles as shown on pages 35–38.

   From 11" x 42" pieces of green check, cut:
      18 off-bias strips, each 2¾" wide,
   From 11" x 40" piece of light mauve, cut:
      10 off-bias strips, each 2¾" wide
   From 11" x 32" piece of purple floral, cut:
      8 off-bias strips, each 2¾" wide

4. Sew Strip Unit I as shown in the diagram, using 10 green checked and 10 light mauve off-bias strips together as shown to form the first strip unit. Cut 36 rectangles, each 2½" x 4½", following the directions on pages 35–38 and using the BiRangle cutting guide designed by Mary Hickey. You may use a plastic cutting template taped to your ruler if you prefer. To make a plastic cutting template for the rectangle, see page 38.

Strip Unit I

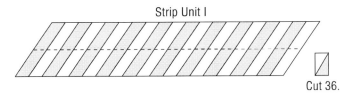

Cut 36.

5. Sew Strip Unit II as shown in the diagram, using 8 green and 8 purple floral off-bias strips. Cut 28 rectangles, each 2½" x 4½". Set them aside for the borders.

Strip Unit II

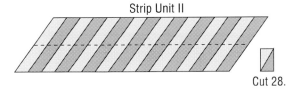

Cut 28.

6. Sew each green/light mauve rectangle to the side of one of the squares made in step 2.

7. Join 1 unit created in step 6 to each green 2½" center square, using a half seam as shown on pages 76–77.

8. Complete the block, following the diagram and adding the triangle/rectangle units one at a time to each side of the center square.

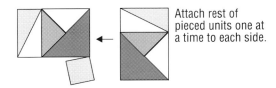

Attach rest of pieced units one at a time to each side.

9. Finish the last half of the first seam to complete each block.

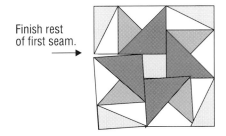

Finish rest of first seam.

10. Assemble the quilt top, referring to "Quilt Top Assembly" on page 95 and ignoring the template references.

11. Finish the quilt, referring to "Quilt Finishing" on page 96.

Country Crossing

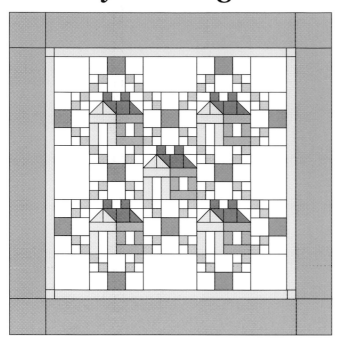

Color photo on page 115.
Finished Quilt Size: 67½" x 67½"
Finished Block Sizes: 12" and 8" x 12"

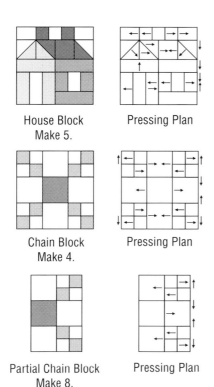

House Block
Make 5.

Pressing Plan

Chain Block
Make 4.

Pressing Plan

Partial Chain Block
Make 8.

Pressing Plan

Template Method

MATERIALS: 44"-WIDE FABRIC

1⅝ yds. black floral for House blocks and outer border
⅞ yd. mauve for House blocks and inner border
⅜ yd. burgundy for House blocks
⅜ yd. medium blue for full and partial Chain blocks
⅜ yd. dark blue for full and partial Chain blocks
2 yds. pale pink for large corner squares, fill-in rectangles, and full and partial Chain blocks
½ yd. for binding
4 yds. for backing

TEMPLATE CUTTING

Templates begin on page 106. If you prefer to rotary cut this quilt, see the directions that begin on page 100.

From the black floral, cut:
  10 Template 14 (T14) for House blocks
  10 Template 16 (T16) for House blocks
  4 Template 24 (T24) for outer border corner squares
  6 strips, each 6½" x 42½", for outer border
From the mauve, cut:
  10 Template 17 (T17) for House blocks
  5 Template 16 (T16) for House blocks
  10 Template 1 (T1) for House blocks
  4 Template 2 (T2) for inner border corner squares
  6 strips, each 2" x 42½", for inner border
From the burgundy, cut:
  10 Template 1 (T1) for House blocks
  5 Template 15 (T15) for House blocks
  10 Template 11 (T11) for House blocks
From the medium blue, cut:
  64 Template 11 (T11) for full and partial Chain blocks
From the dark blue, cut:
  12 Template 18 (T18) for full and partial Chain blocks
From the pale pink, cut:
  15 Template 14 (T14) for House blocks

69 Template 11 (T11) for House blocks and full and partial Chain blocks

10 Template 1 (T1) for House blocks

5 Template 17 (T17) for House blocks

40 Template 18 (T18) for full and partial Chain blocks

4 pieces, each 8½" x 12½", for fill-in rectangles

4 squares, each 8½" x 8½", for plain corner blocks

From the binding fabric, cut:

7 strips, each 2" x 42"

DIRECTIONS

House Blocks

Note: Each House block is made from 4 pieced sections. See the piecing diagram below.

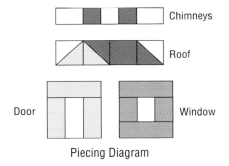

Piecing Diagram

1. Assemble 5 each of the chimney, roof, door, and window sections, following the piecing diagrams below and top right.

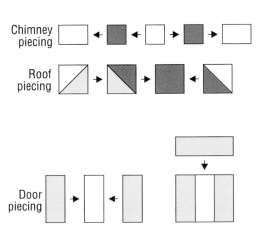

Window piecing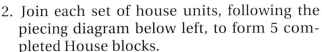

2. Join each set of house units, following the piecing diagram below left, to form 5 completed House blocks.

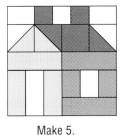

Make 5.

Full and Partial Chain Blocks

1. Join the 64 medium blue squares (T11) to the remaining 64 pale pink squares (T11). Join these units into pairs to form 32 Four-Patch units.

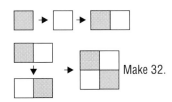

Make 32.

2. Sew 2 four-patch units to the opposite sides of each of 16 pale pink squares (T18) to make 16 double four-patch units. Be careful to position the four-patch units as shown.

Make 16.

3. Sew a pale pink square (T18) to opposite sides of a dark blue square (T18). Make 12.

4. Sew a double four-patch unit to each of the 12 units made in step 3. Set aside 8 of these units for the partial Chain blocks.

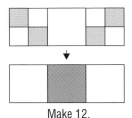

Make 12.

5. Make 4 full Chain blocks, using the 4 remaining double four-patch units and the 4 remaining partial blocks created in step 4.

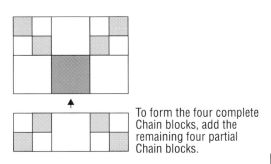

To form the four complete Chain blocks, add the remaining four partial Chain blocks.

Quilt Top Assembly

1. Using House blocks, full and partial Chain blocks, pale pink 8½" squares, and 8½" x 12½" rectangles, assemble the quilt top in horizontal rows as shown. Press seams toward the chain units.

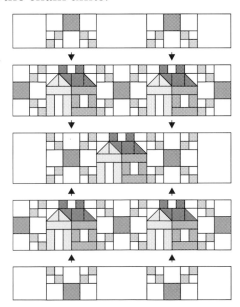

2. Join the rows to form the quilt top.
3. Cut 2 of the 6 mauve inner border strips in half. Sew a half strip to one end of each of the 4 remaining strips. Cut the resulting strips to fit the length and width of the quilt top, referring to the directions for borders with corner squares on page 206. Add the mauve corner squares (T11) to the ends of the top and bottom strips. Press seams toward the borders.

Sew the border strips to the sides of the quilt first, then add the top and bottom borders with corner squares. Press seams toward the borders.

4. Prepare and attach the black floral border strips and corner squares (T24) for the outer border in the same manner.

Quilt Finishing

1. Layer the quilt top with batting and backing; baste. See page 255.
2. Quilt as desired. Refer to "Loving Stitches," beginning on page 225.
3. Bind the edges. Refer to "Happy Endings," beginning on page 275.

Rotary-Cutting Method

Refer to the Materials list on page 98 for required yardage.

ROTARY CUTTING

From the black floral, cut:
2 strips, each 2½" x 42", for Strip Unit V

2 strips, each 2½" x 42"; crosscut into 10 bars, each 2½" x 6½", for windows

6 strips, each 6½" x 42", for outer border

4 squares, each 6½" x 6½", for outer border corner squares

From the mauve, cut:
2 strips, each 2½" x 42", for Strip Unit IV

2 squares, each 8" x 8", for bias squares for roofs

1 strip, 2½" x 33"; crosscut into 5 bars, each 2½" x 6½", for doors

6 strips, each 2" x 42", for inner border

4 squares, each 2" x 2", for inner border corner squares

From the burgundy, cut:
1 strip, 2" x 42", for Strip Unit III

2 squares, each 8" x 8", for bias squares for roofs

1 strip, 3½" x 18"; crosscut into 5 squares, each 3½" x 3½", for roofs

From the medium blue, cut:
4 strips, each 2½" x 42", for Strip Unit I

From the dark blue, cut:
2 strips, each 4½" x 42", for Strip Unit II

From the pale pink, cut:
6 strips, each 2½" x 42", for Strip Units I, III, IV, and V
3 strips, each 4½" x 42", for Strip Unit II
1 strip, 3½" x 42", for Strip Unit III
2 strips, each 4½" x 42"; crosscut into 16 squares, each 4½" x 4½", for Chain blocks
4 squares, each 8½" x 8½", for plain corner blocks
4 pieces, each 8½" x 12½", for fill-in rectangles
2 squares, each 8" x 8", for bias squares for roofs

DIRECTIONS

Note: Cut all strips for the strip-pieced units in half to form half-length strips that are approximately 21" long. If your half-length strips do not measure at least 21" long, you may need to make an additional strip unit to cut the required number of segments. In the directions that follow, the number of strip units you are instructed to make refers to 21"-long strip units. Arrows indicate the direction in which to press the seams.

Full and Partial Chain Blocks

1. Assemble 8 Strip Unit I as shown, using 8 medium blue and 8 pale pink 2½" x 21" strips. Crosscut strip units into 64 segments, each 2½" wide.

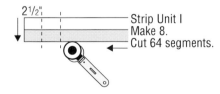

2. Join the 64 segments into pairs to form 32 four-patch units.

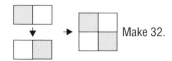
Make 32.

3. Sew 2 four-patch units to opposite sides of each of 16 pale pink 4½" squares to make 16 double four-patch units. Be careful to position the four-patch units as shown.

Make 16.

4. Assemble 3 Strip Unit II as shown, using 1 dark blue 4½" x 21" strip and 2 pale pink 4½" x 21" strips for each strip unit. Crosscut strip units into 12 segments, each 4½" wide.

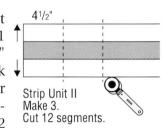
Strip Unit II
Make 3.
Cut 12 segments.

5. Sew a double four-patch unit to each of the 12 units made in step 4. Set aside 8 of these units for the partial Chain blocks.

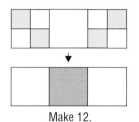
Make 12.

6. Make 4 full Chain blocks, using the 4 remaining double four-patch units and the 4 remaining partial blocks created in step 5.

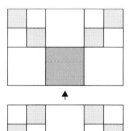
To form the four complete Chain blocks, add the remaining four partial Chain blocks.

House Blocks

Note: As shown in the piecing diagram at right, each House block is made from 4 pieced sections.

1. Assemble 1 Strip Unit III, using 2 pale pink 3½" x 21" strips, 1 pale pink 2½" x 21" strip, and 2 burgundy 2½" x 21" strips. Crosscut this strip unit into 5 segments, each 2½" wide, to form the chimneys.

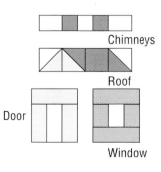
Chimneys
Roof
Door
Window

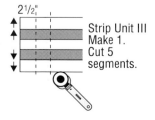
Strip Unit III
Make 1.
Cut 5 segments.

2. Assemble 2 Strip Unit IV, using 2 mauve 2½" x 21" strips and 1 pale pink 2½" x 21" strip for each unit. Crosscut strip units into 5 segments, each 5½" wide.

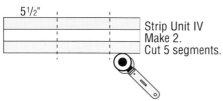

Strip Unit IV
Make 2.
Cut 5 segments.

3. Sew a 2½" x 6½" mauve rectangle to the top of each segment cut in step 2 to form the 5 doors.

4. Assemble 1 Strip Unit V, using 2 black floral 2½" x 21" strips and 1 pale pink 2½" x 21" strip. Crosscut strip unit into 5 segments, each 3½" wide.

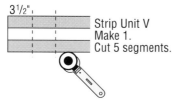

Strip Unit V
Make 1.
Cut 5 segments.

5. Sew a 2½" x 6½" black floral rect-angle to the top and bottom of each segment cut in step 4 to form the completed windows.

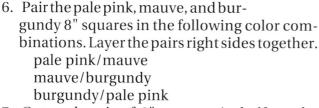

6. Pair the pale pink, mauve, and bur-gundy 8" squares in the following color com-binations. Layer the pairs right sides together.
   - pale pink/mauve
   - mauve/burgundy
   - burgundy/pale pink

7. Cut each pair of 8" squares in half on the diagonal. Then cut a 3¾"-wide strip from each triangle, making the cut parallel to the long edge as shown to create ready-to-sew pairs of bias strips. Discard the small triangles.

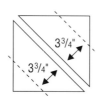

8. Sew the bias-strip pairs to-gether on the long edge. Press the seam in the pale pink/mauve set toward the mauve strip. Press the seam in the other sets toward the burgundy strip.

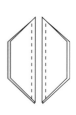

9. Sew the pairs from each color combination to-gether to form a 4-piece multiple strip unit.

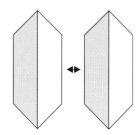

10. Cut 5 bias squares, each 3½" x 3½", from each multiple strip unit.

11. Assemble each of the 5 roof units, using one each of the 3 different 3½" bias squares and one 3½" burgundy square.

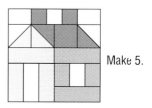

Roof Piecing

12. Join each set of house units, following the piecing diagram on page 101 to form 5 com-pleted House blocks.

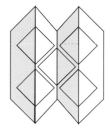

Make 5.

Quilt Top Assembly and Finishing

1. Assemble the quilt top, referring to "Quilt Top Assembly" on page 100 and disregard-ing all template references.

2. Finish the quilt, referring to "Quilt Finish-ing" on page 100.

Ferris Wheel

Color photo on page 114.
Finished Quilt Size: 34½" x 34½"
Finished Block Size: 12"

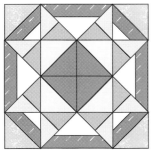

Ferris Wheel Block

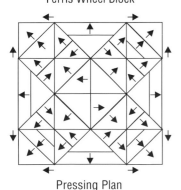

Pressing Plan

MATERIALS: 44"-WIDE FABRIC

¾ yd. plum floral print for blocks and outer border
⅜ yd. mottled gray print for blocks
⅜ yd. green print for blocks
⅜ yd. blue print for blocks
½ yd. plum print for blocks
¾ yd. light teal print for blocks and sashings
⅝ yd. light print for blocks
⅜ yd. for binding
1 yd. for backing

ROTARY CUTTING

Note: No templates are required for this quilt. Using a rotary cutter, mat, and ruler, cut the strips listed in the first column of the cutting chart below. Then cut the pieces listed in the second column. For some parts of the quilt, additional cutting is not required at this time, so no additional information appears in the second column.

	FIRST CUT		SECOND CUT	
	NO. OF STRIPS	DIMENSIONS	NO. OF PIECES	DIMENSIONS
BIAS SQUARES				
Plum Floral Print	1	9" x 19"		
Mottled Gray Print	1	9" x 19"		
SIDE-BY SIDES				
Green Print	1	10" x 30"		
Blue Print	1	10" x 30"		
STRIPED SQUARES				
Plum Print	1	9" x 34"	9	1½"-wide bias strips*
Light Teal Print	1	9" x 34"	5	3⅛"-wide bias strips*
Light Print	1	9" x 28"	5	2"-wide bias strips*
*Discard corner pieces left after cutting bias strips.				
STRIPED TRIANGLES				
Plum Print	2	3" x 42"	4	3" x 21"
Light Print	3	3" x 42"	6	3" x 21"
SASHING				
Light Teal Print	5	2" x 42"	2	2" x 29"
			3	2" x 26"
			2	2" x 12½"
BORDER				
Plum Floral Print	4	3½" x 42"	2	3½" x 29"
			2	3½" x 35"
BINDING				
Binding Fabric	4	2" x 42"		

DIRECTIONS

Bias Squares

1. Layer the plum floral and mottled gray fabrics with right sides up. Cut into 3¼"-wide bias strips.

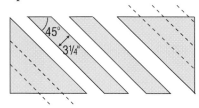

2. Assemble the strips into 2 strip-pieced units. Press the seams on one unit toward the plum fabric and toward the gray fabric on the remaining one.
3. Cut eight 3½" bias squares from each strip-pieced unit

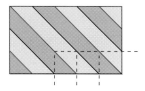

Side-by-Sides

1. Layer the green and blue fabrics, right sides up. Cut into 3½"-wide bias strips.
2. Assemble the strips into 2 strip-pieced units. Press all seams toward the blue fabric.
3. Cut a total of sixteen 3⅞" bias squares from the strip-pieced units. Cut these bias squares in half on the diagonal to make 32 mirror-image, side-by-side triangle units.

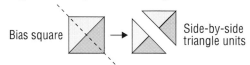

Bias square → Side-by-side triangle units

Striped Squares

1. Sew bias strips of the plum print, light teal print, and the light print into a strip-pieced unit, repeating the sequence shown in the diagram, above right. Press the seams toward the light teal print and the plum print.
2. Cut sixteen 3½" striped bias squares from the strip-pieced unit. Lay the diagonal line of the Bias Square on the seam between the teal and plum strips. There will be a small waste rectangle between the striped squares. Discard these as you cut.

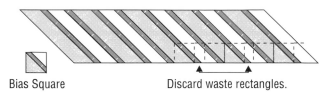

Bias Square   Discard waste rectangles.

Striped Triangles

1. Sew the 3" x 21" plum print strips to the 3" x 21" light print strips, alternating the colors and beginning and ending with a light strip. Offset the strips by 1¼" as shown in the diagram below step 3 to reduce fabric waste. Press the seams toward the plum print.
2. With a washout marker or chalk pencil, draw a line through the center of each plum strip.
3. Cut eight 5⅛" striped bias squares from the strip-pieced unit, aligning the diagonal line of the Bias Square on the line drawn through the plum print strips.

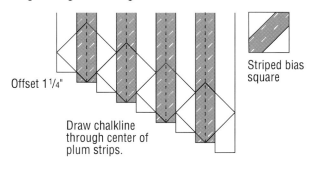

Offset 1¼"

Striped bias square

Draw chalkline through center of plum strips.

4. Cut the 8 striped squares in half through the center of the plum print strip on the chalk line to form 16 striped triangles.

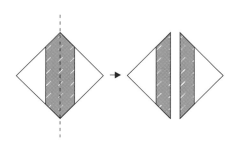

Quilt Top Assembly

1. Using bias squares, side-by-sides, striped squares, and striped triangle units, assemble 4 Ferris Wheel blocks. First, assemble the center section by joining bias squares with opposing seams as indicated by the pressing arrows in the diagram below. (This is why you were instructed to press the seams in the strip-pieced units in opposite directions when you made the bias squares.)

2. Assemble each block, following the diagram.

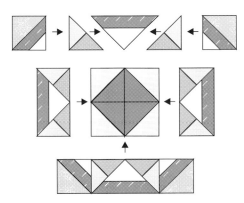

3. Join blocks into 2 pairs, using a 2" x 12½" light teal sashing strip to join each set. Press the seams toward the sashing. Join the rows with a 2" x 26" light teal sashing strip. Press the seams toward the sashing.

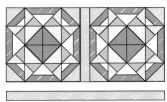

Join blocks in pairs with sashings.

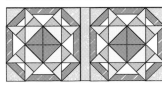

Join rows together with row sashings.

4. Add the 2" x 26" side sashing strips first, then the 2" x 29" top and bottom sashing strips. Press seams toward the sashing.

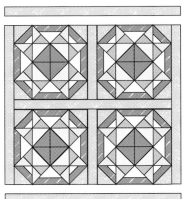

Add side sashings first.

Add top and bottom sashings last.

5. Sew the 3½" x 29" borders to the sides of the quilt top. Then add the 3½" x 35" top and bottom borders. Press the seams toward the borders.

Quilt Finishing

1. Layer the quilt top with batting and backing; baste. See page 255.
2. Quilt as desired. Refer to "Loving Stitches," beginning on page 225.
3. Bind the edges. Refer to "Happy Endings," beginning on page 275.

TEMPLATES

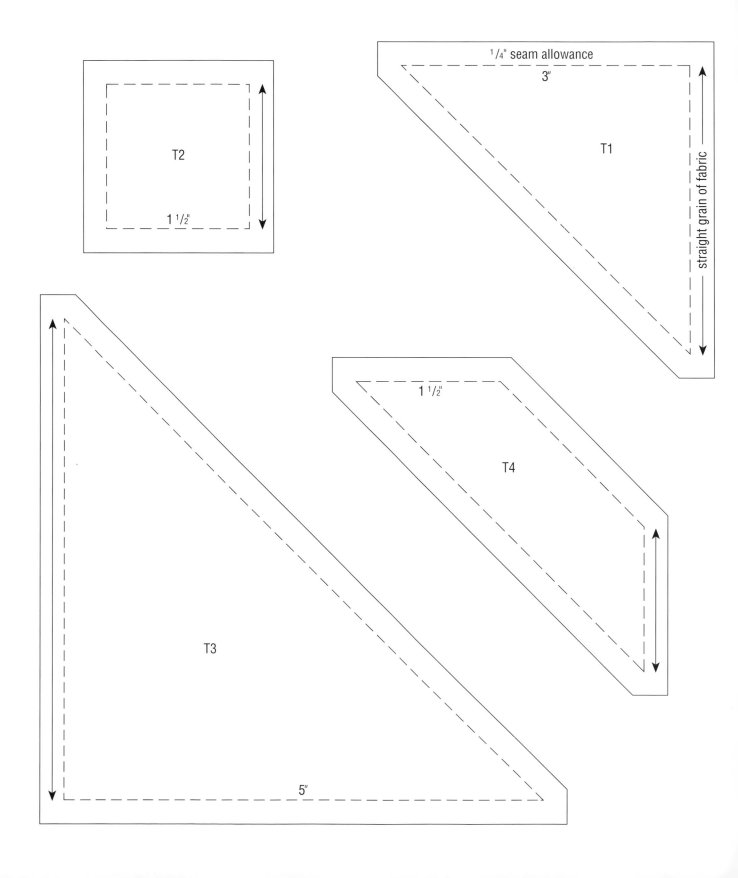

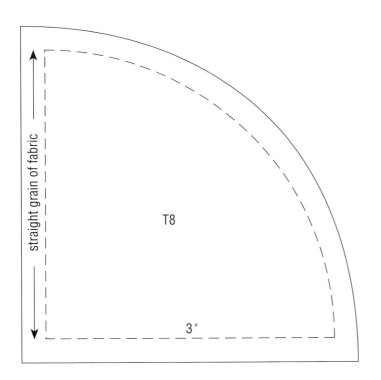

T8

straight grain of fabric

3"

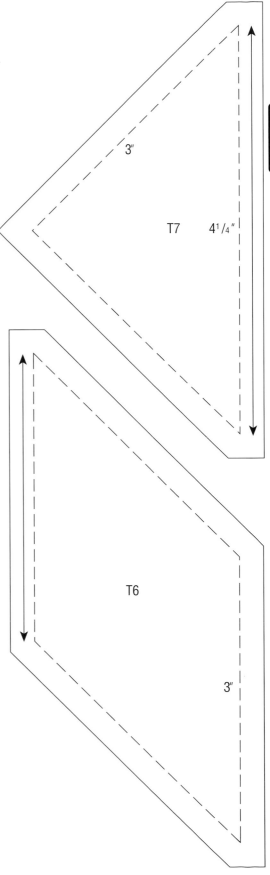

3"

T7   4¹/₄"

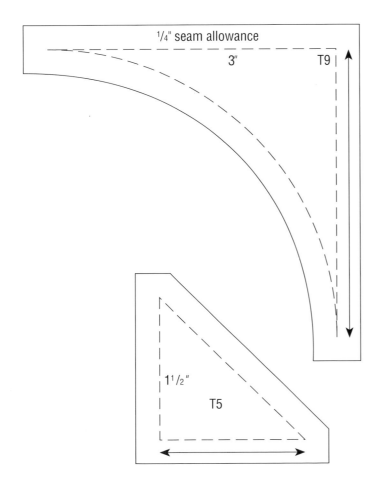

¹/₄" seam allowance

3"

T9

T6

3"

1¹/₂"

T5

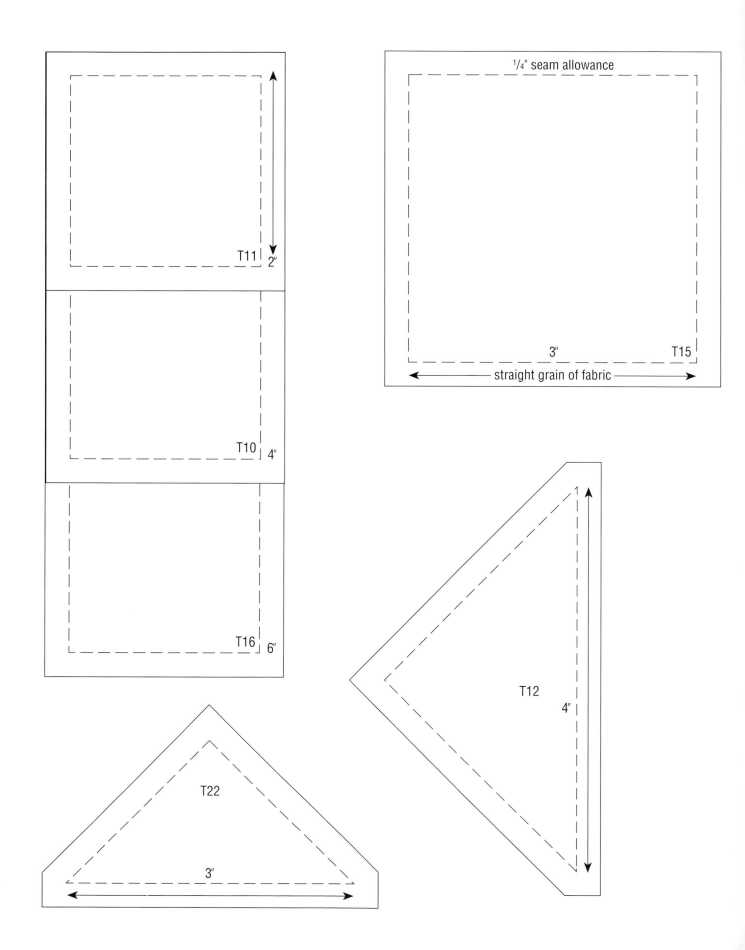

T11 2″

T10 4″

T16 6″

¼″ seam allowance

3″ T15

straight grain of fabric

T12 4″

T22 3″

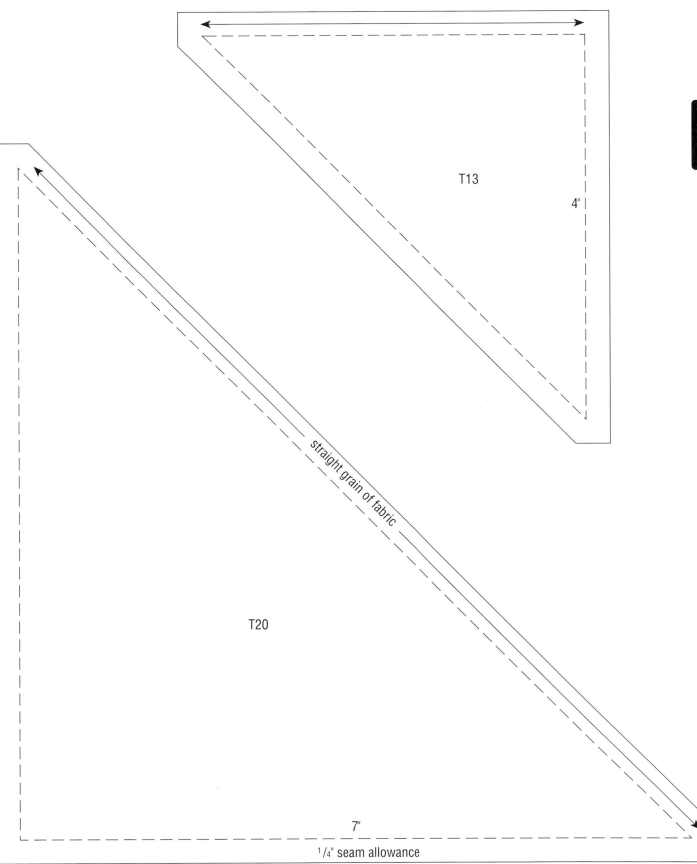

T13

4"

straight grain of fabric

T20

7"

¹/₄" seam allowance

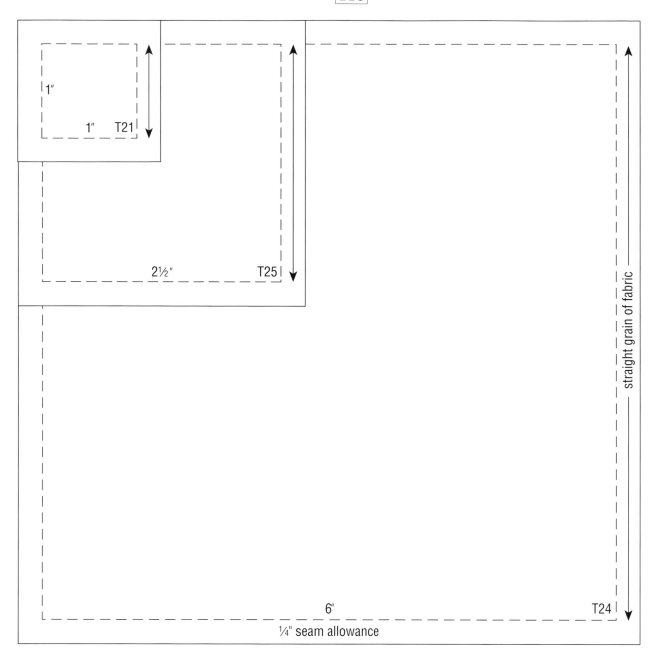

1"

1"   1"   T21

2½"   T25

6"   T24

¼" seam allowance

straight grain of fabric

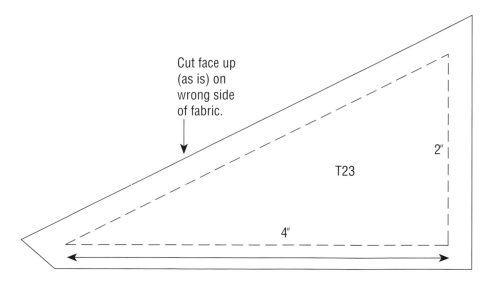

Cut face up
(as is) on
wrong side
of fabric.

T23

2"

4"

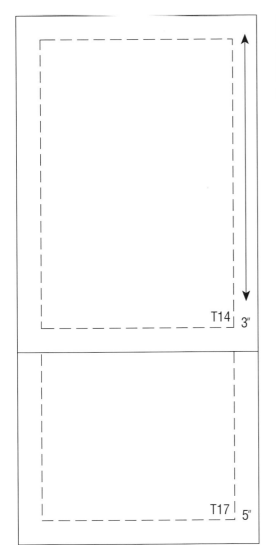

T14 3"

T17 5"

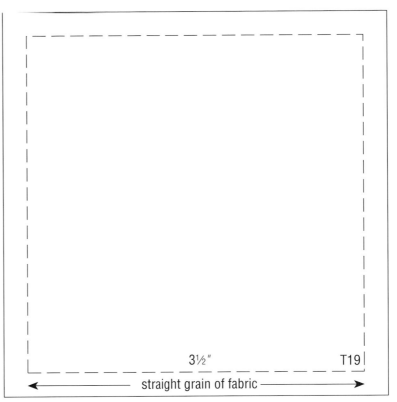

3½"   T19

straight grain of fabric

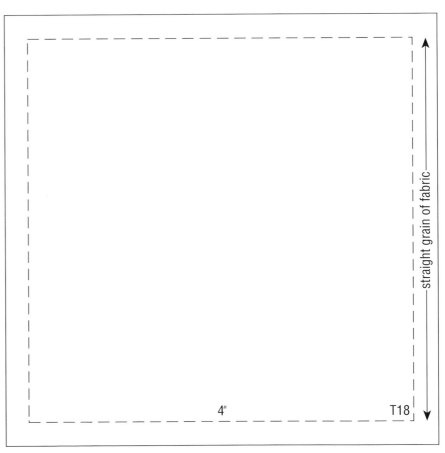

4"   T18

straight grain of fabric

MITERING GUIDES

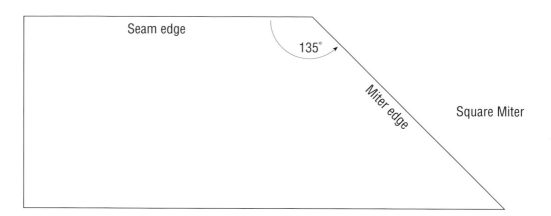

Seam edge

135°

Miter edge

Square Miter

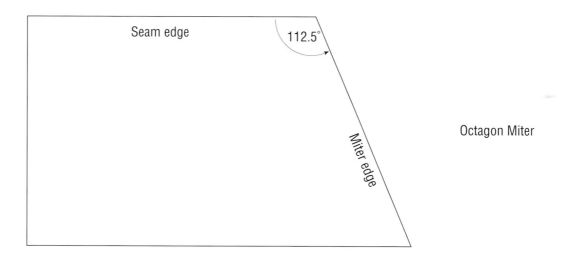

Seam edge

112.5°

Miter edge

Octagon Miter

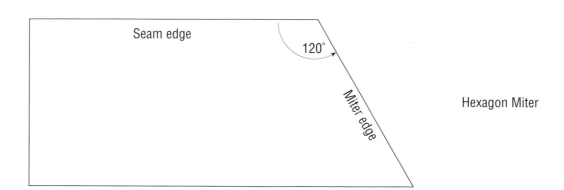

Seam edge

120°

Miter edge

Hexagon Miter

A Perfect Match
GALLERY

Evening Shades by Donna Lynn Thomas, 1992, Dorf-Guell, Germany, 45" x 45". The soft greens and purples help to counterbalance the asymmetry of the stars. The purple stars are obvious, but where the blocks meet, a second set of stars is created. Quilted by Donnas Thomas, Marie-Thérèse Rüthling, and Ann Woodward.

Starpool by Dee Glenn, 1992, Rochester, England, 28½" x 39¾". Diamonds in cool jewel tones and warm reds complement each other beautifully while the butterfly border pulls it all together for an eye-pleasing effect.

Starpool by Donna Lynn Thomas, 1992, Dorf-Guell, Germany, 28½" x 39¾". The curves at the corners of the LeMoyne Star blocks make the stars appear to float in a pool of teal green water, giving this quilt an exotic appeal. Quilted by Roxanne Carter.

Ferris Wheel by Donna Lynn Thomas, 1992, Dorf-Guell, Germany, 34½" x 34½". Cool blues and greens plus warm plums combine to create a striking effect. The striped squares and triangles on the edge of the block add a circular movement to the design. Quilted by Ann Woodward.

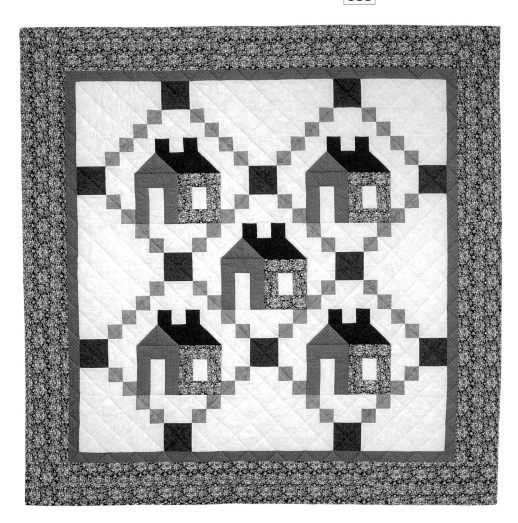

Country Crossing *by Donna Lynn Thomas, 1992, Dorf-Guell, Germany, 67½" x 67½". Two perennial favorites, Schoolhouse and Puss in the Corner blocks, combine to re-create the simplicity of a walk in the country. Quilted by Roxanne Carter.*

Sweetheart *by Donna Lynn Thomas, 1992, Dorf-Guell, Germany, 29" x 39". Always versatile, the traditional Log Cabin Block takes a twist and ends up as a heart. The use of many fabrics makes this quilt as interesting as it is fun to sew. Quilted by Roxanne Carter.*

Ohio Sparkler *by Donna Lynn Thomas, 1992, Dorf-Guell, Germany, 47" x 47". There's a lot to look at in this quilt with Churn Dash Variation blocks and Ohio Star sashings. Changing the colors and using contrast could create a number of different looks to this pattern. Quilted by Roxanne Carter.*

THE Art OF Appliqué
TRIED & TRUE TECHNIQUES FOR HAND & MACHINE

CONTENTS

INTRODUCTION

Appliqué pieces stitched to background fabrics create beautiful designs on the surface of quilts. Instead of sewing fabric pieces together to make patchwork designs, appliqué designs are cut from selected fabrics and sewn to a background fabric. Appliqué makes it easy to create intricate designs with curves and sharp points, something that is often more challenging in pieced work. Traditional appliqué is done by hand, but machine appliqué has gained popularity in recent years.

Mimi's directions for traditional hand-appliqué techniques appear here, followed by Roxi's directions for invisible machine appliqué. In addition, fusible appliqué with machine-stitched embellishment is an alternative for quick and easy appliqué on small items and wall hangings that do not require regular laundering. Basic directions follow the section on invisible machine appliqué.

You can practice the basics of hand or machine appliqué, using the simple heart-shaped appliqué that appears on page 136. You will then know how to appliqué pieces with straight edges, curves, and outside and inside points. Once you have mastered the techniques, make Mimi's "Heart's Desire" quilt on pages 135–36 to experiment with hand-appliqué methods. Then graduate to Mimi's "Hearts and Flowers" quilt on pages 137–42 to learn additional hand-appliqué techniques. If you prefer invisible machine appliqué, practice on Roxi's "Apple Blossoms" quilt on pages 153–60, or use her techniques to make Mimi's quilts or other favorite appliqué designs.

Mimi Dietrich and Roxi Eppler

HAND APPLIQUÉ

Fabrics for Appliqué

When choosing fabrics for appliqué, you need fabric for the background fabric and the appliqué pieces. Appliqué background fabrics are often, but not always, light-colored solids or small prints and stripes that complement the appliqué design. White-on-white printed fabrics make lovely appliqué backgrounds. If you use a bold print, plaid, or striped fabric for the background, it may be difficult to see the appliquéd design.

Choose fabrics for the appliqué pieces that are appropriate for the design. Consider the proper color and print size for the pattern you are stitching. Solid-colored fabrics are always "safe" to use, but printed fabrics are often more exciting and appealing and can be used to create delicate shadings within the design. Little floral prints and geometric calicoes work well in many traditional appliqué designs.

Fabrics printed in shades of one color can be very effective for representing texture in flowers, leaves, and other natural shapes. Large, multicolored fabrics may be too elaborate for small appliqué pieces in traditional designs but are quite acceptable and often desirable in larger, more contemporary designs. The design in a large-print fabric is often lost in a small appliqué piece. However, sometimes you can cut a perfectly shaped and colored design from a specific area of a large print. It's wise to avoid stripes and plaids unless they work well with your design.

When choosing fabrics for the appliqué pieces, 100% cotton fabrics are easiest to handle. Synthetic fabrics tend to fray more easily than cotton and are often slippery. Sometimes, however, a favorite fabric contains synthetic fibers, and it's worth a little extra care to use it in your design. Contemporary appliqué artists often use a variety of fabrics, including lamé and satin, but these are not recommended for the beginner.

To prevent shrinking and bleeding in the quilt, prewash all cotton and cotton-blend fabrics as directed on page 8.

Supplies

Needles. When you choose a needle for hand appliqué, the most important consideration is the size of the needle. A fine needle glides easily through the edges of the appliqué pieces so your stitches are small and inconspicuous. Choose a size 10 or 12 for the best stitching results.

The type of needle you use for hand appliqué depends on personal choice. Some stitchers use short quilting needles (betweens) because they feel closer to the stitching. Longer needles (sharps or crewels) may be easier to thread. An even longer type of needle (milliner's) works well as a tool for "needle-turning" the edges of the appliqué as you apply it to the background.

Quilting needle (between)	————
Sharp	————
Crewel	————
Milliner's	————

Try different types of needles to find the one most comfortable for you. If a fine needle is difficult to thread, use a needle threader to insert the thread through the eye of the needle.

Thread. Thread for hand appliqué should match the color of the appliqué pieces rather than the background fabric. Designs with many different-colored pieces require many shades of thread. If it is not possible to match the color exactly, choose thread that is a little darker than the fabric. If the appliqué fabric contains many colors, choose a neutral-colored thread that blends with the predominant color in the piece.

All-cotton thread works well for hand stitching appliqués. It is very pliable and disappears or blends invisibly into the edges of the appliqués. If cotton thread is not available in just the right color, use cotton-covered polyester thread. Sometimes, it is necessary to use thread that is available in your sewing area. If so, make sure the thread is strong and closely matches the color of your appliqué pieces.

> *Tip* Always use white or light-colored thread for basting. Dye from dark-colored basting thread often leaves small dots of color on light-colored fabrics.

Pins. You may need pins to position appliqué pieces for basting. Small, ½"- to ¾"-long sequin pins are wonderful because they don't get in the way of the thread as you stitch.

Scissors. You will need a small pair of scissors for clipping threads and trimming appliqué pieces. Sharp blades that cut to the point are necessary for clipping inner points on some appliqué pieces.

Glue Stick. Glue stick is handy for "basting" pieces in position instead of basting by hand.

Template Plastic and Permanent Marker. You will need these to make patterns for each piece in the design. You may also make templates by gluing paper patterns to cardboard, but plastic templates are more durable and more accurate.

Fine-lead Mechanical Pencil or Sharp Chalk Pencil. Use this for tracing your design pieces onto the appliqué fabrics.

Freezer Paper. Available at most supermarkets and grocery stores in rolls, this white paper has a plastic coating on one side that adheres to fabric when you apply a warm iron to the uncoated side. You can use it to prepare appliqués with smoothly turned edges.

Silver Marking Pencil. This works well for tracing the appliqué design onto the background to mark the placement of each appliqué piece.

Appliqué Preparation

To prepare for hand appliqué, you must mark the design onto the background fabric, make templates for each appliqué shape, and then trace them onto the selected fabrics and cut them out.

MARKING THE BACKGROUND FABRIC

The background fabric for appliqué is usually cut in a rectangle or square, or for borders, in long strips. If the finished size of an appliqué block is 10" square, cut the block 10½" x 10½" to allow for

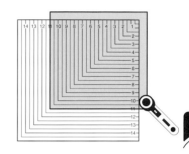

seams. Sometimes, it is better to cut the square an inch larger to start, then trim it to the correct size after completing the appliqué. It is easy to cut accurate background squares, using your rotary cutter, mat, and a large, square acrylic ruler.

In order to place the appliqué pieces onto the background fabric accurately, you will need to mark the design on the fabric. If your background fabric is white or off-white, it's easy to trace the design onto the fabric.

1. Place the fabric right side up over the pattern so that the design is in the correct position on the background piece.
2. Use a silver marking pencil to trace the design. The marks will be dark enough to see easily and will wash out after the quilt is completed. You can also use a water-erasable marker to trace the lines exactly, but test it first on a sample of your fabric to make sure that you can remove the marks with cold water.

As an alternative, you can use a fine-lead mechanical pencil to trace *slightly inside the pattern lines*. When you attach the appliqués, you will cover these lines.

If your background fabric is dark, a light box works well for tracing the design. If you do not have one, tape the pattern and fabric to a window on a sunny day, and trace the design. See page 251 for instructions on how to create your own light box.

Making Templates

For the traditional appliqué method, make templates for appliqué pieces by tracing them onto a sheet of clear plastic. If a design shape is repeated in a quilt, you need to make only one plastic template for it. For example, you need only one heart template to make the nine hearts in "Heart's Desire" on pages 135–36.

1. Place the plastic over the design and trace each piece with a fine-line permanent marker. Do not add seam allowances.
2. Cut out the templates along the traced lines so that they are the *exact* size of the design pieces.

Cutting Appliqués

Appliqué designs do not usually provide grain lines to aid in placing the templates on the fabric. If possible, place the templates on the appliqué fabric so that when the piece is in position its grain line runs in the same direction as the background fabric. In many appliqué designs, you may want the cut piece to include a special design printed on the fabric. In this case, disregard grain lines and enjoy the way that the fabric and the appliqué design work together.

1. Place a sheet of fine sandpaper under your fabric to keep it from slipping while you work. Place the template right side up on the right side of the appliqué fabric.
2. Using a fine-lead mechanical pencil for light-colored fabrics or a sharp chalk pencil for dark fabrics, trace around the template, marking on the right side of the fabric. When tracing several pieces, leave at least ½" between tracings for room to add seam allowances.

Right side
of fabric

3. Cut out each fabric piece, adding a ¼"-wide seam allowance around each tracing. You will turn this seam allowance under to create the finished edge of the appliqué.

Preparing Appliqués

Before you can sew the appliqués to the background fabric, prepare them by turning under the seam allowances smoothly and evenly. Care in this step will help you place the appliqués accurately on the background fabric. Eight different methods for appliqué preparation follow. Each one uses a heart shape for illustration.

METHOD ONE: TRADITIONAL APPLIQUÉ

1. Cut a template for the appliqué shape from template plastic and trace the design onto the *right* side of the fabric.

Right side
of fabric

2. Cut out the shape, adding a ¼"-wide seam allowance all around.
3. Turn under the seam allowances, rolling the traced line to the back of the appliqué piece so it doesn't show on the front or along the edge of the appliqué. Hand baste in place. See "Basting Practice" on page 123.

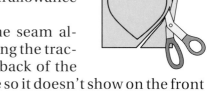

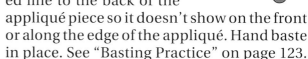
Tip

Try looking at the right side of the piece while you turn under the edge and baste near the fold. This method helps to keep the piece neat and accurate as you concentrate on the smooth shape of the piece. If you keep your stitches near the fold, you will be sure to catch the seam allowance.

4. Hand baste the seam allowance in place, using light-colored thread in the needle. See "Basting Practice" on page 123 to learn how to turn straight and curved edges and how to treat inside and outside corners and points.

(continued on page 124)

BASTING PRACTICE

Practice basting the edges of a heart-shaped appliqué. Use the template on page 136 to cut a heart from scraps. With this simple shape you can practice on straight edges, curves, outside points, and inside points.

1. Thread a needle with an 18" length of thread but do not knot one end as you normally would for basting. (This makes it easier to remove the basting later.)

2. Begin turning under the edge of the heart and baste along the straight edge. To anchor the first stitch, take a few stitches in place. Stop basting just before you reach the point of the heart.

3. Prepare the outside point by first turning it in toward the center of the heart. Fold the right side under, then the left, to form a sharp point.

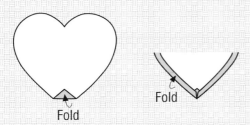

Fold

Fold

The seam allowances may overlap slightly at the point. They will overlap more on a very sharp point. If the point is too thick where the seam allowances cross, trim some of the seam width away to eliminate the bulk, or push the extra fabric under the point with your needle later as you sew. Baste close to the edge.

4. Continue basting the straight edge of the heart until you come to the first curve at the top of the heart. As you baste the curve, ease the seam allowance around the curve. Do not clip the outside curve, as it will result in little bumps along the edge of the appliqué. If your seam allowance is wider than ¼", trim it to a scant ¼" around the curve (more accurately, ³⁄₁₆"). As you baste around the curve, take small basting

stitches. Sew near the fold to keep the shape accurate. If little points appear along the curve, push them under with the tip of your needle when sewing the appliqué to the background.

5. As you finish basting the first curve, you will come to the inside point. Carefully clip the seam allowance so that the fabric will turn under easily. Do not clip all the way into the appliqué design. Stop clipping about two threads out from the marked line. As you baste the inside point, use shorter basting stitches but do not force the threads at the point to turn under. You will push these under with the tip of the needle later as you sew the appliqué to the background fabric. Tack down the seam-allowance edges, taking stitches away from the inside point.

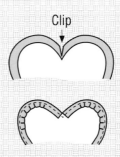

Clip

6. After basting the inside point, baste the second curve at the top of the heart, then overlap the beginning of your basting stitches along the straight edge.

(continued from page 122)

5. Do not turn under edges that will be covered by other appliqué pieces. Each of these should lie flat under the appliqué piece that covers it.
6. Baste the appliqué in place, using hand basting or pins, and appliqué, using the "Traditional Appliqué Stitch" as shown on pages 128–29 or the "Ladder Stitch" as shown on page 131.

METHOD TWO: GLUE-STICK PREPARATION

You can substitute glue basting for hand basting, using a water-soluble glue stick. Using glue saves time when preparing the pieces for appliqué and washes out after the appliqué is finished. Be sure to prewash fabrics (page 8) if you choose this method.

1. Make a plastic template for the appliqué.
2. Trace the design onto the right side of the fabric, using a fine-lead pencil and the plastic template.
3. Cut out the appliqué, adding a ¼"-wide allowance all around.
4. Apply glue stick to the ¼"-wide allowance on the wrong side of the appliqué. Try not to get too much glue in the fold area of the allowance or it will make the edges stiff and difficult to stitch in place.

Glue stick

5. Wait a few seconds for the glue to get tacky, then carefully fold the allowance to the wrong side of the appliqué.

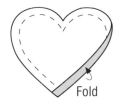

Fold

6. Baste the appliqué to the background fabric with glue. Apply glue to the background fabric in the center of the appliqué location.

Position the appliqué on the background fabric, finger press into place, and allow the glue to dry.

Background fabric

7. Stitch the appliqué in place, using the "Traditional Appliqué Stitch" on pages 128–29, or the "Ladder Stitch" on page 131. When you are finished, soak the appliqué in warm, soapy water to remove the glue. After the piece is dry, press from the wrong side.

METHOD THREE: NEEDLE-TURN APPLIQUÉ

With this method, there is no basting so it saves time.

1. Make a plastic template for the appliqué.
2. Trace the design onto the right side of the fabric, using a fine-lead pencil and the plastic template.
3. Cut out the appliqué, adding a scant ¼"-wide allowance (³⁄₁₆").
4. Position the appliqué on the background fabric and pin or baste it securely in place.
5. Beginning on one edge, use the tip of your needle to gently turn under the seam allowance, about ½" at a time. Hold the turned seam allowance firmly between the thumb and first finger of one hand as you stitch the appliqué securely to the background fabric.

Tip Use a longer needle—a sharp or a milliner's needle—to help control the seam allowance so it will turn neatly.

METHOD FOUR: FREEZER PAPER

Use freezer paper to help you make perfectly shaped appliqués. This technique improves accuracy in repeated designs. You can trace around a plastic template for each shape or simply trace the design onto freezer paper. If the shape is asymmetrical (each half different), trace a reverse image onto freezer paper. Be sure to prewash fabrics (page 8) if you choose this method.

1. Place the freezer paper, plastic side down, on your pattern and trace with a sharp pencil.

Freezer paper

2. Carefully cut out the freezer-paper design on the pencil line. *Do not add seam allowances.*
3. Place the plastic side of the freezer paper against the *wrong side* of the appliqué fabric and iron it in place, using a hot, dry iron.

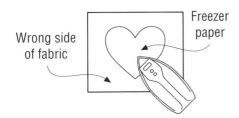

Wrong side of fabric

Freezer paper

4. Cut out the appliqué, adding a ¼"-wide allowance of fabric around the outside edge of the freezer paper.

5. Turn the ¼" allowance toward the freezer paper and baste by hand or use a glue stick to

baste it to the paper. Clip any inside points and fold any outside points.

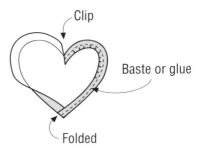

Clip

Baste or glue

Folded

6. Pin or baste the appliqué to the background fabric and stitch in place.
7. After stitching the appliqués in place, remove any basting stitches. Make a small slit in the background fabric behind the appliqué and remove the freezer paper with tweezers. If you have basted with a glue stick, soak the piece in warm water for a few minutes to soften the glue and release the paper. Pull out the paper. After the appliqué dries, press it from the wrong side.

METHOD FIVE: NEEDLE-TURN FREEZER PAPER

This technique eliminates basting when preparing appliqués.

1. Trace the design onto freezer paper and cut it out on the pencil line. If the shape is asymmetrical (each half different), trace a reverse image onto freezer paper.
2. Iron the freezer-paper shape to the *wrong side* of the appliqué fabric.
3. Cut around the freezer paper, adding a scant ¼"-wide allowance. Clip any inside corners, but do not turn under and baste the raw edges of the appliqué.

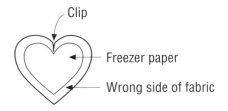

Clip

Freezer paper

Wrong side of fabric

4. Position the appliqué on the background fabric and pin or baste in place.

5. Use the tip of your needle to gently turn under the seam allowance, about ½" at a time. Hold the turned seam allowance tightly between your nonsewing thumb and finger. Stitch this area to the background fabric, then needle-turn the next ½" and repeat. The stiffness of the freezer paper makes it easy to turn under the seam allowances and gives you a smooth edge to work against. The result is a perfectly shaped finished appliqué.

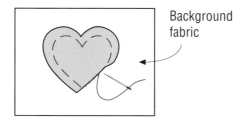

Background fabric

6. Make a small slit in the background fabric behind the appliqué and carefully remove the freezer paper with tweezers.

METHOD SIX: FREEZER PAPER ON TOP

If you do not like the idea of cutting the back of your work to remove the freezer paper, try ironing the freezer-paper design to the right side of the appliqué fabric.

1. Trace the appliqué design onto freezer paper and cut it out on the pencil line. Iron the freezer-paper shape to the *right side* of the appliqué fabric.

   Cut out the appliqué, adding a ¼"-wide allowance around the outside edge of the freezer paper.

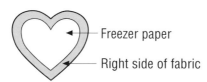

Freezer paper

Right side of fabric

2. Securely baste or pin the appliqué to the background fabric.

3. Following the shape of the paper, use the tip of your needle to gently turn under the seam allowance as shown for traditional needle-turn appliqué (Method Three, page 124) so that the fabric is folded at the edge of the

freezer paper. Use the tip of the needle to smooth the fabric along the edge, then stitch the appliqué to the background fabric.

4. Peel away the freezer paper when you are finished. You can reuse these freezer-paper shapes several times.

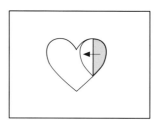

METHOD SEVEN: MACHINE-OUTLINED APPLIQUÉ

Use this machine method to control fraying fabric on inside points. As you stitch the design to the background fabric, turn the machine stitches under at the edge of the appliqué to create a perfect shape.

1. Trace the appliqué design onto freezer paper and cut out on the pencil line.

2. Iron the freezer-paper shape to the *right side* of the appliqué fabric. The freezer paper helps to stabilize the fabric as you sew, and you can reuse it several times for this technique.

3. Using thread that matches the appliqué fabric, set your sewing machine for 15 to 20 stitches per inch. Sew around the outside edge of the paper, overlapping the stitches at the end. Do not catch the paper in the stitching.

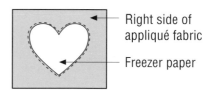

Right side of appliqué fabric

Freezer paper

4. Peel away the freezer paper. Cut out the shape, adding a scant ¼"-wide (³⁄₁₆") allowance beyond the machine stitches.

5. Pin the appliqué to the background fabric.

6. Using the tip of your needle as shown for "Method Three: Needle-Turn Appliqué" on page 124, turn under the allowance until the machine stitches disappear. The machine stitches create a ridge along the outside edge of the appliqué. This ridge will help you keep the piece shaped accurately as you stitch.

7. Appliqué the design to the background fabric. When you get to an inside point, clip the seam allowance all the way to the machine stitches. The small machine stitches will keep the fabric from fraying.

METHOD EIGHT: DOUBLE APPLIQUÉ

With this method, you use a double layer of fabric to create perfect shapes. The added layer gives a slightly padded appearance to the finished work.

1. Cut two pieces of the appliqué fabric, making them slightly larger than the appliqué shape.

2. Trace the appliqué shape onto freezer paper. Cut out on the pencil line.

3. Iron the freezer-paper shape to the *wrong side of one of the fabric pieces.*

4. Place the fabric pieces right sides together with the freezer paper facing you.

5. With your sewing machine set for 15 to 20 stitches per inch, stitch completely around the edge of the paper design, overlapping the stitches where you started. Peel away the freezer paper.

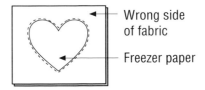

Wrong side of fabric

Freezer paper

6. Cut out the shape ¼" away from the stitching. Clip corners and curves as needed.

7. Carefully make a small slit in the center of one layer of fabric. Turn the shape right side out through the slit.

8. Finger press the seams flat along the edge, then press with a hot steam iron.

9. Pin the completed, double-layer appliqué to the background fabric, with the slit side against the background fabric.

10. Appliqué the design to the background, catching the top layer with the stitches.

SUMMARY OF THE METHODS

Now that you have tried several different methods of preparing appliqués for hand stitching, you can choose the technique you like best for your appliqué projects. Some methods work better than others in different situations and with different fabrics.

The traditional methods are tried and true, but you may find the freezer-paper techniques more accurate. Using the freezer paper on top may be better if you do not want to clip the back side of your work. The machine-outlined or double-layer method may be your favorite because you enjoy using the sewing machine. Choose your favorite technique and enjoy it with the knowledge that you can always substitute another when it will provide better results.

Stitching Appliqués in Place

Before appliquéing, baste the appliqué pieces to the background fabric. Most stitchers pin-baste their appliqués in place, one or two pieces at a time. Use several pins to attach the appliqué pieces to the background so they will not slip. If you have trouble with threads tangling around pins as you sew, pin the appliqués in place from the wrong side of the background fabric.

Hand basting is another option. This method is very secure. Use light-colored thread and position the basting stitches near the turned edges of the appliqués.

You may also baste the pieces in place with a water-soluble glue stick. Apply glue to the background fabric, keeping it toward the center of the design. Do not apply glue along the outer edges where you will stitch as it will stiffen the fabric and make it more difficult to sew to the background fabric. After applying the glue, position the appliqué and allow the glue to dry before sewing. If you use a glue stick, you will need to wash the finished piece to remove the glue, so be sure to prewash your fabrics (page 8).

To attach the appliqués permanently, use either the "Traditional Appliqué Stitch" or the "Ladder Stitch." Directions for each follow.

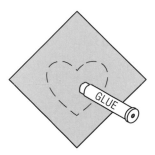

TRADITIONAL APPLIQUÉ STITCH

The traditional appliqué stitch works well on straight areas as well as sharp points and curves. As you stitch various shapes in place, you will encounter straight edges, points, curves, and inside corners. Refer to the box on page 130 for tips on handling these design features.

1. Thread your needle with a single strand of thread approximately 18" long and tie a knot in one end. To hide your knot, slip your needle into the seam allowance from the wrong side of the appliqué piece, bringing it out along the fold line. The knot will be hidden inside the seam allowance.

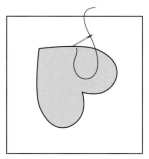

2. If you are right-handed, stitch from right to left. If you are left-handed, stitch from left to right. Start the first stitch by moving your needle straight off the appliqué, inserting the needle into the background fabric.

Let the needle travel under the background fabric, parallel to the edge of the appliqué, and bring it up about ⅛" away. As you bring the needle back up, pierce the edge of the appliqué piece, catching only one or two threads of the folded edge.

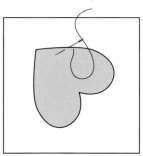

3. Move the needle straight off the appliqué into the background fabric. Let your needle travel under the background, bringing it up about ⅛" away and again catching the edge of the appliqué. Give the thread a slight tug and continue stitching. The only visible parts of the stitch are small dots of thread along the appliqué edge.

The part of the stitch that travels forward will be seen as ⅛" stitches on the wrong side of the background fabric. The length of your stitches should be consistent as you stitch along the straight edges. Smaller stitches are sometimes necessary for curves and points.

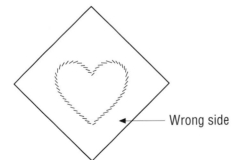

— Wrong side

4. When you reach the end of your stitching or run out of thread, pull your needle through to the wrong side. Behind the appliqué piece, take two small stitches, making knots by pulling your needle through the loops.

Tip   Before you cut the thread, take a moment to see if the thread end will shadow through your background. If you think it will, take one more small stitch through the back side of the appliqué to direct the thread tail under the appliqué fabric where it won't show through to the right side.

STITCHING OUTSIDE POINTS

As you stitch toward an outside point, make the stitches smaller. Start taking smaller stitches within ½" of the point. If the seam allowance is too thick, you may need to trim the seam allowance or push the excess fabric under the point with the tip of your needle. Smaller stitches near the point keep any frayed edges of the seam allowance from escaping.

At the point, place your last stitch on the first side very close to the point. Place the next stitch on the second side of the point. A stitch on each side, close to the point, will accent the outside point. Do not put a stitch directly on the point, as that will flatten it.

STITCHING ALONG A CURVE

If the curve is very round, use the tip of your needle to arrange the fabric along the curve as you sew. To keep little points of fabric from sticking out, push the fabric under with the tip of your needle, smoothing it out along the folded edge before sewing.

Keep your stitches fairly small so that those fabric points cannot escape between the stitches.

STITCHING INSIDE POINTS

On inside points like the one at the top of a heart shape, make the stitches smaller as you sew within ½" of the point. Stitch past the point, then return to add one extra stitch to emphasize the point. Come up through the appliqué, catching a little more fabric in the point (four or five threads instead of one or two). Make a straight stitch outward, going under the point to pull it in a little and emphasize its shape.

If an inside point frays, use a few closely spaced stitches to tack the fabric down securely. If you use thread that matches the appliqué fabric, these stitches will blend in with the edge of the shape.

LADDER STITCH

The ladder stitch is another appliqué stitch that works well along straight edges and curves. When you stitch inside points or tight outside points, you may want to switch to the traditional appliqué stitch to create more durable stitches.

1. Bring the needle and thread out through the folded edge on one side of the appliqué. Make a very small stitch by moving your needle straight off the appliqué and inserting it into the background fabric. Travel along the pattern line under the background fabric about ⅛"; bring the needle out.

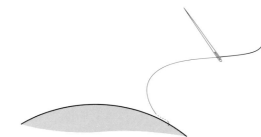

2. Place your needle into the appliqué directly across from where you brought the needle out of the background. Travel through the fold of the appliqué about ⅛" and bring the needle out.

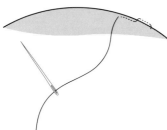

3. Move straight off the appliqué and take another stitch in the pattern line on the background fabric. Repeat until you have five or six stitches between the appliqué and the background fabric. The visible stitches will resemble the rungs on a ladder.

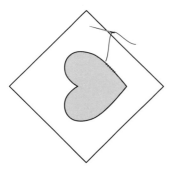

4. Tug gently on the thread until the stitches disappear, attaching the appliqué neatly and invisibly to the background. The wrong side of your work will look like a running stitch with a series of stitches and spaces.

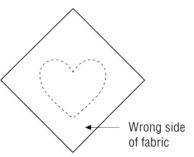

Wrong side
of fabric

Appliquéing Special Shapes

STEMS

To make stems for appliqué, you must cut bias strips of fabric. Do this quickly and easily with rotary-cutting tools. Refer to page 28 for complete directions on cutting bias strips.

To prepare and apply stems for your project, choose one of the following methods:

Method One

1. Determine how wide the finished stem should be and cut the bias strips four times the finished width.
2. Fold the bias strip in half lengthwise, *wrong sides together,* and press with a steam iron.

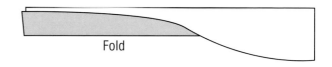

Fold

3. Cut pieces from the bias strip for the stems, cutting them the measurement of the finished stem plus a ¼"-wide seam allowance on each end to layer under other appliqué pieces.
4. Position the raw edges of the strip just inside one of the marked stem lines. If the stems must curve, as in a wreath shape, position the raw edges of the strip just inside the outer (longer) curved line.

Using small running stitches, sew the strip to the background through the center of the strip. Actually stitch slightly toward the raw edge. Backstitch every few stitches to secure the stem to the background.

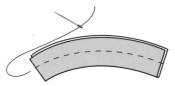

5. Roll the folded edge over the seam allowance. Appliqué the fold to the background fabric to create a smooth, even stem.

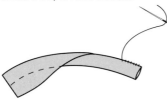

Method Two

1. Cut bias strips that are twice the desired finished stem width.
2. Fold raw edges in to meet in the center and baste along the folded edges. These neatly basted strips are great for straight or curved stems.

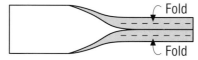

Method Three

You can use Bias Bars™ or Celtic™ bars to make stems of a uniform width. These are available at quilt shops in several sizes, from ⅛" to ½" wide. Choose the one that matches the finished width of the stems in your design.

1. Determine how wide the finished stem should be and cut bias strips twice this width, plus ½" for seam allowances.
2. Fold the strip in half lengthwise, wrong sides together, and machine stitch a scant ¼" from the raw edges to make a tube.

3. Slip the Bias Bar into the tube and position it with the seam centered on one side of it. Press the tube flat, with the seam allowance

to one side. If necessary, trim the seam allowance so it does not extend past the folded edge of the strip. Remove the bar.

4. Cut the tube into the required stem lengths. Position on the background fabric and pin in place. On curved areas, use the steam iron to shrink out any excess fullness on inside curves. Stitch the inside curve in place first and then the outside curve.

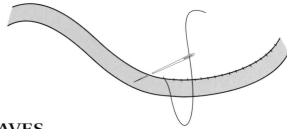

LEAVES

Treat sharp points on leaves as you would outside points as shown on page 130.

1. Turn the point in toward the leaf, then fold the two sides in to form the point. Trim excess seam allowance to eliminate bulky points.

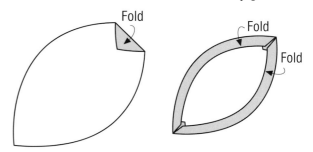

2. As you baste along curves, keep the stitches close to the fold to keep the shape accurate.

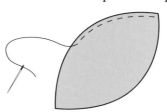

3. As you appliqué the leaves, place stitches on either side of the point to emphasize it.

FLOWERS

To keep flower-petal shapes consistent, try "Method Four: Freezer Paper," on page 125, or "Machine-Outlined Appliqué" on pages 126–27.

1. Carefully clip the seam allowance between the "petals." Clip to within two or three threads of the inner point to eliminate "fuzzies" between the petals.

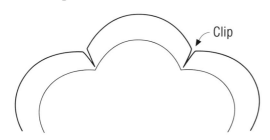

2. As you appliqué, use the tip of the needle to push under the threads and take very small stitches at the inner points to control the threads.

> As you appliqué the inner points, put a dab of glue stick on the tip of your needle. Then, as you sweep the "fuzzies" under with the needle, the glue will help control these little troublesome threads.

FLOWER CENTERS (PERFECT CIRCLES)

1. From heavy paper, such as a manila folder, cut circular templates the *exact* size of the finished circle.
2. Trace around the template onto the fabric. Cut fabric circles, adding ¼" around the edge of the template.
3. Sew with a small running stitch around the fabric circle. Keep the stitches within the seam allowance but not too close to the edge.

4. Place the paper template in the center of the fabric circle. Pull the thread ends to draw the seam allowance in around the template.

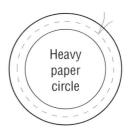

5. Steam press the circle, then let it rest a minute to cool. Carefully peel back the fabric and remove the paper circle. Gently pull the basting threads to tighten the seam allowance and make it lie flat.
6. Pin the circle to the center of your flower (or in another desired location) and appliqué with smaller-than-usual stitches.

BOWS

Appliqué a bow in five pieces: two streamers, two loops, and a circle for the center.

1. Appliqué the streamers first, with the top edges inside the placement line for the bow center.

2. Appliqué the loops, using the "Machine-Outlined Appliqué" technique on pages 126–27 for the inside curves. Machine stitch around the paper on both the inside and outside curves.

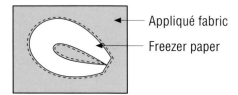

Appliqué fabric

Freezer paper

3. Appliqué the outside edges first, then clip the inside curves in the center.

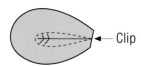

Clip

4. As you stitch, use the tip of the needle to turn under the fabric threads. Take very small stitches on the inner curve.

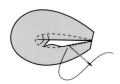

5. Finish the bow by stitching the circle over the raw edges of the other pieces. See "Flower Centers" on page 133.

SWAGS

1. Turn under the ¼" allowance on the top and bottom edges of each swag. It is not necessary to turn under the ends of the swags because the raw edges will be covered by other appliqué pieces.

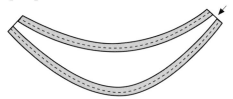

2. Appliqué the swag to the background fabric, using your favorite appliqué stitch.

Heart's Desire

Color photos on pages 163–64.
Finished Quilt Size: 27½ x 27½"
Finished Block Size: 4"

Fall in love with a multicolored floral or paisley fabric, then select colors from the print for the hearts and borders. This lovely quilt contains nine appliquéd hearts. It is a wonderful project for a beginner. If this is your first hand-appliqué project, use each of the eight methods that begin on page 122 to prepare hearts. Use your favorite of these for the ninth heart.

If you are already skilled at hand appliqué but haven't yet tried machine methods, this is also a good first machine-appliqué project. See pages 144–52 for machine-appliqué preparation methods.

Once you have completed this quilt, you can go on to new appliqué projects, sure of your "heart's desire!"

MATERIALS: 44"-WIDE FABRIC

⅜ yd. background fabric for the hearts
½ yd. for hearts and middle border
¾ yd. floral or paisley print for piecing and outer border
⅜ yd. for inner border and binding
1 yd. for backing
30" x 30" square of batting

CUTTING

Use the heart template on page 136.

From the background fabric, cut:
9 squares, each 4½" x 4½". If you wish, you may cut the squares larger and trim them each to a 4½" square after completing the appliqués.

From the fabric for the hearts and middle border, cut:
2 strips, each 2" x 18½", for the middle side borders
2 strips, each 2" x 21½", for the middle top and bottom borders
Set aside the remaining fabric for the hearts.

From the floral or paisley print, cut:
4 squares, each 4½" x 4½", for the alternating squares in the quilt top
2 squares, each 4⅞" x 4⅞"; cut twice diagonally for 8 side setting triangles
2 squares, each 3¾" x 3¾"; cut once diagonally for 4 corner setting triangles
2 strips, each 3½" x 21½", for the outer side borders
2 strips, each 3½" x 27½", for the outer top and bottom borders

From the fabric for the inner border, cut:
2 strips, each 1" x 17½", for the side borders
2 strips, each 1" x 18½", for the top and bottom borders
3 strips, each 2" wide, for the binding (Cut the strips across the fabric width.)

DIRECTIONS

1. Trace the heart pattern onto the background squares.

2. Appliqué a heart to 8 of the background squares, using a different method for each heart. See pages 122–27. Use your favorite method to appliqué the ninth heart.

3. Following the diagram, sew the completed heart squares together with the alternating print squares in a diagonal setting, adding the side setting and corner setting triangles as shown.

Quilt Top Assembly

4. Sew the inner border to the sides and then to the top and bottom edges of the quilt top. Press seams toward the border. Repeat with middle and outer border strips, always stitching the side borders to the quilt top before adding the top and bottom borders.

5. Beginning in the corners, trace the quilting design shown on page 143 in the middle and outer borders. Mark quilting lines ¼" inside the hearts and inside the background squares as shown in the pattern below.

6. Layer the quilt top with backing and batting; baste. See page 255.

7. Quilt around the hearts on the quilting lines and on either side of the narrow inner border. Refer to "Loving Stitches," beginning on page 225.

8. Bind the edges. Refer to "Happy Endings," beginning on page 275.

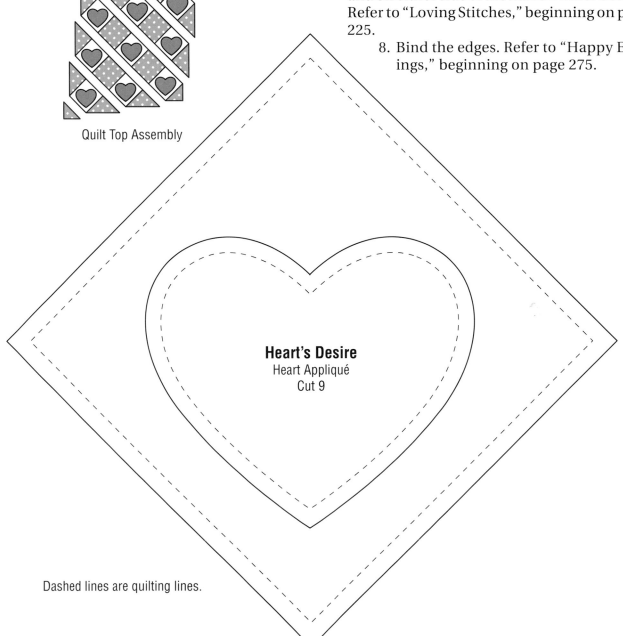

Heart's Desire
Heart Appliqué
Cut 9

Dashed lines are quilting lines.

Hearts and Flowers

Color photo on page 165.
Finished Quilt Size: 31¼" x 31¼"
Finished Block Size: 10"

Making this traditional flower-wreath quilt will give you lots of practice using appliqué techniques to create thin stems, pointed leaves, layered designs, curved flowers, and perfect circles.

Select a light, solid-colored fabric or a white-on-white print for the background fabric and select traditional red and green for the appliqués. Of course, you can break tradition and use soft pastel shades for the appliqués instead.

MATERIALS: 44"-WIDE FABRIC

1⅜ yds. light fabric for background
¾ yd. red for flowers, hearts, bows, inner border, and binding
½ yd. green for leaves, stems, and border swags
⅛ yd. yellow or gold for flower centers
1 yd. for backing
35" x 35" square of backing

CUTTING

From the light background fabric, cut:
4 squares, each 10½" x 10½". (If you wish, you may cut 11½" squares and trim them to size after completing the appliqué.)
2 strips, each 5½" x 21¼", for the side outer borders
2 strips, each 5½" x 31¼", for the top and bottom outer borders

From the red fabric, cut:
2 strips, each ⅞" x 20½", for the side inner borders
2 strips, each ⅞" x 21¼", for the top and bottom inner borders
4 strips, each 2" x 42", for the binding. Cut these strips across the fabric width. Reserve the remaining fabric for appliqués.

From the green fabric, cut:
1 strip, 4½" x 42". From this strip, cut 8 bias strips, each ¾" wide. Use your rotary-cutting tools to do this quickly and easily. See pages 13–14.

Fold each bias strip in half lengthwise, wrong sides together, and press with a steam iron. Set aside.

Fold

Make appliqué templates, using the appliqué placement guides on pages 139–41. Trace a flower and a leaf from the placement guide onto a sheet of clear template plastic. Cut out the templates along the traced line so they are the exact size of the design. You do not need a template for the stems that create the circle in each wreath.

Cut and prepare the wreath appliqué pieces from the red, green, and yellow fabrics. Use "Method Four: Freezer Paper" on page 125, to help keep identical pieces accurate. Set remaining fabric aside for the border appliqués.

DIRECTIONS

Blocks and Borders

1. Fold each of the 4 background squares in quarters to find the center point. Match this point to the center point of the wreath pattern on page 139 and trace the wreath onto each square.

2. To appliqué the stems, cut 3" lengths from the folded green bias strips. You will need a total of 16 pieces. Appliqué stems, following the directions on pages 131–32. Roll the folded edge over the seam allowance. Appliqué the fold to the background fabric to create a smooth, even stem.

3. Stitch the appliqués in the following order: leaves, flowers, flower centers. For appliquéing these shapes, see pages 131–33.

4. Referring to the quilt plan on page 137 and using the appliqué and quilting designs on pages 140–41, center the outer border strips over the design and trace the swags and hearts onto the fabric. Do not trace the bows for the corners onto the fabric yet.

   Trace the swag, the heart, and a bow onto a sheet of template plastic to make the border appliqué templates. You will appliqué the bow in five pieces: 2 streamers, 2 loops, and a circle. Cut the border appliqués from the border fabrics and prepare the hearts as you did the wreath appliqués.

   To prepare the swags, baste under the seam allowances on the top and bottom edges. The hearts will cover the short ends of the swags.

Raw edge

5. Appliqué the border swags. Carefully position the hearts to cover the raw ends of the swags and stitch in place.

Quilt Top Assembly and Border Finishing

1. If you cut the background blocks oversize, trim them all to 10½" square, being careful to keep the wreath centered in each block.

2. Using ¼"-wide seams, sew the blocks together in 2 rows of 2 blocks each. Then join the sets to complete the center of the quilt.

3. Sew the ⅞" x 20½" red inner border strips to the sides of the quilt top. Press the seam allowances toward the border strips. Sew the ⅞" x 21¼" red border strips to the top and bottom edges of the quilt top. Press.

4. Sew the short appliquéd border strips to the sides of the quilt top and press the seams toward the red inner border strips. Sew the remaining appliquéd border strips to the top and bottom edges of the quilt top and press the seams toward the red inner border strips.

5. Trace bow design in each corner of quilt top.

6. Following the directions on pages 133–34, appliqué the bow.

Quilt Finishing

1. Trace the feather-wreath quilting design on page 142 in the center of the quilt. To mark the background quilting design, place dots at 1" intervals along the edges of the 10" blocks. Then use a long ruler and marking pencil to connect the dots with diagonal lines.

2. Mark quilting lines 1" apart on the sides and top and bottom of the border and radiating from each inner corner as shown on the border pattern on pages 140–41.

3. Layer the quilt top with batting and backing; baste. See page 255.

4. Quilt on all marked quilting lines, on either side of the inner border, and around all appliqué pieces. Refer to "Loving Stitches," beginning on page 225.

5. Bind the edges. See "Happy Endings" beginning on page 275.

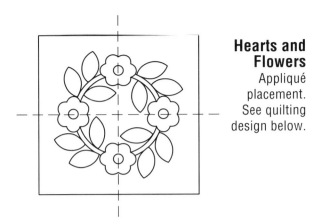

Hearts and Flowers
Appliqué placement. See quilting design below.

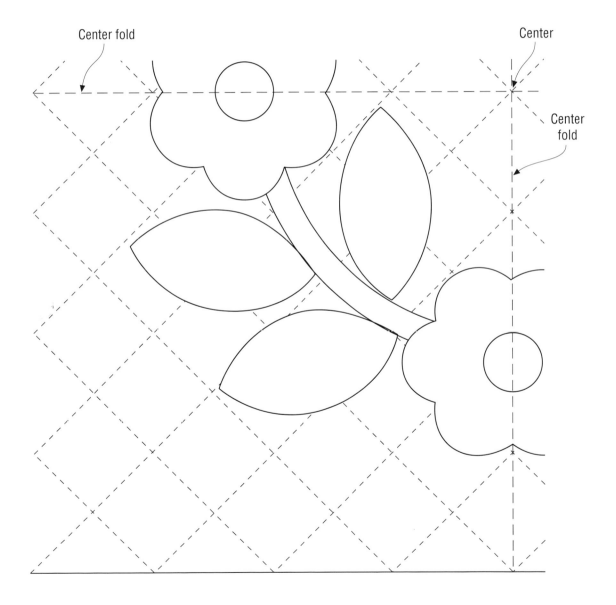

Center fold

Center

Center fold

Hearts and Flowers
Appliqué placement
and quilting design
for border

Hearts and Flowers
Appliqué placement
and quilting design
for border corners

Hearts and Flowers

Feather wreath
quilting design.
Trace in center
of quilt.

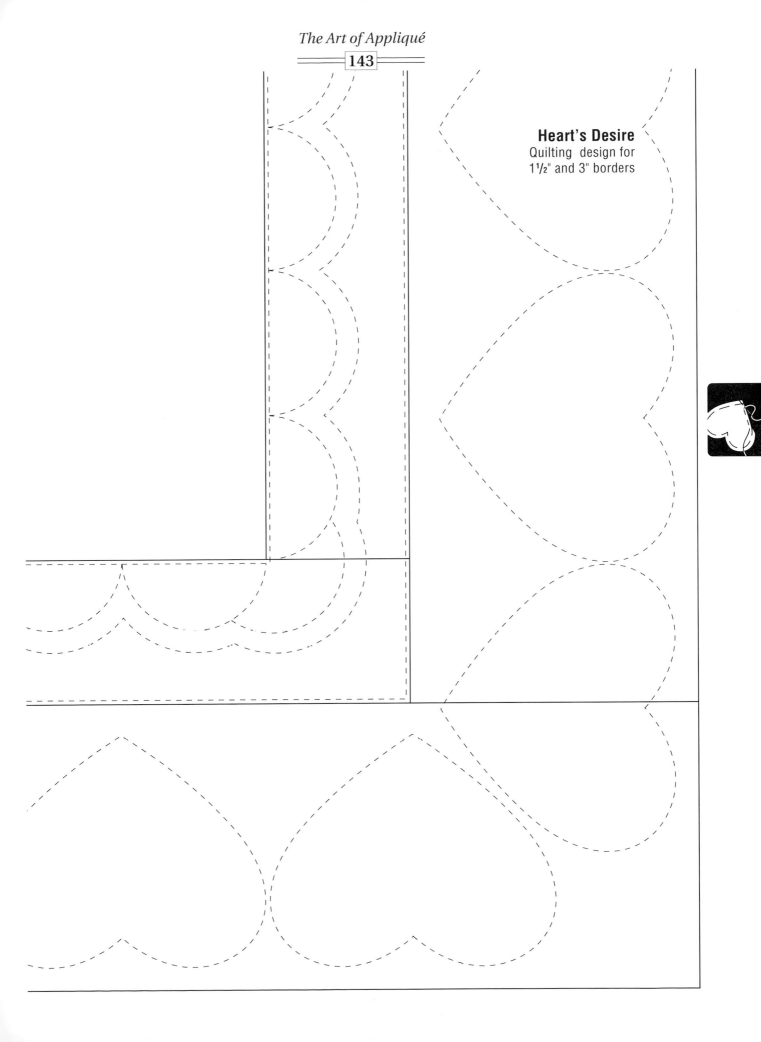

Heart's Desire
Quilting design for
1½" and 3" borders

INVISIBLE MACHINE APPLIQUÉ

If you have admired hand appliqué but felt it was too difficult or too time-consuming to add to your quilting repertoire, I know you will enjoy using my Smoothstitch™ technique to do machine appliqué that looks like it was done by hand. I have perfected this machine-appliqué technique to make it more invisible and more secure than previous methods I have tried. The results will amaze you! Not only will your appliqué look as though it were hand stitched, but it will also take a lot less time than hand appliqué.

Step-by-step directions for two methods of preparing appliqués, plus a special beginners' technique, are included in this section, along with instructions for sewing, cutting multiple pattern pieces, and adapting other patterns to this technique. It is easy to adapt Smoothstitch techniques to almost any appliqué pattern.

Roxi Eppler

Fabrics

Choose fabrics made of 100% cotton. They are easier to handle than cotton/polyester blends. It is often difficult to turn a smooth edge with a blend. I have found very few fabrics, however, that will not work with this method. For additional information on selecting fabrics for appliqué, see page 120.

Machine appliqué stitching is most invisible on printed fabrics. If you intend to use a solid-colored fabric, do a test strip (page 149) to be sure you like the results.

Prewash all fabrics to eliminate the possibility of shrinkage and of dyes running. See page 8. If using Appliqué Preparation Method II, page 147, you must dampen the fabric to remove the paper. This may cause color bleeding even if your fabric has been prewashed. To be safe, do a test block.

Supplies and Tools

Needle and Thread. Start with a sharp, new, size 75 (11) or 60 (10) needle in your machine. For nearly invisible machine-appliqué stitches, thread your machine with extra-fine, .004, invisible nylon machine quilting thread on top. Use cotton-covered polyester thread or 3-ply, mercerized cotton thread, size 50, in the bobbin. If you have tension difficulties with your machine, such as bobbin thread showing on top after all adjustments have been made (pages 149–50), use a finer thread in your bobbin. Try serger thread or fine machine-embroidery thread.

Presser Foot. Use an open-toe appliqué foot for a clear, unobstructed view of the appliqué edge as you stitch.

Open-toe appliqué foot

Freezer Paper. Use freezer paper (plastic coated on one side) for appliqué pattern pieces. Your local quilt shop may carry a similar product for this purpose.

Pencils. Use only a pencil, never a pen, for tracing patterns onto the freezer paper. Make sure it is sharp or use a mechanical pencil.

Iron. Try using a small travel-size iron for preparing appliqué pieces. It is so lightweight that your wrist and arm won't get tired. Place the temperature setting on WOOL. Press over a piece of the nylon thread to be sure it doesn't melt. If it does, lower the temperature. You don't want to "unstitch" all of your beautiful work.

Ironing Board. Use an ironing board with a firm surface for the best results, especially when preparing the appliqué pieces in Method I. If it is too soft, work on a flannel-covered board or a piece of firm, smooth-surfaced cardboard.

Glue Stick. When using a glue stick, be sure it's fresh and keep the cap on when not in use so it doesn't become gummy.

Appliqué Preparation

Use the following key for distinguishing the right and the wrong sides of fabric and freezer paper.

| Right side of fabric | Wrong side of fabric | Uncoated side of freezer paper | Shiny (coated) side of freezer paper |

There are three ways to prepare appliqué pieces before stitching them to the background fabric.

Beginner's Method: This technique incorporates a little of Method I and Method II, making it easier if you've never worked with freezer-paper appliqué.

Method I: This technique is best for simple shapes, such as hearts, leaves, or swag border pieces.

Method II: Use this method for very small or complex shapes that have tight curves and that will require a lot of clipping.

BEGINNERS' METHOD

If you have struggled with freezer-paper appliqué in the past, or if you have never tried it, I encourage you to try this method, using the heart appliqué shape on page 136.

1. Fold a piece of freezer paper in half, shiny, coated side in. Trace the pattern onto one side. Staple and cut through *both* layers to get two freezer-paper pieces per appliqué. This gives you a mirror image (the side not traced on), plus the true pattern.

2. With your iron set on WOOL, no steam, press the mirror-image piece of freezer paper, shiny side down, to the wrong side of a piece of fabric. Cut out the shape, *cutting ¼" away from the edge of the freezer paper to add a seam allowance to turn under.*

Press to adhere and cut out.

3. Position the other freezer-paper piece, shiny side up, on top of the mirror-image piece you just ironed to the fabric. Both should be touching, uncoated side to uncoated side. Glue the two together with a few dabs from your glue stick, just enough to hold the top one in place.

Position on top and glue in place.

Clip corners where needed, to within one or two threads of the paper. Clip concave curves (never convex curves), being careful not to clip all the way to the paper. The more clips, the smoother the curve.

Do not clip convex curve.

Clip concave curve.

4. Use the tip of the iron to press the appliqué seam allowance onto the shiny side of the paper.

Remember to work on a firm surface. (See "Supplies and Tools" on page 144.) Apply pressure to make the fabric adhere to the paper. If you accidentally press in a tuck that creates a point where the edge should be smooth, gently loosen the seam allowance from the paper and press again, redistributing the fullness of the fabric.

If your pattern has 90° corners or sharper points, secure loose corners with a small dab of glue from the glue stick. Do not trim the corners.

5. Continue with Appliqué Preparation, Method I, step 6 on page 147.

The advantage of this method is that you have a stiffer paper edge to press against and the fabric won't shift as you work with it. The disadvantage is that you need twice as many freezer-paper pieces.

APPLIQUÉ PREPARATION— METHOD I

This method is best for uncomplicated appliqué shapes, such as hearts, simple leaves, or swag borders. With this method, you turn the appliqué seam allowances to the back onto the shiny (coated) side of a freezer-paper pattern piece of the desired finished shape and size.

Note: For Method I, consider the uncoated side of the freezer paper the same as the right side of the fabric.

1. Position a piece of freezer paper, *shiny side down,* over the chosen appliqué design. Using a pencil only, trace the shape(s) onto the freezer paper and transfer the number(s) indicating the sewing sequence. *Do not add seam allowances.* Draw small arrows on each shape to indicate which edges are to be turned and pressed.

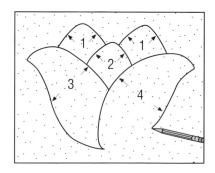

2. Carefully cut the traced pattern into individual pieces, making sure the edges are smoothly cut. If the edges are jagged, the finished appliqué edges will not be smooth. Place the freezer-paper pattern, *shiny side up,* on the wrong side of the fabric and pin.

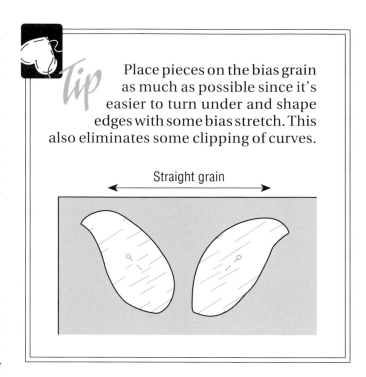

Tip — Place pieces on the bias grain as much as possible since it's easier to turn under and shape edges with some bias stretch. This also eliminates some clipping of curves.

Straight grain

3. Cut the appliqué from fabric, *adding a ¼"-wide seam allowance on all edges.*

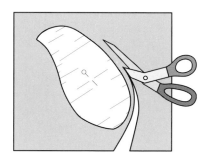

Add ¼" seam allowance all around.

4. Use the tip of the iron (dry iron, WOOL setting) to press appliqué seam allowances onto the shiny side of the freezer paper. Apply pressure to make fabric adhere to the paper. You may use the COTTON setting to press appliqué seam allowances onto freezer paper if you prefer, but be sure to lower the iron temperature when pressing close to already-stitched appliqués.

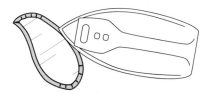

5. Clip curves as needed for a smoothly turned edge, being careful not to clip all the way to the paper. If you accidentally press in a tuck that creates a point where the edge should be smooth, gently loosen the seam allowance from the paper and press again, redistributing the fabric fullness. *Do not press seam allowances under if they will be covered by another piece of the appliqué.*

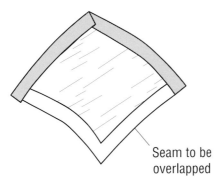

Seam to be
overlapped

If the pattern has 90° corners or sharper points, secure loose corners with a small dab of glue from a glue stick. Do not trim the corners.

6. Notice that the shiny side of the freezer paper is exposed in the center of the appliqué. Position the appliqué, right side up, on the background fabric and fuse in place with a dry iron. Press until the plastic coating on the freezer paper softens and the appliqué adheres. If the appliqué is so small that very little freezer paper is exposed on the underside, use a small dab of glue to hold it in position.

Fuse in place on
background fabric.

7. Stitch appliqué in place, referring to "Attaching Appliqués" on pages 149–51.

8. After each appliqué is stitched in place, remove the freezer paper, using one of the following methods:

a. Reach under an unstitched edge of the appliqué, loosen the freezer paper from the seam allowance, and gently pull it out.

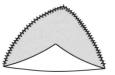

Loosen and remove paper
from the front.

OR

b. Carefully cut away the background fabric behind the appliqué, leaving a ¼"-wide allowance of background fabric all around.

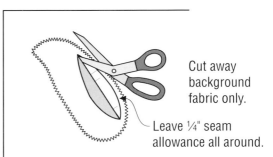

Cut away
background
fabric only.

Leave ¼" seam
allowance all around.

Gently loosen the fused seam from the freezer paper, using your fingernail, an orange stick (from your manicure supplies), or the blade of a small screwdriver. Gently remove paper.

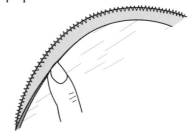

APPLIQUÉ PREPARATION— METHOD II

Use this method for more complex appliqué shapes. With this method, you fuse the freezer-paper pattern to the wrong side of the appliqué fabric, then turn and glue the appliqué edges to the uncoated side of the freezer-paper pattern.

Note: For Method II, consider the shiny side of the freezer paper the same as the right side of the fabric.

1. If the appliqué shape is symmetrical (both halves identical), use a pencil to trace it onto the freezer paper as directed in Method I.

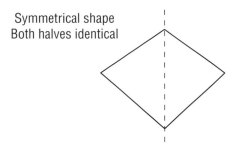

Symmetrical shape
Both halves identical

If the shape is asymmetrical (each half different), trace a reverse image onto freezer paper. Do not add seam allowances. Use arrows on each piece to indicate which edges to turn under.

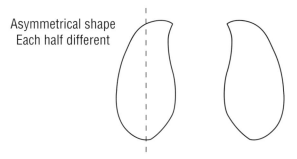

Asymmetrical shape
Each half different

Reverse image

2. Carefully cut the traced freezer-paper pattern into individual pieces, making sure the edges are smoothly cut. (If the edges are jagged, the finished appliqué edges will not be smooth.)

3. Position the freezer-paper pattern, *shiny side down*, on the wrong side of the fabric. Fuse the paper to the fabric with the iron (dry iron, WOOL setting).

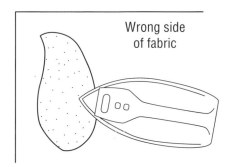

Wrong side
of fabric

4. Cut the appliqué shape from the freezer paper–backed fabric, adding a ¼"-wide allow-ance all around. Clip curves and corners where necessary, being careful not to clip all the way to the paper pattern.

Clip corner.

5. Use a glue stick to apply a small amount of glue to the seam allowances. Fold them over onto the paper pattern and finger press in place.

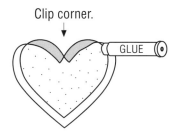

Clip corner.

GLUE

Tip

For points with one flat side and one rounded side, glue the flat side down first. Then ease rounder side onto freezer paper.

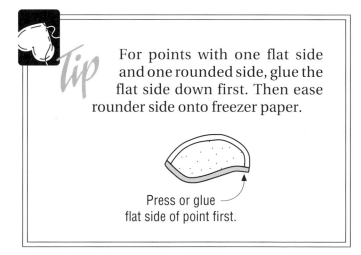

Press or glue
flat side of point first.

6. Using a glue stick, apply a small amount of glue to the exposed freezer paper on the wrong side of the appliqué. Position appliqué, right side up, on the background fabric. If the appliqué is a fairly large piece, apply glue to the edges where fabric touches fabric. This will prevent the background piece from shift-ing as you stitch.

7. Sew appliqué in place, referring to "Attaching Appliqués" on pages 149–51.

8. Remove the freezer paper after stitching each appliqué in place. Unless you can reach and remove the paper from the front as shown on page 147, carefully cut away the background fabric behind the appliqué, leaving a ¼"-wide allowance of background fabric all around the piece.

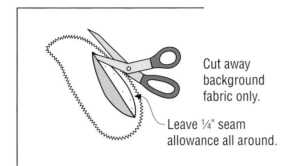

Cut away background fabric only.

Leave ¼" seam allowance all around.

Spray the seam allowance area on the back side of the appliqué with water until wet but not dripping. Allow to sit for 7–10 minutes so the glue softens. Then, gently loosen the paper and slowly peel it away, using tweezers to get into tight spots. Allow to air dry before adding the next appliqué layer or carefully block and dry with your iron from the wrong side (or use a press cloth).

TRANSFERRING APPLIQUÉ PLACEMENT LINES

The appliqué pattern for "Apple Blossoms," (pages 153–56) appears on pages 157–60. The pattern has dotted lines that indicate center and diagonal lines. Adapt other appliqué designs that you wish to machine appliqué by adding these lines to the pattern to help you position the design accurately on the background fabric.

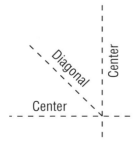

Diagonal

Center

Center

1. Fold the background fabric into fourths and finger press the fold lines.
2. Unfold and lay the fabric over the master pattern, lining up folds and lines; pin.

3. Place on a light box or tape to a window to transfer the design onto the background fabric. (Directions for making a simple light box appear on page 251.) Trace over the lines only where two pieces touch each other. Mark ⅛" to ¼" inside at other points around the outside edge.

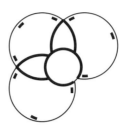

Heavy lines indicate transferred design to background fabric.

Attaching Appliqués

1. Thread the sewing machine with regular thread on the top and in the bobbin and adjust the machine for a zigzag stitch 1 to 1½mm long (approximately 16 stitches per inch) and a little less than 1mm wide. Test the stitch for a balanced zigzag.
2. Thread the machine with invisible nylon monofilament thread on top. On the bobbin, use cotton-covered polyester or mercerized cotton thread in a color that matches the background fabric. *Make a test strip to check your stitch and adjust tensions as needed.* To determine the correct tension, this test strip should consist of a background piece and a sample appliqué piece with freezer paper adhered to it. It may be necessary to loosen the top tension so the bobbin thread does not pull up to the top and show on the right side of your work. After loosening the top tension, make sure the bobbin thread still forms a zigzag stitch on the back.

On some machines, the bobbin case has a special eye for the bobbin thread to add extra tension. If your machine has this feature, thread the bobbin thread through the eye and test the stitch quality before adjusting the top tension.

Thread through extra eye.

Tip If you cannot adjust your machine enough to keep the bobbin thread from showing on top, try using serger thread or fine machine-embroidery thread in the bobbin.

3. Position your work under the presser foot so the left swing position of the needle will stitch into the appliqué, and the right swing position will stitch into the background fabric just at the outer edge of the appliqué piece.

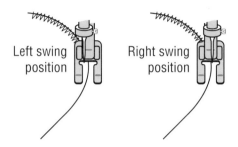

Left swing position   Right swing position

Tip The most invisible stitch is narrow enough to catch only a few threads of the appliqué. All machines are different, but the width setting best for my machine is halfway between .5 and 1mm.

To lock the beginning and the end of the stitching, backstitch two or three stitches. (If tension and stitch width and length are set correctly, this will be very difficult to rip out!) Stitch slowly since you are taking such tiny bites into the appliqué.

4. When approaching an inside corner, decrease the stitch length to almost 0 for the last few stitches before and after turning the corner. This will create a tiny satin stitch in the corner. Return to the original stitch length and continue stitching.

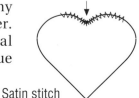

Satin stitch

Use the same technique for stitching around small, tight inside curves.

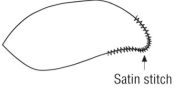

Satin stitch

5. When stitching around sharp points, manually position the needle for the stitches at the very tip of the point.

6. When layering appliqué shapes, remove the freezer paper from each piece *after it is sewn in place and before adding the next layer on top;* reach under the unstitched edge of the appliqué to grasp it and pull it out. (If you forget to do this, you can cut away the background fabric as shown on page 149 and remove the paper from behind.)

7. Press completed appliqué from the back side, using the WOOL setting on the iron, or use a press cloth on top. An iron that is too hot will melt the nylon thread holding the appliqués in place. Test press over a piece of the nylon thread. The thread should be soft (not brittle) but should not melt. If necessary, lower the iron temperature.

UNIT APPLIQUÉS

When appliquéing a multi-layered piece, you may appliqué the piece as a whole unit.

1. Trace or photocopy your design onto a piece of typing paper.

2. Press prepared appliqué pieces to paper and stitch them to it, just as if it were the background fabric, stitching only where one appliqué touches another.

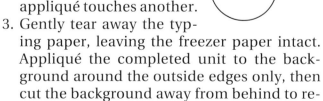

3. Gently tear away the typing paper, leaving the freezer paper intact. Appliqué the completed unit to the background around the outside edges only, then cut the background away from behind to remove the paper.

The advantage to this method is that you can press all the pieces at once to the paper background. Also, it is easier when working on a large background piece, such as long border strips.

The only disadvantage is the need to tear the typing paper away from the stitching. Use tweezers to grasp and remove stray pieces of paper caught under the stitches.

BIAS STRIPS

When your appliqué pattern calls for stems or narrow strips, it is important to cut them from the true bias so that you can shape them to curved areas of the design. You may cut and prepare the stems using one of the methods for hand appliqué shown on pages 131–32, or you may use the alternate method below.

1. Cut bias strips twice the desired finished width, plus ½" for seam allowances. For example, for a ½"-wide finished strip, cut the bias strips 1½" wide. Sew strips together if necessary for the required length. (See "Cutting and Sewing Binding Strips" on page 285.)

2. Fold each bias strip in half lengthwise, *right sides together*. Stitch ¼" from the raw edges.

3. Turn right side out, using a turning tool, such as Fasturn®. Press, keeping the seam on the underside of the tube you have created.

4. Use glue to position the completed stems or strips on the background material and machine appliqué in place.

Adapting Appliqué Patterns

Appliqué shapes with sharp points and curves should be rounded out, so to speak. For easier stitching, sharp points and corners should be closer in shape to a 90° angle.

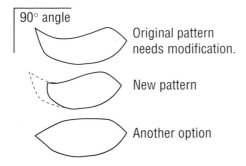

90° angle — Original pattern needs modification.

New pattern

Another option

Expand tight curves as shown below.

Turn one shape with a very sharp angle into two shapes with no angles.

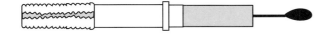

Note: You can also appliqué shapes with very sharp points. Turn and press the seam allowance along both edges of the point, accordion-fold the loose corner, and apply a little glue from a glue stick to each fold to secure it.

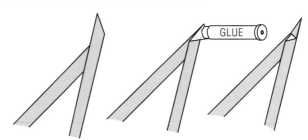

Accordion fold and glue sharp points.

CUTTING MULTIPLE APPLIQUÉ PATTERNS

Some appliqué projects require pattern shapes that are used repeatedly. To make quick work of cutting symmetrical pattern shapes (both halves identical) in multiples, trace the pattern several times along one edge of a piece of freezer paper. Accordion-fold the paper to four thicknesses with the designs still visible and staple paper layers together inside each pattern outline. Carefully cut out pattern pieces.

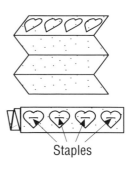

Staples

To cut multiples of pattern shapes that are asymmetrical (each half different), trace the pattern several times onto the *uncoated* side of a piece of freezer paper. Stack this piece on top of three additional layers of freezer paper, shiny sides down, and staple the layers together as before. Use enough staples to prevent shifting during the cutting process. Cut out the pattern pieces.

CUTTING "SNOWFLAKE" APPLIQUÉ PATTERNS

You can use the Smoothstitch appliqué method to appliqué snowflake and Hawaiian-style motifs. Use the following technique to cut accurate freezer-paper shapes for this type of design.

1. Cut a square of freezer paper the size of the quilt block. Fold in half and finger press the crease.

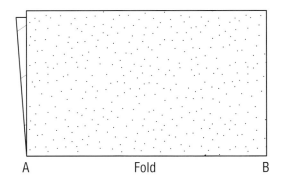

A   Fold   B

2. Fold in half again, bringing A and B together.

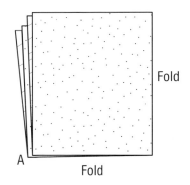

Fold

A
Fold

3. Unfold and place over the appliqué pattern with the uncoated side facing up. Trace the design onto two adjacent quarters.

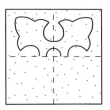

4. Fold in half and staple. Do not fold and cut more than two thicknesses, or your pieces may not be accurate.

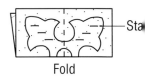

Sta

Fold

5. Cut out the appliqué shape and remove staples. Use Method II on pages 147–48 to cut and prepare appliqués.

SMOOTHSTITCH APPLIQUÉ AS AN ALTERNATIVE TO CURVED PIECING

You can use this invisible machine-appliqué method to create blocks for a Drunkard's Path quilt, eliminating the tedious curved seaming that is typical of this traditional pieced design.

1. Appliqué a circle to a square, using the appliqué preparation method of your choice.

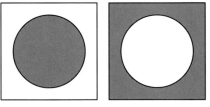

2. Cut the square into four quarters and reassemble the quarters to make a traditional Drunkard's Path or one of its many variations.

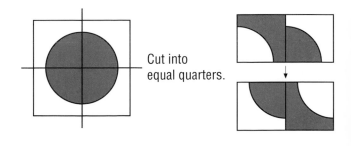

Cut into equal quarters.

Apple Blossoms

Color photo on page 166.
Finished Quilt Size: 34" x 34"
Finished Block Size: 11½"

Make 4.

MATERIALS

1½ yds. fabric A (print) for background
1 yd. fabric B (green) for stems, leaves, triangles, and binding
⅓ yd. fabric C (purple print) for large petals and border strip
⅛ yd. fabric D (pink) for small petals
⅛ yd. fabric E (gold) for flower centers
1⅛ yds. for backing

CUTTING

Use block pattern on pages 157–60.

From freezer paper, cut the following appliqué templates. See pages 145–49.
   4 each of Templates 2, 3, 3r, and 5
   8 of Template 4
   24 of Template 6
From Fabric A (background), cut:
   4 strips, each 3⅜" x 42", for border strips B and C. See step 4 in "Quilt Top Assembly and Finishing" on page 156 for additional cutting directions.
   1 piece, 12" x 26"; for half-square triangle units, if using quick bias square method (pages 154–55)

OR

   14 squares, each 3¼" x 3¼", if using traditional method (page 155) to make half-square triangle units.
   2 squares, each 7⅝" x 7⅝"; cut once diagonally for 4 corner setting triangles A.

   4 squares, each 12" x 12", for the background blocks
From Fabric B (green), cut:
   3 bias strips, each 2" wide, for binding (See page 28 for information on cutting bias strips.)
   1 piece, 12" x 26"; for half-square triangle units, if using quick bias square method (pages 154–55)

OR

   14 squares, each 3⅛" x 3⅛", if using traditional method (page 155) to make half-square triangle units
   4 bias strips, each 1½" x 10", for stems
   4 squares, each 3⅛" x 3⅛"; cut once diagonally for 8 triangles

   24 of Template 6 for leaves

From Fabric C (purple print), cut:
  4 each of Templates 2, 3, and 3r
  2 strips, each 1" x 23½", and 2 strips, each
    1" x 24½", for the narrow border surround-
    ing the appliquéd blocks
From Fabric D (pink), cut:
  8 Template 4
From Fabric E (gold), cut:
  4 Template 5

DIRECTIONS

Bias Squares

Make bias squares for this quilt, using the traditional method on page 155 or the quick bias square method below. My favorite is Mary Hickey's method, a variation of the one designed by Nancy J. Martin. Mary's method first appeared in her book *Angle Antics*.

Quick Bias Square Method. For this method, you will need a Bias Square ruler in addition to a longer acrylic ruler.
1. Stack the 2 large rectangles (12" x 26") of fabrics A (background print) and B (green) with *right sides facing up.*
2. Make a 45° bias cut at one corner. Cut 4 bias strips, each 2½" wide and parallel to the first cut.

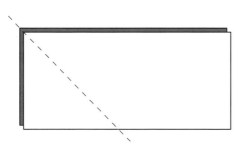

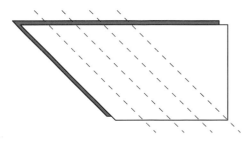

3. Sew the strips together along the bias edge, alternating the two colors and positioning the strips so that the top edge is even. Press

the seams toward the darker fabric or press them open.

Sew strips into a unit.

4. Position the Bias Square with its diagonal line on one of the seams. Place the long ruler across the top. Remove the Bias Square and cut along the ruler edge.

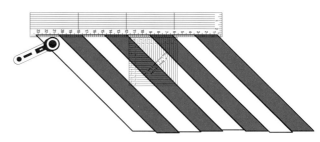

5. Cut 5 strips, each 2¾" wide, parallel to the first cut.

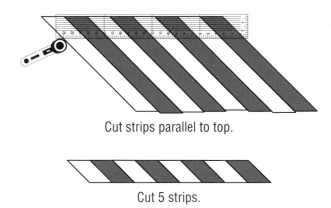

Cut strips parallel to top.

Cut 5 strips.

6. Place the Bias Square with the diagonal line on the seam line and one edge of the square on the cut edge of the strip. Cut one side.

7. Rotate the fabrics and place the diagonal line of the Bias Square on the seam line with one edge of the square on the cut edge of the strip.

Line up the edges of the square with the 2¾" markings on the Bias Square and cut the other side. Continue cutting squares from the strip-pieced unit. You need a total of 28 squares, each composed of 2 triangles.

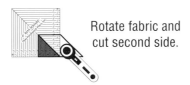

Rotate fabric and cut second side.

Traditional Method. If you prefer to cut individual triangles and join them into bias-square units, use the following method.

1. Cut each of the 14 light and 14 dark 3¼" squares once diagonally to yield 28 light and 28 dark triangles.

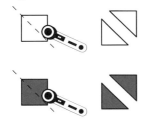

2. Join each light triangle to a dark triangle along the bias edge to make 28 bias-square units.

Make 28.

Blocks

1. Prepare the appliqué pieces, using the method of your choice. See pages 145–49.
2. Mark the appliqué placement lines on each of the 12" squares of background fabric.

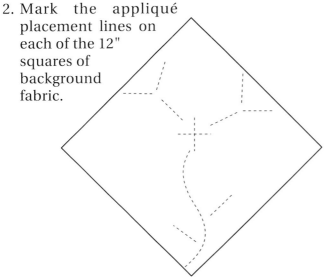

Mark appliqué placement lines.

3. Attach appliqués in numerical order, using the Smoothstitch appliqué techniques beginning on page 149.

Note: If you prefer, prepare the pieces for appliqué using the unit method shown on page 150.

Tip
When appliquéing stems by machine, place a sheet of paper underneath the block to stabilize and prevent puckering while stitching. Carefully tear away the paper after appliqué is completed.

4. Remove all freezer paper. Press the finished blocks from the wrong side.

Quilt Top Assembly and Finishing

1. Sew 4 blocks together with stems pointing toward the center.
2. Add the 1" x 23½" purple border strips to opposite sides of the quilt top. Add the remaining purple strips to the remaining sides.

3. Following the piecing diagrams below and using the bias square units and the loose green triangles, make 4 of each unit shown.

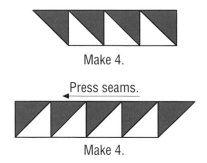

Make 4.

Press seams.

Make 4.

4. Crosscut 2 of the 3⅜"-wide strips of background fabric into 4 rectangles, each 3⅜" x 15". Position the Bias Square ruler with the diagonal line at the top edge of the rectangles as shown. Cut off and discard the corner triangle. The resulting pieces are border strip B.

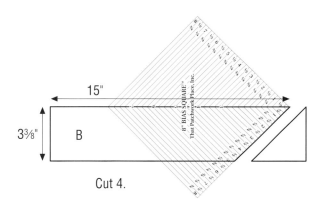

15"

3⅜"

B

Cut 4.

Cut the remaining 2 strips into 4 rectangles, each 3⅜" x 17⅞". Position the Bias Square ruler with the diagonal line at the top edge of the rectangle as shown. Cut off and discard the triangle. The resulting pieces are border strip C.

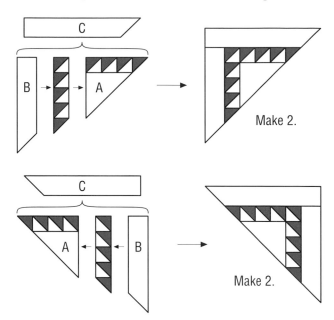

17⅞"

3⅜"

C

Cut 4.

5. Sew one of each unit made in step 3 to each corner setting triangle as shown, adding border strips B and C on the outer edges.

C

B   A

Make 2.

C

A   B

Make 2.

6. Sew the corner units to the quilt top.

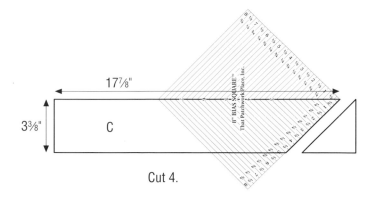

7. Layer the quilt top with batting and backing; baste. See page 255.
8. Quilt as desired. Refer to "Loving Stitches," beginning on page 225.
9. Bind the edges with bias strips of green fabric. Refer to "Happy Endings," beginning on page 275.

A

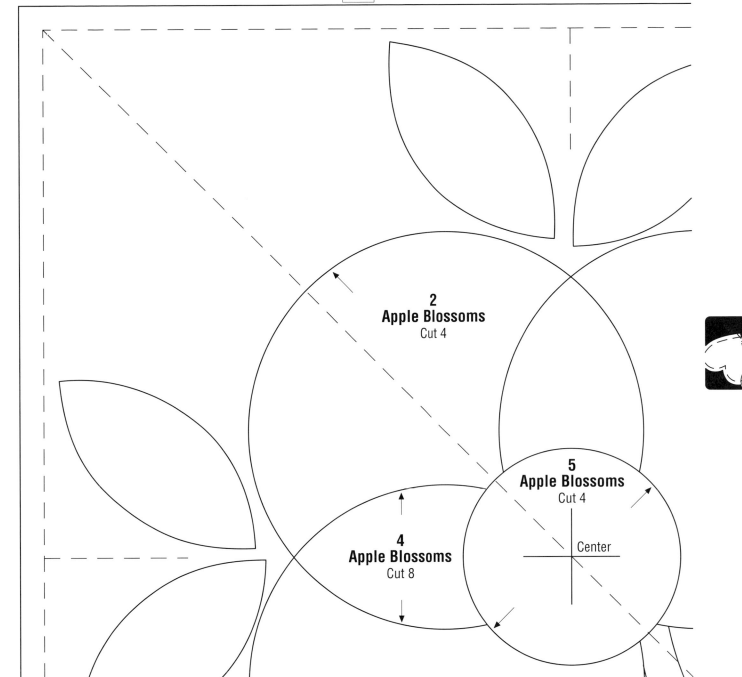

2
Apple Blossoms
Cut 4

5
Apple Blossoms
Cut 4

Center

4
Apple Blossoms
Cut 8

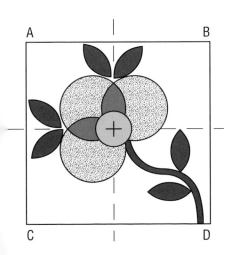

A   B

C   D

To make complete pattern, trace each quarter
(pages 157–60) matching the center marks.

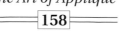
B

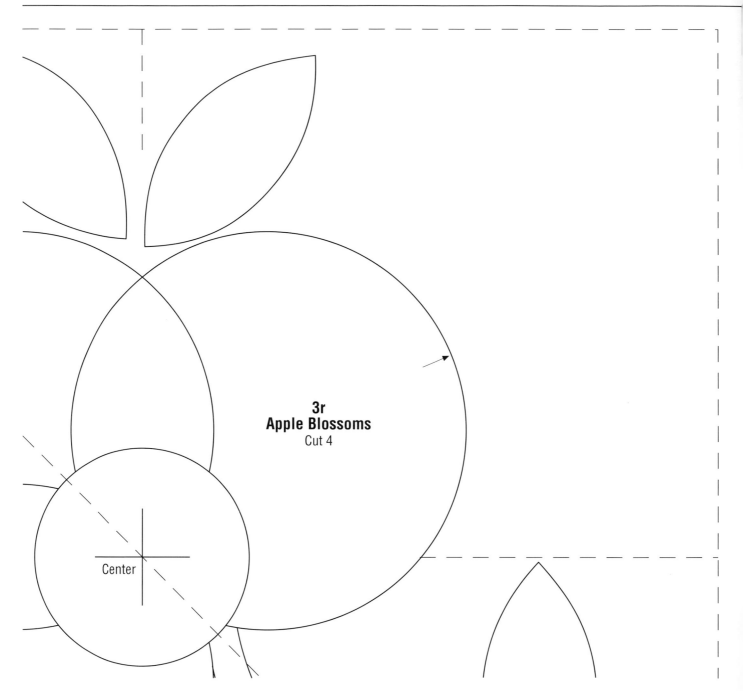

3r
Apple Blossoms
Cut 4

Center

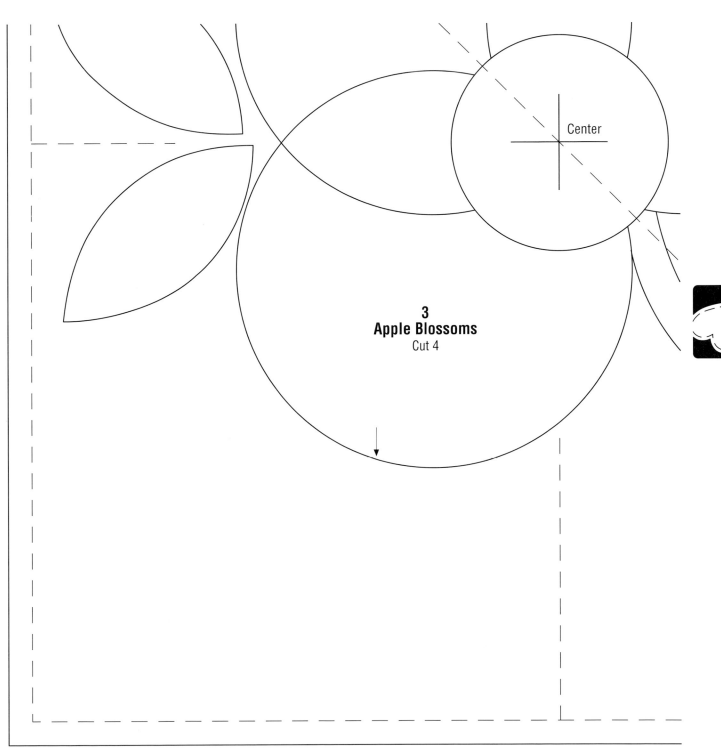

Center

3
Apple Blossoms
Cut 4

C

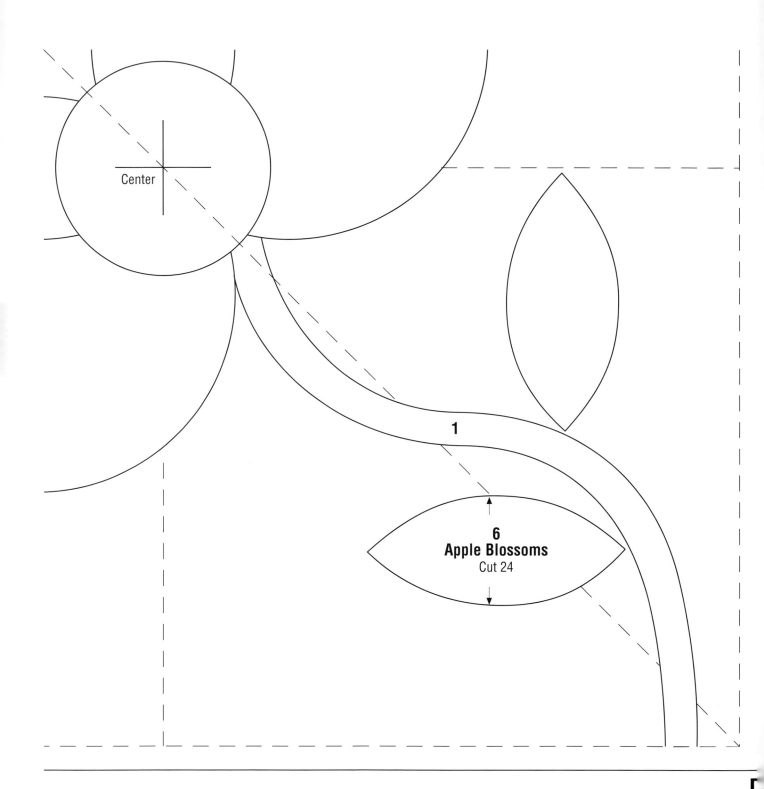

Center

1

6
Apple Blossoms
Cut 24

FUSIBLE APPLIQUÉ

If you like the look of hand and machine appliqué, but do not want to invest too much time in a wall hanging or other project that will not receive much wear, consider fusible appliqué. In addition to the fabrics for the background and the appliqués, you will need a paper-backed fusible web, such as Wonder-Under™ or HeatnBond™.

Fusible webs are made of thermoplastic fibers temporarily caught to a piece of release paper. When you position the web against the wrong side of a piece of fabric and apply the heat and the pressure of an iron to the paper side for a few seconds, the web adheres to the fabric. When you remove the paper backing, you can permanently fuse the piece of fabric to another layer of fabric. When allowed to cool, the melted fibers of the web form a thin, permanent bond between the fabrics, which is desirable when doing machine appliqué as it eliminates slipping and puckering while you stitch the fabric shapes in place. The only disadvantage is that the fused shapes are a little stiffer than two layers of fabric without the web between them.

For some fusible appliqué projects, you might want to simply cut and fuse the appliqué shapes in place on the background fabric. This is particularly appropriate for wall hangings. For a more durable and more decorative effect, use the web as a bonding agent so that you can machine stitch easily and smoothly around the outer edges of the appliqués to make them more permanent. Depending on the stitch and the thread you choose, this stitching can be decorative or almost unnoticeable.

To apply appliqués with fusible web:
1. Position the fusible web over the appliqué pattern piece with the *paper side up.*
2. Trace the appliqué shapes onto the paper, using a pencil.
3. Cut the appliqué shape from the fusible web, cutting just outside the marked line.

4. Place the shape, *fusible web down,* on the wrong side of the appropriate appliqué fabric. Following the manufacturer's directions, fuse in place. Allow to cool before handling.

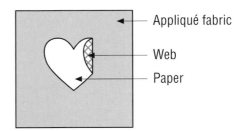

Appliqué fabric
Web
Paper

5. Cut out the shape on the drawn line. Do not add seam allowances to the edges of the shape.
6. Peel away the paper backing. If it is difficult to grasp the edge of the backing to tear it away, tug gently to make the paper rip so you can grasp a torn edge.
7. Arrange the fusible-backed appliqué(s) in position on the right side of the background fabric and fuse in place, following the manufacturer's directions. Allow to cool before handling.

To stitch appliqués in place:
1. Thread the machine with a thread that matches the color of the appliqué. Replace the regular presser foot with an open-toe appliqué foot if available for your machine.

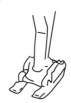

Open-toe appliqué foot

2. Set the machine for a tiny satin stitch (short, narrow zigzag stitch). If you have adjusted the stitch correctly, it will be about $\frac{1}{16}$" wide and very closely spaced. Test the stitch on scraps and adjust the tension so it is slightly looser on top. See step 2 under "Attaching Appliqués," page 149, for information on adjusting tension so bobbin thread won't show on top.

Tip Place a piece of tear-away stabilizer on the wrong side of your work for more stability while you stitch. Remove only when you have completed all stitching.

3. Place the appliqué under the needle and satin stitch over the raw edges. The right swing of the needle should penetrate the background fabric; the left swing of the needle should go through the appliqué. Make sure all raw edges of the appliqué are covered with stitches.

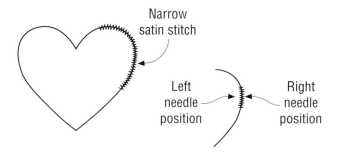

You may embellish the edges of fused appliqués with hand embroidery stitches, such as the blanket stitch.

On some machines, you can duplicate the look of hand blanket stitching. Consult your sewing machine manual or your dealer for details. As with the satin stitch, you will need to experiment with the machine settings and practice stitching around curves, corners, and points to obtain the best stitch quality and finished appearance.

Stitching Tips

When stitching around curves, stop every few stitches with the needle down in the fabric and lift the presser foot so you can turn the piece ever

so slightly before taking the next few stitches.

When stitching around points, try gradually decreasing the stitch width as you reach the point and then stitch away from it. Return the stitch to the original setting. Practice this adjustment on scraps first.

To stitch an outside corner with a secure overlapping zigzag:

1. Stitch the first side of the appliqué, ending at the outside corner with the needle in the background fabric at the outside edge of the appliqué. Raise the presser foot and rotate the fabric to a ready-to-stitch position; stitch. The first few stitches you take will overlap the stitches at the corner.

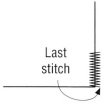

To stitch an outside corner with a mitered zigzag stitch that isn't quite as thick as the overlapped corner, above:

1. Complete step 1, above.
2. Raise the presser foot, rotate the fabric halfway, and take 1 stitch over the previous stitches.

3. Raise the presser foot, rotate the fabric so you are ready to stitch the next side; continue stitching.

The Art of Appliqué
GALLERY

Mama's Jewels *by Marion L. Shelton, 1991, Redmond, Washington, 26" x 26". Marion created a loving showcase to display some her mother's jewelry using Mimi Dietrich's "Heart's Desire" pattern on page 135.*

Hearts Galore *by Monica L. Doramus, 1993, Everett, Washington, 27½" x 27½". This adaptation of Mimi Dietrich's Heart's Desire pattern is Monica's first quilted creation.*

Hearts and Flowers *by Mimi Dietrich, 1989, Baltimore, Maryland, 31¼" x 31¼". Traditional red and green are always a perfect choice for a beautiful appliqué wreath design.*

Apple Blossoms *by Roxi Eppler, 1993, Lubbock, Texas, 34" x 34". Stylized blossoms float in a medallion setting that breaks into the borders of this dynamic little quilt.*

Sensational Settings

OVER 80 WAYS TO ARRANGE YOUR QUILT BLOCKS

CONTENTS

INTRODUCTION

We all know one when we see one, a quilt that reaches out and speaks to us, asking us to linger and enjoy its beauty for just a little longer. In this chapter, we will explore a variety of ways to set quilt blocks together in a pleasing overall design to create a stunning quilt that is a joy to behold.

Coming up with an idea for a quilt happens in many different ways. Perhaps you have received a set of friendship blocks that need to be set or inherited some from a relative. You may have won a set of blocks at a guild meeting or made a set of sampler blocks in a class. Maybe a beautiful block in a book or magazine caught your eye and you know you have to make a quilt using that pattern. You might have fabrics in your collection that you want to use in a quilt or perhaps you want to make a baby quilt or a wedding quilt for a special friend. A collection of fabrics from various trips would make a wonderful travel quilt. Or, you may simply have a bed in your home that needs a quilt.

Turning your initial enthusiasm into a successful quilt takes some thought and planning. For me, designing the setting and choosing the fabrics are among the most exciting and important steps in producing a stunning quilt. Following the step-by-step plan presented in this book will enable you to start cutting and stitching your way to the quilt of your dreams. Sometimes, you will decide not to make a particular quilt after working your way through the planning stage. Consider the time well spent as you will have made that decision before investing your time and fabric in a quilt that might have been a disappointment.

When you start a project, you will probably have one or more "givens" with which to work. Perhaps the finished quilt needs to be a certain size to cover a particular bed or wall space, or you have a given number of blocks and want to end up with a quilt of a particular size. You can plan a quilt setting to stretch blocks to cover a bigger area or squeeze them into a smaller area.

Many variables come into play when you decide how to set blocks into a quilt. Some blocks must be set horizontally, such as House blocks, while other blocks are designed for a diagonal set, also called "on point." Many Basket blocks are designed on point. A variety of blocks, such as Star blocks, can be oriented either horizontally or diagonally with dramatically different results. As a general rule, remember that horizontal lines are calming and restful, while diagonal lines give movement and add drama to your design.

Peaceful

Dramatic

Don't hesitate to branch out and try setting a quilt in a way you haven't tried before. It's easier than you may think!

As you look through the settings that follow, consider them as a beginning to spark your own ideas. Try combining elements of several of these setting ideas to come up with your own variations. Remember, there are no hard and fast rules here. Some of the best quilt settings are just waiting to be tried, so don't hesitate to break out and reach for them.

Joan Hanson

QUILT SETTINGS

Side By Side

> ### CONSIDER THIS SETTING FOR:
>
> ▶ Log Cabin, Drunkard's Path, Double Wedding Ring, and Kaleidoscope
>
> ▶ Blocks that form a secondary design when joined together
>
> ▶ Appliqué blocks that "float" on the background

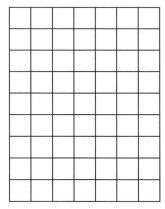

Side-by-side Horizontal Setting

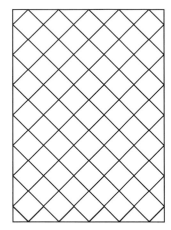

Side-by-side Diagonal Setting

This setting is probably the most used and overused because it is easy and the first one that comes to mind. Just line up your blocks in neat rows and sew them together. We are used to organizing things in this way. It is a way to get a set of blocks made into a quilt quickly without giving much thought to how they could be set to their best advantage.

When set side by side, many blocks gain an unexpected graphic punch. They form a secondary pattern as the boundary of one block blurs together with its neighboring blocks, causing a new and unexpected design to appear. Try changing the colors in the blocks from the center to the edges of your quilt (light to dark), or change the background fabric in each block to set it off.

Another option along these lines is to change the color arrangement in every other block. If a block is asymmetrical, such as a Log Cabin block, try turning the blocks in different directions to create a variety of results. The old-time favorite settings for Log Cabin blocks—Streak of Lightning, Sunshine and Shadows, Barn Raising, Straight Furrows, Light and Dark, and Pinwheel—are accomplished this way.

Appliqué blocks that "float" on the background fabric are very effective set side by side. If you are considering this setting, try placing your blocks on point to see how this affects the look of your blocks. Many blocks take on a new and dramatic appearance when set this way.

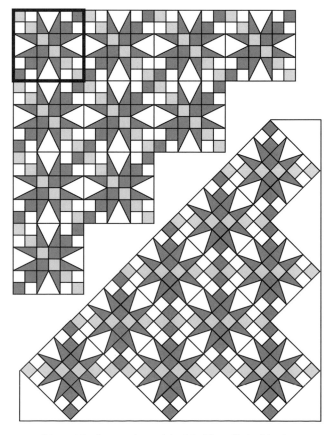

Many blocks, such as this 54-40 or Fight block, change dramatically when rotated from a horizontal to a diagonal setting.

The same block set side by side becomes more interesting when the background fabric changes from block to block.

This Pinwheel block forms a secondary pinwheel when blocks are set side by side.

Ocean Waves blocks are usually set in a side-by-side setting so that the design flows over the quilt. (This diagonal setting with two corner blocks accommodates seventeen blocks.)

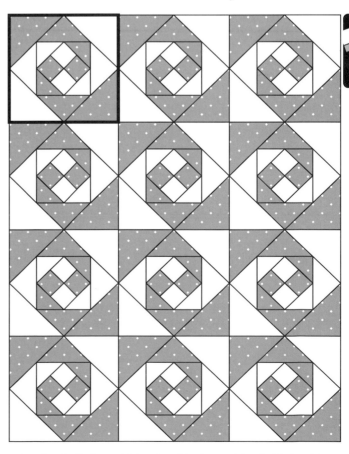

The Snail's Trails multiply when blocks are joined side by side.

This Rail Fence–Flying Geese variation creates
a woven look when the blocks alternate
directions, adding movement and drama.

This Anvil block not only changes direction with
every other block, but the color scheme
changes from block to block as well.

This is another example of an appliqué block that floats on
its background fabric. The diagonal set allows space in the
side and corner triangles for a fancy quilting design.

The outer flowers on this appliqué wreath create a
secondary design when they meet in the corners.
The wreaths "float" on their plain block backgrounds.

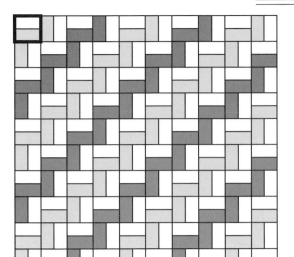

Rotating a simple Rail Fence block in a side-by-side setting creates a zigzag design.

Alternating the direction of these Spool blocks sets off each block. (See color photo on page 221.)

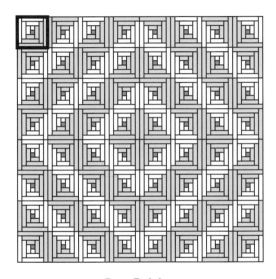

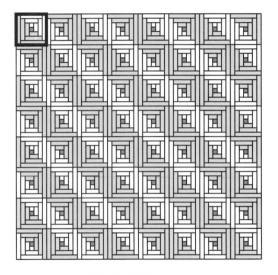

Barn Raising

Straight Furrows

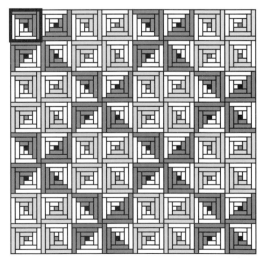

Light and Dark

Pinwheel

Endless setting variations are possible when you change the orientation of the light and dark sides of Log Cabin blocks.

Alternating Plain Blocks

CONSIDER THIS SETTING FOR:

▶ Ninepatch or other designs that connect at corners to give diagonal movement

▶ Complex pieced or appliquéd blocks

▶ Stretching a few blocks into a bigger quilt

▶ Creating a space to show off quilting

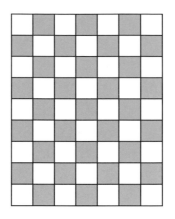

Side-by-side Horizontal Setting
with Alternating Plain Blocks

Side-by-side Diagonal Setting
with Alternating Plain Blocks

If you have a limited number of blocks and want to stretch them into a larger quilt, alternating your design blocks with plain blocks can do the trick. Just remember that all those plain blocks will probably require a greater amount of quilting. The time you don't spend piecing additional blocks will be spent quilting later.

Many blocks connect visually at the corners and add diagonal movement to a quilt when alternated with a plain block, such as a simple Ninepatch alternated with a plain block that has the same background fabric. When you use the same background fabric for the plain block as you do in your design blocks, the design blocks appear to "float" on the surface of the quilt.

Plain blocks cut from a floral print or a dark solid might also be a good choice for setting off your blocks to their best advantage. An easy way to get the look of a medallion setting is to change the color of the alternating plain block from the edges to the center. When you are using alternating blocks, you will want an odd number of blocks in each row and an odd number of rows so that you end up with the same type of block in each corner.

Alternating lovely appliqué blocks with plain blocks that have been enhanced with elaborate quilting can be stunning.

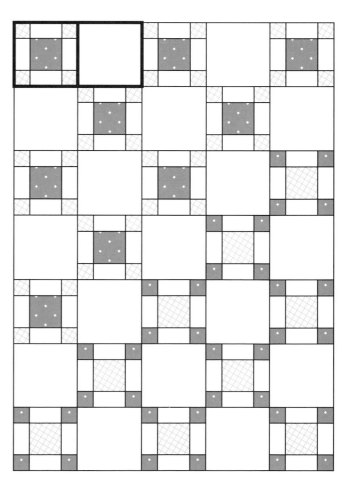

Puss in the Corner connects in the corners,
wherever the lights and darks are placed.

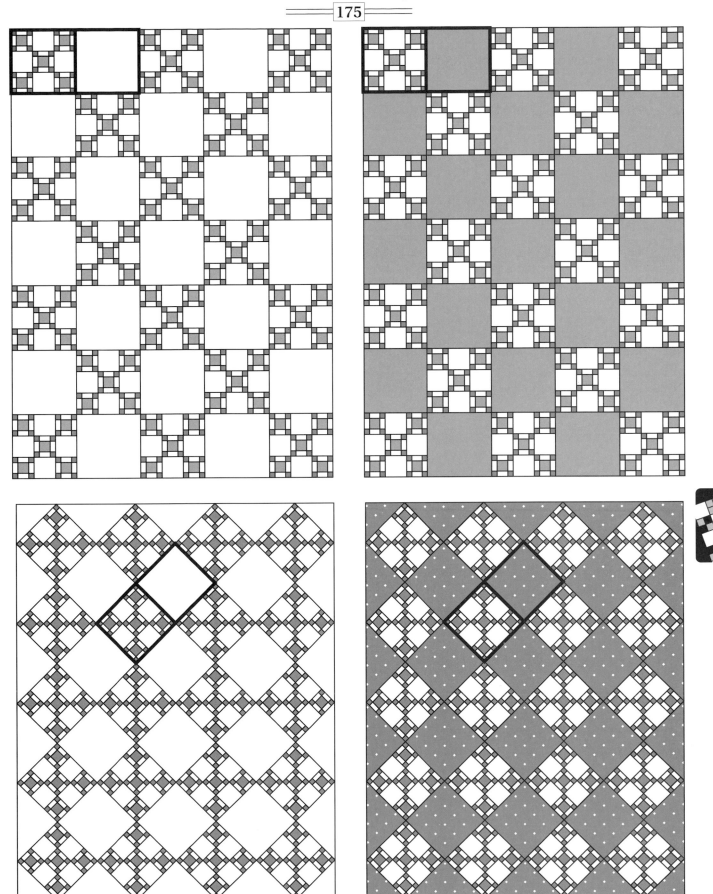

Small blocks can be grouped into larger Four Patch or Ninepatch blocks with
alternating plain blocks, then combined with a large alternating block.

This Star block takes on a variety of looks, depending on the fabric used in the alternating block.

Appliqué blocks and elaborate hand quilting seem to complement each other. To highlight quilting stitches, use a solid color for the alternating blocks, or a print to conceal them.

These baskets float in the center and are framed by contrasting fabric in the side and corner triangles.

Alternating Design Blocks

> ## CONSIDER THIS SETTING FOR:
>
> ◗ Irish Chain or other "A" block/"B" block designs
>
> ◗ Appliqué blocks
>
> ◗ Complex blocks that relate to a simple companion block

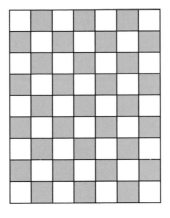

Side-by-side Horizontal Setting
with Alternating Plain Blocks

Side-by-side Diagonal Setting
with Alternating Plain Blocks

Many interesting combinations happen when you combine two different pieced or appliquéd blocks. Usually one of the blocks is more complex than the other and, for pieced blocks, both blocks have the same divisions, such as in Ninepatch, sixteen-patch, or twenty-five-patch, so that some of the intersections line up and carry the eye across the quilt.

Examples of some simple alternating blocks include Snowball, Churn Dash, and Puss in the Corner. Some patterns, such as Irish Chain, use an "A" block that alternates with a "B" block to create a pleasing overall design. If you are setting an appliquéd quilt, consider using a simple pieced or appliquéd design that relates to the main blocks.

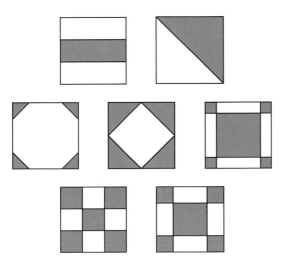

These simple pieced blocks can be
used as alternating blocks.

Double Irish Chain relies on an alternating block
with a square in each corner to carry the design
across the surface.

Although one design is set horizontally and the other is set diagonally, these two designs both use a Puss in the Corner as an alternating block with background fabric matching the background fabric in the main block.

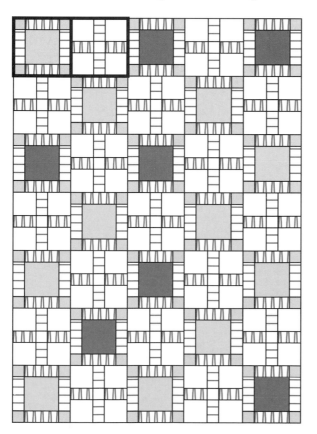

This design also uses a Puss in the Corner alternating block, but since the segments are shaded differently, the effect is quite different.

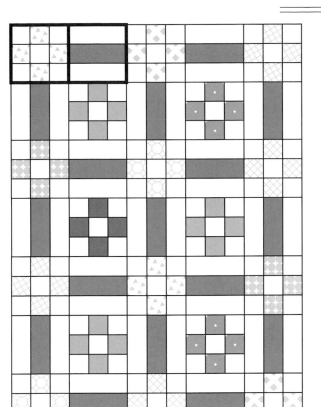

These two very simple blocks combine with very satisfying results. (Note how
the lights and darks in the Ninepatch blocks change in each quilt.)

Snowball blocks combined with other blocks create diagonal
movement across the quilt surface.

Simple Sashing

CONSIDER THIS SETTING FOR:

◗ Sampler or friendship blocks

◗ Blocks that stand on their own

◗ Picture blocks, such as Basket blocks

Side-by-side Horizontal Setting
with Sashing

Side-by-side Diagonal Setting
with Sashing

Many blocks look best when set apart and allowed to stand on their own without interfering with neighboring blocks. Sampler blocks are often set with simple sashing between blocks to add a unifying element to blocks that don't hold together on their own. This works especially well if the sashing fabric contains colors from each of the blocks.

Experiment with the width of sashing—narrow sashing lets the design jump easily from block to block, while wider sashing sets the blocks apart. Wider sashing can also stretch a limited number of blocks into a larger quilt.

Using sashing that matches the background fabric in the blocks causes the blocks to "float" on the surface of the quilt. Using a printed sashing fabric helps to blur the seams, while a solid fabric shows off a beautiful quilting design.

When you are cutting sashing, cut short strips the same size as your block to fit between the blocks in each row and then cut long sashing strips to join the rows. When you are assembling the rows, make sure the blocks and sashing strips line up from row to row.

When sashings match the background fabric in the blocks,
the blocks are separated and appear to float.

Changing the sashing fabric gives two different
looks to these blocks.

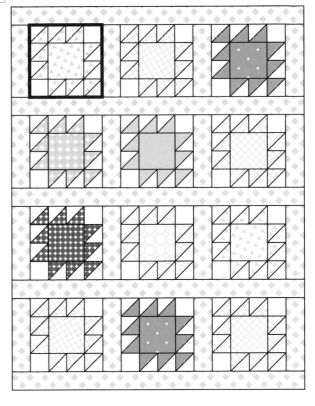

Wide sashing in a print helps to unify
these scrappy Anvil blocks.

This appliqué sampler is held together with
a narrow printed sashing.

These sampler blocks are surrounded by a narrow frame
(to bring the blocks all up to the same size)
and then a wide sashing.

Sashing and Cornerstones

CONSIDER THIS SETTING FOR:

▶ Blocks that stand alone but need a unifying effect

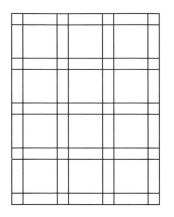

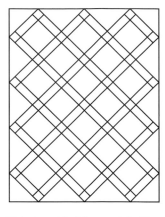

Side-by-side Horizontal Setting with Sashing Strips and Cornerstones

Side-by-side Diagonal Setting with Sashing Strips and Cornerstones

Once you've completed a set of blocks, you may find piecing the sashings and cornerstones too much trouble, but they can really enhance the look of your blocks. Cornerstones help connect blocks to carry the eye across the quilt surface. Sometimes, they simply add more design interest. You can also piece the sashing and/or cornerstones to contribute to the overall design.

You may want to design a sashing that joins up with the intersections in your blocks (Ninepatch, sixteen-patch, twenty-five-patch) and helps connect the blocks. Try sashing that uses the background fabric with a contrasting cornerstone to give a floating effect, or strip piece the sashing, using two strips of the background fabric with another fabric. Place the background strips on either side of the contrasting strip. This format opens up the visual space around each block.

Try using a design element from a pieced or appliquéd block; use it in the cornerstone in its original size or reduce it in scale. Four Patches, Ninepatches, and Puss in the Corner are good choices for pieced cornerstones. Sometimes, the sashings and borders blend together for an effective look. Try repeating the cornerstone design in the corners of the border, for example.

Cornerstones in each of these quilts match the background of the blocks. Wider contrasting sashing separates the pieced blocks, while the narrow sashing in the appliqué sampler draws the blocks together.

These two quilts have sashings that match the background of the blocks and cornerstones that contrast. In the quilt on the right, note how four Pinwheel blocks are joined together with narrow sashing and cornerstones into a larger block, and then wider sashing and cornerstones are used to join them into rows.

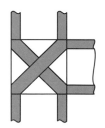

Detail of Garden Path
Sashing and
Cornerstone

This setting is called Garden Path and is usually used with floral appliqué blocks.
It can be used for either a horizontal or diagonal setting.

There are several alternatives for ending the rows of sashing and cornerstones on a diagonal setting. The appliqué quilt (above, left) has whole cornerstones along the outside edges. The cornerstones are cut in half along the outside edges on the Star quilt (above, right). The Basket quilt (right) was designed with the sashing and setting squares on the diagonal in the center of the quilt instead of centering the block at the corner as in the Star quilt (above, right). In the pieced Star quilt (above, right), the setting squares were cut in half at the outside edges.

Ninepatch cornerstones combine with pieced sashing to surround blocks in different ways in these three quilts (above and left).

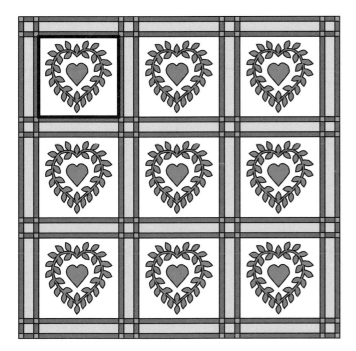

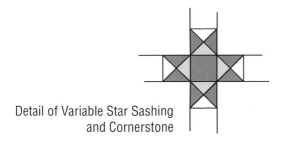

Detail of Variable Star Sashing and Cornerstone

The pieced sashing and cornerstones in this Variable Star quilt repeat the star design, only in a slightly smaller scale.

A plain sashing and a pieced cornerstone that repeats an element found in the block design help to carry the design across each of the quilts shown here.

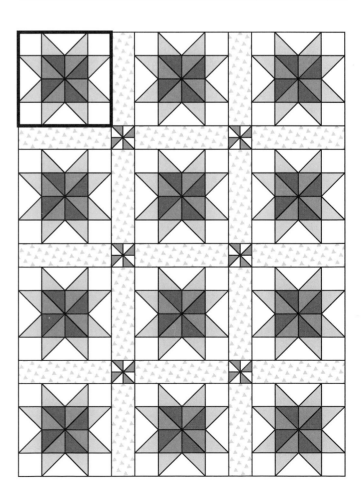

Framed Blocks

CONSIDER THIS SETTING FOR:

◗ Sampler blocks

◗ Friendship blocks

◗ Blocks that aren't quite the same size

This setting is one of my favorites because you can use it to standardize the size of blocks that would otherwise be difficult to join. It is great for sampler or friendship blocks or any other group of blocks that are not all the same size and/or shape.

You can standardize blocks that are each a different size by adding an oversized border or "frame" to each block, then trimming them all down to the same size. The width of the frame may vary slightly, but you will be working with blocks that are easy to join because they are all the same size.

There are several frame variations from which to choose. Use the same fabric to go halfway around each block, then choose another fabric to frame the other half. Then alternate the blocks, or use a dark fabric for two adjoining sides and a light fabric for the remaining two sides. This arrangement requires that you miter the corners, but when you put all the blocks together, it creates the illusion that light is shining on your quilt. Attic Windows is a variation of this idea.

Another possibility is to add sashing and cornerstones to each block. When you join these blocks, you create a Four Patch at each intersection. (Your blocks must be a consistent size for this strategy to work.) Add triangles to each side of your blocks to frame them and change their orientation from horizontal to diagonal or the other way around. Try framing your blocks, then combining them with sashing and cornerstones for a more elaborate effect.

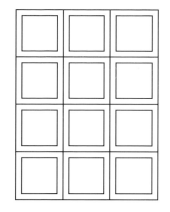

Framed Blocks in Side-by-side Horizontal Setting

Framed Blocks in Side-by-side Diagonal Setting

Examples of Frames

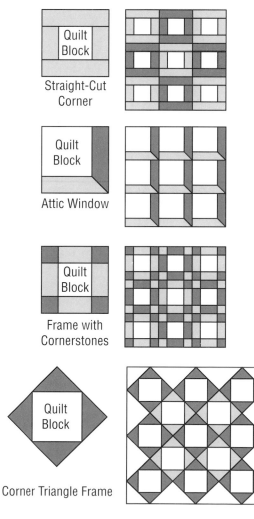

Straight-Cut Corner

Attic Window

Frame with Cornerstones

Corner Triangle Frame

Mitered Corner

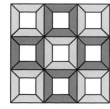

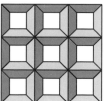

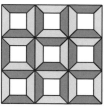

Narrow framing sets off the blocks, which appear to "float" between the wider sashing strips.

Two prints alternate to frame these appliqué blocks.

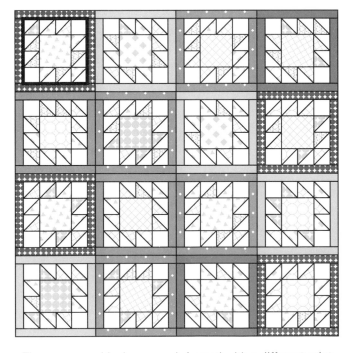

These scrappy blocks are each framed with a different print to add to the scrappy look.

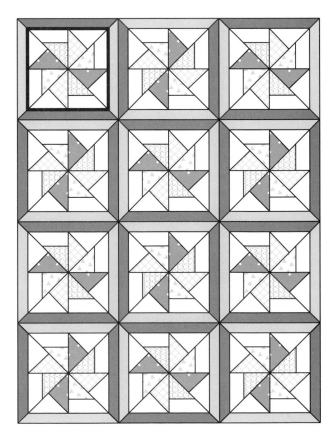

Each block is framed with a light fabric on opposite sides and a dark fabric on the other two sides, which gives a three-dimensional effect.

Blocks in both these quilts are framed with corner triangles in alternating colors. Notice that the appliqué Basket quilt started out with diagonal blocks and became a horizontal setting, while the appliqué Heart blocks change from a horizontal orientation to a diagonal setting.

Two-color frames with Four-Patch cornerstones tie these sampler blocks together.

This quilt combines simple framing and corner triangle framing. This would be a good choice for sampler blocks or any group of blocks where some of the blocks are oriented horizontally and some are oriented diagonally.

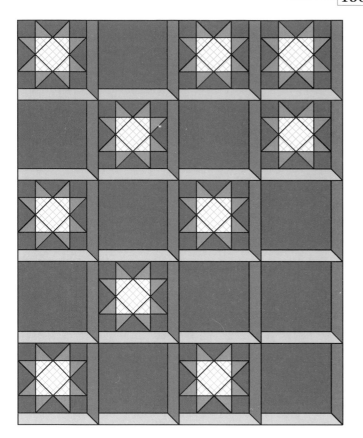

Attic Windows frame these Star blocks. Add blank window blocks at random to stretch fewer pieced blocks into a larger quilt or to set an odd number of blocks together.

This quilt combines two framing options: a box-shaped frame and a simple frame in two alternating colors.

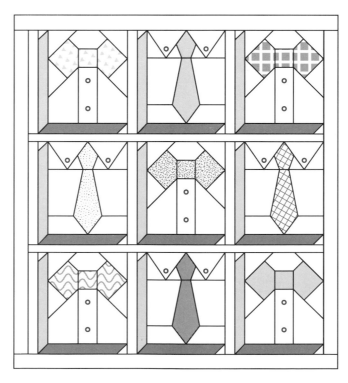

A dark box-shaped frame surrounds two adjacent sides of these shirt blocks to give the illusion of shirt boxes. Simple sashing separates the blocks.

Stripped Sets with Sashing

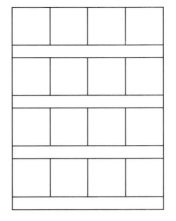
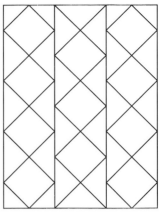

CONSIDER THIS SETTING FOR:

▶ Flying Geese blocks

▶ Picture blocks, such as trees, houses, bunnies, cats, cars, and trains

▶ A diagonal set to which you want to add movement

Side-by-side Stripped Setting
with Horizontal Sashing

Diagonal Setting
Creating a Zigzag

In this setting, your blocks touch each other in one direction and are separated by sashing in the other direction. For horizontally set quilts, the sashing can run crosswise or lengthwise.

If the sashing runs crosswise, it creates a "landscape" for houses, bunnies, cats, cars, trains, or other objects in your quilt. Your sashing could be grass, sidewalk, highway, flowers, or a train track, just to name a few examples.

An example of sashing running lengthwise would be a Flying Geese quilt. Keep your eyes open for lovely vine-type floral prints that you can use for a vertical sashing treatment. When this idea is carried over to a diagonal setting, it produces a zigzag effect. To do this, move every other row up half a block, and use an odd number of rows to balance each side. This is a good way to set an odd number of blocks, such as seven, eleven, or eighteen blocks.

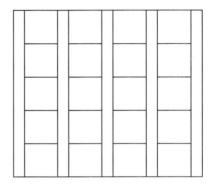

Side-by-side Stripped Setting
with Vertical Sashing

Vertical sashing in strippy quilts can be wide or narrow, with blocks set horizontally or on the diagonal with side triangles.

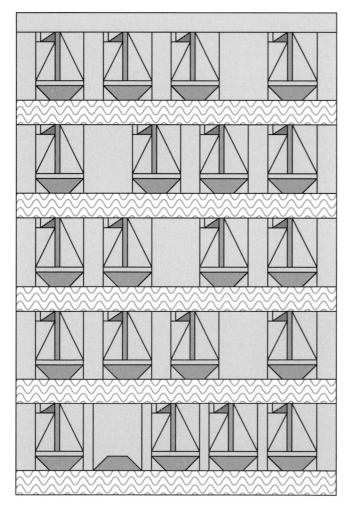

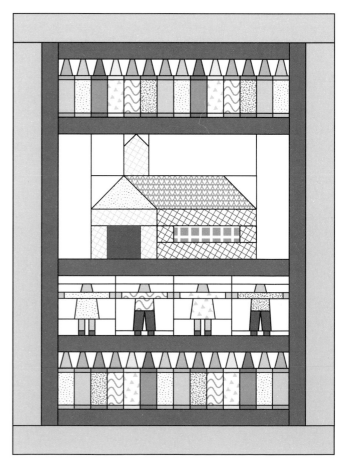

Crosswise sashing creates a landscape for houses, bunnies, boats, kids, and crayons.

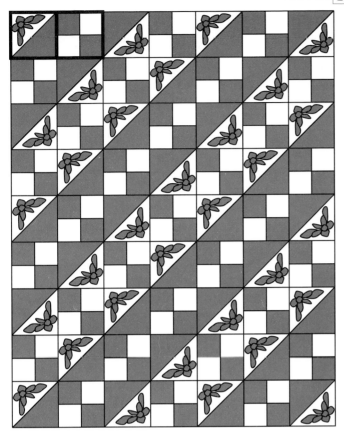

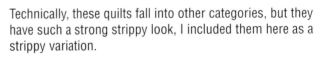

Technically, these quilts fall into other categories, but they have such a strong strippy look, I included them here as a strippy variation.

A diagonal strippy setting has diagonally set blocks in rows
that begin and end with a half block to create a zigzag effect.
Side and corner triangles complete the set.

Medallion Sets

> ## CONSIDER THIS SETTING FOR:
>
> ◗ A central block
>
> ◗ A group of blocks that create a focal point

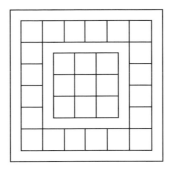
Straight-Set Medallion

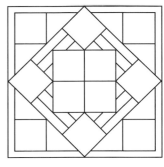
Diagonally Set Medallion

This setting has many different variations. Included here are some basic ideas to use as a starting point. Medallions usually have one or more blocks as a central focus. From there, you add borders, blocks, or other elements. You can piece or appliqué these elements or use a combination of both.

Often, the various elements switch from a diagonal setting to a horizontal setting, creating the illusion that one part sits on top of another. This is a good option for a large central block or if you don't want to make the same block over and over.

There are many variations on the medallion setting. Included here are examples that use multiples of blocks of the same size. Perhaps more than any of the other settings, this one takes some planning with graph paper, but the results are well worth the effort!

If you are switching from a diagonal to a horizontal orientation in your design, it may be helpful to cut out the design area that is oriented in one direction and glue it onto a new sheet of graph paper when you change to the other orientation, so that you are always working with graph paper that lines up with your design. For example, if you set the center blocks diagonally and add corner triangles, then set more blocks horizontally, you should use graph paper oriented in the same way as the blocks, diagonally and horizontally.

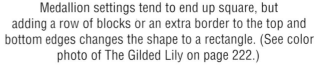
Medallion settings tend to end up square, but adding a row of blocks or an extra border to the top and bottom edges changes the shape to a rectangle. (See color photo of The Gilded Lily on page 222.)

Four appliqué blocks form the center of this medallion setting with eight more blocks used around the edges.

Twelve appliqué blocks surround a large central block in this medallion setting.

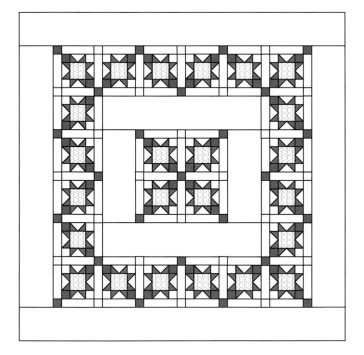

These settings include sashings and cornerstones.

Design elements can be changed easily when working with graph and tracing paper. These two quilts start out with the same center design elements and show how the basic format can be changed from a square to a rectangle, with other elements changing as well.

These four Basket blocks, framed with sashing and cornerstones, can stand on their own or form a center for a larger medallion setting by adding more borders.

Change this star setting by putting four blocks in the center or set one block diagonally.

DESIGNING QUILT SETTINGS

Blocks. If you are starting with a stack of blocks, have them handy. You'll want to know how many you have, what their finished sizes are, and how true to size each block is. If your blocks vary in size more than ¼", you may want to design a setting where the blocks do not meet side by side.

Books, Magazines, Photos, Quilt Sketches. There are many examples of different setting possibilities in this book, but keep your eyes open for settings that please you. Take your camera or a pad of paper to quilt shows and guild meetings to record settings that you like. When you are looking through quilt books or magazines, use "sticky notes" to mark pages that have appealing settings.

Graph Paper. You'll find graph paper in notebook-sized tablets and in large single sheets (usually 17" x 22"). The smaller size is handy to carry with you for sketching, and the large sheets work well for planning large projects at home. The most common scale of graph paper is four squares to the inch, but it also comes five, six, and eight squares to the inch. These scales come in handy when you are working with blocks based on Ninepatch or twenty-five-patch grids and you want to draft blocks to scale. If you are working with blocks based on a Ninepatch, use graph paper with six squares to the inch so that divisions in the block match up with lines on the graph paper. When I'm working with a stack of blocks, I usually use a 1" or ½" square to represent the block and determine the size from there.

Tracing Paper. Use this see-through paper over the top of graph paper for sketching quilt settings. This method not only saves graph paper but keeps the extra lines on the graph paper from interfering with the quilt design. It also makes it easier to include both horizontal and diagonal design elements in your sketch by changing the orientation of the graph paper under the tracing paper. This method works especially well if you are planning a medallion-style setting, where the block

Equipment

As with any task, gathering your supplies and having a good work space with adequate lighting make the job go more smoothly. Try to find a table or desk where you can leave your work in progress (also known as mess!) and come back to it when you have a few minutes or a new idea comes to mind. You will get a lot more done and use smaller bits of time if you don't have to get everything out each time you want to work and then put everything away when you are finished.

The following supplies are helpful when designing quilt settings.

orientation can change from horizontal to diagonal and back again.

See-Through Ruler. A 2" x 18" thin, clear acrylic ruler is useful for drafting designs and making templates. It is marked with ⅛" divisions. These rulers are not made to be used with a rotary cutter as they are too thin and the cutting blade will roll up on top of the ruler and ruin the edge. The 1" x 6" and 1" x 12" sizes are handy for sketching smaller shapes.

Lead Pencils. Mechanical pencils are preferable because they consistently give you a sharp, fine line, but any sharp pencils will work. Be sure to keep a good supply on hand.

Erasers. A big eraser is to sketching what the seam ripper is to sewing. Don't be without one!

Glue Stick. Anything sticky will do, but glue sticks are so easy to use.

Paper Scissors. Use these as you cut and paste designs together; don't use your good fabric scissors!

Colored Pencils or Markers. After sketching a design, I use colored pencils to color it in. I like to use a wide assortment of colors, either pencils or markers, but I find it easier to use pencils to get light and dark color variations.

Calculator. Since this process does involve some math, a calculator is helpful. To convert decimals to inches and fractions of inches for quiltmaking, use the conversion chart on page 211.

Mirrors and Fresnel® Viewing Lenses. Two 12"-square mirrors placed at right angles to each other can give you an idea of how your design will look repeated over and over again. Place the mirrors at the center of your design and see what happens. It's magic! Looking at a block through a Fresnel viewing lens repeats it over and over to give you a sense of its overall design.

Flannel Board. Placing your blocks on a flannel board or even a piece of batting tacked to the wall allows you to stand back and squint at them and audition different arrangements, fabrics, borders, and sashing treatments. What looks wonderful on paper might not look so wonderful in real life, so this is a good way to test your ideas "in the flesh."

Designing on Paper

1. By now, you have some idea of settings that you like. Your first sketches will probably be quite crude. Don't worry about using a ruler at this point. The main thing is to get your ideas down on paper—any kind of paper—before you forget them. I like starting out with the "paper-napkin approach," where you get the creativity flowing and focus on getting several possibilities down that you feel have some merit. Don't worry about being neat and tidy or coloring in your design. That can come later, in the fine-tuning stage.

2. Before going any further, you may want to sketch out your block design. If you are working with a pieced block, use graph paper in whichever scale matches your block. If you are making a large quilt with many repeating blocks, sketch your block so that 1½" is equal to one block. That way, graph paper that is divided into ⅛" squares will match a variety of blocks (including Ninepatch and sixteenpatch). If you are working with a complex block, a large block, or a block that doesn't repeat very much, use 2" or 3" to equal one block. This is up to you and how big you want your working drawing to be; you will work out the scale later. Make enough copies of your block so that you can cut them out and arrange them into various designs.

3. Place a piece of tracing paper over your graph paper. Choose the horizontal or diagonal, depending on the orientation you are using. Use a few small pieces of tape to hold it in place. If you are planning a medallion-style setting where orientation changes, start with the center and tape your tracing paper onto the appropriate graph paper as you go along. Using your see-through ruler and a sharp lead pencil, sketch out your design, leaving blank spaces for your blocks so you can tape or glue copies of them in place. This is the point where you can audition various options, such as different alternating blocks, framing ideas, or different sashing widths. If your quilt must be a predetermined size for a certain wall space or bed size, adjust the width of sashings, frames, borders, or other components so your quilt will be the required size. For more information on bed sizes, see page 211. Use two mirrors or the Fresnel viewing lens (page 199) to see how your design will look repeated.

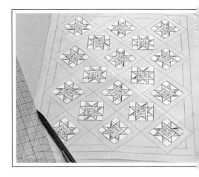

4. When you are pleased with a design, tape or glue the copies of your block design into place.

Make several copies of your finished design. Get out your colored pencils or markers and color in your design in various ways. Keep in mind that dark colors come forward while light colors tend to recede. If you want to use a strong color, try using it in smaller amounts so it won't overpower other parts of your design. This is your opportunity to try changing colors from the center to the edges of your design, or to try "floating" the blocks with sashing or alternating blocks. Don't forget that each setting you design has a number of color-choice possibilities. After you have finalized your setting design and color scheme, plan the borders. (See pages 204–8.)

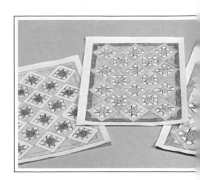

5. Using the size of your block as a guide, determine the size of the other parts of your setting. Make a list of component parts that you will need to complete your top. Decide which fabrics you will use for each component of your design. Fill in the work sheet on page 209 with this information, making it as detailed or as sketchy as you wish. By now, you should have a good idea of the size of your quilt so you can determine how much fabric you will need for the binding and backing and what size the batting should be. Refer to the handy charts on pages 211–13 for help with the calculations.

6. The next step is to figure out how much of each fabric you need. Once you have decided which parts of your quilt you will cut from which fabric, use the fabric-cutting diagrams on page 210 and the chart on page 213 to calculate your fabric needs. You may duplicate the fabric-cutting diagrams to plan the yardage needed for each fabric. I usually buy at least ½ yard extra to allow for mistakes and in case I change my color choices along the way. Planning a fabric layout for each of your main fabrics not only tells you how much fabric you need but also the best way to cut it. Begin by positioning borders and long sashing strips along the lengthwise grain (which has less stretch) so you can avoid seaming strips together to get the correct length for each border. Then fill in with smaller shapes. Check the chart on page 213 if you just have small shapes and no long strips. These diagrams are based on a fabric width of 40" of usable fabric after preshrinking, folded in half lengthwise. That means that each piece on your layout will yield two pieces when cut.

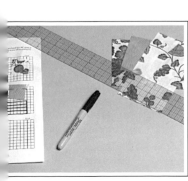

7. You may want to make templates for any unusual shapes in your design. Cut them out of template plastic, X-ray film, or graph paper mounted on cardboard. Be sure to add a ¼"-wide seam allowance to each side. Most of the shapes you will be working with will be squares, rectangles, and triangles. To figure the cut size for squares and rectangles, add ½" to the length and width for seam allowances. There are two types of triangles used in quilt settings.

Half-Square Triangles: These triangles are half of a square, with the short sides on the straight grain of the fabric and the long side on the bias. To cut these triangles, cut a square and then cut it in half diagonally. Cut the square ⅞" larger than the finished short side of the triangle to allow for seam allowances. Each square makes two triangles.

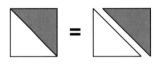

Cut square ⅞" larger than finished size needed.

Half-Square Triangles

Quarter-Square Triangles: Quarter-square triangles are usually used along the outside edges of blocks and quilts. Cut squares twice diagonally so their short sides are on the bias and their long side is on the straight of grain. These triangles are easier to handle and keep the outside edges of your quilt from stretching. Cut the square 1¼" larger than the finished long side of the triangle to allow for seam allowances. Each square makes four triangles.

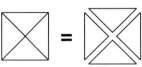

Cut square 1¼" larger than finished size needed.

Quarter-Square Triangles

Special Considerations

Let's take a look at several common problems you might run into when working with actual blocks, such as setting blocks that aren't quite the same size, or setting an unusual number of blocks together.

BLOCKS THAT AREN'T QUITE THE SAME SIZE

Sometimes, no matter how hard you try, a set of blocks just doesn't end up all the same size. This often happens with sampler blocks or friendship blocks that are made by many different people. First, square up the blocks, using a 12" or 15" acrylic square and a rotary cutter. Trim off the uneven parts along each side and try to end with all the blocks as close to the same size as possible.

FUDGE TO FIT

If the difference in sizes ranges from no more than ⅛" to ¼", you will probably be able to join them, using the "fudge to fit" method.

1. If possible, arrange the blocks so that the smaller blocks are at the top of the quilt and the larger ones are at the bottom so less easing will be necessary.
2. As you piece the blocks together, place the smaller of the two blocks on top, right sides together. Pin the ends and any intersecting seams and points that need to match along the way. If things don't quite match up, you will need to decide which seams are going to show the most and match those, settling for "just close" on the others.

3. As you stitch, keep the smaller block on top so that the feed dog on your sewing machine will ease the larger block in on the bottom. Hold onto each end of your blocks and pull gently to stretch them as you stitch.

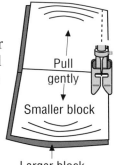

Pull gently

Smaller block

Larger block

FRAME TO FIT

You can standardize blocks that vary too much in size to fudge together by adding a frame around them. Choose the approximate frame width, adding ½" for seam allowances, plus another ½"–1" for trimming, depending on the difference in size between the smallest and largest blocks. The wider the frame, the less the difference in size will show. Some frames that work well for squaring up blocks are noted in the framed-block section on pages 187–90. After stitching the frames onto the blocks, use a 12" or 15" acrylic square to trim them all down to a uniform size. Center the block in the frame and trim away an equal amount from each side of the frames.

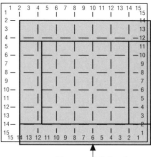

Framed block

Another option is to add oversized triangles around your blocks. Then trim the resulting blocks to a standard size. If the fabric you use is the same as the background fabric in the blocks, the blocks will appear to float. You can set the framed blocks horizontally or diagonally.

Adding oversized triangles that are the same fabric as the block background makes the design appear to float.

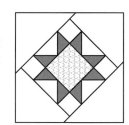

THE MEDALLION CONNECTION

If most of your blocks are the same size with only a few oddballs to worry about, consider a medallion setting.

1. Stitch together either the four largest or four smallest blocks for the center medallion. Hopefully, the remaining blocks will be fairly close in size.
2. Frame the medallion with borders or corner triangles, or both.
3. Add the remaining blocks around the edges.

Medallion Setting

Refer to "Medallion Sets" on pages 195–97 for additional ideas.

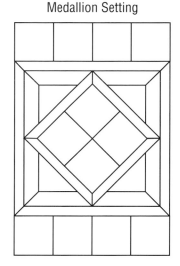

Blocks Across	Rows Down	No. of A Blocks	No. of B Blocks	Total No. of Blocks
3	5	7	8	15
5	7	17	18	35
7	9	31	32	63
9	11	49	50	99

SETTING AN UNUSUAL NUMBER OF BLOCKS

It's easy to figure how to set thirty blocks together. You can set them in six rows with five blocks in each row, but what do you do with twenty-six blocks? Thirteen rows of two blocks in each row isn't too practical. An odd number of blocks, such as seven or seventeen, also presents a challenge. There are several solutions.

Alternating Plain or Design Blocks

When a main block alternates with another block, you usually set them with an odd number of blocks and an odd number of rows so that the same block will end up in each corner.

5 blocks

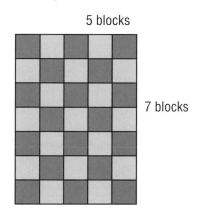

7 blocks

5 x 7 = 35 ÷ 2 =
17 blocks + 18 blocks

If you multiply the odd number of blocks in a row by the odd number of rows, you will end up with an odd number of total blocks needed. Now divide the total number of blocks needed in two equal groups and you will have one group with one more block than the other. Perhaps the number of blocks you have will work into one of the following arrangements:

Diagonal Settings

Diagonal settings, with blocks set side by side or with alternating blocks, can also accommodate an unusual number of blocks. If you orient your blocks horizontally, add corner-triangle framing around them to change them to a diagonal orientation. A good example of this is "Class Heroes" (page 220), where twenty-six students made blocks to set together. Here are some other possibilities:

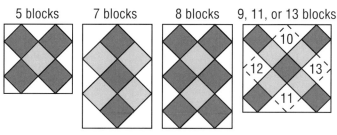

5 blocks　　7 blocks　　8 blocks　　9, 11, or 13 blocks

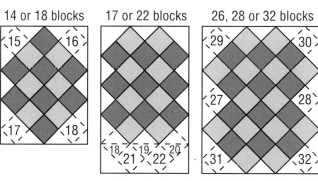

14 or 18 blocks　　17 or 22 blocks　　26, 28 or 32 blocks

31 blocks

Medallions

A medallion setting might be the answer when you have an unusual number of blocks. Take another look at some of the medallion settings on pages 195–97 and the number of blocks in each.

BORDER BASICS

Like the mat and frame on a favorite piece of art, a quilt needs a border to contain the design elements you have used to create it. A beautiful border draws the eye of the viewer into the center of the quilt top, where you have focused most of your stitching time and energy.

It is ideal to plan the borders as part of your quilt before purchasing fabrics, but often borders are planned and purchased after the piecing or appliqué is completed. It is particularly important to plan ahead if you wish to repeat any of the fabrics you used in the quilt top in the border. You will want to buy enough for the border when you buy fabrics for the quilt top. (You can always change your mind later, but it is often impossible to find the same fabric at a later date.) Use the "Set Design Work Sheet and Inventory" and the cutting diagrams on pages 209 and 210 to determine the required border yardage if you are planning and designing your own borders rather than following a specific quilt plan.

When determining yardage, you will need to decide how you will cut the border strips from your fabric. Borders with mitered corners require a little more yardage than those with straight-cut borders. (See pages 206–8.)

You may cut border strips from either the crosswise or lengthwise grain of the fabric. Usually, borders cut across the width of the fabric (crosswise grain) require less yardage than those cut along the lengthwise grain. If you cut border strips for a quilt with dimensions larger than 42" x 42", you will probably need to piece strips into longer lengths to fit your quilt top.

Some quiltmakers simply do not like the piecing seams required when you cut borders on the crosswise grain. Although it requires additional yardage, you may prefer to cut borders from the fabric length because the lengthwise grain has less stretch and is therefore more stable.

You may sew border strips together in one of two ways. A seam stitched at a 45° angle is less noticeable than a straight seam. To piece borders at an angle, place the short ends of the strips at right angles as shown above right and stitch from intersection to intersection. Trim excess, leaving a ¼"-wide seam. Press the seam open.

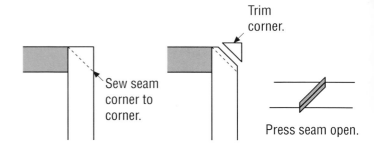

Trim corner.

Sew seam corner to corner.

Press seam open.

If you are short on yardage, you may need to join the short ends of the strips instead. Be sure to press the seams open.

Before You Begin

Be sure to straighten the edges of your quilt before adding the borders. Little or no trimming should be necessary for a straight-set quilt. However, a diagonally set quilt is often constructed with oversized side triangles, and these may need to be trimmed down to size. Align the ¼" line on the ruler with the block points and trim the quilt edges to ¼" from these points. Always position a ruler along the block points of the adjacent edge at the same time so the corner will be square when you have completed the trimming.

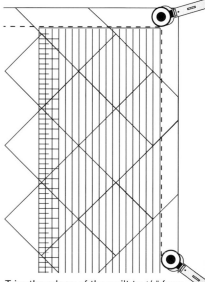

Trim the edges of the quilt to ¼" from block points, using ruler to square the corners.

Borders with Straight-Cut Corners

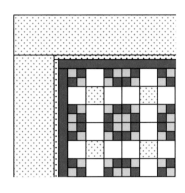

Straight-cut borders are the easiest and fastest borders to add to your quilt top. They require a little less yardage than borders with mitered corners. You may add them to the sides and then to the top and bottom edges of the quilt top, or vice versa.

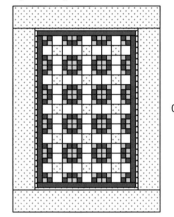 or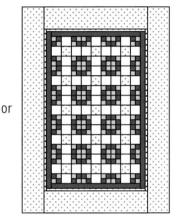

Add side borders first.   Add side borders last.

It requires a little less yardage to add straight-cut borders to the sides of a rectangular quilt first, and then to the top and bottom. This may be an important consideration if you are short on fabric. It makes no difference in yardage for a square quilt.

To add borders with straight-cut corners:

1. Measure the length of the quilt top through the center, from raw edge to raw edge. Cut two border strips to match this length. Cut them the width specified in your quilt plan or the desired finished width plus ½" for seam allowances.

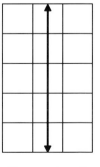

Measure length at center.

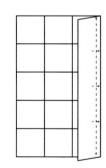

Tip
Do not measure the outer edges of your quilt top—unless you want to know how uneven they are. Due to stitching inaccuracies and stretching, the outer edges of a quilt top are often not the same. If you measure each side of the quilt and cut your borders to match, the finished quilt will not be "square."

2. Fold the quilt top in half crosswise and then in half again and mark the center and quarter folds with straight pins. Repeat with the border strips.

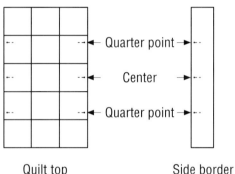

Quilt top   Side border

3. Pin each border strip to the quilt top, matching the center and quarter pins and raw edges. Use additional pins as needed to hold the layers together for stitching.

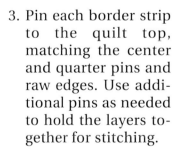

Stitch side border.

4. As you stitch, ease or stretch the border as needed for a smooth fit. Sometimes it is necessary to ease the border strip on one side and slightly stretch the other border strip to fit the other side.

5. Press seams toward the side borders.

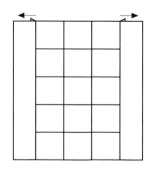

Press seams toward borders.

6. Measure the quilt top's width at the center from raw edge to raw edge, including the two side border strips. Cut top and bottom border strips to match this measurement, cutting them the desired finished width plus ½" for seam allowances.

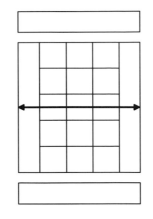

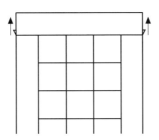

Measure width at center after adding side borders.

7. Mark the top and bottom edges of the quilt top for centers and quarters as you did for the side borders. Repeat with the borders.

8. Pin and stitch the top and bottom borders to the quilt top as described for the side borders. Press seams toward the borders.

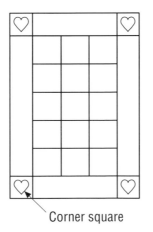

Borders with Corner Squares

One way to add design interest to a border is to add corner squares. For a corner square, you may use a square of a solid color or a pieced or appliquéd block that repeats or complements a design in the quilt. Using a corner square is particularly appropriate when you wish to cut the border strips across the fabric width, but they are not wide enough to match the quilt dimensions. In this case, you might even wish to cut the corner square from the same fabric used for the borders.

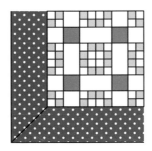

Corner square

To attach borders with corner squares:

1. Complete steps 1–5 for "Borders with Straight-Cut Corners," on page 205.

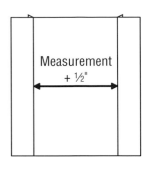

Measurement + ½"

2. Measure the width of quilt top across the center *from border seam line to border seam line* to determine the width. Add ½" for seam allowances. Cut top and bottom border strips.

3. Cut, piece, or appliqué 4 corner squares that are equal in size to the cut width of the border strips.

4. Sew a corner square to each end of the top and bottom border strips. Press seams toward the squares.

5. Sew the top and bottom borders to the quilt top as described for the side borders. Press seams toward the borders.

Borders with Mitered Corners

Mitered corners are not difficult, but they do require a little extra fabric and a little extra time to finish. They are especially effective when using a stripe or other linear, one-way design, such as a border print for the border fabric.

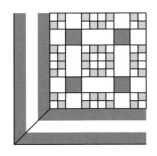

Border with mitered corners | Mitered corners are especially effective with striped fabric.

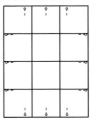

Some quiltmakers prefer to use mitered corners when adding several borders to the quilt top. Rather than sewing each border to the quilt separately, which also requires mitering each new border at each corner, you can sew all the border strips for each side of the quilt together first. Then you simply sew each of the strip-pieced border units to the quilt top and you have only four corners to miter. This is a real time-saver and helps to eliminate inaccuracies.

To cut border strips for mitered corners:

1. Decide how wide you want the finished border to be.
2. Measure the quilt top through the center to determine the width and length of the quilt top without borders.
3. Add two finished border widths to each dimension. This gives you the estimated *finished* size of your quilt, *including borders.*

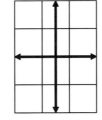

4. For two seam allowances and an extra allowance for safety's sake, add 2"–3" to each dimension. Cut border strips to match these dimensions.

    For example, if your quilt measures 75" x 90" and you want a 6"-wide finished border, you would cut the top and bottom border strips 90" long and the side border strips 105" long.

QUILT TOP	LENGTH	WIDTH
	90"	75"
Finished Border Width x 2	12"	12"
Seam-Allowance Safety Factor	3"	3"
	105"	90"

To attach borders with mitered corners:

1. Fold the quilt top in half crosswise and then in half again and mark the center and quarter points along each side with straight pins. Fold in half lengthwise and then in half again and mark the folds with pins.

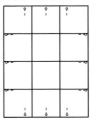

Mark centers and quarter points on all four edges of the quilt top.

2. Fold the side borders in half crosswise and mark the center fold with a pin. Then, with the border lying flat on a smooth surface, measure and mark half the length of the quilt top in each direction from the center pin.

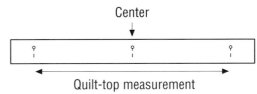

Center

Quilt-top measurement

3. Fold the border strip in to the center pin, so the end pins meet in the middle, and mark the quarter points with pins.

Quarter point | Center | Quarter point

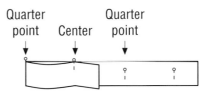

4. Repeat steps 2 and 3 with the top and bottom border strips.
5. Pin each border strip to the quilt top, matching centers and quarter points. *The raw edges of the quilt top should match the outermost pin in the border strip.* An equal length of border strip should extend at each end of the quilt top. Stitch, being careful to begin and end stitching ¼" in from the corners of the quilt top.

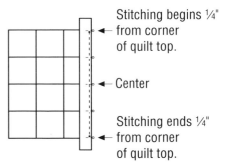

Stitching begins ¼" from corner of quilt top.

Center

Stitching ends ¼" from corner of quilt top.

6. Place one corner of the quilt on the ironing board, right side up. Anchor the quilt top to the ironing board cover with a few pins to keep it from shifting while you work.

7. Turn under one border strip at a 45° angle and pin in place. Check the angle with the 45° line on your rotary ruler or the diagonal line on the Bias Square. If you have multiple borders or a striped border fabric, be sure that the seam lines or stripes match. Also check to make sure that the outer corner is square. When you are happy with the mitered fold you have created, press the fold line.

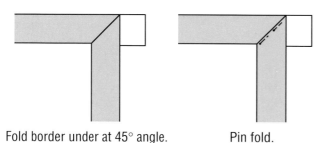

Fold border under at 45° angle.   Pin fold.

8. Center a piece of 1"-wide masking tape over the pressed fold, removing pins as you place the tape on the fold line.

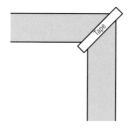

Remove pins as you tape corner.

9. Remove the quilt from the ironing board and fold it, right sides together, with the folded edge extending straight out from the crease line. Stitch on the crease line and remove the masking tape from the right side. Draw a light pencil line on the crease line to make it easier to see while you stitch. Begin stitching at the inside corner, folding the border strips out of the way.

10. Press the seam toward the border.

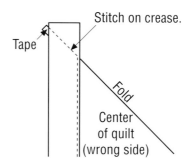

11. Trim away the excess border fabric, leaving a ¼"-wide seam allowance. Press seam open.

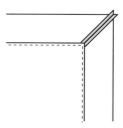

12. Repeat steps 6–11 with remaining corners.

SET DESIGN WORK SHEET AND INVENTORY

Fill out this work sheet in as much detail as you wish. Use the completed work sheet, along with the fabric cutting diagrams, to determine how much of each fabric you will need to complete your quilt, including the binding, batting, and backing. Not all categories will apply to each quilt, but you can organize each component of your quilt and record which fabric you plan to use for each. Use the reference charts, beginning on page 211, to determine your fabric requirements. The goal is to complete the section below so you can go shopping!

Fabric #

Type of Setting _____

Finished Size of Quilt _____

Block Design _____

Size of Block _____

Additional notes:

Number of Main Blocks _____ _____

Number of Alternating Blocks _____ _____

Number of Sashing Strips (short) _____ _____

Number of Sashing Strips (long) _____ _____

Number of Cornerstones _____ _____

Number of Side Triangles _____ _____

Corner Triangles _____ _____

First Border (Inner) _____ _____

Second Border (Middle) _____ _____

Third Border (Outer) _____ _____

Binding _____ _____

Backing _____ _____

Yardage for Each Fabric: (Use the fabric-cutting diagrams on page 210 to help you estimate your yardage requirements.)

Fabric #1 | Swatch | Yardage _____   Fabric #4 | Swatch | Yardage _____

Fabric #2 | Swatch | Yardage _____   Fabric #5 | Swatch | Yardage _____

Fabric #3 | Swatch | Yardage _____   Fabric #6 | Swatch | Yardage _____

Permission is granted to photocopy this work sheet for your personal use only.

FABRIC CUTTING DIAGRAMS

Draw in the border strips and large blocks first. (Run border strips along the lengthwise grain of fabric whenever possible.) Then start with other large pieces and work your way down to smaller shapes.

These cutting layouts are based on a 40" width of usable fabric (after preshrinking), folded in half, so you will be cutting two of each piece. Each square = 2".

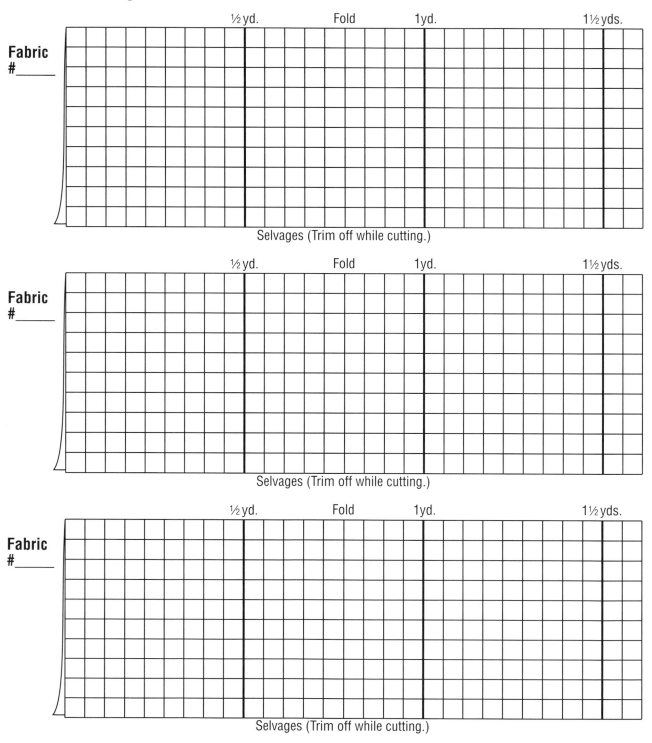

Permission is granted to photocopy this work sheet for your personal use only.

QUICK REFERENCE CHARTS

These cutting layouts are based on a 40" width of usable fabric (after preshrinking), folded in tions you will need when designing quilts and figuring yardage requirements.

COMMON BED SIZES

If you are designing a quilt for a specific bed, it is best to measure the actual bed, but if this isn't possible, use the chart at right.

BED	MATTRESS SIZE
Crib	23" x 46"
Youth	32" x 66"
Twin	39" x 75"
Double	54" x 75"
Queen	60" x 80"
King	78" x 80"
Calif. King	72" x 84"

DECIMAL TO INCH CONVERSIONS

When you are using a calculator, you will run into fractions given as decimals. Use this chart to convert to fractions or to round them to the nearest ⅛".

.125	=	⅛"
.25	=	¼"
.375	=	⅜"
.50	=	½"
.625	=	⅝"
.75	=	¾"
.875	=	⅞"
1.00	=	1"

DIAGONAL MEASUREMENTS OF STANDARD-SIZE BLOCKS

When you are setting blocks diagonally, it is helpful to know the diagonal measurement of the block so that you can figure the quilt size. To figure this yourself, multiply the length of one side of the block by 1.414, or use the chart at right.

2" block	=	2⅞"
3" block	=	4¼"
4" block	=	5⅝"
5" block	=	7⅛"
6" block	=	8½"
7" block	=	9⅞"
8" block	=	11¼"
9" block	=	12¾"
10" block	=	14⅛"
12" block	=	17"
14" block	=	19⅞"
16" block	=	22⅝"
18" block	=	25½"
20" block	=	28¼"
24" block	=	34"

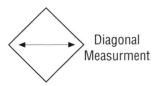

Diagonal Measurment

CALCULATING CORNER AND SIDE TRIANGLES

It is important to cut corner and side triangles so that the grain lines run vertically and horizontally. This stabilizes the quilt, prevents sagging, and makes the borders go on more smoothly.

Corner Triangles

Corner triangles are made from a square cut diagonally in one direction so that one square yields two corner triangles. To calculate the size of square needed, divide the finished block size by 1.414 and add .875" (⅞") for seam allowances. Round this up to the nearest ⅛".

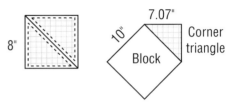

$$10" \div 1.414 = 7.07 + .875 = 7.95" \text{ or } 8"$$

Side Triangles

Side triangles are made from a square cut diagonally in two directions so that one square yields four side triangles. To calculate the size of the square needed, multiply the finished block size by 1.414 and add 1.25" (1¼") for seam allowances. Round this up to the nearest ⅛".

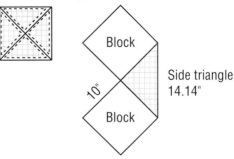

$$10" \times 1.414 = 14.14" + 1.25 = 15.39" \text{ or } 15½"$$

The chart at the top of page 212 gives you the measurements for corner and side triangles for the most common quilt-block sizes. However, you may overcut your squares by ½"–1" if you prefer and trim them down once you've pieced your top together.

CORNER AND SIDE TRIANGLES

FINISHED BLOCK SIZE	CUT SQUARE SIZE FOR CORNER TRIANGLE	CUT SQUARE SIZE FOR SIDE TRIANGLE
2" Block	2⅜"	4⅛"
3" Block	3"	5½"
4" Block	3¾"	7"
5" Block	4½"	8⅜"
6" Block	5⅛"	9¾"
7" Block	5⅞"	11¼"
8" Block	6⅝"	12⅝"
9" Block	7¼"	14"
10" Block	8"	15½"
12" Block	9⅜"	18¼"
14" Block	10⅞"	21⅛"
16" Block	12¼"	23⅞"
18" Block	13⅝"	26¾"
20" Block	15⅛"	29⅝"
24" Block	17⅞"	35¼"

ESTIMATING YARDAGE REQUIREMENTS

The chart at the bottom of page 213 is based on a 40" width of fabric. Most 100% cotton fabrics used for quiltmaking measure 42"–44" wide, but after preshrinking and trimming off the selvages, I consider anything over 40" a bonus. Therefore, you might get a few more pieces than I have estimated, but you won't be short.

Even though this chart only gives yardage requirements for squares, you can easily use it for other shapes. For half-square triangles, multiply the number of squares by two. For quarter-square triangles, multiply the number of squares by four.

For rectangles, figure how many will fit into a square and calculate from there.

For irregular shapes, figure how many will fit into a certain size square and go from there.

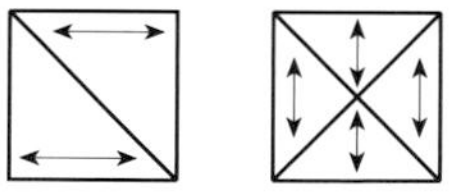

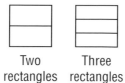

Arrows indicate straight of grain.

Two rectangles   Three rectangles

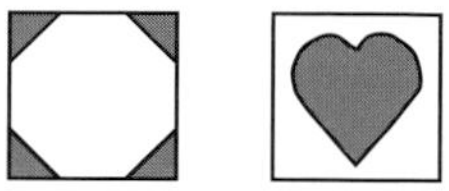

Backing and Binding Yardage Requirements

You will need to piece the backing for most quilts larger than crib size, using two or more strips of 42"- to 44"-wide fabric. The piecing seams may run horizontally or vertically in the backing as long as the fabric isn't a directional print. Look for 90"-wide 100% cotton in solid colors so you won't have to piece the backings for large quilts. Avoid the temptation to use a bed sheet for a backing as it is difficult to hand quilt through the weave of sheeting fabric.

If you are planning to put a sleeve or rod pocket on the back of your quilt so you can hang it, buy a little extra backing fabric so that the sleeve and the backing match. Once you know the finished size of your quilt, refer to the following diagrams to plan how to lay out the backing and determine how much fabric you need. Be sure to trim off the selvages before seaming pieces together. See "Adding a Sleeve" on page 307.

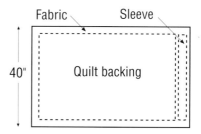

Up to 40" width or length
Example: 60" (length or width) + 18" (½ yd. for trimming and sleeve) = 78" (2⅛ yds.)

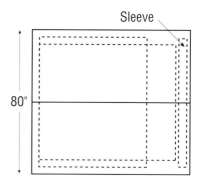

Up to 80" width or length
Example: 2 x 100" (length or width) = 200" + 27" (¾ yd. for trimming and sleeve) = 277" (6⅓ yds.)

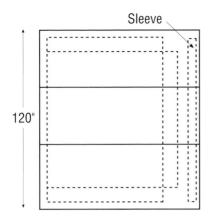

Sleeve

120"

Up to 120" width or length
Example: 3 x 100" (length or width) =
300" + 36" (1 yd. for trimming and
sleeve) = 336" (9⅓ yds.)

See pages 284–85 in "Happy Endings" for directions on calculating binding yardage requirements.

YARDAGE CHART FOR SQUARES

SIZE OF SQUARE		YARDAGE NEEDED (40" OF USABLE FABRIC)							
CUT	FINISHED	¼ YD.	½ YD.	¾ YD.	1 YD.	1¼ YDS.	1½ YDS.	1¾ YDS.	2 YDS.
1½"	1"	130	286	416	572	702	858	1066	1144
2"	1½"	80	160	240	320	400	480	620	640
2½"	2"	48	96	160	224	272	320	400	448
3"	2½"	26	65	104	143	195	221	260	286
3½"	3"	22	55	77	110	132	165	187	220
4"	3½"	20	40	60	80	110	130	150	170
4½"	4"	8	27	40	56	72	88	104	112
5"	4½"	8	24	40	56	64	80	96	112
5½"	5"	7	21	28	42	56	63	77	84
6"	5½"	6	12	24	30	42	48	60	66
6½"	6"	6	12	24	30	36	48	54	66
7½"	7"	5	10	15	20	25	35	40	45
8½"	8"	4	8	12	16	20	24	28	32
9½"	9"		4	8	12	16	20	24	28
10½"	10"		3	6	9	12	15	15	18
11½"	11"		3	6	9	9	12	15	18
12½"	12"		3	6	6	9	12	15	15
13½"	13"		2	4	4	6	8	8	10
14½"	14"		2	2	4	6	6	8	8
15½"	15"		2	2	4	4	6	8	8
16½"	16"		2	2	4	4	6	6	8
17½"	17"		2	2	4	4	6	6	8
18½"	18"			2	2	4	4	6	6
19½"	19"			2	2	4	4	6	6

Too Fruity

Color photo on page 217.
Finished Quilt Size: 58" x 75"
Finished Block Size: 8"

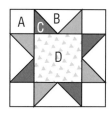

Finished block: 8"

You will need to make a total of 18 blocks. They may be the same block, or you may use a variety of your favorite 8" Star block designs and make this quilt in true sampler style. *The directions given are only for the Star block shown at left.*

Note: There are patterns for several Star blocks in the Shortcuts Sampler quilt on pages 44–58. You can adapt these blocks to an 8" size by using ¾" as the size of each square in the grid on which you draw the blocks. See the note on page 44 for more information.

This is a wonderful way to set sampler blocks, particularly if they vary in size. Simply adjust the width of the frame on each block so the framed blocks all finish to the same size. The frames set the blocks apart so each can stand on its own, and they help give a unifying look to dissimilar blocks. Alternate blocks in the setting are framed with triangles. Combining the framed blocks with these alternate blocks creates a dynamic setting. The framed blocks are set on point, and the alternate blocks end up in a horizontal position. The beauty of this setting is that it allows you to combine blocks that have a horizontal orientation, such as the Schoolhouse block, with blocks that usually have a diagonal orientation, such as the Basket block.

MATERIALS: 44"-WIDE FABRIC

1¼ yds. white for background in blocks
¼ yd. pieces of 10–15 assorted fabrics for the scrappy stars
2¼ yds. for the block frames (pink)
2¼ yds. background print for the side and corner setting triangles and the framing triangles for some of the blocks (fruit fabric)
1 yd. for borders (green)
½ yd. for binding
4 yds. for backing

CUTTING

Cut all strips across the fabric width (crosswise grain).

Blocks
From the white background fabric, cut:

5 strips, each 2½" x 40"; crosscut strips into a total of 72 squares, each 2½" x 2½", for A
3 strips, each 5¼" x 40"; crosscut strips into a total of 18 squares, each 5¼" x 5¼"; cut twice diagonally to yield 72 quarter-square triangles for B

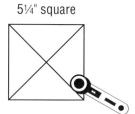

5¼" square

From the assorted star fabrics, cut:
a total of 72 squares, each 2⅞" x 2⅞"; cut once diagonally to yield 144 half-square triangles for star points C

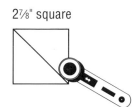

2⅞" square

a total of 18 squares, each 4½" x 4½", for star centers D*

*You may make some of the square centers, substituting four-patch units composed of four 2½" squares, and some of them as pinwheels, using 8 half-square triangles in each. For half-square triangles, cut 2⅞" squares; then cut once diagonally.

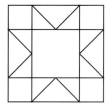 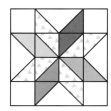 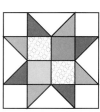

Square Center   Pinwheel Center   Four Patch Center

Frames and Borders
From the framing fabric, cut :
3 strips, each 12" x 40"; crosscut strips into a total of 48 strips, each 12" x 2¼".

From the background print, cut:
2 strips, each 6⅝" x 40"; crosscut strips into 12 squares, each 6⅝" x 6⅝"; cut once diagonally for 24 half-square triangle "frames" (for 6 of the Star blocks)

6⅝" square

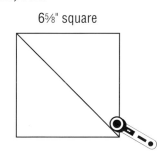

3 squares, each 13¼" x 13¼"; cut twice diagonally for 12 side setting triangles (You will use only 10 of these.)

13¼" square

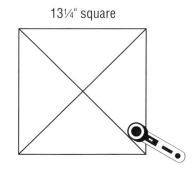

2 squares, each 4⅞" x 4⅞"; cut once diagonally for 4 corner setting triangles

4⅞" square

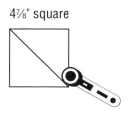

From the border fabric, cut:
1 strip, 17" x 30"; crosscut strip into 10 strips, each 2¾" x 17"
1 strip, 9" x 25"; crosscut strip into 8 strips, each 2¾" x 9"

DIRECTIONS
Piecing the Blocks and Setting Triangles
1. Piece 18 Star blocks, following the piecing diagram and placing the pieces in pleasing combinations.

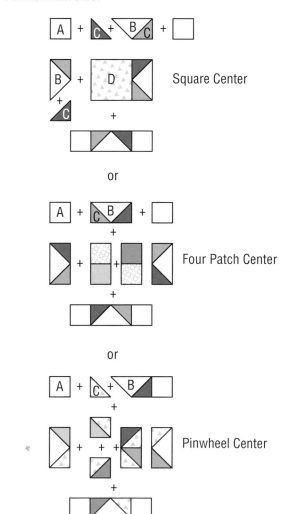

2. Referring to the quilt plan on page 214, lay out the blocks in a pleasing arrangement. Identify the 6 that will be framed with triangles.

3. Sew half-square triangles to opposite sides of each of the 6 blocks, then add the remaining half-square triangles to each block.

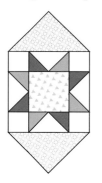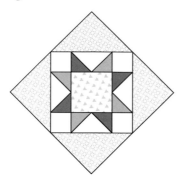

4. Using a 12" or 15" square ruler, square up the 6 triangle-framed blocks so they are all the same size, making sure you leave a ¼"-wide seam allowance all the way around.

5. Sew framing strips to each side of the remaining 12 blocks, using either straight-cut or mitered corners.

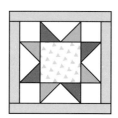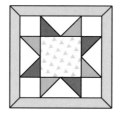

Straight-cut Corners   Mitered Corners

6. Using a 12" or 15" square ruler, trim the framed blocks to match the size of the 6 triangle-framed blocks. Be careful to trim them equally on each side so that the frames are the same width all the way around the block. Since the framing strips are oversized, you should have plenty of fabric to trim away to make all 18 blocks the same size.

7. Sew a 2¾" x 17" border strip to the long edge of each of the 10 side setting triangles, matching the center of the strip to the center of the long edge of the triangle. Trim excess as shown.

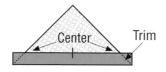

Center   Trim

8. Sew 2¾" x 9" border strips to the short sides of each of the 4 corner setting triangles, using either straight-cut or mitered corners. Trim the excess from the border strips as shown.

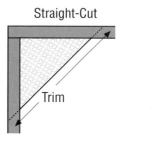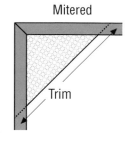

Straight-Cut   Mitered

Trim   Trim

Assembling and Finishing the Quilt Top

1. Assemble the quilt top in diagonal rows as shown, adding the corner triangles last. Press the seams between blocks in opposite directions from row to row.

2. Layer the quilt top with batting and backing; baste. See page 255.

3. Quilt as desired. Refer to "Loving Stitches," beginning on page 225.

4. Bind the edges. Refer to "Happy Endings," beginning on page 275.

Sensational Settings

GALLERY

The quilts in this gallery are examples of many of the settings shown throughout this chapter. They are for inspiration only.
(No patterns given except where noted.)

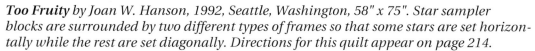

Too Fruity *by Joan W. Hanson, 1992, Seattle, Washington, 58" x 75". Star sampler blocks are surrounded by two different types of frames so that some stars are set horizontally while the rest are set diagonally. Directions for this quilt appear on page 214.*

Spring Baskets I *by Joan W. Hanson and Needle & I Guild Members, 1986, Seattle, Washington, 42" x 58".*
When these diagonally oriented blocks are set side by side, eight blocks are required.

***Spring Baskets II** by Joan W. Hanson and Needle & I Guild Members, 1988, Seattle, Washington, 58" x 58". When the same Basket blocks are alternated with a plain block, nine Basket blocks are needed. There is plenty of room for hand quilting in the plain blocks.*

Class Heroes *by Joan W. Hanson and the Fourth Grade Class of Jody Lemke, View Ridge Elementary School, 1992, Seattle, Washington, 62" x 76". This setting was designed to accommodate the blocks made by the twenty-six students in the class. Framing the blocks with corner triangles of two alternating colors forms a star around the heroes.*

Friendship Spools *by Joan W. Hanson and fifty-six quilter friends, 1988, Seattle, Washington, 54" x 60".*
In this side-by-side setting, the spool blocks alternate directions so that they appear to float on a
light background.

The Gilded Lily *by Joan W. Hanson, 1987, Seattle, Washington, 48" x 56". This quilt commemorates the Washington State Centennial. The four center blocks are named for the state of Washington. Since each one has twelve set-in corners, I only made four and decided on a medallion setting.*

Garden Girls *by Dorothy Everett Whitelaw and Joan W. Hanson, 1930s, 1989, Seattle, Washington, 41" x 45".
My mother made these blocks as a young girl. As a surprise for her seventieth birthday, I made her this quilt. I
chose a pieced sashing with pieced setting squares to set it, using soft shades of light blue so that the blocks
wouldn't be overwhelmed.*

Star Light, Star Bright by Joan W. Hanson, 1986, Seattle, Washington, 54" x 72". Scrappy pink stars and scrappy green Puss in the Corner blocks alternate to form this twinkling design.

Dutchman's Puzzle by Tecla Coffee Rippeteau, 1898, 75" x 88". The diagonal strippy setting adds movement to these blocks.

Loving Stitches

A GUIDE TO FINE HAND QUILTING

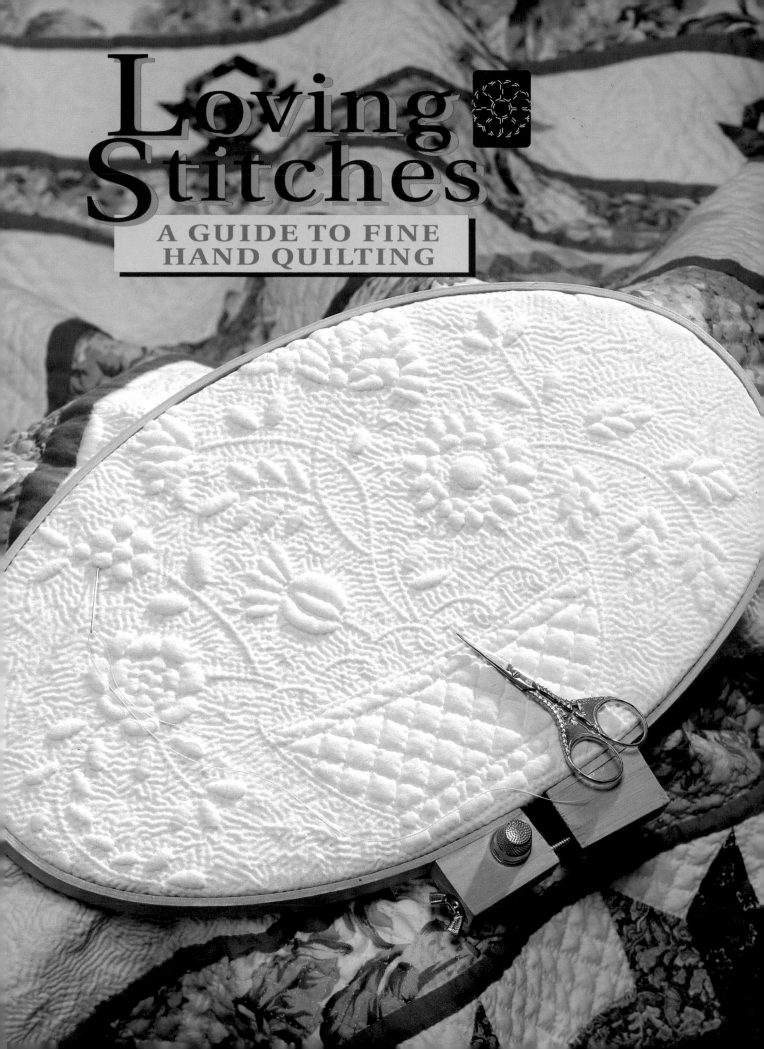

CONTENTS

INTRODUCTION

The day a quilt top was stretched on the quilting frame was always an exciting time for me as a small child. First, it meant all of the furniture in the living room was pushed back, making the room look large and impressive. Next, the long rails and stands were set up with the quilt stretched over them, making a perfect playhouse for me and my younger sisters. And, best of all, it meant that Grandma and some of the aunts would come by to "help with the quilting," sometimes for as many as three or four days in a row. What a treat it was to play with our dolls under the frame or quietly listen to the grown-up talk going on overhead. Occasionally, if we were very good, we could have a tea party under the quilt canopy.

As I grew older, I was glad quilting days came only once or twice each year. When I became a teenager, I was capable of and expected to help with the quilting or take over daily household chores. My older sister wisely adapted to quilting at the frame with the ladies, but I had a more difficult time. Sitting in a straight-backed chair with one arm on top and one underneath the quilt was uncomfortable for me. But worst of all was never knowing when the next prick of the needle would come, whether it would draw blood, or worse yet, whether the prick would hurt. All this time, I was trying to keep a thimble on my middle finger and remember to use it once in a while. All in all, quilting made me fidget and wish I were someplace else. Fixing meals, washing dishes, and folding laundry was preferable to quilting back then. Years later, I learned that there is more than one way to stabilize the quilt "sandwich" while putting in quilting stitches to avoid the dreaded needle pricks. Now I prefer quilting to any household chore!

Next best to the quilting is planning what to quilt. There is nothing like finishing a quilt top and standing back to take a look. It is time to savor and appreciate what you have done and look forward to the next process—quilting. Quilting adds a new dimension of texture and motion to the quilt, like adding the frosting to a cake.

Unfortunately, many quilters find it difficult to choose a quilting design. A debate begins within: How much is enough quilting? Are straight lines or curved ones better? Should I follow the outline of the pattern or impose a secondary design over the quilt surface? The debate goes on and on and sometimes the quilting never gets started, let alone finished!

The good news is there is no right or wrong way to quilt a quilt. You are the creator and can make up the rules as you go along. When my mother, grandmother, and aunts sat down to quilt a top, the decision was easy: Avoid the seams as much as possible, choose a quilting format that several people could easily work on at the same time, and select a design that could be completed in the shortest amount of time.

Before you begin, you will find that you have certain criteria for your quilting design. The focus of this chapter is to help you recognize your own criteria, to point out considerations, traditions, and options, and to help you with your decision of how to quilt your top. There is also lots of information about quilting tools, patterns, and different ways to stitch. Now there is no need to procrastinate any longer—just get started!

Jeana Kimball

QUILTING YOUR QUILT

When planning how to quilt your top, do not underestimate its importance! At one quilt show I attended—as is often the case—one quilt received more attention than the others. The pieced design was well done, but the quilting was extraordinary, the subject of many compliments. If the quilt had not been so finely quilted, it would not have been noticed by most visitors. To make your quilt a "show stopper," the quilting should enhance and add texture to the pieced or appliquéd design of the quilt top.

On a patchwork top, the quilting design should complement but not detract from the lines of the patchwork unless it is intended in the overall effect of the quilt design. Keep in mind that the quilting stitches and design will stand out more on areas of solid-colored fabric than the quilting stitches on patchwork areas. For example, the quilting on the body of a scrap bag–type quilt is not nearly as evident as the design chosen for a plain border that surrounds it. The viewer's eye will follow the patchwork pattern over the patchwork surface, but when there is a plain area, the secondary quilting design stands out more, inviting the viewer to study it. Quilting designs on these plain areas must be carefully chosen to complement the rest of the quilt top. Since many appliqué quilts have white or very light backgrounds, the quilting pattern choice is as important as the appliqué.

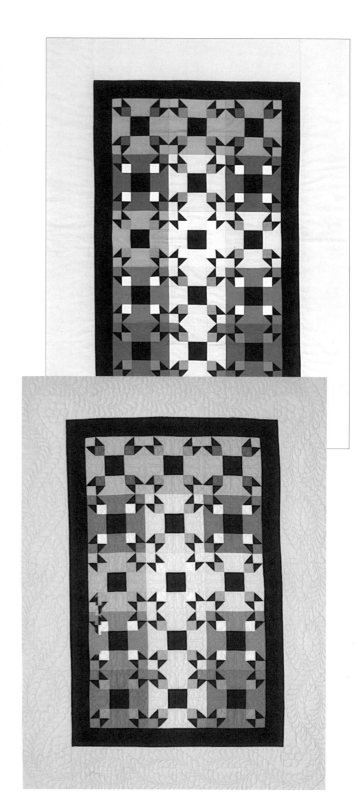

Rabbit's Paw, 1985 top, 1992 quilting, Jeana Jones Kimball and Loraine Hoyt Jones, Utah, 46" x 64". As can easily be seen when comparing the two photos of this quilt, the quilting is truly the "frosting on the cake." Notice how much texture and depth is added to this quilt once the quilting is applied. (Collection of Jeana Kimball)

PREPARING FOR QUILTING

Following is a checklist and some suggestions for preparing your quilt top so that the finished quilt will look its very best.

1. Clip stray threads. This step is especially important if a light fabric is used next to a dark one, and dark thread is used to sew the two together. If the thread strays to the "light" side of the seam, it will cause a shadow, detracting from the seam line.

2. Trim points and seams. Check the back of the quilt top for seam-allowance points that need to be clipped.

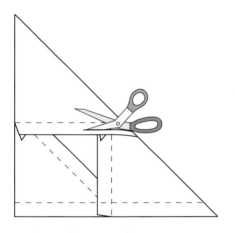

Trim all patchwork seams to an even width—usually ¼"—before layering and quilting the top.

The shadowing of a point or seam that should have been clipped or trimmed cannot be remedied once the quilt is layered and the quilting begins, so be sure to double-check for any protruding points or seams before layering your quilt.

If the two seam allowances within a given seam are not the same width, be sure to trim them evenly before quilting the top.

3. Press seams. On a patchwork quilt, the same seams on all blocks should be pressed in the same direction to give the surface a smooth continuity. All border seams should also be pressed in the same direction, either all toward the center or all toward the outside edges. Generally, seams are pressed toward the darker fabric to make them less conspicuous. Usually, a seam is stronger if both seam allowances are pressed together to one side of the seam. However, it is sometimes appropriate to press seams open. One example is in the center of a pieced Star block, where several points meet, or when multiple layers would make the quilt bulky. Another exception is when joining blocks and borders of an appliquéd quilt top, where background quilting will cover the quilt surface and you want the seams to be completely flat and unnoticeable. The seams joining the blocks of the Dresden Plate wall quilt on page 269 were pressed open.

Preparing Antique Tops

If you are planning to quilt an antique quilt top, there are a few additional considerations. If the quilt top is musty, air it out instead of washing it to remove the odor. Washing any antique quilt top before quilting may cause all the exposed seams to fray. Many antique quilt tops were pieced with very narrow seam allowances, some as narrow as ⅛" or ¹⁄₁₆", and even minor fraying could be disastrous. If laundering is necessary, do it after the quilting is finished and the seam allowances are protected and reinforced with the quilting stitches.

PLANNING THE DESIGN

Following is a list of factors to consider when making decisions about the quilting design for your quilt top.

What is the quilt's intended function? A utility quilt needs only enough quilting to hold the layers together securely, and it is possible that a tied finish would be sufficient. On the opposite end of the spectrum is a masterpiece quilt or your very best quilt. This type of quilt warrants lavish quilting, much more than is necessary to hold the layers together. The more quilted detail added, the better the "masterpiece" effect will be.

"When it comes to quilting, too much is not enough," is a quote I heard when I first started quilting. In studying old quilts over the years, I've come to agree; the ones I admire the most are usually very lavishly quilted. The next time you visit a quilt show, pay attention to the winners. I am sure you will find that they have much more quilting than is required to simply hold the layers together. If you plan to enter your quilts in competition, you will want to keep this in mind while you plan the quilting design and placement.

Is the quilt a gift? Who will use it and how? A majority of the quilts being made today are given as gifts. If the quilt is for a child, remember that the quilt will probably be used and loved with little respect for the time you spent quilting. Therefore, do not put so much quilting into it that you will be offended or unhappy if the quilt is "used up" in a few years.

Will the recipient (or spouse of the recipient) respect, appreciate, and take care of your gift? We have all heard horror stories of a lovely quilt gift being used as a dog bed, picnic blanket, or padding for moving furniture. Even though it sounds cold and calculating, consider how this quilt will be cared for in its new home.

How much time do you have to complete this quilt? Do you have a required completion date? If so, the decision of how much quilting to use may already be made for you. Many of us work best, or at least faster, under pressure, but only so much is possible in a given time period. Don't start a quilting format that you will be unable to complete in the time allowed.

Will more than one person work on this quilt at the same time? If it will be quilted by a group, plan a quilting format that several people can easily follow without having to shift seating positions. The fan pattern (page 239) is an old-time favorite for church-group quilters because the lines form an arc, and one person can complete several lines of stitching without having to physically move to a new position.

Do you enjoy the quilting process? We all have our favorite and least-enjoyed parts of the quiltmaking process. If your favorite is the rhythmic stitching of the layers together, quilt as densely as you like. When Marella Baker shared her mother's quilts with me, she said that as a girl she was embarrassed to invite her friends to her house because her mother, Florence Jane Stockdale, always had a quilt on the frame. The quilt frame took up the entire dining room and, in her mind, looked shabby.

As Marella grew older and wiser, she realized that the quilt on the frame served two important roles for her mother. First, it provided artistic expression while designing and drafting the patchwork and quilting patterns, and second, the hours her mother spent stitching at the frame were part of a healing process from some deep emotional pain.

Florence Stockdale's quilts are beautifully and densely quilted, with approximately fifteen stitches per inch. The "Winding Ways" quilt on page 271 was made by Florence for her second grandchild in 1930. If your least favorite part of quiltmaking is the quilting process, you may want to plan your quilt top to minimize quilting detail. Some ways to minimize the quilting are: (1) use fewer plain fabrics that would highlight quilting stitches, substituting two-color fabrics that look like solids from a distance; (2) plan narrow borders that do not require large amounts of quilting to fill them, and (3) choose quilting formats that avoid seams to make the stitching go faster. Outline quilting and straight-line quilting are two examples. See pages 235–36.

Types of Quilting Designs

There are three basic types of quilting designs from which to choose for each quilt you make.

Plain block designs

These designs are used to fill in large, plain areas, such as a plain block set between two patchwork or appliqué blocks in the quilt setting. There are many good reference books with quilting patterns and designs for these large areas. Check your local quilt-shop personnel for their favorite quilt pattern books.

Border designs

The purpose of border quilting is to fill plain border strips with interesting quilting detail that highlights and complements the pattern used in the body of the quilt. There are some good reference books and plastic templates available to make this selection process easier for the quiltmaker. For a discussion of how to make templates for transferring your design to the quilt top, see page 251. A selection of cable designs for quilting is shown on pages 262–63.

Fill-in designs

A fill-in design is used over the entire quilt top to tie together plain block designs with quilting on the patchwork blocks and border. Also included in this general heading of "fill-in designs" is quilting done on patchwork blocks to enhance the patchwork design. The most commonly used fill-in designs are cross-hatching or diagonal lines, but there are other possibilities. On pages 235–40, you'll find several familiar and some seldom-used fill-in patterns.

PLAIN BLOCK DESIGNS

Plain block designs were traditionally derived from nature themes. Leaves were gathered and arranged in a pleasing format and then traced for quilting. In *Quilts in America,* Patsy and Myron Orlofsky (New York: McGraw-Hill Book Company, 1974, p. 146) tell of one quilter whose "mother and grandmother used to pick sprays of oak leaves, ivy, clover, and thistles, bringing them home to study in the evening, before making the decision of which should form the basis for a quilting design." They also state that "acan-

thus leaves were a much-used motif by early American craftsmen. Many late eighteenth-and nineteenth-century houses have acanthus carvings around their fireplaces and on the inside of the front door."

Other American motifs with symbolic traditions, such as the pineapple, lyre, and eagle, were favorite quilting design inspirations. Very early whole-cloth quilts often started with a bouquet of flowers in a medallion quilting format.

The "rose" is a traditional English quilting motif. It often resembles an American Dresden Plate patchwork-and-appliqué quilt pattern. Plain spaces on the Dresden Plate quilt, shown on page 269, were filled with such a rose pattern. A template for that rose appears on page 264.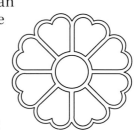

Another traditional English plain block design from the "North Country" is the True Lover's Knot. As you can guess from its name, the True Lover's Knot was frequently used on a wedding quilt. Other traditional wedding-quilt motifs include baskets of flowers for happiness, grapes symbolizing plenty, and a chain continued unbroken around the corners to give a long life, with horseshoes to bring good luck. (Rosemary E. Allan, *North Country Quilts and Coverlets from Beamish Museum County Durham* [Stanley, England: Beamish North of England Open Air Museum, 1987], p. 18) There are patterns for a Pineapple and an 8" True Lovers' Knot on pages 264 and 266.

One trick used by skilled quiltmakers to make their quilting motifs stand out is to stitch a second row, or double quilt, around the motif's outside edge. Stitch the second line (or double line) about ⅛" to ¼" away from the first line for the best effect of setting the motif off from the fill-in quilting format.

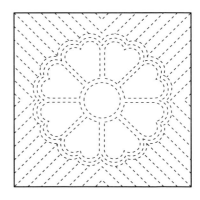

Double Quilting

When deciding whether to use a motif with rounded or angular edges for plain areas in your quilt, try cutting a template from paper for each type and placing it on the quilt top to see the mood each creates. Rounded shapes, such as the rose mentioned earlier, will soften sharp points of pieced designs, while angular shapes, such as a star, heighten the effect of piecework. In general, most quilting motifs have rounded edges to make the quilting stitch flow smoothly. See pages 251–52 for further information about template making and marking quilting designs onto the quilt top.

BORDER DESIGNS

Quilting designs used in border areas can make a quilt look well planned. If poorly done, however, they can cause the entire quilt to look unfinished. There are three types of border formats.

A fill-in format can be used to fill an area with straight lines of stitching. Below are two examples of diagonal-line designs for borders. Diagonal lines change direction along the border length on Quilt A and in the corner on Quilt B.

Quilt A

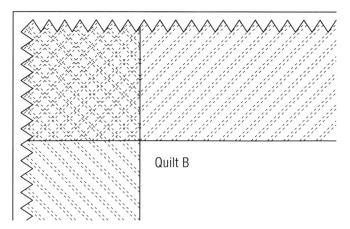

Quilt B

In studying antique appliqué quilts, I found that the entire surface of the quilt center was usually filled with one kind of quilting format, such as cross-hatching, but in the border, the quilting pattern changed to something else,

such as diagonal lines. It seems that the quiltmaker wanted to distinguish the border from the quilt center, even though the same background fabric was used throughout. This method was followed almost without exception on all antique appliqué quilts that I studied.

The advantage of using a fill-in border format is that corners are easily managed when straight lines are used. See the illustration below left for two methods of turning the corners with diagonal lines.

When using diagonal lines on a quilt, in the border or as a background fill-in, it is important that the diagonal lines change directions rather than running in one direction only around or across the entire quilt. If the lines are all stitched from the top right corner to the lower left corner, for example, it can cause the entire quilt to pull off-grain in the direction the quilting lines were stitched. This kind of distortion is common in needlepoint. Finished needlepoint can be blocked to square the shape, but a quilt cannot be rigidly blocked without breaking threads in some of the quilting lines. Therefore, when planning to use diagonal lines, remember to change directions at regular intervals, usually once on each side, as shown in the illustrations at left.

Most likely, the measurement of lines will not work out perfectly so that they all come together at exact required intervals when meeting to change directions. Some "fudging" is usually required to make lines match up. To mark lines for the plain border as shown in the illustration of Quilt A at left:

1. Start drawing lines in one corner and work toward the border center.
2. About 3"–4" before reaching the center, stop and measure the actual distance from the last line drawn to the center. If the measurement is not an even multiple of the spacing width you're using, start "fudging" as you mark each of the next few lines so that they are wider or narrower than the regular intervals to make up the difference.

By "fudging" a little on each line, you can "ease in" the marking so that the measurement works out correctly without being noticeable.

A second type of border design is a disjointed border, where a motif is repeated along the length but does not touch the motifs on either side of it. Again, corners are easily managed because the space between motifs can be expanded or shortened, depending on the area to fill. Below is a traditional Acanthus Leaf used in a disjointed border. The diagram shows how to turn the corner using this motif. A full-size pattern for the Acanthus motif is found on page 265.

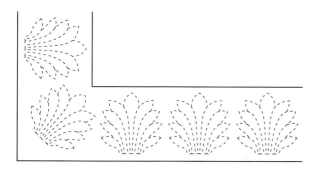

Evenly space large motifs in the borders.

The third and most common border design is the cable. This border must be planned in advance to make corners turn smoothly. However, that advance planning is not as difficult as many believe. There are many variations of this linked-type border. Eight examples of cables appear on this page and in template form on pages 262 and 263.

The shaded area on each template shows how to make a single template you can use to repeat the design along the border. Enlarge designs of your choice on a photocopy machine to a size that will fit your border. If there is any distortion of the design in the enlarging process, reshape it when tracing it to make your template. Use the notches to guide you in the placement of the design. The corner requires special attention.

At right, you will find six suggested strategies for making the corner design flow smoothly. Advance planning is required to make the motifs "land" at the corner in the proper position. Examine the photograph on page 234 for an example of a cable design that flows smoothly around the corner and one that does not. If the cable you are using is very large, or the repeats are some distance apart, such as 4" or more, you must measure the length of the border before beginning to mark and adjust the size of the template so that the repeats will work out correctly. You can use the enlarging or reduc-

ing features on a photocopy machine in five or ten percent increments to adjust the size of the template. For example, if you have a 6" repeat and the border measures 50" in length, adjust the template so that it repeats every 5" instead, and then ten repeats will work out perfectly.

Cable Border Designs

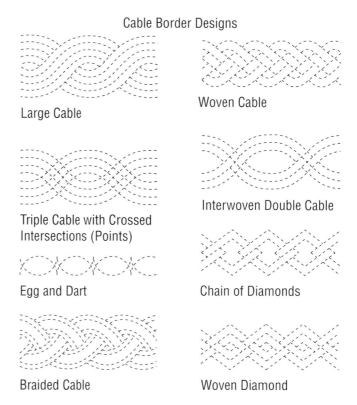

Large Cable

Woven Cable

Triple Cable with Crossed Intersections (Points)

Interwoven Double Cable

Egg and Dart

Chain of Diamonds

Braided Cable

Woven Diamond

Cable Corner Designs

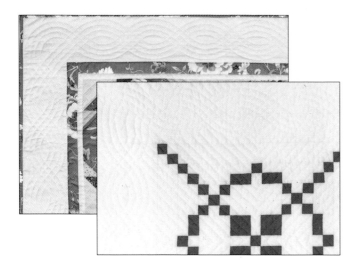

3. Draw a line through the center of the length of the master pattern. Next, draw a line that flows evenly through the divided sections.

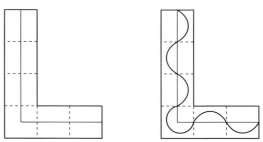

4. Use a light box to transfer the flowing center line to quilt-top border before joining the top with the batting and backing. See page 251 for light box suggestions.

5. Use an appropriate feather template from the three provided on page 265 to mark the feather along the flowing center line you have traced from the paper pattern.

When the repeats are closer together, adjust the cable so it is in the correct position to turn the corner. Begin marking at one corner; continue marking across two-thirds of the border. Then, stop and measure the distance to the next corner. Divide that number by the measurement of the repeat. Either expand or condense the marking of the template to "ease in" the extra inches. This method is successful, and because you begin adjusting early, the "fudging" is not noticeable. The quilted design is secondary, and you can easily disguise minor adjustments.

The feather is similar in nature to cable designs. You can plan feather borders to fill a very wide border, or straighten them out to fill a narrow border. A simple feather vine and an appliqué border are planned the same way.

1. Use butcher paper or smaller sheets of paper taped together to make a paper pattern that equals one-quarter or one-half of the quilt's finished border. (See illustrations at right.)

2. Fold paper pattern into equal sections. The folds divide the master pattern into sections that will be filled proportionately with the feather design.

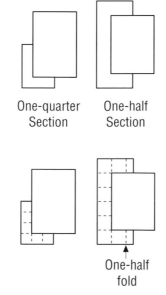

One-quarter Section

One-half Section

One-half fold

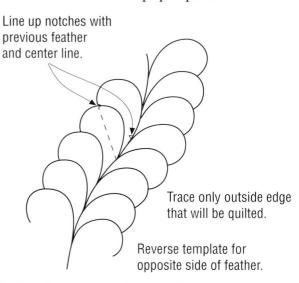

Line up notches with previous feather and center line.

Trace only outside edge that will be quilted.

Reverse template for opposite side of feather.

The feather can run in one direction continuously around the border or change directions at the corners. When changing directions at the corners, the feather line must stop halfway along the length of the border, making a broken feather border like those often used in Amish quilts.

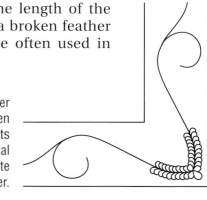

Begin making feather in corner. For broken feather arrangements such as this, individual feathers go in opposite directions from corner.

Trace the feather template directly onto the quilt top. You may mark the individual feathers along the premarked, flowing center line before the quilt is put on the frame, or you may mark it as you quilt, marking a few plumes at a time just ahead of your stitching. It is preferable to mark as you stitch, using light marking lines, since there is no risk of the lines fading or flaking off before you quilt them. Begin marking in the corner and continue around the quilt. Many variations in feather quilting are possible when you use a disjointed vine that turns up, down, and back on itself, as shown in the illustrations below and on page 234. Experiment with a few variations that fit your border before settling on the best one.

FILL-IN DESIGNS

Use fill-in designs to provide background fill between other quilted elements, or as unobtrusive quilting in areas where the patchwork design is meant to dominate. The eighteen designs that follow are fill-in designs. You can mark many of them with a ruler, but some must use a template. The shaded area in the accompanying diagram indicates the template shape. Notice how different the same pieced block looks with different fill-in quilting designs.

Quilting-in-the-Ditch

Quilting-in-the-ditch is a name used to describe an outline quilting method in which a quilted line follows the patchwork seams. It is stitched in the well of seam lines so it is almost invisible on the quilt top. Plan this type of quilting so you are stitching along the seam line on the side where there are no seam allowances. (Seams are pressed to one side in most patchwork piecing.)

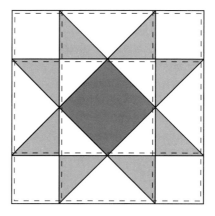

Quilting-in-the-ditch is done along patchwork seam lines where there are no seam allowances.

Outline Quilting

The quilted line in this method is placed approximately ¼" from the pieced seam line. There are two reasons for using this method. First, it allows you to avoid stitching through any seam allowances. Also, the quilted line stands out and adds texture to the patchwork surface by echoing the lines in the patchwork. Outline quilting is also often used around appliqué shapes.

Outline quilting ¼" from seam line echoes and enhances the shapes.

Straight-Line Quilting

Another kind of quilting line used to avoid seams is straight lines stitched through the center of patchwork pieces, making a simple grid across the patchwork surface. This kind of quilting is minimal and appropriate for utility-type quilts. Some quilt designs that lend themselves to this quilting format include Ocean Waves, Trip around the World, and Double Irish Chain.

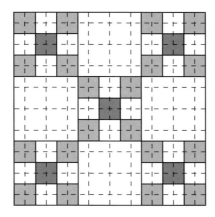

Straight-line quilting is a good quilting format for utility quilts.

Diagonal Lines

A diagonal-line format is most often used to fill border areas. Occasionally, it is used as fill-in quilting too. When using this format, be sure to change the direction of the diagonal lines at regular intervals to avoid distortion of the quilt. If you stitch diagonal lines across the surface in one direction only, the stitching will pull the quilt surface on the same slant, distorting the quilt so it is no longer square or rectangular.

Plan diagonal-line quilting so the lines change direction in order to avoid distorting the quilt top when stitching.

Echo Quilting

Echo quilting is traditionally used on Hawaiian quilts and occasionally on other appliqué quilts. In fact, it is often referred to as Hawaiian quilting. Quilted lines begin at the edge of the appliqué, and successive rows of stitching beyond the first row echo the shape. The rule-of-thumb for spacing this kind of quilting is a "finger's width" apart. However, any distance less than that is also acceptable. Spacing rows of stitching any farther apart than a finger's width may cause the echo effect to disappear.

Echo quilting echoes the appliqué shape in each successive row.

Cross-Hatching

Cross-hatching describes diagonal quilting lines that create squares on the quilt. First, mark a large X on the quilt top, drawing the lines from corner to corner across the center surface of a square quilt or a square portion of a rectangular-shaped quilt. Then, draw additional lines parallel to the center lines. The most commonly used distance between lines for this type of quilting is ½" to 1".

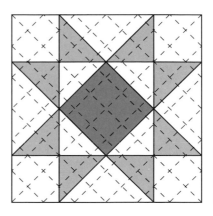

Cross-hatching covers the quilt with closely spaced rows of diagonal quilting stitches.

Straight-Grid Quilting

In this method, a grid of quilting lines is drawn on the quilt top with the lines parallel to the sides and the top and bottom edges. Stitching must be done on the straight of grain. You may find it more difficult to make even stitches that are visible in this format.

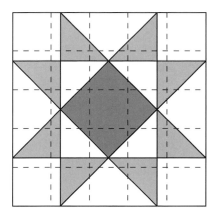

Straight-grid cross-hatching follows the lengthwise and crosswise grain of the quilt top.

Cross-Hatching Variations

Sometimes double lines, and occasionally triple lines, are used in cross-hatching to emphasize the quilting. Another variation is to create a "plaid" by varying the number of lines and the distance between them. This variation can either be set on the diagonal or in straight lines parallel to the quilt-top edges.

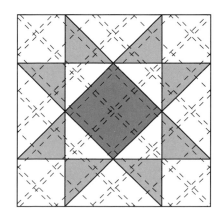

Closely spaced double rows for cross-hatching add more emphasis to the quilted surface. When double rows are used alternately rather than over the entire surface, a "plaid" quilting design emerges.

Uncrossed Lines

This method of fill-in quilting is done in a grid of straight lines, but none of them ever cross each other. When quilt blocks are placed next to each other and quilted in this format, it creates an interesting surface.

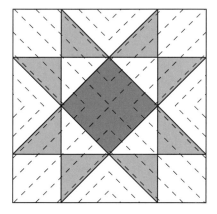

Uncrossed lines of diagonal quilting create an interesting surface texture.

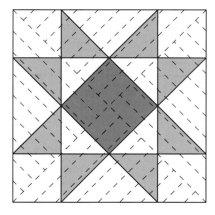

Changing the direction of uncrossed lines adds visual movement to the quilt surface.

Hanging Diamonds

This diagonal-line quilting format creates a diamond pattern on the quilt surface. It is an easy pattern to mark on the quilt top. First, draw parallel lines along the length of the quilt top and then draw a second set of lines on the diagonal across the surface. Space the lines in both directions the same width apart. Double lines, approximately ⅛" apart, were used to emphasize the format in the diagram.

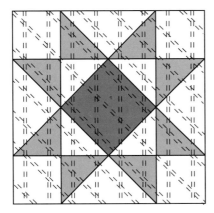

A hanging diamond quilting pattern is easy to mark on the quilt top.

Diamonds

In this format, a true diamond shape is created on the surface of the quilt.

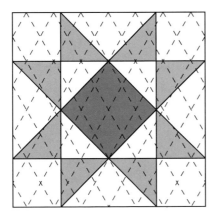

Trace diamond-shaped template in center of quilt, then extend lines to outer edges.

To establish the line spacing and the correct angle, draft a diamond-shaped template in the size desired. Then place the template in the center of the quilt top and trace. Using a yardstick, extend the lines to the outer edges of the quilt top. Continue drawing parallel lines across the

surface of the quilt, making the space between the lines the same as the length of one leg of the diamond.

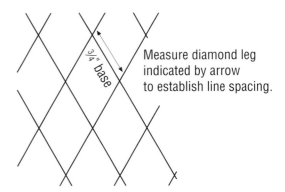

Measure diamond leg indicated by arrow to establish line spacing.

Wave or Herringbone

This is an undulating design based on an equilateral triangle (all three sides equal). Make a template for the design, adding a "base" to the triangle. The template used to mark the example shown has a ¾" base, making each row approximately ½" apart. For spacing rows farther apart, enlarge the base. Align the template by placing the base on the "valley" points of the previously marked line. Mark in one direction, working from the bottom to the top of the quilt top.

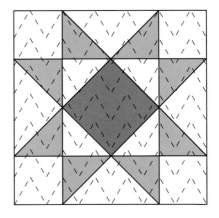

Wave or Herringbone

Basket Weave or Splint

In *Old Patchwork Quilts and the Women Who Made Them*, Ruth Finley says that the basket-weave design required so much accuracy in marking that it was very early discarded as too difficult to be worthwhile (Newton Center, Mass.: Charles T. Branford Company, 1929, p. 146). It is true that it is difficult to mark, but careful planning and marking make a very charming finished result. Choose one of the two variations that follow, leaving spaces and marking lines as indicated. This design looks especially nice on a basket or floral appliqué quilt.

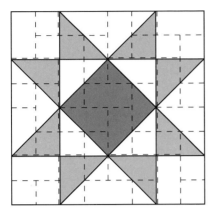

Marking the basket weave design requires patience and precision.

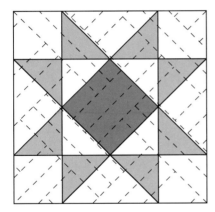

Basket Weave or Splint Variation

Fan

This design is frequently found on old scrap-bag quilts because this type of quilt was often the subject of a quilting bee. The fan format allowed many people to work at the quilting frame at the same time without having to frequently shift positions.

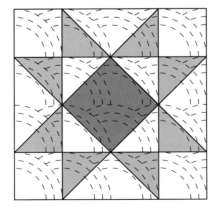

The fan shape was a popular quilting pattern on scrap-bag quilts finished at quilting bees.

The fan is also very easy to mark, using either a string and a pencil or a series of fan-shaped templates in increasingly larger sizes. To mark with a pencil and string, first tie knots along a length of string, evenly spacing the knots ½" apart. Then wrap the end of the string around a pencil with enough of the string let out to reach the first knot. Draw the arc. Then, unwrap the string to the next knot. Start in a corner of the quilt and mark along one side. Continue until you have marked the desired number of fan repeats.

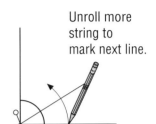

Unroll more string to mark next line.

Clamshell

Clamshell is a traditional fill-in design that gives a pleasing curved effect to a quilted surface. A half-circle template with a notch placed in the middle of the arc makes marking this design an easy task. A single arc or several connected arcs can be used as a template for this type.

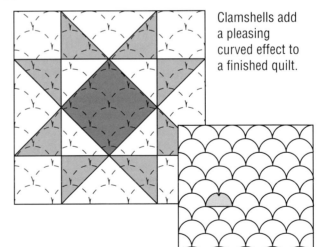

Clamshells add a pleasing curved effect to a finished quilt.

Teacup or Wineglass

In this design, a series of overlapping circles creates the optical illusion of a four-petal flower at first glance. At second glance, circles appear. Early methods of marking this format employed a teacup or wineglass, hence the name. Ruth Finley reminds us that older teacups had no handles to get in the way of marking (*Old Patchwork Quilts*, 1929, p. 142). The template used to mark this design has four notches at equal intervals around the circle. They indicate when the overlap is in the correct position.

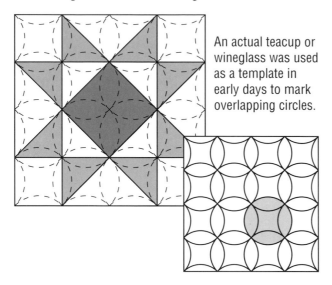

An actual teacup or wineglass was used as a template in early days to mark overlapping circles.

Stipple Quilting

Stipple quilting is for those who truly enjoy the quilting process. To stipple quilt means to cover the entire surface with quilting stitches so densely spaced that hardly a stitch can fit between quilting lines. One method of stipple quilting is to echo quilt with only 1/16" between each row of stitches. Another method is random stitching over the surface until the entire area is filled. Jeanne Huber quilted a meandering, wavy line throughout plain areas on the example shown below and then filled in with echo lines between the wavy lines. Stipple quilting is most often found on appliqué and whole-cloth quilts.

Continuous Line Designs

Continuous cable and vine and other similar patterns most often used to quilt borders can also be used to quilt the entire surface of a quilt. Judy Hopkins calls these designs two-way repeat designs and recommends placing them in vertical, horizontal, or diagonal rows across the quilt top. Eight of her original two-way repeat designs are included in her book, *Rotary Riot,* which she wrote with Nancy J. Martin. An example of one of her designs is shown below.

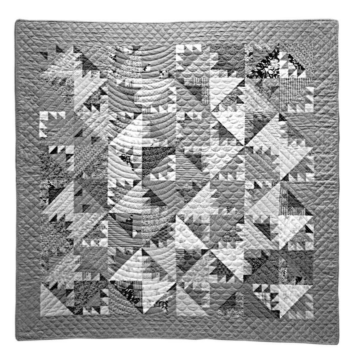

Consider using several of the different quilting formats discussed here on one quilt top. Nancy Martin's Kansas Troubles quilt was divided into several areas of unequal size, and a different pattern was used in each area. Straight-line, Clamshell, and Fan quilting patterns flow across the surface of this quilt.

Trapunto

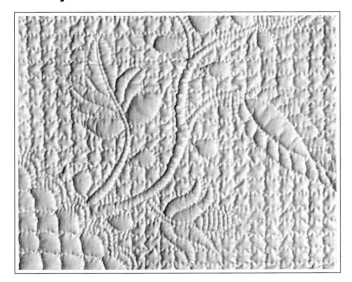

If you wish to add extra dimension and texture to a quilt, you may use a technique called trapunto or stuff work. In this method (also known as "Italian" quilting), two layers of fabric are sewn together along selected design lines to outline the area that will be stuffed. Then the area is stuffed with a lightweight padding or cording from the back of the quilt.

Trapunto was frequently used on whole-cloth "best quilts" in previous centuries. Traditionally, a fine, tightly woven grade of fabric was used for the quilt top, and backing was of a coarser, loosely woven quality, sometimes hand woven by the quiltmaker. After the outline of the stuffed design was quilted, the threads of the quilt backing were separated with a stiletto (a sewing tool with a pointed end about the length of a toothpick), and tiny bits of stuffing were inserted into the desired areas.

After the stuffing was completed, the backing fibers were manipulated back into place with the stiletto point so that little or no evidence remained to indicate how the stuffing was inserted. Some quiltmakers would cut a slit through the backing, insert the stuffing, and then use a whipstitch to rejoin the cut edges of the backing. This last method took less time but was considered less desirable because the quilt back was not as attractive.

To stuff narrow, linear, or curved areas, such as flower stems and basket handles, or self-contained designs with curved channels, such as a

True Lover's knot motif, (page 266), a slightly different method was used. First, the design lines were quilted through both layers of fabric. Then a blunt-pointed needle, such as a tapestry needle, was threaded with yarn and inserted into the stitched channel through the quilt backing. After guiding the needle and yarn through the channel, the needle was gently pushed out through the backing and the yarn cut at both ends. The yarn ends were manipulated into the channel, using the stiletto or the point of the needle. When carefully done, no sign existed of where the yarn entered or left the channel.

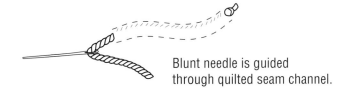

Blunt needle is guided through quilted seam channel.

Both of these trapunto techniques are still in use today. Another variation called shadow work is also popular. A sheer or transparent fabric is used for the quilt top, and the design areas are stuffed with brightly colored yarns. The color that shadows through the quilt top is a pastel version of the yarns used.

Jeanne Huber's beautiful "Bountiful Baskets" quilt, shown on page 267, is an excellent example of a modern quilt featuring trapunto. Some trapunto techniques she used are different than those described above but are more applicable for today's quiltmaking because the types of fabrics used by earlier quiltmakers are no longer available. Jeanne does the trapunto on the completed quilt top *before* layering the top with batting and backing. When you use her method, there is no need to make holes or cut slits in the quilt backing in order to add the stuffing.

1. For each design area selected for trapunto quilting, cut a piece of very fine, lightweight cotton fabric, such as lawn or batiste, making it slightly larger all around than the actual design motif.
2. Using a pencil, trace the selected design onto lightweight fabric and baste it in place on the back of the quilt top, with pencil tracing face up. It is important to note that if the design is asymmetrical, you will need to make a reverse tracing; otherwise, the fin-

ished design on the quilt top will be a reverse image of the design you've chosen.

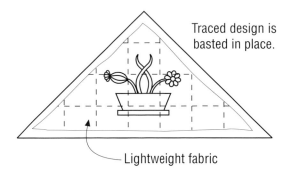

Traced design is basted in place.

Lightweight fabric

3. Thread a needle with thread in a light, but contrasting, color and tie a knot at one end. Insert needle on right side of quilt top at the end of one of the pencil lines so the knot will be on the surface of the quilt. Bring the thread to the wrong side of the quilt top and outline the trapunto motif with fairly small basting stitches. Do not make these stitches as small as your hand-quilting stitches. The basting stitches will be replaced with actual quilting stitches when the rest of the top is being quilted.

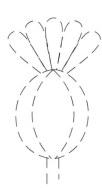

Basting lines that will later be replaced with quilting stitches.

4. To stuff basted areas, carefully make small slits in the lightweight fabric only. Then stuff small bits of polyester batting through the slits or draw cording through basted channels. Jeanne recommends using the points of a small pair of embroidery scissors to gently push the batting into place. Note that overstuffing areas with batting or using a yarn that is too large in diameter causes design distortion and a lumpy appearance. The goal is a softly stuffed look.

Use scissors points to stuff motif.

5. Loosely whipstitch the slits back together to keep the batting in place. In the case of cording, it is not necessary to manipulate the yarn ends into the channels, since the back of the work will be completely covered by the quilt batting and backing.

6. Layer the quilt top with batting and backing and baste. Quilt as desired. In the areas where the trapunto has been done, stitch just inside the basted lines. After these quilting stitches are completed, carefully remove the basting around each motif.

Tip When inserting cording in designs with tight curves or when turning sharp corners, bring the needle with yarn out of the channel on the wrong side of the quilt top. Reinsert needle in the same hole, leaving a small loop of yarn on the back side of the work. This technique makes it easier to insert the cording and helps prevent puckers and pulls on the surface.

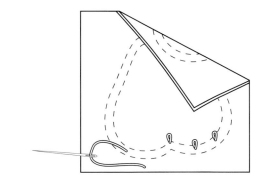

More Quilting Design Ideas

The designs discussed above are based on traditional quilt designs and sets, but what if yours is a nontraditional quilt? A quilt with no set format allows freedom to relay subliminal messages or to create additional illusions with the quilting stitches. This type of quilt lends itself to freehand drawn lines and shapes that need not follow or repeat a particular format. Since you have shown the creativity necessary to conceive and stitch such a quilt top, you will no doubt have ideas of how the quilting should enhance your design. Follow your instincts, on paper first, if necessary, and add the kind of texture and statement you want your quilt to convey.

Although many traditional designs are shown here, they may not be exactly what you want for your quilt. Don't be discouraged; there are design sources everywhere. You just need to educate your eye to find them in your surroundings. While working in downtown Salt Lake City, I spent one lunch hour walking up and down Main Street with my camera, looking for designs in the old buildings. To my surprise, I found many wonderful ideas that I could use for quilting patterns—lovely fruit and floral moldings and geometric shapes on windows and carved doors. Even ironwork motifs on fences and railings provided inspiration. Architecture where you live can provide some wonderful ideas for enhancing the surface of your quilt.

Quilt magazines and books are full of ideas. Antique quilts also contain a wealth of ideas. Many ideas being used today had their origins in an old quilt.

The patchwork quilt you are working on may also provide ideas. Why not repeat the patchwork grid of the pieced block in plain squares, or parts of it in the border? Consider using fabric from the quilt top as inspiration. If there is a floral arrangement or a geometric pattern in the fabric that you like, simply enlarge that design at the photocopy machine to create a quilting design for your quilt.

Last, but not least, many beautifully designed quilting patterns are available in books or as precut stencils. With all the resources discussed, you will surely find something that is just right for your quilt.

QUILTING TOOLS

Relatively few tools are required to quilt, but it is important that the tools you use are comfortable and appropriate for your stitching method. Because each quilter uses her hands differently, what is comfortable for one quilter might not be satisfactory for another.

Basic Supplies

Needles. When I took my first quilting class, one of the things I learned was that the needles called "betweens" are designed for quilting. Betweens are shorter, thicker, and stronger than regular sewing needles. I was also told that the accepted theory is "the shorter the needle, the smaller your stitches will be." In needle sizing, the higher the number, the shorter and thinner the needle.

What this means is that many believe a size 12 between is the best needle to use for quilting. However, since each quilter uses her hands differently, and threading a size 12 between might be difficult for those with "mature eyesight," no one needle size is exactly right for everyone. Experiment with several different needle sizes and brands until you find one that works best for you. As your skill develops, your needs may also change.

Recently, I have come to prefer milliners' needles instead of betweens for quilting. The extra length and thinner needle shank of the size 8 milliner gives me more control to manipulate the needle through the layers and causes fewer callouses on my fingers with the lap quilting method I use. In *Old Patchwork*

Quilts and the Women Who Made Them, Ruth Finley says that early quilters used a "fairly long needle" for quilting. She also says that a curved needle was even better for quilting and that "women always 'broke in' quilting needles by using them first on the coarser every-day patchwork. Those that became nicely bent were jealously saved for the curves and flourishes of the intricate needlework that was lavished on best quilts" (pp. 140–41). Other research supports Mrs. Finley's needle theory. For example, in *Traditional British Quilts*, Dorothy Osler says that when talking with one Welsh quilter, "she opened a piece of unfinished quilting, stored away since the 1930's to reveal a long Sharp needle still threaded to the last line of stitches!" (London: B.T. Batsford Ltd., 1987, p. 20).

I also suggest that you try different brands of needles to find one you prefer, because not all needles are equal from manufacturer to manufacturer, even though the size is the same. Recently, as an experiment, I supplied my mother, who quilts nearly every day, with nine different brands of quilting needles in her favorite size. The needles she tried were manufactured in England, Japan, Korea, and the United States. After trying them all, she decided on two brands that she liked best.

Needle Threader. If you have difficulty threading the small eye of the needle you use, a needle threader may be appropriate. Here are a few suggestions for the threading process that may eliminate the need for a needle threader.

1. Always thread a fresh cut. The thread fiber will be less worn at the newly cut end of an 18" length than on the end that has been exposed on the spool for a time.

2. Make the fresh cut on the diagonal instead of straight across because a diagonal cut is easier to thread through the eye of the needle.

3. Instead of trying to carefully guide thread through the needle's eye, try holding the thread stationary in your nonsewing hand, with only a little thread protruding between your fingers. Place the eye of the needle, which you hold with your sewing hand, over the thread. In other words, "needle the thread" instead of threading the needle. This technique is recommended for threading yarn into needles for crewel embroidery and needlepoint, but I have found it makes threading with all kinds of thread easier.

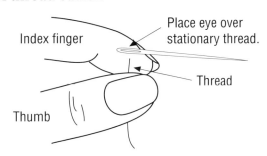

Index finger

Place eye over stationary thread.

Thread

Thumb

4. If you've tried all the tips above and are still having difficulty, try turning the needle around to thread the other side of the eye. During manufacture, the needle's eye is punched through the needle shank in one direction and the front, or first side, is larger than the back. The thread will fit through the front side much easier.

If all else fails, use a needle threader to save your sanity!

Scissors. Keep a 3"-long embroidery scissors handy for cutting thread. I wear mine on a 36"-long ribbon around my neck while quilting. That way, I never have to search for them when I need them. Another option is thread clips. Thread clips have short blades, and some types come with blunt ends so that you are less likely to slip and snip the fabric while clipping a thread close to the surface of the quilt.

Beeswax. Thread made specifically for quilting is thicker and stronger than regular sewing thread to hold the layers together. But, each time the thread is pulled through the fabric when making quilting stitches, the thread is worn a little. Wax thread before you begin to stitch, to retain the original strength of the quilting thread. As you stitch, the wax wears away, leaving the thread strong. Wax also helps prevent the thread from tangling. For the strongest wax application, pull the thread through a cake of wax to coat it. Then, place it between two sheets of typing paper and press with a warm iron. The wax will penetrate and coat the thread so it glides smoothly through quilt layers without shedding small chunks of wax as you stitch.

Beeswax is the traditional favorite for waxing quilting thread. However, if you are concerned about discoloration from the yellowish beeswax color, try using paraffin (canning wax) instead. Since paraffin is white, it won't discolor the thread or fabric.

Lamp and Magnifier. If you have difficulty seeing your stitching, especially when natural light is not available, invest in a good portable lamp. Some of the new quilting frames have a special fitting for attaching a portable lamp. Also available is a lamp that hangs from a strap around your neck to aim light directly onto your stitching.

Another wonderful stitching aid is a large magnifying device. These, too, can be worn around the neck to magnify the area on which you are working. Check the ads in quilting magazines for sources for these special lamps and magnifiers.

Thimbles. The thimble you choose depends on the way you quilt. Some thimbles have a brass fitting or built-in ridge on the top edge to give extra leverage to push the needle through the quilt layers.

Some quilters prefer to use the side of their thimbles and find traditionally shaped thimbles best for this method.

Others never become accustomed to wearing a traditional metal thimble at all and choose a soft leather thimble or a tailors' thimble. A tailors' thimble is metal with an open end so the finger protrudes slightly, allowing the quilter to use the finger while pushing the needle with the side of the thimble.

Some quilters do not use a thimble at all, but the majority agree that some kind of thimble is necessary if you plan to quilt for any length of time without causing extremely sore fingers.

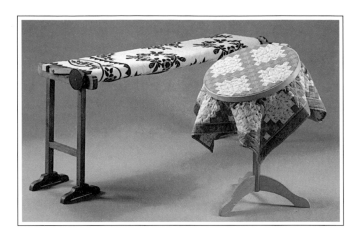

Quilting Hoops and Frames

Quilting hoops and frames are designed to hold the quilt layers taut while stitching. There are many brands and sizes available. Smaller hoops are hand-held and larger ones attach to a frame for supporting the hoop and quilt while working. Diameters of 16" and 18" are most frequently used for hand-held, hoop quilting. A 22" hoop with a supporting stand is standard. Large, round hoops are also available in a 29" size, but unless you have long arms, you may have difficulty reaching to the center of the hoop. Oval hoops are also available on stands, but some quilters find that tension is uneven across the quilt surface when stretched in an oval hoop.

Quilting frames are also available in a variety of sizes and types. The traditional quilting frame is constructed of four long rails supported by stands, or chair backs if you must improvise.

Attach a quilt to a frame in one of two ways. Some quilters prefer to layer and baste the quilt first—quilt top, batting, and backing—and then stretch and attach the basted layers all at once to the quilt frame. For this method, see pages 255–56. Others baste the layers together after attaching them to the quilt frame as follows:

1. Prepare backing, making sure it is "square," with all corners being true 90° (right) angles. Use a large, square rotary-cutting ruler or a T-square to check the corners. See "The Quilt Backing," beginning on page 252.

2. With the wrong side facing up and working from the center out to the corners, tack the two short sides of the quilt backing to opposite rails first. As an alternative, permanently thumbtack or staple strips of heavy muslin to the rails. (Long, folded strips of muslin are more durable than a single-layer strip.) Then pin the backing to the muslin strips, using quilting pins or safety pins.

Thumbtack or staple muslin strips to the rails.

Pin quilt to muslin strips.

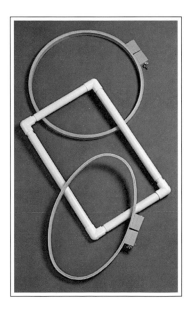

3. Place the remaining rails on the stands and then clamp the rails with the quilt backing to them.

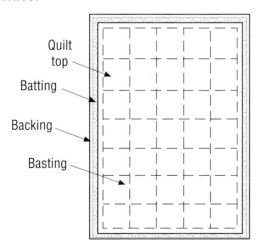

4. Stretch the remaining long edges of the quilt backing taut and attach to the side rails.
5. Layer the batting (pages 253–54) and then the quilt top on the backing and pull taut. Pin the layers together around the outside edges.
6. Baste the quilt layers together, using a very long doll-making needle (about 4" long). These needles allow you to make long basting stitches from the top. Place rows of basting stitches 2" apart in a grid over the entire quilt surface.

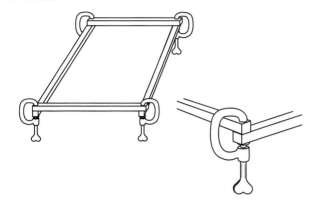

Quilt top
Batting
Backing
Basting

Step 6 is optional when you plan to quilt on the frame. I baste my large quilts as shown above for lap quilting and then remove the quilt from the frame.

Once stretched in this manner, you are ready to quilt, working from the outside edges toward the center. Stretching a quilt on a frame is particularly well suited to group projects because several people can quilt toward the center from all four sides at the same time.

After the top and bottom sides have been stitched an arm's length toward the quilt center, the quilt is ready to be "rolled." Release two clamps at one end and roll the quilted portion onto the rail, moving toward the quilt's center. Reattach the clamps and continue quilting.

Most quilting projects today are solo efforts, and many of us do not have houses large enough to accommodate the large quilt frame described above. Many quilt-frame manufacturers make different versions of a "full-sized" frame that does not take so much room. These frames are based on the width of the quilt but are only approximately 36" long. They fit very nicely in a sofa-sized space. The added advantage, besides the reduced size, is that all three layers are attached and rolled onto the quilt frame at once with specially designed rollers, and there is not as much "setup" time required. Prices vary, depending on the model you choose and whether the frame is made from hardwood or pine.

In addition to the traditional wooden hoops and frames, new, lightweight ones made of PVC plastic tubing are also available in lap and floor-frame sizes. Each easy-to-assemble frame is composed of four plastic tubes, which are connected with corner joints. The quilt is wrapped over each tube, pulled taut, and snapped in place with a white plastic "sleeve." Many quilters prefer them because they are relatively inexpensive, easy to handle, and easy to disassemble for storage or for packing in a suitcase. And, because the parts are interchangeable, it is possible to invest in small and large frames to make ones that will hold quilts of varying sizes.

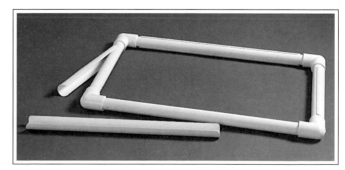

Tip

To make it easier to center the quilt backing on the rails, permanently attach two tape measures to each rail with the beginning of the tapes meeting at the center as shown.

1" mark
Attach two tape measures, end to end, to each rail.

Fold the quilt backing in half and mark the center on each edge. Then unfold the backing and attach it to the rails, lining up the center mark on each side of the backing at the point where the two tapes butt next to each other on the rail.

When you have finished attaching the backing to rails, all four corners should line up with the same number on the tape measure. If not, remove the backing and adjust as needed so they do.

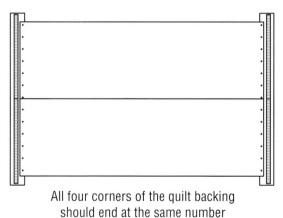

All four corners of the quilt backing
should end at the same number
on the tape measures.

Marking Tools

When marking the quilting pattern onto the quilt top, the marked stitching lines must be dark enough to see "a stitching distance" away, using a marking method that can be removed easily. First, choose a marking method. Choices include:

Lead Pencil. I think a fine, lightly drawn pencil line is the best way to mark a quilt top. It is important to use a light touch when marking the quilting lines. It is easy to go back over a line that is too light if necessary, but it is very difficult to remove a pencil line that is so dark that the lead is actually embedded in the fibers.

I recommend a mechanical pencil, size 0.5mm with a 2H lead. This is a hard lead, which breaks easily when too much pressure is used. That forces you to mark lightly to avoid breaking the lead. In addition, a mechanical pencil never needs sharpening, and the width of the line it draws is similar to the width of the quilting thread. A regular #4 pencil has the same lead hardness, but it loses its sharp point quickly so the pencil lines become thicker the longer you use it between sharpenings. It is easy to disguise a pencil line if the stitches hide all or half of its width but very difficult to hide if marked line is thicker than the thread is.

Colored Pencils. A variety of white, blue, silver, and yellow marking pencils are available for marking on dark fabrics when lead pencil marks don't show up. My favorite for this purpose is the Berol® Prismacolor, #916 Canary Yellow. This pencil has more wax in its lead than other colored pencils have, so it glides more smoothly and marks more easily on fabric. EZ marking pencils are also highly recommended. They are available in quilt and fabric stores and are available in pink, blue, and green. This type of pencil is thicker than a regular pencil and the point dulls faster. The lead in both the Berol and EZ marking pencil flake off fabric quickly and easily, and you can easily remove any residue with gentle laundering.

Soap Slivers. Soap slivers are also effective for marking on dark fabrics. The soap is easy to remove, but the marking edge dulls fairly quickly.

Chalk Markers. Chalk markers are also useful for marking on dark fabrics. The powdered, colored chalk is dispensed through a small container with a wheel at its base. A small amount of chalk is released as the wheel rolls across the fabric. It should be noted that colored chalk is sometimes difficult to remove from white and light-colored fabrics.

Water-Soluble Marking Pens. These pens are available in a variety of colors, including pink, blue, and purple, making it possible to mark clearly visible lines on a variety of colors. Instructions for removing the marks after the stitching is complete are included with each pen. *It is important to test these pens on your fabric first to make sure you can remove the color.* The ink is a chemical that may not react favorably with the fabric and batting combination you have chosen for your quilt.

Sometimes, the ink reappears months or years later, in the original color or as a brownish color. It is also important to note that pressing over marks made with these pens sometimes sets the color, making it impossible to remove.

Kitchen Products. Some old-time quiltmakers used cornstarch or spices to mark quilting designs. You may find the method just as suitable. To give it a try:

1. Draw the desired quilting design on heavy paper. A brown paper grocery bag is ideal.
2. Using an unthreaded size 90 or 100 needle on the sewing machine, stitch on the traced lines to make perforations in the paper.
3. Place the perforated-design paper on the quilt top and carefully rub cornstarch through the holes in the paper. When the paper pattern is removed, a trail of cornstarch remains on the quilt surface, outlining the design. Cornstarch works well on darker colors. For lighter colors, use cinnamon.

This marking method works best on a stationary quilt that is mounted in a frame. You simply brush or blow away the cornstarch or cinnamon when the stitching is finished!

Stiletto or Blunt Needle. Another marking method that leaves no colored mark on the quilt surface was used by old-time quiltmakers on their all-white, whole-cloth quilts. They used a blunt or pointed instrument to mark indentations in the quilt surface. This type of marking can be done only on a small area at a time and is most visible when a cotton or cotton-like batting is used in the quilt.

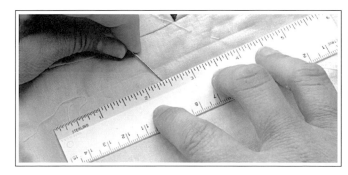

To duplicate this method:

1. Place quilt-design template or a ruler along the area to be marked.
2. Then run a stiletto, a tapestry needle, or the eye end of the quilting needle along the template or ruler, exerting enough pressure to make a visible indentation in the surface of the quilt.

Tip

If you choose to use a water-soluble pen, remove the ink as you go rather than waiting until all the quilting is finished. To aid in the removal of the markings, wash the completed quilt in cold water with gentle agitation, allowing it to sit in the water after agitation for twenty minutes. Flush the water from the machine and repeat the process three more times. Then flush the water and spin dry.

Obviously, this method allows you to mark a quilt without leaving permanent marks, but, if you mark more than you can stitch in a short period of time, the remaining marks will probably disappear.

Masking Tape. Masking tape is another alternative for marking straight quilting lines without leaving a visible mark on the quilt top. Tape in widths of 1", ¾", and ¼" are most useful for this type of marking.

Place a ruler on the quilt top to locate the line to be quilted. Lay the masking tape alongside the ruler on the quilt top. Use the ¼"-wide tape when you wish to mark single straight lines or double lines, spaced ¼" apart. The ¾" and 1" widths are good for marking crosshatching.

Use this method of marking in small areas and remove tape at the end of the day when you stop quilting. Leaving tape in place for long periods of time might leave a sticky residue that is difficult to remove and that will pick up dirt and lint. Avoid using old masking tape as adhesive becomes gummier with age and often leaves a residue.

MAKING TEMPLATES

After you choose the quilting format you wish to use, you may need a template or stencil to transfer the quilting design to the quilt top. Template plastic, X-ray film, or clear plastic are suitable materials for templates. Lightweight cardboard is also appropriate, although you would not be able to see through the cardboard to check correct placement. Pictured are cardboard templates that belonged to Marie A. Ehst, a quiltmaker from the 1930s.

Make templates or stencils for the section that will be repeated. Cut the outside edges of the template the actual size. To mark detail lines inside the template, use a tool designed for cutting out pencil-line widths to indicate stitching lines. An electric hot pen can be used to "melt away" the strategic marking areas on plastic templates. However, be careful not to melt away too much of the plastic. A double-bladed X-acto knife can cut a pencil-line width also, but be careful to cut smoothly. As with any new technique, practice improves your skill, so work slowly and patiently and don't give up if your first try is not perfect when using these tools.

You can use a template or stencil to mark fairly simple repeat designs, but if the design you choose is more complex, such as a floral arrangement with many flowers and leaves, marking with a light box may be a better choice. Office and architectural supply stores usually stock light boxes. You can also make your own.

To make your own light box:

Separate your dining-room table as if adding an extra leaf. Then place a piece of glass, plastic, or Plexiglas over the opening. (I use the removable glass from a storm door.) Have the glass (or glass substitute) cut to fit your table at a glass shop, if desired, and frame or tape the edges to avoid cut fingers. For an added fee, you can have glass edges finished to eliminate the sharp edges. Once the glass is in place, position a table lamp on the floor beneath it, and you have an instant light table. If your table does not separate, use two card tables or end tables of the same height to create a support for the glass.

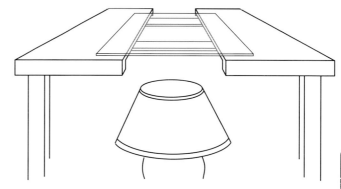

Make your own "light box."

To use a light box, prepare a master pattern of the design on plain paper. Tape the master pattern to the light-box surface, layer the portion of the quilt top to be marked over the master pattern, and use a gentle touch to trace the quilting lines with the marker of your choice. It is a common tendency to mark more heavily when using a light box because you cannot see the line you are drawing as easily with the light behind it. Occasionally, slip a white piece of paper between the light box and quilt top to check the lines and to make sure you are not tracing too darkly or too lightly.

MARKING THE QUILT TOP

To mark quilting lines on a quilt top, choose one of the following methods.

Mark the entire quilt top *before* layering with the batting and backing. This method takes more time at the beginning, but it allows stitching to progress without interruption. If you plan to quilt in a hand-held hoop or to lap quilt without a hoop (pages 259–61), some of the premarked lines may wear off before you are finished, and some remarking may be necessary.

Mark the quilting lines as you go. A few of the marking methods described on pages 248–50 can be used only in this way. I prefer to mark as I quilt because I can use very light marking lines, making it easy to make changes as the stitching continues.

The third method is a combination of the above two methods. Plan and mark continuous areas, such as borders, in advance. Mark complex motifs in plain areas in advance over a light box and then mark fill-in formats as stitching progresses.

THE QUILT BACKING

The back of a quilt can add another dimension or point of interest to your quilt design. A very plain backing shows off quilting stitches. There are several factors to consider when choosing backing.

Selecting a Backing

First, do not sacrifice quality or cut corners when choosing fabric for backing. The strength of a quilt is dependent on both the front and the back for support, and each should wear at the same rate.

Second, keep in mind the overall color tone of the quilt top and choose backing fabric in the same value range. For example, a light backing is more appropriate for a white quilt than a dark one. A darker-colored backing may shadow through to the right side of a light-colored quilt. In the case of a dark quilt, a dark backing and batting are more appropriate because there can then be no risk of white filling bearding through the quilt surface. It also eliminates shadows on the back of the quilt.

Beginners may want to choose a quilt backing that is a printed fabric. Quilting stitches do not show up as well against a printed surface, helping to disguise less-than-perfect stitches.

Another reason to choose a printed backing is to disguise several different colors of quilting thread. Some quiltmakers prefer to match the color of the thread to the individual patchwork pieces so that the quilting stitches are unobtrusive. A printed backing helps to camouflage the different colors of thread.

Some quiltmakers like to add a "surprise" to the quilt back by piecing together large leftover scraps from the fabrics used to make the quilt top. When planning this type of quilt back, remember that you will be quilting over the seams on the back. Quilting through several layers of fabric is always more difficult than quilting through only two layers.

Preparing the Backing

To prepare the backing fabric, preshrink it first and then press to remove all wrinkles and fold lines. Even though the backing may be stretched taut on the quilt frame, fold lines and major wrinkles will not "ease out" with quilting. If you don't press first, they will become a permanent part of your quilt!

Sometimes it is necessary to piece the fabric to make it wide enough to match the quilt-top dimension. There are two basic ways to do this. One method is to piece two lengths of fabric together, press seam open, and then center the seam on the quilt top. Trim the same amount of excess from both sides, leaving an extra 3"–4" all around. The extra is "insurance" in case the layers shift toward one side or corner during quilting.

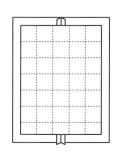

Center quilt and trim away any excess, leaving 3"–4" all around.

You can also piece a quilt backing in three sections, using one full width of fabric and splitting the second width down the center for the remaining sections. Press the seams open; then center and trim as described above. Make sure that you center the quilt top on the pieced backing so each side section of the backing is the same width.

Both of these methods distribute pieced fabric evenly on the quilt back.

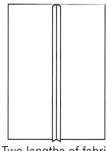

Two lengths of fabric seamed in the center

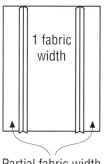

Partial fabric width

BATTING

Past generations had only two choices—cotton or wool—for filler in the quilts they made. Cotton batting required careful carding and cleaning to remove the tiny, hard cottonseeds. Wool batting required extensive cleaning to remove the dirt and animal oils. Today, no such labor is required for batting preparation, but it's important to know about the types available and their effect in a finished quilt. Since there are so many different manufacturers and each one makes several different batting products, the choices can be confusing. Following is a discussion of batting types available, but it's a good idea to experiment until you find the particular brand and type you prefer.

Cotton Batting

Magnificent antique quilts that are heavily quilted most often contain 100% cotton batting. Quilts with cotton batting have a very desirable soft look and feel. These quilts are cool in summer because the natural fibers are able to "breathe" and are warm in winter due to the density of cotton batting. Batting of the same heirloom-quality, 100% cotton fiber is still available. However, this kind of batting must be closely quilted with only ½" to 1" between stitching lines to keep fibers from shifting or migrating when laundered. If you enjoy the quilting process, you will probably like this type of batting best. It is my personal favorite.

Contemporary batting manufacturers have recognized quiltmakers' desire for the look of a cotton batting but also realize that many of us do not want to quilt so densely. As a result, they have developed a batting that is 80% cotton and 20% polyester. Quilting stitches can be spaced as far as 2" apart with this batting. Some manufacturers have recently perfected a manufacturing process for cotton batting that locks fibers in place by bonding the surface with a glaze. Quilting at 2" intervals is also appropriate with this batting.

Polyester Batting

Many quiltmakers do not enjoy quilting through a cotton batting because the cotton fibers are compact and require more force to manipulate the needle through the layers. To solve this problem, batting manufacturers now produce a lightweight polyester batting. This thinner polyester batting is easy to needle and has a similar look to cotton batting. However, polyester fibers tend to beard or pill. Some brands are worse than others. If the polyester fibers are heat bonded rather than chemically bonded, the batting is less prone to bearding. Check the packaging for the method used in bonding the fibers.

If you prefer a full or puffy look to your quilt, regular-weight polyester batting is the best choice. My local quilt shop sells more of this type of batting than any other because many quilters prefer the look of a down-filled quilt. When using a standard-weight polyester batting, you can place quilting lines as far as 3" apart.

Other Batting

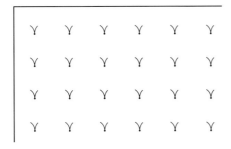

Comforter Batting. Batting manufacturers produce a thicker polyester batting that is suitable for this fuller look. Comforter-style quilts are usually tied rather than quilted. The ties or tacks can be placed at 4" intervals on comforter-weight batting.

Note: Tying a quilt is a speedy alternative to hand quilting.

Needlepunch. For clothing, a polyester batting called needlepunch is available. The density of this batting gives warmth with minimum bulk. Many prefer it for quilted clothing construction.

Silk and Wool. Silk and wool are other natural fibers that are made into batting, but they are expensive and usually more difficult to obtain. Check ads in quilting magazines for sources and availability.

Wool is very easy to needle but has a tendency to beard. Encase wool batting in a cheesecloth casing to keep the bearding to a minimum. Wool batting provides warmth and a soft look like cotton batting.

Silk batting is very fine, extremely lightweight, and easy to quilt. However, it is very expensive and much more difficult to locate. Silk batting is desirable in clothing because it offers texture and warmth without added weight.

Some of the above-mentioned batting types can be split into two layers for a still flatter look. Wall hangings and clothing are good candidates for split battings. Polyester fleece, available by the yard, is another option for a smooth, flat batting. Some quilters prefer it for wall quilts.

Batting is available in various sizes from crib- to king-size. Be sure to check the package for the appropriate size before purchasing.

PREPARING TO QUILT

First, mark all or part of the quilt top for quilting, choosing the appropriate method from those listed. See pages 248–50 and page 252.

Next, prepare the quilt backing (pages 252–53), making sure it is 3"–4" larger than quilt top. Excess backing is necessary for the following reasons:

1. When quilting on a full-size frame, you can tack or pin excess backing to the long rails. If there is any pulling or stretching when attaching the quilt to the rails, the fabric will pull around the tack or pin, leaving a small hole in the backing. When the backing is purposely cut larger, you can pin through the excess and cut away the holes after quilting is complete and before binding has been added.

2. When using quilting frames with rollers, all three layers of the quilt are rolled into the frame at the same time. If the top shifts to one side or the other during this process, the excess backing is there to accommodate the shifting.

3. When hoop or lap quilting, you can wrap the excess backing over to the front of the quilt top and baste it in place to prevent the quilt and batting from fraying during quilting.

Batting should be cut larger than the quilt top for the same reasons. Occasionally, you will need to splice batting to make it large enough for the quilt you are making. Splice as you layer the batting on top of backing. First, butt the two pieces of batting next to each other; then, using white thread and a herringbone or ladder stitch, join the two pieces together.

The method for layering the quilt "sandwich" when quilting on a frame is described on pages 246–47. However, many quilters prefer to hoop quilt or lap quilt. When using one of these quilting methods, prepare the quilt sandwich as follows, working on a large carpeted or padded surface, if possible. It is easier on your back and knees if the surface is waist level, but the floor is acceptable, although much less comfortable for long periods of work.

1. Place the prepared backing right side down on the work surface, smoothing out wrinkles as you work. Secure backing to the padded surface with pins or masking tape to keep it stretched smooth, taut, and straight, with all four corners at 90° angles.

2. Smooth quilt batting in place on top of the backing, splicing the batting if necessary to make it large enough, as shown below left. Remember that the batting, like the backing, should be larger than the quilt top to allow for some shifting during quilting.

3. Smooth the quilt top in place on top of the batting, carefully centering it. Pin all three layers together at 6" to 8" intervals around outside edge, making sure that there are no wrinkles in any of the layers and that the top is smooth and flat.

4. Baste layers together with long stitches, using a 3"- to 4"-long needle. Look for long needles in quilt and fabric stores that sell doll-making supplies. Space basting stitches 2" apart across the width and length of the quilt top.

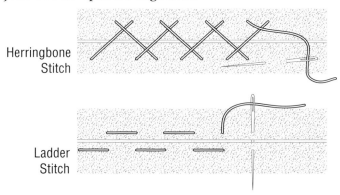

Herringbone Stitch

Ladder Stitch

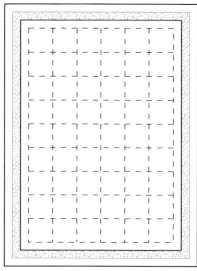

Baste the layers together with a long doll-making needle.

I lap quilt without a hoop, so whenever I baste a large quilt, I stretch the layers on a full-size quilt frame and invite my quilting friends to a basting party. In a few hours, the entire quilt is basted and I serve lunch as a thank-you, knowing full well that my guests will invite me to return the favor. If you do not own a full-size frame, borrow one from a friend or fellow guild member, or better yet, encourage your guild to invest in a full-size frame to loan or rent out for basting parties.

5. After completing the basting, remove the quilt from the work surface or the quilt frame. Then fold the excess backing and batting onto the quilt top and baste in place. This step creates a temporary binding that keeps the batting in place and prevents the edges of the quilt top from fraying while you quilt. At this point, you're ready to begin quilting.

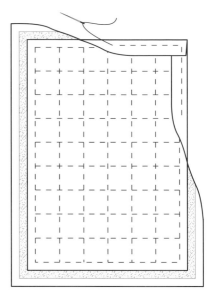

Fold excess backing over raw edges of quilt top and baste in place.

HAND QUILTING

Hand-Quilting Standards

One mark of beautiful quilting is short, evenly spaced stitches. However, when you first begin hand quilting, it's more important to concentrate on making even stitches that follow the quilting design without "wobbling" off the marked line. "Even" quilting stitches are also evenly spaced; that is, the length of the stitch is the same as the length of the space between stitches. Short stitches come with practice as you become more comfortable with the process and develop your own stitching rhythm. Needle size (page 244) can also affect the length of your stitches.

One way to measure your progress is to count your stitches. Place a ruler on the quilt top along a quilted line and count the stitches in an inch. Seven to nine stitches per inch is the standard for good-quality quilting. Excellent quilting has nine to twelve stitches per inch. Any more than that per inch is exceptional! With lots of practice, your quilting stitches will be equally beautiful on the front and back of your quilt. Master quilters make such even stitches that it's impossible to distinguish the back from the front of a whole-cloth quilt.

Hand-Quilting Thread

Hand-quilting thread is heavier than regular sewing thread because it must be strong enough to keep layers together and to withstand wear if put into daily use on a bed. Check the label to be sure you are buying "quilting" thread. Choose from 100% cotton quilting thread or cotton-wrapped polyester quilting thread.

I prefer 100% cotton thread because all of the components in my quilts—quilt top, batting, and backing—are also 100% cotton. However, many quilters prefer cotton-wrapped polyester because they believe it is stronger. Try both types in different brands and choose your favorite.

Thread the Needle and Knot the Thread

The process of pulling the thread through all the layers wears on the thread. Using a short length keeps this wear to a minimum. Waxing the thread, as discussed on page 245, also minimizes excessive wear and helps the thread glide through the quilt layers more easily. See pages 244–45 for information on quilting needles and needle-threading tips.

To thread your needle, cut an 18" length of quilting thread. Next, knot the thread end. Tie the knot securely so that it doesn't come undone. It must also be small enough so you can "pop" it from the surface of the quilt down into the batting. That way, it doesn't show on either the quilt top or the backing.

To make a quilter's knot:
1. Hold the threaded needle in your right hand, between thumb and forefinger. With the thread tail in your left hand, point needle toward the thread tail.

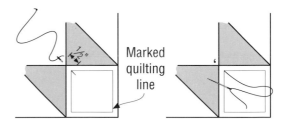

2. Grasp the thread tail in the fingers holding the needle and use the left hand to wrap the thread around the needle two or three times.
3. Hold the wraps with the right thumb and forefinger and pull the needle through the wraps with the left hand. Hold wraps tightly until you have pulled the thread all the way

through. This procedure should result in a small, firm knot, similar to a French knot. Don't be concerned if there is a bit of a tail beyond the knot; cut it off close to the knot.

Tip   Consider threading as many as ten needles at a time, before a quilting session, to save time and frustration.

Bury the Knot

To begin stitching, you must bury the knot by "popping" it into the batting layer.

1. Insert the needle in the quilt top approximately ½" ahead of where you wish to begin stitching. If possible, insert the needle in a seam line to anchor it more securely. Push the needle point between the quilt top and batting and bring it out on the marked quilting line.

2. Give a gentle "tug" on the thread to pop the knot below the surface. If the knot pops down and then back out again, start over, this time aiming deeper into the batting where the knot will become entangled in the fibers. Then tug more gently to pop the knot inside.

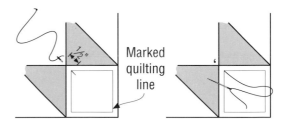

Marked quilting line

3. If a thread protrudes on the surface after popping the knot, insert the needle between the quilt layers and rotate it toward and past the tail to catch the tail and pull it between the layers. I call this "swishing."

With needle between the layers, rotate it from side to side to pull the tail between the quilt layers.

4. Stitch on the marked quilting lines, using one of the quilting methods described on pages 259–61.

5. When you reach the end of the thread or the end of the stitching line, tie off the thread with another knot. I recommend the colonial knot.

The colonial knot is especially good for quilting because it is an elongated knot that is easier to pull through the quilt layers than a rounder, heavier knot.

To make a colonial knot:

1. Pull the thread taut toward your body with your free hand.

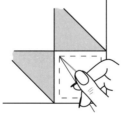

2. Point the threaded needle toward the quilt top, keeping it parallel to thread.

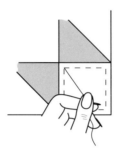

3. Angle the needle over the top of the thread and wrap once around the needle point.

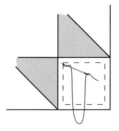

4. Use your free hand to wrap the thread around the needle point a second time.

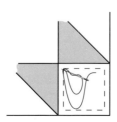

5. Reinsert the needle point into the same hole. Then run the needle through the layers for about ½" and pull it through until the knot is lying on the quilt surface where the needle and thread entered.

6. Give a tug to the thread, and the knot will "pop" below the quilt top and into the batting. Snip the thread, leaving a short tail, and use the needle to "swish" the tail into the batting as described on page 257.

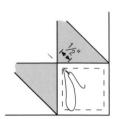

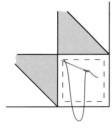

Tip   Some quilters prefer quilting from both ends of the thread rather than beginning with knotted thread. To try this method, insert the needle in the quilting line you wish to stitch and pull it through so that half of the thread length extends on each side of the initial stitch. Then quilt along the line until you run out of thread; knot and bury the knot as described above. Remove the needle and thread it with the remaining half of the thread and quilt in the other direction. In this case, you can start with a 36" length of thread.

Quilt from the center of the thread length to each end and bury the knot.

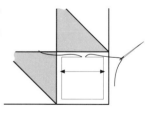

The Quilting Stitch

The quilting stitch is a short, evenly spaced running stitch, which is made through all three layers of the quilt to hold them together and to add depth and surface design to the finished quilt. How you prepare the quilt for quilting determines the method of stitching. Experiment with the three basic methods described on pages 259–61 to find the one you like best.

QUILTING WITHOUT A HOOP

Lap quilting is done without a frame or hoop. Many quilters favor this method because the work is very portable and they can quilt in a variety of positions—on the floor, at a table, in an easy chair, or a car. Most important, they find it easier to take small stitches when they use this method. In contrast, it may be more difficult to quilt in straight lines. In addition, when not stretched taut, the layers can shift, resulting in permanently stitched-in wrinkles on the back of the quilt. If you have a lot of hand-sewing experience, you might find this method best suited to your stitching style and skill level.

To lap quilt:

1. Layer and baste the quilt sandwich as shown on pages 255–56.
2. Place one hand underneath the basted quilt and the other on top, smoothing the front and back surfaces so there are no wrinkles. Repeat this process every time you begin a new line of stitching.

   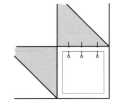

   To ease in any fullness you find or to prevent it from developing while you stitch, place a few straight pins through layers across the line about to be quilted.

   The pins are, in essence, a substitute for the quilting frame or hoop that holds the layers together. It's not necessary to pin on every line of stitching, only where there are not yet any other lines of quilting to help stabilize the layers. Don't neglect the pins; they are a necessary supplement to the basting that is already in place.
3. Next, with your free hand, grasp the quilt in the area to be stitched with the thumb on top and the other four fingers underneath as shown (top right). Hold the quilt this way when working on a small quilt or when working near the outer edges of any size quilt. (When working in center areas, the thumb will be underneath the quilt with the other four fingers and will grasp a "handful" of quilt. In middle and bottom right photos, the thumb is underneath the quilt.)

4. Bury the knot as described on pages 257–58. Insert needle into the quilt a stitch length away from where the needle is coming out. As the needle goes through the layers, it slants back toward the thread. This angle helps you make stitches on the quilt back the same length as the front.

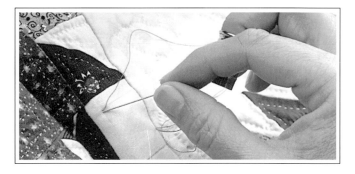

As the needle comes out on the back, move your fingers out of the way to avoid being pricked. Half of the length of the needle should be pushed through to the quilt back.

Turn the needle horizontally and pull it back toward the first stitch, dragging the needle point along the backing fabric and following the "backing up" with the fingers underneath the quilt.

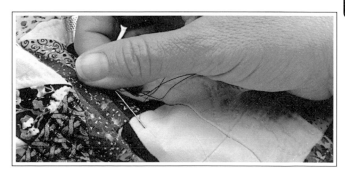

When the needle reaches the spot where you want it to come back through the top, push the needle point with the fingers underneath and at the same time, use the fingers on top to pull needle upward. Strive to make the needle come as straight up (vertically) through the layers as possible to ensure evenly spaced stitches.

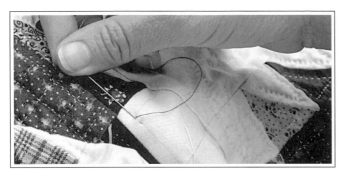

To make the next stitch, repeat the above process, putting as many stitches on the needle as is comfortable for you before pushing needle and thread through with the thimble on your middle finger.

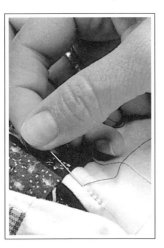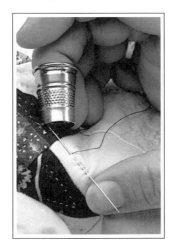

QUILTING IN A FRAME OR HOOP

The stitching method most commonly used when quilting in a frame or hoop is called "rocker" quilting. To stitch this way, you must hold quilt layers taut and smooth. Using this method, you guide the needle through the quilt layers with the thimble in a rocking motion. A short "between" needle is easier to manipulate with the rocker method. A long needle was used in the following photos for better visibility.

To rocker quilt:

1. Stretch the quilt layers taut in a frame or hoop.
2. Work with your sewing hand on top and your free hand beneath the quilt. Use the thumb and index finger on your sewing hand to place the needle in the correct position to make a stitch (photo below), having your middle finger with the thimble ready at the eye end of the needle. The eye end will rest in an indentation in the top of the thimble after you have begun the first stitch.

3. Begin to load short, evenly spaced quilting stitches onto the needle. As the needle starts through the layers, let go of the needle with the thumb and index fingers and use the thimble finger to push and guide it through in a "rocking" motion (photos below).

4. As soon as you feel the needle point coming through on the back side of the quilt (usually with the longest finger of the hand underneath the quilt), release the pressure of the thimble finger. Then use the fingers underneath to guide the needle, pushing it back up through the layers to the top of the quilt in the correct position.

5. As you guide the needle to the top, apply pressure with the thimble to help force the needle through the layers. At the same time, use the thumb of the sewing hand to apply downward pressure on the top of the quilt to assist in forcing the needle point as straight up through the layers as possible.

6. When the point comes back through the quilt top, use the thimble finger to push the needle forward a stitch length. Then apply downward pressure with the thimble to push the needle underneath, setting up the "rocking" motion again to accumulate several stitches before being pulled all the way through the quilt layers (photos below and top right).

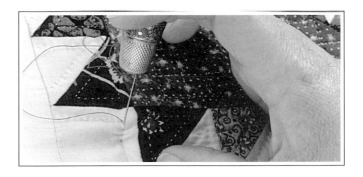

STAB STITCHING

The alternative stitching method for frame quilting is stab stitching. As the name infers, you insert the needle or "stab" it vertically through the layers from the top to the back of the quilt. You use the hand underneath to pull the needle all the way through and then complete the stitch by guiding the needle vertically up through the top.

This stitching method takes longer than the lap-quilting method and "rocker" quilting, since you complete each stitch individually rather than loading several stitches on the needle before completing them. In addition, quilters often find it difficult to make the stitches on the back even and straight. It takes much control and coordination with the hand underneath the quilt to make beautiful quilting stitches this way.

IN CONCLUSION

Remember, "practice makes perfect." If you quilt a little every day, your stitches will positively improve, becoming smaller and easier to make. The added bonus is that your fingers will not be sore because small calluses will form on the fingers that get the most pressure or wear.

I truly enjoy the rhythmic process of quilting a little every day and am often amazed at the volume of work that can be produced by spending only an hour or two each day stitching. Time spent hand quilting is never wasted. The stitches you take will always be there as tangi-

ble evidence of at least one thing you did each day. Aunt Jane of Kentucky expressed similar sentiments when she said ". . . when I am dead and gone there ain't anybody goin' to think o' the floors I've swept, and the tables I've scrubbed, and the old clothes I've patched, and the stockin's I've darned. But when one o' my grandchildren or great-grandchildren sees one o' these quilts, they'll think about Aunt Jane, and, wherever I am then, I'll know I ain't forgotten."

Happy stitching!

TEMPLATES

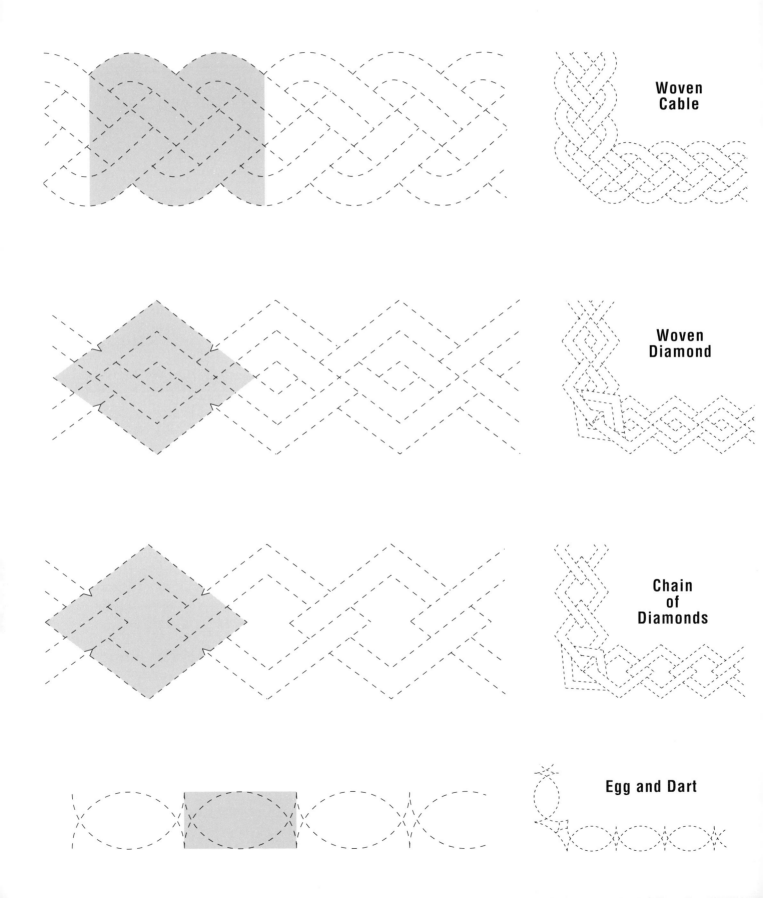

**Woven
Cable**

**Woven
Diamond**

**Chain
of
Diamonds**

Egg and Dart

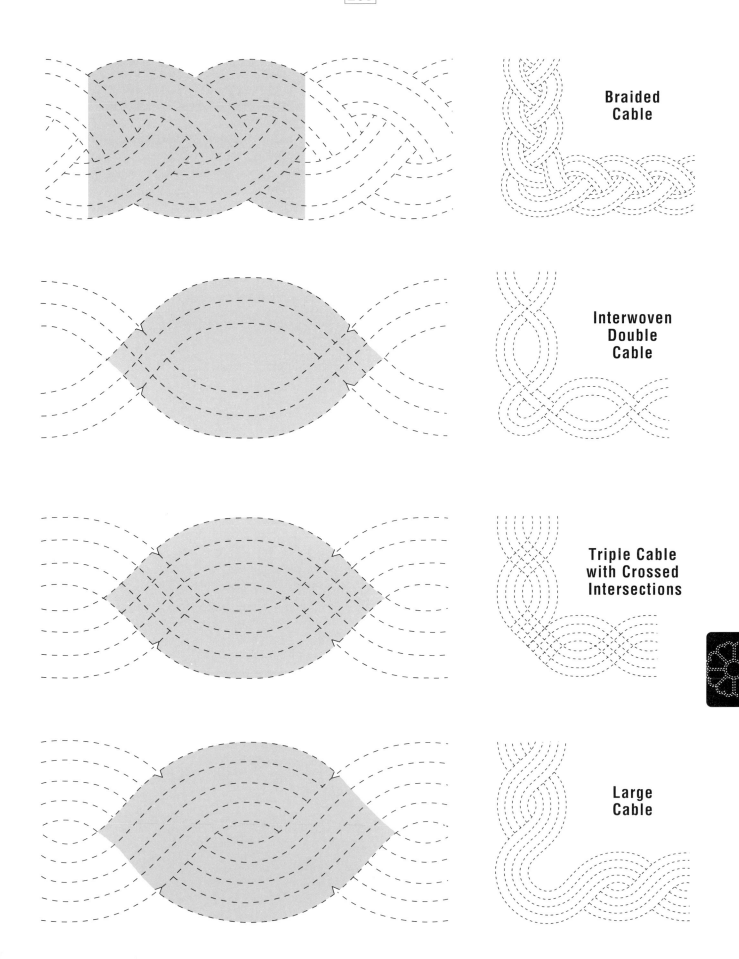

Braided Cable

Interwoven Double Cable

Triple Cable with Crossed Intersections

Large Cable

Rose Pattern Template

Pineapple Template

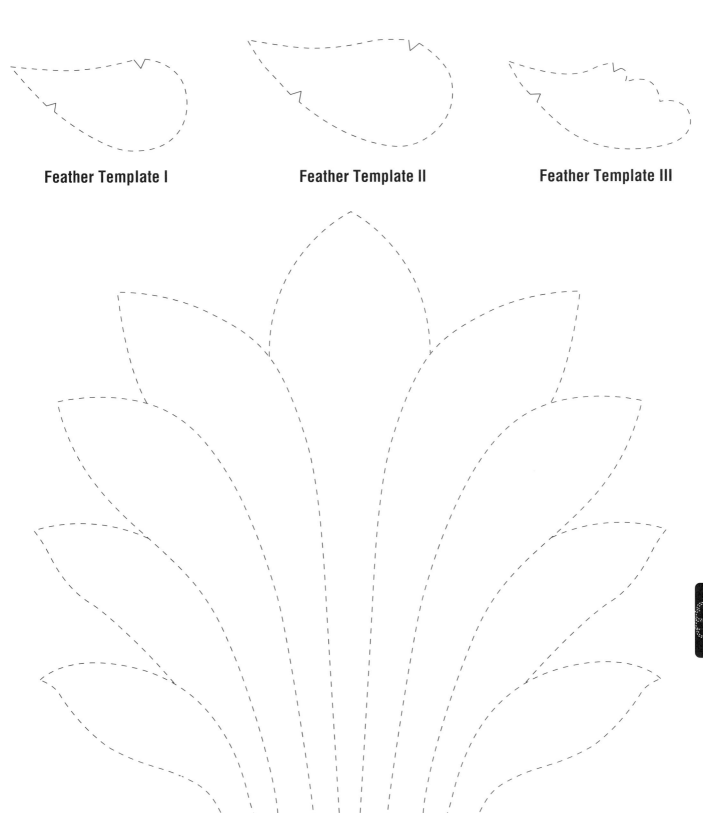

Feather Template I

Feather Template II

Feather Template III

Acanthus Leaf Template

True Lover's Knot Template

Loving Stitches
GALLERY

The quilts pictured in this gallery are examples of effective quilting.
(No patterns are given.)

Bountiful Baskets *by Jeanne Huber, 1989, Bountiful, Utah, 94" x 94". This basket medallion quilt is a true masterpiece. Jeanne's combination of several different basket patterns in both the piecing and the quilting displays her remarkable needlework skills. (Collection of Jeanne Huber, Bountiful, Utah)*

Evening Star Quilting Sampler *by Jeana Kimball, 1992, Salt Lake City, Utah, 34" x 42". Each block of this wall quilt is quilted in a different format, giving its surface a varied texture. A contrasting solid fabric on the quilt back makes an interesting mosaic. (Collection of Jeana Kimball)*

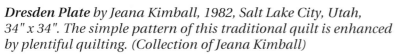

Dresden Plate *by Jeana Kimball, 1982, Salt Lake City, Utah, 34" x 34". The simple pattern of this traditional quilt is enhanced by plentiful quilting. (Collection of Jeana Kimball)*

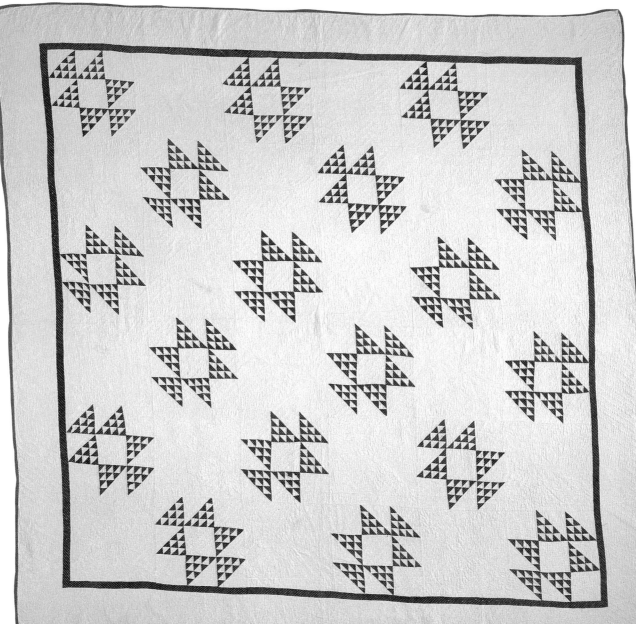

Birds in the Air, *maker unknown, c. 1870, 84" x 85".*
The pristine two-color theme of this quilt shows off the
finely stitched triple rows of quilting. It is in excellent
condition, indicating, perhaps, that it was a "best"
quilt, used only on special occasions. (Collection of
Rose B. Gallo, Yardley, Pennsylvania)

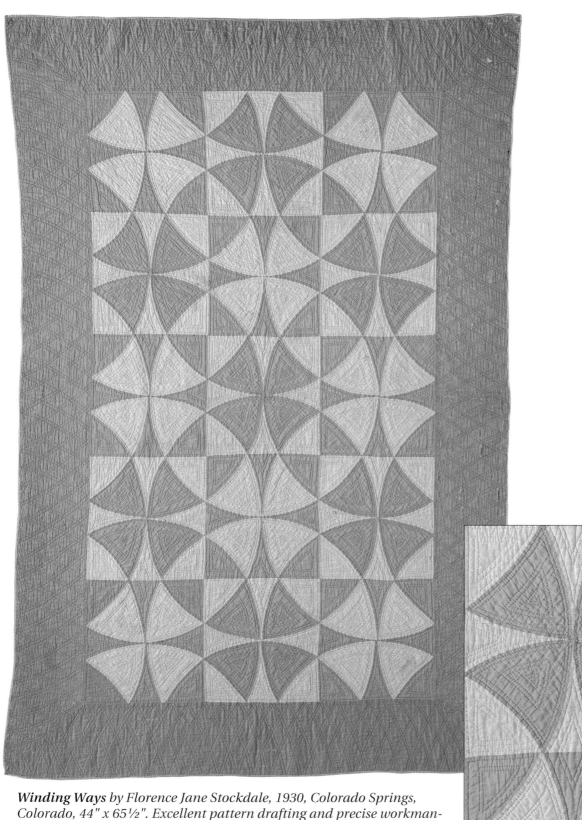

Winding Ways *by Florence Jane Stockdale, 1930, Colorado Springs, Colorado, 44" x 65½". Excellent pattern drafting and precise workmanship make this deceivingly simple-looking quilt a work of art. Mrs. Stockdale made this quilt for her second grandchild. (Collection of Marella Baker, Salt Lake City, Utah)*

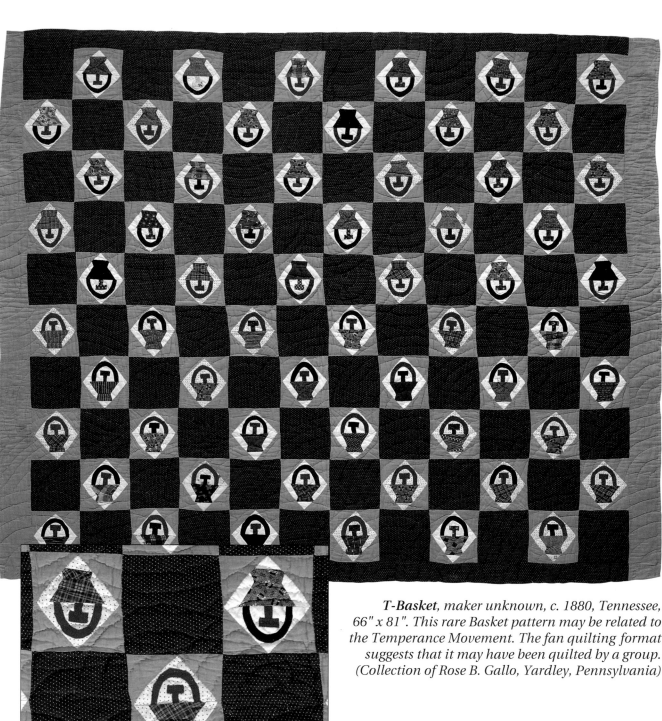

T-Basket, *maker unknown, c. 1880, Tennessee, 66" x 81". This rare Basket pattern may be related to the Temperance Movement. The fan quilting format suggests that it may have been quilted by a group. (Collection of Rose B. Gallo, Yardley, Pennsylvania)*

Tall Trees *by Jeanne Huber, 1987, Bountiful, Utah, 94" x 94". A graceful pieced Tree pattern is beautifully framed with a pieced Maple Leaf border. Again, Jeanne shows her amazing talent at combining piecing and quilting skills to create an heirloom quilt. (Collection of Jeanne Huber, Bountiful, Utah)*

Paradise Lost *by Charlotte Warr Andersen, 1989, Salt Lake City, Utah, 80" x 66". This is a pieced depiction of Saltaire, a resort built in 1893 on the shores of the Great Salt Lake. The pieced blocks along the bottom border combine the Exquisite and Lady of the Lake traditional patterns. Notice that the quilting lines in the background areas do not follow the pieced format but create an additional dimension to the sky. Also, note how perspective is created by the spacing of the wavelike quilting lines in the water. (Collection of Charlotte Warr Andersen, Salt Lake City, Utah)*

Happy Endings

FINISHING THE EDGES OF YOUR QUILT

CONTENTS

INTRODUCTION

As quiltmakers, we love to choose fabric colors, textures, and prints to create new designs for our quilts. We find a wonderful peace in quilting the layers of soft fabric, but many of us hastily complete the last step of the quiltmaking process—finishing the edges. In this chapter, you will find directions for a variety of edge finishes and guidance in choosing the perfect one for your quilt.

As you plan your quilt, it's a good idea to consider the technique you will use to frame your design. How you plan to use the quilt is one factor to consider as well as your available time and fabric.

A brief description of the types of finishes included in this book follows. Keep in mind that you can use many of the techniques included in this book to finish the edges on other quilted projects. Vests, jackets, and tote bags often require binding or finished edges.

Color photos of the edge finishes described below begin on page 309.

Some quilts are finished without a binding. Very often comforters are finished by placing the front and back of the quilt right sides together on the batting and sewing around the edge, then turning the quilt right side out. A row of quilting near the edge gives the illusion of binding.

If you prefer to quilt the layers first, you can finish the edges in a fashion similar to the stitch-and-turn method by turning under the front and back of the quilt and stitching the edges together by hand. Choose either of these two finishing techniques when you do not want a bound edge along the edge of the quilt, or if you do not have a binding fabric in the desired color. Directions for methods of finishing a quilt without binding begin on page 278.

Using the backing fabric of your quilt to create binding is an easy, quick, and inexpensive way to complete your quilt. It requires extra backing fabric extending beyond the front of the quilt in all four directions to turn over the cut edges of the front. This is a fast way to finish your quilt. Directions for this method begin on page 281.

For a more professional finish, you can make your own binding. It requires extra fabric to make the binding, so you need to plan ahead and save fabric for this last step. Use custom-made binding to add a final frame to the outer edge of your quilt in a matching or coordinating fabric.

You can cut binding on the straight grain or on the bias. You can also take advantage of directional prints by cutting strips for your binding on either the straight or bias grain. For example, if the binding fabric is printed with straight rows of little flowers or hearts, you can cut the binding strips so the design lines up along the edges. When you cut bias strips from a striped fabric, the stripes will spiral around the edge of the quilt. Cutting binding strips across a striped fabric gives an entirely different look to the bound edge. You can also cut striped fabric so that a single stripe accents the edge of the quilt all the way around.

For yet a different look, sew small pieces of several different fabrics together, patchwork-style, to create a rainbow-colored binding. Directions for finishing a quilt with binding begin on page 283.

Special edge finishing techniques begin on page 299. For a very special quilt, you can use prairie points—small folded triangles caught in the seam at the outer edge of the quilt. Directions begin on page 301. Prairie points require extra fabric, but they add a unique finish.

Consider adding a *ruffled-edge finish* to a baby quilt or one with a feminine design. This also requires extra fabric. Use a favorite fabric from the quilt top for the ruffle, or use purchased, gathered eyelet, lace, or other trim. You can also pleat rather than gather the ruffle for a slightly more tailored look. *Adding cording to the edge is another way to create an interesting edge finish* that complements one of the colors in your quilt.

Whether you choose a quick front-to-back finish, use the back of the quilt to bind your edges, make your own binding, or add special effects, may you discover a Happy Ending for your quilting project!

Mimi Dietrich

FINISHING WITHOUT BINDING

You may finish your quilt without binding by sewing the quilt layers together by hand or machine along the outer edges to enclose the batting. Use this technique when you do not want a row of binding on the edge. It's also a good technique to use when you cannot find binding fabric in the desired color.

Hand-Finished Edges

If you wish to quilt the layers together before finishing the edges, be sure to end your quilting ½" from the quilt edge to allow room for the finishing seam. Then hand finish the outer edges in the following manner.

1. Trim the front and back of the quilt so that the cut edges are ¼" larger than the finished size of the quilt. Trim the batting ⅛" smaller than the finished size of the quilt.
2. Fold the front of the quilt over the batting, turning under the ¼"-wide seam allowance.

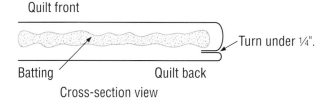

Quilt front

Turn under ¼".

Batting
Quilt back
Cross-section view

3. Turn the back of the quilt under ¼" and pin the folded edge to match the front of quilt.
4. Slipstitch the front and back folds together to complete your quilt.

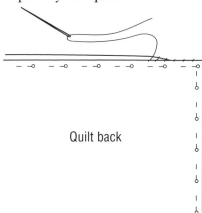

Quilt back

Machine-Finished Edges

If you prefer to sew the edges together by machine, do it *before* you quilt. This method works best if you plan to tie your quilt or to quilt lightly for a puffy effect. It is difficult to closely quilt a large area after the edges have been stitched. Use this method for a child's fluffy quilt or for a comforter.

1. Place the quilt top and backing right sides together.
2. Pin the edges together, then trim the edges of the front and back so they are even.
3. Beginning in the center on one side of the quilt, stitch ¼" from the edges. Backstitch at the beginning and end, leaving an opening for turning. For a small quilt, the opening should be 6"–10"; for a large quilt, it may need to be as large as 20". This keeps the front and back of the quilt together as you attach the batting.
4. Smooth out the batting on a flat surface and pin the quilt top/backing unit to it with the wrong side of the quilt top next to the batting. Pin around all edges of the quilt and batting, allowing the batting edges to extend beyond the quilt. (You will trim them later.)
5. Sew the quilt to the batting from the backing side, following the previously stitched ¼" seam line and leaving the same opening as before.

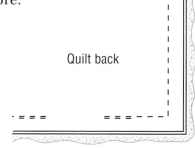

Quilt back

6. Trim the batting close to the stitching, making sure you do not cut the quilt top or backing fabric.

7. To turn the quilt right side out, reach through the opening between the front and back of the quilt. Pull the corners through the opening, one corner at a time, and turn the quilt right side out. As you turn each corner, fold the two seam allowances over the batting before you pull them out.

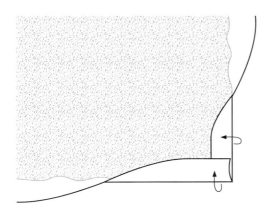

8. To close the opening, trim the batting to the finished size of the quilt. Fold the front seam allowance over the batting. Turn under ¼" at the edge of the quilt backing and pin it to the front. Slipstitch the open edges together.

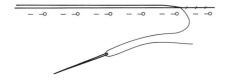

9. Quilt or tie your quilt.

Tip Before quilting or tying your quilt, straighten out the layers of a small quilt on a tabletop. You may need to smooth a large quilt out on the floor with the help of a friend. Tug on opposite sides of the quilt to straighten the three layers so that the front, back, and batting lie smoothly. Baste or pin the three layers together before quilting or tying.

Rounded Corners

If you wish, you may round off the square edges of your quilt or comforter for a softer look. Do this before sewing the outer edges together by hand or machine. This treatment is best if your quilt has wide borders or a wide area of background fabric in the corners. If your quilt has a definite square pattern in the corners, it will look better if you keep the corners square.

To round off the corners, use a round piece of dinnerware. Use a cup for a slightly rounded corner, or a saucer for a more rounded curve. Use a dinner plate to round off the corners on a large quilt.

1. Position the plate in one corner so that the circle touches both sides of the quilt.

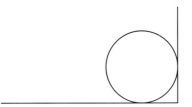

2. Using a pencil, draw along the curve from side to side, creating a perfectly rounded corner.

3. Cut along the line; repeat on all corners on the front and back of your quilt.

4. Sew the front and back of the quilt together by hand or machine as described above, being careful not to stretch the curved edges of the fabric as you stitch.

Imitation Binding

After you have stitched the front and the back of the quilt together and have turned it right side out, you can create the look of binding along the edge. Simply quilt by hand or machine, placing the stitches ¼" to ½" from the finished edge.

This row of quilting makes a ridge along the edge that gives the illusion of binding. It also flattens down the puffy edge. This looks especially nice when the quilt backing matches the border fabric.

To give the appearance of wide binding, add a 1"- to 2"-wide border to your quilt top before you finish the edges. Then sew the layers together by hand or machine, and hand or machine quilt along the border seam.

Appliquéd Border

To create a very unusual finishing touch, appliqué a curved or scalloped border to the edge of your quilt top before finishing the edge. Your border will have the soft look of scallops without the work of binding curved edges. Sew the front and the back of the quilt together along the straight edges and quilt along the appliqué curves for a very special quilt finish.

FINISHING WITH BACKING

Some quilts appear to have binding along the edges but are actually finished without making a separate binding. You simply turn the backing fabric over the batting and front edge of the quilt for a quick and easy edge finish with the appearance of binding.

To finish your quilt with backing, you must cut the quilt backing larger than the front of the quilt. Very often in planning a quilt, the backing fabric is already longer and wider than the front. This finish is an economical way to use up that excess fabric rather than trimming it and throwing it away. It's a good method to use when you do not have extra fabric to make binding. Make sure that your backing fabric coordinates with the quilt design. If not, you may want to reverse the process, turning the quilt-front fabric to the back to create the finished edge.

1. After completing the quilting, trim the batting even with the front cut edge of the quilt, being careful not to clip through the quilt backing.
2. Lay the quilt on a flat surface and baste ¼" from the cut edge of the quilt top, stitching through the quilt front, batting, and backing to hold all the layers together and prevent shifting while you finish the edges.

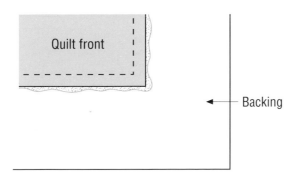

Quilt front

Backing

3. For a finished "binding" width of ½", you will need 1" of backing fabric extending beyond the front of the quilt. Use a clear ruler to measure 1" of extra fabric around all edges of the quilt, then trim the backing carefully. For binding wider than ½", cut the extending fabric two times the desired finished binding width.

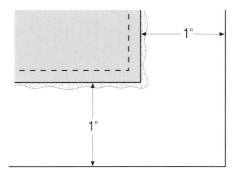

1"

1"

4. Fold the backing fabric in half, wrong sides together, so that the cut edge of the backing meets the cut edge of the front.

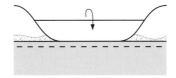

5. Fold again along the front edge of the quilt to form the finished edge. This encases the batting and covers ½" of the front edge. Pin along the first fold to hold the finished edge in place. Decide whether you will use overlapped or mitered corners. See the box on page 282. Then finish by hand or machine as shown below.

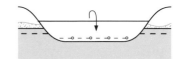

Binding Corners

To overlap binding corners:

1. Continue folding the corners as you fold the sides. Fold the first side, extending the folds to the corners.

2. Fold the second side, overlapping the first.

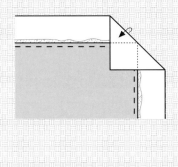

This method is the fastest; however, it can be bulky. To prevent stray threads from sneaking out at the corners, slipstitch the corners closed.

To miter binding corners:

Mitered corners are more attractive and less bulky than overlapped corners. They only take a few extra minutes. Remember there are only four corners on your quilt! In this method, you fold the corners first, then the sides.

1. Fold the corner of the quilt backing over the point of the quilt front, so the fold touches the corner of the quilt top.

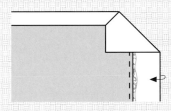

2. Fold the sides, so that the edge of the back meets the edge of the front as before.

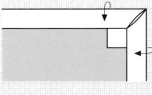

3. Fold once more to create the binding and a miter at the corner.

4. Trim out the small square that extends onto the quilt and pin the folds securely before sewing.

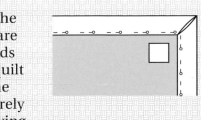

Backing-to-the-front "binding" can be stitched by hand or by machine.

To finish by hand:

1. Thread a needle with an 18" length of thread that matches the backing fabric. Sew the binding to the front of the quilt, using the blind stitch or slip stitch and taking care that the stitches do not go all the way through to the backing.

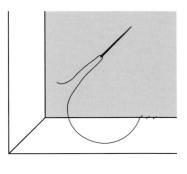

2. Blindstitch the corners closed.

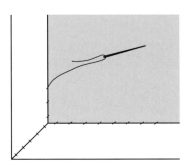

3. Do a row of quilting stitches right next to the inner edge of the "binding," sewing through all three layers of the quilt.

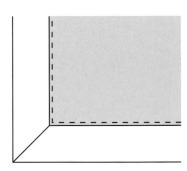

To finish by machine:

Pin binding in place and stitch around the edges of the quilt on the folded edges of the "binding." It is not necessary to do a row of quilting stitches next to the binding when you finish by machine. Use a blind stitch to stitch mitered corners in place.

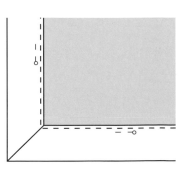

FINISHING WITH BINDING

After completing the quilting, take a little time to prepare your quilt for the binding.

Basting

It is very important to baste the edges together, so that the quilt top, the batting, and the quilt backing become one unit along the edges. It is much easier to sew the binding to one edge rather than to three unattached layers.

1. Lay your quilt on a flat surface with the quilt top facing up.
2. Pin the layers together around the outer edges. Baste by hand ¼" from the cut edge of the front, stitching all around the quilt. You may stitch by machine but be careful that the layers do not shift. Check the opposite sides of your quilt to make sure they are even. You can adjust the length of the quilt edges by tightening or loosening the basting stitches.
3. After completing the basting, trim the batting and the backing so that they are even with the front edge of the quilt. Use a rotary cutter for a clean, accurate edge. Also trim any threads that may be hanging from the front edge of the quilt to create a nice clean edge so that you are ready to apply the binding.

Making Binding

Making your own binding is fun and creative. You can use packaged binding, but binding made from your own fabric is a perfect match to the quality fabric used in your quilt. It gives a coordi-

Tip — Use a walking foot or a built-in, even-feed feature on your sewing machine to help keep the layers from shifting as you baste by machine.

Tip — If you do not plan to use your binding immediately after you make it, store it by winding it carefully around a paper tube. Wind it flat, not folded, and try not to stretch it.

nated look to your project and adds a special touch. Handmade binding is usually more durable than commercially made binding, but you will need to purchase extra fabric to make it. To prevent shrinking and puckering, always preshrink binding fabric before making your own binding.

Determining Binding Size

To determine the cut length for your binding strip, measure the distance around your quilt. Add 9" to this measurement to allow for turning corners and the finishing seam. If your quilt has scalloped edges, be sure to measure around the curves. It takes more binding to finish a curved edge than a straight edge.

When you determine the width of the binding, first choose the method that you will use to apply it. Traditional binding covers the edge with a single layer of fabric that finishes to approximately one-fourth of the cut width.

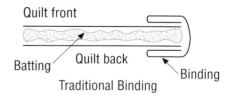

Quilt front

Batting   Quilt back   Binding

Traditional Binding

Traditional binding cut 2" wide allows for two ½"-wide seam allowances, ½" showing on the front of the quilt, and ½" showing on the back. If it is cut 2½" wide and you use ⅝"-wide seam allowances, you will have a finished width of ⅝". If it is cut 3" wide and you use ¾"-wide seam allowances, the finished width will be ¾". The seam allowances change with the width of the binding. If you are using thick batting, add ¼" to the cut size to allow the binding to turn over the thickness of the batting.

French binding is a double layer of fabric that finishes to approximately one-sixth of the cut width.

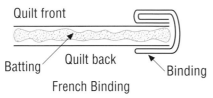

Quilt front

Batting Quilt back

Quilt back

Binding

French Binding

French binding cut 2" wide allows for two ¼"-wide seam allowances, ⅜" showing on the front and back of the quilt, and ⅜" for the front and back of the quilt on the inside layer. If the binding is cut 3" wide, the finished size will be ½", using ½"-wide seam allowances. If you are using thick batting, add ¼" to the cut size to allow for the batting thickness.

In this book, *directions for marking, cutting, and sewing binding are given for binding that is cut 2" wide.* This size makes traditional binding that finishes ½" wide or French binding that finishes ⅜" wide. This measurement is easy to mark and cut, using a 2"-wide, clear acrylic quilter's ruler. The binding width is easy to handle as you apply it to the quilt and turn it to cover the edges. Some quiltmakers prefer wider bindings to provide a wider "frame" at the outer edge of the quilt and are more comfortable handling a wider strip.

Tip

If there is a ¼"-wide seam allowance at the outer edge of your completed quilt and you want a wider binding, allow the batting and backing to extend beyond the quilt top to the desired finished binding width.

Quilt front

Batting and Backing Extended

If you prefer a wider binding, cut the fabric strips wider, being sure to allow for the thickness of the quilt and the wider seam allowance. For traditional single-layer binding, cut the binding four (4) times the desired finished width, plus an allowance for the thickness of the quilt layers. For double-layer French binding, cut binding strips eight (8) times the desired finished width, plus an allowance for the thickness of the quilt.

No matter which binding method you choose, it is important to prepare your quilt so that the batting extends to the edge of the binding to evenly pad it and give it body along the edge.

Determining Binding Fabric Requirements

After you have measured the distance around your quilt and determined the width of your cut binding, you are ready to calculate the amount of extra fabric you will need to cut a separate binding. Use either a rectangle or square to do these calculations.

To determine the amount of fabric, using a rectangle of fabric:

You can cut binding strips from a rectangle along the straight or off grain or on the bias.

1. Divide the length of binding you need by the width of your fabric. (If you are planning to piece your strips together, subtract 3" from the width of your fabric to allow for diagonal seams.) Round off to the next highest number. This will tell you how many strips you will need to cut across the rectangle.
2. Multiply the number of strips by the width of the strips to determine how many inches of fabric you will need to cut enough binding. If you don't want to figure it out, Chart A on page 285 gives you the length of fabric you need if you have 40"-wide fabric (44"-wide fabric minus shrinkage and 3" for seam allowances). The quilt sizes in this chart are based on standard mattress sizes, with 12" added to the sides, top, and bottom to determine the finished quilt size.

For example, if you are making a baby quilt with binding cut 2" wide, you will need 12" of 44"-wide fabric to cut enough binding.

To determine the amount of fabric, using a square of fabric:

1. Multiply the width of your cut binding times the length (in inches) needed for your quilt. This gives you the total number of square inches of binding (the area of fabric needed from which to cut it).

2. Find the square root of this number. (Don't faint! Just get out a small calculator, enter the number, and press the square root button for the answer!)

3. Round off this number to the next highest even number to allow extra for seam allowances. This number is the size of the square you will need, to cut enough binding.

If you don't want to figure it out, Chart B below will help. The quilt sizes in the chart are based on standard mattress sizes, adding 12" to the sides, top, and bottom for the quilt size.

For example, if you are making a baby quilt with 2"-wide cut binding, you will need a 22" square of fabric to cut enough binding.

Cutting and Sewing Binding Strips

When you finish your quilt without binding or use the back of your quilt to finish the edges, your quilt is naturally finished with fabric that is cut on the straight of grain. That means the threads in your binding fabric run parallel to the edges of your quilt. When you finish your quilt with separate binding strips, you may cut the strips on the bias or on the straight of grain.

Binding strips cut along the lengthwise grain are somewhat stronger, with almost no stretch as compared to those cut on the crosswise grain. However, it is often more economical to cut the strips across the fabric width. Straight-cut binding has very little stretch and works best on straight edges and square corners.

Cut strips straight across the width or length of your piece of binding fabric, then sew them together to make a strip long enough to bind the edges of your quilt. See "Sewing Binding Strips Together" on page 287.

You can also cut straight-grain binding in a continuous strip. See "Cutting Continuous Binding," pages 286–89.

Bias binding is cut on the diagonal grain of the fabric and takes a little longer to make, but it has some definite advantages. Bias binding cut on the true bias grain contains built-in stretch so the binding lies smoothly and turns curves easily. It is easy to miter corners in bias binding. When applied to the edge of your quilt, the bias threads crisscross the edge, creating a durable finish. Unlike bias-cut binding, straight-grain binding has a single thread running along the folded edge that will weaken with wear.

Chart A				44"-WIDE FABRIC LENGTH FOR BINDING WIDTH		
EXAMPLE:	STANDARD SIZE QUILT		AMOUNT OF BINDING (LENGTH PLUS 9")	2"	2½"	3"
Baby Quilt with 2" Binding	Baby	45" x 60"	219"	12"	15"	18"
Length of binding ÷ width of fabric	Twin	63" x 99"	333"	18"	22½"	27"
219 ÷ 40 = 5.4	Double	78" x 99"	363"	20"	25"	30"
Round off 5.4 to 6 strips	Queen	84" x 104"	385"	20"	25"	30"
6 strips x 2" width = 12" fabric needed	King	100" x 104"	417"	22"	27½"	33"

Chart B				SQUARE FOR BINDING WIDTH		
EXAMPLE:	STANDARD SIZE QUILT		AMOUNT OF BINDING (LENGTH PLUS 9")	2"	2½"	3"
Baby Quilt with 2" Binding	Baby	45" x 60"	219"	22"	24"	26"
Cut binding width x length	Twin	63" x 99"	333"	26"	30"	32"
2" x 219" = 438"	Double	78" x 99"	363"	28"	32"	36"
438" = area of fabric needed	Queen	84" x 104"	385"	30"	34"	36"
√438 = 22" square	King	100" x 104"	417"	32"	36"	38"

To cut binding strips on the true bias:

1. Begin in a corner, next to a selvage edge if possible. Using a ruler, make a mark 6" from the corner on each side. Connect these marks.

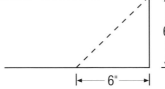

2. Draw a parallel line 2" away to make your first bias strip. Continue drawing parallel lines until you have enough binding strips to go around the edges of your quilt.
3. Sew bias strips together as shown on page 287.

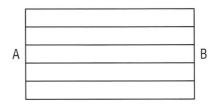

Cutting Continuous Binding

It is possible to cut one long continuous binding strip from a large piece of fabric, eliminating the need to sew many shorter strips together. You can cut straight-grain binding, off-grain binding, or true-bias binding.

Use straight-grain binding to bind straight edges and square corners. It has very little stretch and will not lie flat around curves.

Off-grain binding is cut slightly off grain and has some stretch. It is appropriate for straight edges and moderately curved corners. It takes more care to avoid puckers.

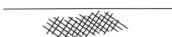

True bias binding, cut on the 45° diagonal grain of the fabric, has the most stretch. It is appropriate for binding any edge—straight or curved.

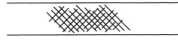

To cut straight-grain continuous binding:

1. Determine the size of the square or the rectangle required to make enough binding for your quilt. See pages 284–85. Cut from the binding fabric.
2. Mark lines 2" apart and parallel to one long side of the square or rectangle of fabric. If there is any excess after marking the entire piece, cut it off along the last marked line.

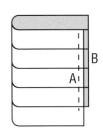

3. With right sides together, bring side A and side B together, shifting the top edge of A down so it lines up with the first drawn line on B. At the other end of the seam, the bottom end of B should match last line on side A.

4. With the machine set for 12 to 15 stitches per inch, stitch ¼" from the raw edges. Press the seam open.
5. Using sharp scissors, start at one end and cut along the marked line. When you reach the seam, you will have moved down one line and can continue cutting in this manner until you reach the end. You will have one long strip of binding long enough to finish the edges of your quilt.

To cut off-grain continuous binding:

1. Determine the size of the square or the rectangle required to make enough binding for your quilt. See pages 284–85. Add 2" (or the cut width of your binding strips if different than 2"). Cut from the binding fabric.
2. Place the fabric square or rectangle on a flat surface, right side up. Along sides A and B, place a mark every 2" (the binding width). Draw a line from the top edge on A to the first mark on B. Continue drawing lines parallel to

(continued on page 288)

Sewing Binding Strips Together

If you cut binding strips from a square or rectangle of fabric, you will need to join them into one continuous strip before sewing them to the quilt top. The total length of the cut strips should be longer than the distance around your quilt to allow for seam allowances.

The easiest way to sew the strips together is to connect the pieces with straight seams. This method, however, creates bulky areas when folded and stitched as binding. The seam overlaps itself and creates a thickness of many layers that is difficult to sew, especially on small projects. However, you may need to do this to conserve fabric.

1. Place the strips right sides together, end to end, and stitch ¼" from the raw edges.

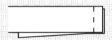

2. Press the seam open.

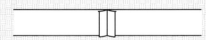

Diagonal seams in your binding are more attractive when finished. In addition, the thickness of the seam allowances is distributed more evenly when applied to the quilt top. Diagonal seams in bias-cut binding are on the straight of grain, which prevents stretching. There are two ways to join strips on the diagonal.

Cut the ends of the strips diagonally at a 45° angle so that they fit together as shown. Then sew them together with raw edges even and the points extending an equal amount on each side so that they cross ¼" from the cut edges. Press the seams open.

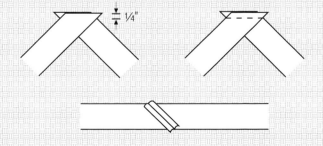

OR

Working on a flat surface, place two strips right sides together with ends crossing at right angles. Imagine the strips as the legs of a giant letter "A." Draw a line across the pieces to "cross the A," then sew on the line. Cut away the excess fabric, leaving a ¼"-wide seam allowance; press the seam open.

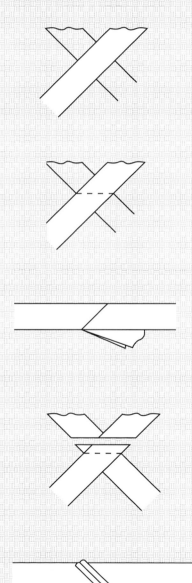

(continued from page 286)

the first one you drew until you reach the bottom of the fabric.

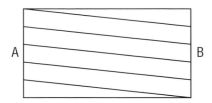

3. Cut away the resulting triangles at the top and bottom edges of the fabric.

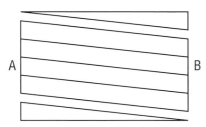

4. With right sides together, bring side A and side B together, shifting the top edge of A down so it lines up with the first drawn line on B. At the other end of the seam, the bottom end of B should match the last line on side A.

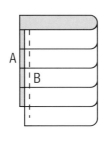

5. With the machine set for 12 to 15 stitches per inch, stitch ¼" from the raw edges. Press the seam open.

6. Using sharp scissors, start at one end and cut along the marked line. When you reach the seam, you will have moved down one line and can continue cutting in this manner until you reach the end. You will have one long strip of binding long enough to finish the edges of your quilt.

To cut true-bias continuous binding:

1. Determine the size of the square or the rectangle required to make enough binding for your quilt. See pages 284–85. Cut from the binding fabric.

2. Place the binding fabric right side up on a flat surface and mark it as shown.

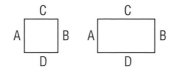

Use a water-erasable pen, or label and attach small pieces of masking tape.

3. If you are using a square, fold square in half diagonally; press lightly. Cut along the fold to create two triangles.

You now have two bias edges. Place sides A and B right sides together and sew ¼" from the raw edges, using 12 to 15 stitches per inch. As you position the two pieces for sewing, make sure the raw edges cross exactly ¼" from the cut edges. Press the seam open.

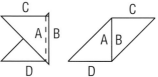

If you are using a rectangle, fold side A down to match side D.

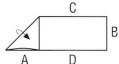

Press the diagonal fold lightly and cut along the fold to create two bias edges.

Place sides A and B right sides together and stitch ¼" from the raw edges, using 12 to 15 stitches per inch. Press the seam open.

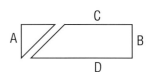

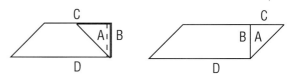

4. Draw a parallel line 2" (the binding width) from the bias edge (one that is not marked with a letter). Continue drawing parallel lines 2" apart on the whole piece of fabric. Trim away any excess fabric that extends beyond the last drawn line. Be careful not to stretch your fabric as you draw the lines.

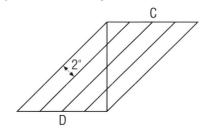

5. Bring sides C and D together to create a tube of fabric.

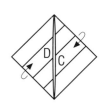

6. Pin the seam together, but first shift one edge of C down so that it matches the first line marked on D.

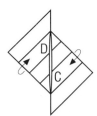

7. At other end, the end of D will match the last line on C. With the machine set for 12 to 15 stitches per inch, stitch ¼" from the raw edges. You are making a tube while you sew, so the fabric will not lie entirely flat while you stitch. Press the seam open.

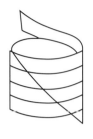

8. Begin cutting at one end along the marked line. When you reach the seam, you will have automatically moved down one line. Keep cutting until you reach the end. You will have one continuous piece of bias binding for your quilt.

Tip: To cut binding for a large quilt, place the binding over your ironing board. Keep turning the tube of fabric as you cut the binding.

Special Binding Treatments

PRINT BINDING

You can use fabrics with small, evenly spaced designs to create very special bindings for your quilt. Look for printed design motifs that repeat in straight or diagonal patterns. Then cut the binding strips to take advantage of the print. For example, cut a print with rows of flowers so they will line up all the way around your quilt.

The method that you use to apply your binding determines how wide to cut binding strips. The width of one design row will equal the width of the finished binding (and, therefore, the width of the seam you will stitch). Traditional, single-layer binding will have a design row on the front and the back of the quilt if there are four rows of the design in the cut strip width.

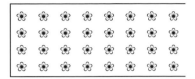

For double layer French binding, six design rows should appear in the strip width. *It may be necessary to adjust binding widths and seam widths to accommodate the design rows.*

Cut strips of fabric to make enough binding for your quilt, making sure that each strip has the same design rows. Cut strips on the straight grain or bias, depending on how the design was printed on the fabric. Some diagonal designs may not be printed on a true bias. If that is the case, cut the fabric along the design and don't worry about the "true" bias. It will still have some bias give and will look beautiful if you apply it carefully. Sew the strips together as shown in "Sewing Binding Strips Together," on page 287.

RAINBOW BINDING

Make a unique patchwork binding for your quilt by piecing together fabrics left over from your quilt top. Cut patches of the same or varying sizes. If you hand sew the edge of the binding in place, choose a thread in a color that blends with a medium color in the binding or one that matches the quilt backing. Choose one of the following methods for making rainbow binding.

Method One: Random-Patch Rainbow Binding

1. Cut single patches and piece them together to form the binding. Cut each patch the width of the binding. Cut pieces in random lengths or the same size as one of the pieces used in the quilt top. Remember to add two ¼" seam

allowances to each patch so you can sew them together.

2. Sew the patches together ¼" from the raw edges and press seams open.

3. Continue adding patches until you have a piece long enough to bind the entire quilt.

Method Two: Strip-Pieced Rainbow Binding

This method makes a rainbow binding that has regular repeats of the fabrics chosen for the binding.

1. Cut strips of the desired fabrics, making them ½" wider than the desired finished width.
2. With the machine set for 12 to 15 stitches per inch, stitch the strips together in the desired order to make a strip-pieced unit of "striped" fabric. Press seams open.

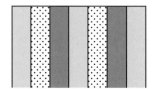

3. Use scissors or a rotary cutter and ruler to cut binding strips of the desired width from the strip-pieced unit.

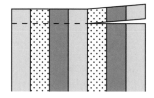

4. Sew binding strips together to make enough binding to finish the edges of your quilt.

STRIPED BINDING

There are several ways to use striped fabric to create special accents for the edge of your quilt.

Method One: Cutting Strips on Crosswise Grain

Cut binding strips across the stripes on the crosswise grain and piece together for a continuous piece of binding. When applied to the quilt,

colors and designs from all of the stripes will appear on the binding edge.

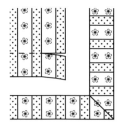

Method Two: Cutting Strips on Lengthwise Grain

Cut binding strips parallel to the striped design, being sure to allow a ¼"-wide seam allowance beyond the design motif you wish to show in finished binding.

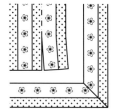

Method Three: Cutting Strips on the Bias

Cut binding strips on the bias. When applied to your quilt, the diagonal stripes will spiral around the edges. This is a dynamic and eye-catching edge finish.

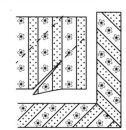

Attaching the Binding

Before you begin to sew the binding to your quilt, take a moment to think about the starting point. Do not start in a corner unless you are planning to overlap the corners. For most binding treatments, it is easier to start beyond a corner on one edge of the quilt and it is also easier to start on a straight edge than on a curve.

Do not start exactly in the center of one side. Each time that you fold your quilt in half, it will weaken at this spot.

The best place to begin sewing the binding is somewhere between the corner and the center of a side. On a large quilt, it may not matter where you start, but on a small wall hanging, you will want to choose a starting point that will not show later. The top edge is a good place to begin.

On a large quilt, it is good to start approximately 10" away from a corner. You may want to start sewing at the beginning of a side and sew the binding to most of the side before you face sewing the corner curve or miter. Or, you might want to sew the first corner right away and save the long edge for last. It's up to you.

Here are some things to remember as you begin to attach the binding:

- When you start to sew, do not start right at the beginning of the binding. The unstitched end will be attached at the end of the binding process. Instead, leave an unstitched "tail" about 2" long. It is unnecessary to backstitch when you begin to attach the binding.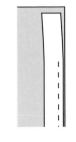

- Do not pin the binding to the entire quilt before sewing. It's very uncomfortable to sew with all of those pins sticking you. Instead, as you sew, concentrate on the 3" of binding directly in front of the sewing machine needle. Lay the 3" length of binding in position and stitch. Then go on to the next 3" length. Before long, those little 3" lengths will add up to the entire distance around the quilt! Be careful not to let the binding stretch as you apply it.

- Keep the long piece of binding in your lap as you sew, rather than letting it fall to the floor, to prevent stretching and puckering.

- If the two layers of binding shift as you sew, use a long straight pin to control the layers in front of the presser foot and needle. This will prevent you from sticking your finger under the needle; the straight pin fits under there much easier.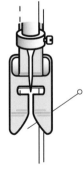

- Before applying the binding by machine, you may want to baste it to the edge of the quilt to hold it in place and prevent stretching while you stitch.

- You may stitch the binding to the quilt by hand if you prefer, using a small, evenly spaced running stitch through all three quilt layers. Backstitch every 2" to secure the stitches.

Use one of two methods to attach the binding to the edges of the quilt, depending on how you prepared the binding strips. Remember that tra-

ditional binding (below) covers the edge of your quilt with a single layer of fabric. A cross section of the quilt looks like this:

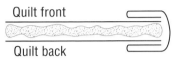

Quilt front

Quilt back

Traditional Binding

French binding (page 292) covers the edge of your quilt with a double layer of fabric. A cross section of the quilt looks like this:

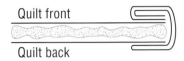

Quilt front

Quilt back

French Binding

French binding is more durable than traditional binding because it places a double layer of fabric along the edge of the quilt.

To apply traditional binding:

1. Cut and prepare binding strips for your quilt, following the directions that begin on page 285.

2. Fold the binding strip in half lengthwise with wrong sides together and press.

3. Fold each cut edge toward the center fold and press again.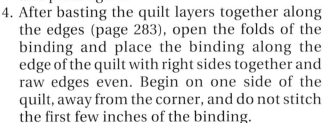

4. After basting the quilt layers together along the edges (page 283), open the folds of the binding and place the binding along the edge of the quilt with right sides together and raw edges even. Begin on one side of the quilt, away from the corner, and do not stitch the first few inches of the binding.

5. Stitch through all layers ¼" from the raw edge, using the fold in the binding as a guide. Do not stitch the first few inches of the binding. To miter the corners as you apply the binding, see pages 292–95. When you reach the point where the binding begins, finish the ends, using one of the two methods for "Connecting the Ends" on pages 297–98.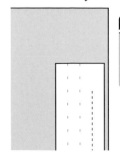

6. Fold the binding over the edge to the back. The folded edge of the binding should just conceal the stitching on the back of the quilt. If it does not, trim the quilt edge slightly.

7. Sew the folded edge of binding to the quilt by hand, using a slip stitch or blind stitch.

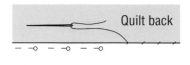

Quilt back

To apply French binding:

1. Cut and prepare French binding strips for your quilt, following the directions that begin on page 284.

2. Fold the binding strip in half lengthwise with wrong sides together and press, allowing the bottom layer to extend slightly beyond the top along the raw edges.

   Don't take the time to measure this; just eye it as you press. When you sew the binding to your quilt, you will be able to see both layers of the strip so that you can control it while stitching. Pressing the strip in half with a steam iron also helps the two layers stay together while you sew.

3. After basting the front, batting, and backing of your quilt together along the outer edges (page 283), position the binding on quilt with raw edges matching. Make sure that the wider half of the binding is on the bottom. Begin on one side of the quilt, away from the corner.

4. Stitch the binding to the quilt, using a ¼"-wide seam, but do not stitch the first few inches of binding.

   To miter the corners as you apply the binding, see pages 292–95. When you reach the point where the binding begins, finish the ends, using one of the two methods for "Connecting the Ends" on pages 297–98.

5. Fold the binding over the edge of the quilt to cover the raw edges. The folded edge of the

binding should cover the stitching on the back of the quilt. You may need to trim the edge of the quilt slightly if the binding will not cover the seam. Hand stitch the folded edge of the binding to the back of the quilt, using a blind stitch or slip stitch.

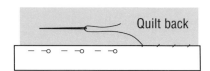

Quilt back

Tip If you prefer, you can stitch traditional binding or French binding completely by machine. Sew the binding strip to the *back* side of the quilt first. After turning it to the front of the quilt, stitch by machine along the pressed fold of the binding. See "Machine-Finished Binding" on page 298.

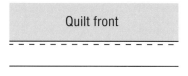

Quilt front

Binding Corners and Curves

There are three methods for turning the binding on square corners: folded mitered corners, stitched mitered corners, and overlapped corners. You may also choose to round the corners on your quilt as discussed on page 296, or you may want to create a scalloped edge (pages 296–97).

FOLDED MITERED CORNERS

Folded mitered corners have a diagonal fold in the binding and give a professional finish to your binding. It only takes a few minutes to fold the miters in the corners as you stitch the binding to the quilt. Small quilts, wall hangings, quilts with narrow borders, and quilts with square designs in the corners look especially nice with mitered corners. With only four corners to do, you'll be an expert by the time you get to number three!

1. Prepare the binding and sew to the first edge of the quilt as shown for either traditional or French binding on pages 290–92. If you are using French binding, stop stitching *exactly ¼" from the raw edge* at the corner and backstitch carefully to secure.

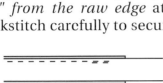

If you are using traditional binding, stop stitching ½" from the edge, or whatever the width of the finished binding will be if you are using a different finished binding width.

Use a straight pin to mark the place to stop stitching. Turn your quilt to the wrong side and stick a pin into the corner so that it is ¼" from each of the edges. Push it straight through all thicknesses (quilt plus binding). The place where the pin comes out on the top marks the place where you will stop stitching. Take another pin and insert it from the front in this spot, using this second pin to hold the binding and quilt together. "Where the pin goes in" signals your place to stop stitching.

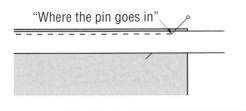

2. Fold the binding back on itself as shown, creating a 45°-angle fold. If you fold it back far enough, you can see the last stitch. When you are folding your miter, if there is a

binding seam near the fold, ignore it. Do your best to pretend that it's not there and continue.

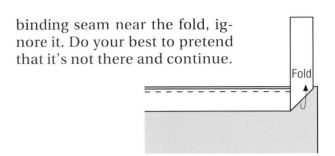

3. Fold the binding so it is even with the second edge of the quilt, and the fold is even with the first edge. Pin in place.

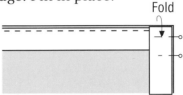

4. Begin stitching ¼" from upper fold, backstitching carefully.

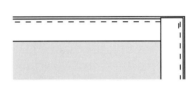

5. Continue in the same manner around the remaining corners of the quilt. When you reach the point where you started, refer to "Connecting the Ends" on pages 297–98.

6. To turn the binding to the wrong side of the quilt, tuck your finger under the corner fold and push the fabric toward the point.

7. Fold the binding over the edge of the quilt and toward the back. On the front, the fabric automatically folds into a miter.

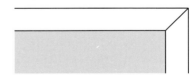

8. On the back, fold the binding flat over one edge of the quilt. At the end of the side, it will form a diagonal fold.

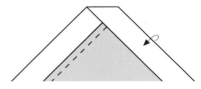

9. Turn under the second half of the binding, creating a miter on the back of the quilt. Hand stitch the binding in place on the back of the quilt, taking three or four stitches along the mitered fold. Then stick the needle through to the front and stitch the mitered fold in place on the front. Push the needle through to the back of the quilt and continue stitching binding to the back of the quilt.

STITCHED MITERED CORNERS

Stitched mitered corners look like folded and stitched mitered corners but are made by machine stitching 45°-angle seams in two binding strips that meet at each corner. To do this, you apply a separate binding strip to each side of the quilt.

1. Cut binding strips to fit each side of the quilt, cutting each one 4" longer than the quilt side measures. See pages 285–89 for directions on how to cut binding strips for your choice of traditional or French binding.

2. Position each binding strip along the edge of the quilt, allowing 2" of the binding to extend at each end of the quilt.

3. Stitch the binding to all four sides of the quilt, stopping ¼" from the ends (or the width of your binding seam) and backstitching.

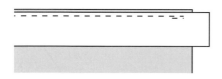

4. Fold the binding away from the center of the quilt, lapping the two strips at each corner at right angles. If you are applying traditional binding, fold under the second seam allowance.

5. Mark each strip where they cross each other at point A.

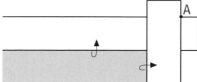

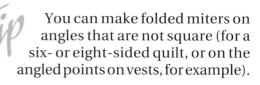

You can make folded miters on angles that are not square (for a six- or eight-sided quilt, or on the angled points on vests, for example).

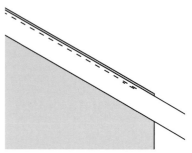

As you fold the binding the first time, make sure that the binding strip extends straight back and lines up with the second edge of the quilt.

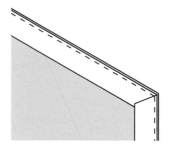

As you fold it down, the fold at the top edge of the binding may not be perfectly even with the first edge because of the different angle. It should still touch the first side at the point, creating a small tuck when you continue stitching the binding to the quilt.

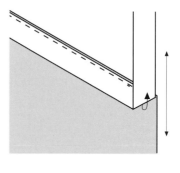

6. On the wrong side of the binding, draw a line from point A into the corner seam at point B.

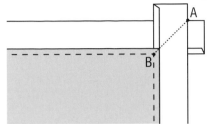

7. Place your ruler along the stitching line and make a mark at the folded edge of your binding, directly across from the corner seam at point C.

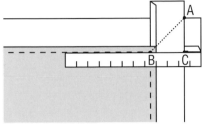

8. Lay your ruler so that it touches point C and the diagonal line. Draw a line from point C to the line at point D.

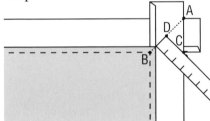

9. Place the binding strips right sides together, matching points A.

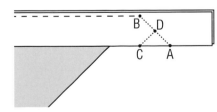

10. Stitch from B to D to C as shown.

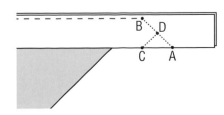

11. Trim the seam to ¼" and finger press it open. Turn the binding over the edge to the back of the quilt, forming miters on the front and back.

12. Slipstitch the binding to the back of the quilt.

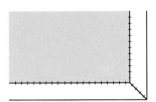

OVERLAPPED CORNERS

Overlapped corners are an option if you do not want to apply the binding in one long piece.

1. Cut binding strips to fit each side of the quilt, cutting each one 4" longer than the quilt side measures. This allows extra fabric to overlap at the corners. See pages 285–89 for directions on how to cut binding strips for your choice of traditional or French binding.

2. Stitch a binding strip to two opposite sides of the quilt, stitching from one cut edge to the other.

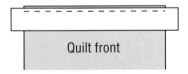

3. Fold the binding over the edge to the back of the quilt and slipstitch in place. Trim excess fabric at each end.

4. Stitch binding strip to each of the two remaining sides of the quilt, having 2" of binding extend at each end.

5. Trim away excess binding strip at each end, leaving a ¼"-wide seam allowance at each end.

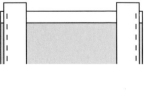

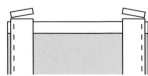

6. Fold the cut ends of the binding over the first binding strips to the back of the quilt.

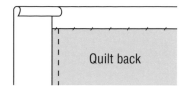

7. Fold the binding to the back of the quilt, enclosing all cut edges. Sew remaining binding to the back of the quilt, stitching the corners with a blind stitch.

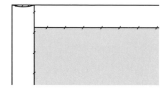

ROUNDED CORNERS

Rounded corners are easy to bind with bias-cut binding. There's no stopping to turn and miter corners, so they take less time. To round off the corners of your quilt before applying the binding, see page 279.

1. Baste the quilt top, batting, and backing together at the outer edges. See page 283.
2. Cut and prepare the binding, following the directions for the method of your choice (traditional or French binding.)
3. Position the binding on the quilt top with raw edges even. Do not clip the binding to make it fit around the curve. Instead ease binding onto the curve. Stitch the binding to the quilt, following the directions for the type you are using. At the curve, be careful not to stretch binding as you position and stitch it in place. If the binding is stretched, the corner will not lie flat when it is finished.

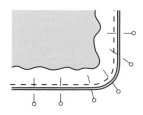

Tip Use a long straight pin to ease the binding under the presser foot on your sewing machine. Take a minute to pin the binding around the curve before you sew. Easing the fabric around the curve provides adequate fabric to allow the binding to lie flat along the edge when you turn it to the back of the quilt.

4. Turn the binding to the back of the quilt and stitch in place by hand.

SCALLOPED EDGES

Scalloped edges create a beautiful finish, especially on appliquéd quilts. Scallops along the edge may reflect part of the pattern, as in some Dresden Plate quilts, or you may want to use scallops to accent the style of your quilt. Always cut binding for curved edges on the true bias so it will fit around curves smoothly.

Sewing binding to scalloped edges combines two processes: applying the binding around a curve and turning an inside corner. If you have rounded off the corners of a quilt to apply binding, then you are halfway there!

1. Baste the three layers of the quilt together, ¼" from the outside edges. This is especially important when working with curves, because bias edges will slide under the presser foot as you sew on the machine.

Tip If your scalloped curves are marked on the quilt top but have not been cut, you can first apply the binding to the marked fabric and later trim the curves.

2. Begin applying the binding on one side of a curve, never at an inside corner, to avoid difficulty finishing the ends where they meet.

Do not start on the outer, most rounded edge of a scallop either, as a joining seam will be more noticeable in that location.

As you position the binding around the curve, do not stretch the binding. Place the binding so that the cut edge of the binding matches the cut edge of the curve.

As you pin the binding around the curve, ease the fullness in the binding so that it matches the seam line of the quilt. Pin the binding around one curve at a time before you sew.

Begin stitching, leaving the first inch of binding free. Stop stitching at inside corner.

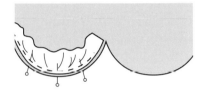

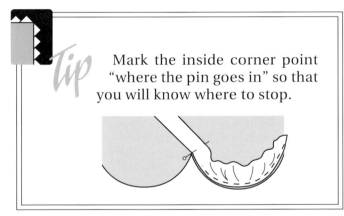

> Mark the inside corner point "where the pin goes in" so that you will know where to stop.

As you sew around the curve, use a long straight pin to help you maneuver fabric under the presser foot on your sewing machine. The small amount of easing around the curve of the scallop allows binding to turn over the curve of the scallop and lie flat when it is finished.

3. Do not stop and backstitch when you reach the inside corner. Leave the needle in the fabric and lift the presser foot. Turn the binding so that it is ready to apply to the next scallop. Pivot and continue stitching for 1".

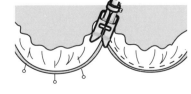

While the quilt is still under the needle, pin the binding to the next scallop and continue stitching to the next inside corner.

4. To turn the binding to the back of the quilt, turn one scallop at a time. When you get to the inside corner, turn one side of the corner to the back and pin it on the back. As you turn the second side of the corner, a folded miter will form. The deepest part of the tuck will be at the outer edge of the binding. As the binding turns to the back of the quilt, the fold will taper to lie flat along the sewing line.

5. Stitch the inner edge of binding to the back of the quilt, stitching the mitered fold in place with a few blind stitches.

Connecting the Ends

When using a continuous strip of binding to finish the edges of your quilt, you will need to finish the ends where they meet on one side of the quilt. Choose one of the following methods.

Method One

1. Stop sewing approximately 4" from the starting point. Cut the end of the binding so that it overlaps the beginning piece by 1".

2. Turn under ½" at the end of the binding.

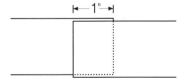

3. Insert the beginning "tail" inside the fold.

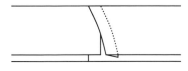

4. Continue stitching, overlapping the beginning stitches to secure both ends of the binding.

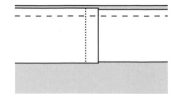

5. Turn binding to the back of quilt and stitch in place. It may be a little thicker where the two ends of the binding overlap, but this is not very noticeable on a large quilt.

Method Two

To avoid a bulky area where the binding ends meet, try this method.

1. Apply the binding to the quilt edge and stop stitching 4" from the point where binding begins.
2. Cut the end of the binding so it overlaps the beginning of binding by 2". 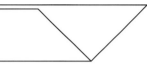 Cut end diagonally, with the shortest end of the diagonal on top, nearest to you.
3. Turn under ¼" at the diagonal edge.

4. Insert the beginning "tail" inside the binding at its diagonal end.

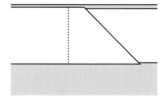

5. Continue stitching, overlapping the beginning stitches to secure both ends of binding.

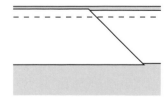

6. Turn the binding to the back of quilt and stitch in place. You may leave the diagonal folded edge loose, or you may blindstitch it to the binding.

Machine-Finished Binding

It is possible to apply the binding entirely by machine.

1. Sew the binding to the back of the quilt rather than to the front.
2. Turn the binding to the front. Carefully pin all around the quilt to keep the binding in place and prevent it from slipping. Pin the mitered corners securely. Make sure that the binding covers the machine stitches.
3. Machine stitch the binding to the quilt along the fold at the inner edge of the binding. You will be sewing through the binding and the three quilt layers. This may be bulky, but you can use a long pin to control it while you stitch. The machine stitches produce a nice finished edge on the front of the quilt, but it's difficult to control the position of the stitches on the back of quilt.

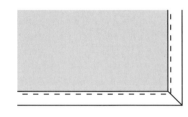

4. If your quilt has mitered corners, ignore the miters as you sew around the binding by machine. Pivot at each inside corner and continue stitching. The miter will survive if you just leave it folded, but you may want to close the miter with a few small blind stitches done by hand. See page 295.

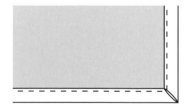

5. As you stitch around the quilt, continue sewing over the point where the binding overlaps the beginning point. Backstitch. Blindstitch the binding layers together at the overlap if you wish.

SPECIAL
FINISHING TECHNIQUES

There are several special finishing techniques that are fun to add to your quilts. Prairie points, pregathered lace, ruffles, pleats, and covered cording all create special effects as a frame for your quilt.

If your quilt is already quilted, apply these special finishing touches to the front of the quilt and batting. Move the backing out of the way as you sew.

Attach the prairie points, lace, ruffles, pleats, or covered cording (without binding) to the right side of the quilt front, using a ¼"-wide seam allowance and stitching through the batting.

After stitching the trim in place, trim the batting close to the seam. Then fold the trim out away from the quilt, turning the seam allowance in toward the quilt.

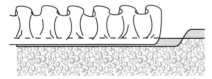

Turn the seam allowance of the backing fabric under ¼" and pin the back of the quilt to the back side of the trim, covering the seam and the machine stitches.

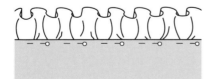

Sew the backing to the trim, using a blind stitch or slip stitch.

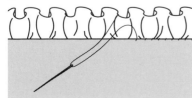

If you are sewing the trim to your quilt before you quilt or tie it, first sew the trim around the front edge of the quilt only. Then place the front and back of the quilt right sides together, sandwiching the trim inside. Stitch ¼" from the edge, sewing with the front on top and leaving an opening to turn the quilt right side out later. Attach the batting, referring to the machine-finishing directions in "Finishing without Binding" on pages 278–80, to complete your quilt.

Covered Cording

Add a very special tailored effect to your quilt by inserting covered cording between the quilt top and the binding. You can also finish the edge of a quilt with cording only, inserting it between the front and back of the quilt to add a colored accent and create the illusion of a very narrow binding.

To make covered cording:

1. Purchase cording of the desired diameter in the length required to fit around the outer edge of the quilt, plus ¼ yard extra.
2. To cover the cording, cut and join strips of fabric as you would cut binding strips. Cut the strips on the bias or straight of grain in a width that will fit around the cording, plus two seam allowances. See pages 285–89. If you are applying cording to curved edges, cut the strips on the bias.
3. To cover the cording, fold the fabric strip, wrong sides together, around the cording, pushing the cording snugly into the center of the strip.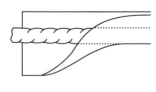
4. Set the sewing machine for 6 stitches per inch. Using a zipper foot with the needle set in the left-hand notch, stitch close to cording.

5. When you have enclosed the entire piece of cording, trim the seam allowance to an even ¼" width. *If you plan to apply cording with binding (below), cut the seam allowance to the desired finished width of the binding.*

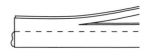

ATTACHING COVERED CORDING

Use one of the following methods:

Method One: With Binding

1. Baste the three layers of the quilt together around the outside edges.
2. Sew the cording to the quilt with raw edges even, using a zipper foot to stitch close to the cording.
3. Apply binding to quilt, positioning it on top of cording and stitching through all layers.
4. Turn the binding to the back of the quilt over the edge of the seam allowance and stitch in place. The cording will appear as a fine line of color between quilt and the binding.

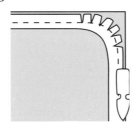

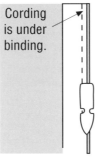

Cording is under binding.

Cording
Binding

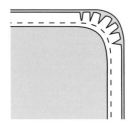

Tip When sewing cording around a curve, avoid stretching it as you stitch. It does not require easing like binding does. However, you may need to clip the cording seam allowance a few times so it will lie flat. Do not clip past the stitching line.

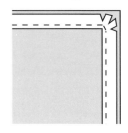

If you are sewing cording around a square corner, stop sewing 1" from the corner. Clip the cording seam allowance three or four times near the corner. Continue stitching to the corner. Stop with the needle in the fabric and lift presser foot. Turn the fabric slightly and take two small stitches across the corner. Lift the presser foot again and turn the fabric to sew the next side.

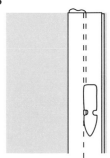

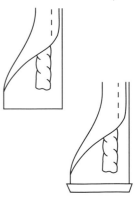

Method Two: Without Binding

1. Lay the cording along the edge of the quilt so that the cut edge of the cording and the cut edge of the quilt are even. Using the zipper foot, sew cording to the quilt, using a ¼"-wide seam allowance.
2. When you reach the starting point, cut the cording so that the two tails overlap 1". Open stitches on the end tail and cut off 1" of the inside cording.
3. Turn under ¼" at the cut edge of the cording fabric, cutting either straight or diagonally as you prefer.

Tip This finish adds thickness at the edge of the quilt. When planning the binding width, add an extra ¼" so it will turn easily over the edge of the quilt. You may need to trim the edge of the quilt slightly after you apply the binding if it does not adequately cover the stitching line on the back of quilt. Before you attach the binding to the back of the quilt, examine cording seam carefully. You may want to redo some sections to cover any stitches you may have missed.

4. Insert the beginning end of the cording, covering all raw edges.

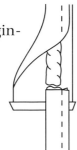

5. Stitch the remainder of the seam.

6. Sew the front and the back of the quilt together by hand or machine as shown on pages 278–79. If you sew them together by machine, continue to use a zipper foot. It will ride easily next to the cording thickness and position your stitches correctly. Sew with the front of the quilt on top so you can see the previous stitching. Sew just to the left of these stitches to hide them in the seam.

Prairie Points

Prairie points are small folded triangles placed along the edge of the quilt. They may repeat a triangular motif in the design of your quilt, duplicate the color scheme, or accent the design. They may all be made from a single fabric or from several that were used in the quilt top.

1. To make 1 prairie point, start with a 3" fabric square. Fold the square in half diagonally, wrong sides together.

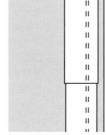

Note: Every 20" of quilt edge takes approximately twelve prairie points of this size when they are overlapped. It will take approximately 1½ yards of fabric to make enough points for a large quilt.

2. Fold it diagonally again, forming a smaller triangle.

3. Make another prairie point, then slip the fold of one point into the opening of the other.

You may overlap the points a little or a lot, depending on the look you want or on the amount of available fabric.

4. To position the points on the edge of the quilt, place one in the center of one side of your quilt, with the long cut edge of the triangle even with the cut edge of the quilt top.

5. Position a point at each end of the side, making sure that the folded edges of the triangles point in the same direction as the first one.

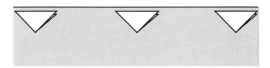

6. Place another point between these triangles, then continue to arrange more triangles in between until the side of the quilt is filled with points. Tuck each prairie point inside the next to make a continuous line. Overlap them a little or a lot; just make sure they are evenly spaced.

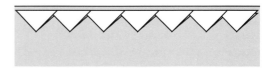

7. At the corners, place two triangles as shown so that they fit together side by side. They should not overlap. When you sew them to the edge of the quilt, pivot where the prairie points meet at the corner.

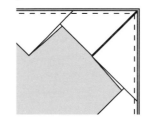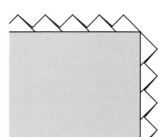

Tip It's easy to make a long string of prairie points to attach to a large quilt. Make the points, then start feeding the first point into your sewing machine, placing the cut edges on the right as you sew, and the folded tip under the needle.

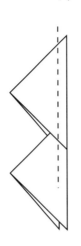

Machine baste for 1", then feed the next point into the first one, overlapping approximately ¾".

Continue sewing and feeding points until you have a chain of points long enough for one side of your quilt. Repeat for the remaining sides.

8. To sew prairie points to the quilt, first pin the cut edge of the points to the cut edge of the quilt top. If you have made a long string of points, make sure that you have the same number of points on opposite sides of the quilt. You may need to shift a few end points to fit the side of the quilt accurately.

9. Stitch ¼" from the edge all around the quilt top. To complete your quilt, refer to the directions on page 299.

Ruffles

Add a gathered or pleated ruffle to your quilt for a special, feminine touch. You can purchase ready-made ruffling or gathered lace trims and eyelet by the yard, or you can make your own to coordinate with the fabrics in your quilt. See the directions on pages 303–4. For a more tailored look, pleat the ruffle as shown on pages 304–5 instead of gathering it.

If you are purchasing ruffling or lace, buy enough to fit around the outer edge of your quilt, plus ¼ yard.

ATTACHING PURCHASED RUFFLING

1. Beginning several inches from one corner, place the ruffling at the outer edge of quilt top, right sides together, with the edge of the ruffling even with the raw edge of the quilt top.

2. Stitch, leaving a 2"-long tail unstitched at the beginning. Use a ¼"-wide seam, sewing along the inside edge of the gathers to make sure that the ruffled binding is completely caught in the seam.

3. Stop stitching 1" from the second corner. Use a long straight pin to push the ruffling under the presser foot, adding more fullness to the gathers there.

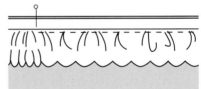

4. When you reach the corner, leave needle in the fabric, lift the presser foot, and pivot to stitch the next side. Continue adding fullness to the gathers for the first inch from the corner. This trick gives your ruffle enough fullness to "fan out" around the corner when you turn it away from the edge of the quilt. Even if you have rounded the corners, it is still helpful to add some fullness as you sew the ruffling or lace around the curve.

5. When you reach the place where the ruffling started, choose one of the following ways to finish the ends. Then complete the quilt, following the directions on page 299.

Make a Seam in the Ruffle

1. Cut the two ends of the ruffling so that they overlap ½".

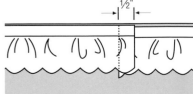

2. With ruffling ends right sides together, stitch ¼" from the raw edges.

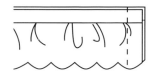

3. Finish stitching the ruffling to the quilt top.

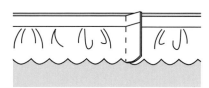

OR

Turn Under the Beginning Tail

1. Turn back 1" on the beginning tail of the ruffling. Stitch the ruffling to the quilt top ¼" from the raw edge.

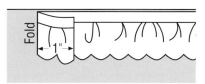

2. Trim the end of the ruffling so it overlaps beginning tail by 1".
3. Finish stitching the ruffling to the quilt top. The fullness of the ruffle will hide the cut edges on the wrong side of finished ruffle.

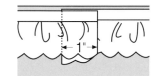

OR

Tuck in the Tail

1. If your ruffle is made of a double layer of fabric, you can conceal the cut edges by cutting the tails so that they overlap 2".
2. Turn under the cut edge ½" on one tail and tuck the other tail inside.
3. Finish stitching the ruffling to the quilt top; you have a finished edge on the front and back of the ruffle.

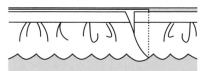

MAKING GATHERED RUFFLING

1. Cut fabric strips for custom-made ruffling on the bias or straight grain of the fabric. For a pretty doubled ruffle, cut the strips twice the desired finished width of the ruffle, plus ½" for two seam allowances. For example, if you want a 2"-wide finished ruffle, cut 4½"-wide strips of fabric, which allows 2" for the front half of the ruffle, 2" for the back half, and two ¼" seam allowances. A double ruffle is attractive on the front and the back. When you make a double ruffle, you also avoid the necessity of hemming yards and yards of fabric.

   You will need to cut enough strips to equal at least twice the distance around the quilt top for a full, beautiful ruffle. Less fullness looks skimpy.

> *Tip* If you own a serger, you may want to make a single-layer ruffle with a decorative, rolled edge finish. If so, be careful to choose fabric for the ruffle that is attractive on the right and wrong sides. Many printed quilting fabrics have wonderful, rich color on the right side but are washed out on the wrong side and are, therefore, not very attractive.

2. Stitch the fabric strips together to make one long strip. Use ¼"-wide seams and press them open.

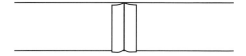

3. Sew the two short ends of the strip together to make a continuous circle.

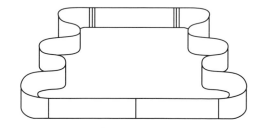

4. Fold the strip in half, wrong sides together, with cut edges even. Steam press the two layers together for easier handling.

Fold

5. Divide the strip into halves and then quarters; mark these four points with pins.

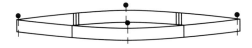

6. Prepare the strip for gathering, using one of the methods in the box below.

7. Divide the distance around the edge of the quilt into quarters and mark these points with pins.

8. Pin the strip to the quilt top with raw edges even and center- and quarter-point pins matching.

9. Gather the strip to fit the quilt top, working from pin to pin and adjusting the gathers evenly. Allow a little extra fullness at each corner so the ruffle will lie smoothly without pulling when turned away from the quilt top. Pin.

10. Stitch the gatherd ruffle to the quilt top ¼" from the raw edges. Finish your quilt, following the directions on page 299.

MAKING PLEATED RUFFLING

Instead of gathering your ruffling strip, you may pleat it for a more tailored look. As you consider using pleats along the quilt edge, remember that pleats are easy to apply if the square corners of your quilt have been rounded off. Refer to "Rounded Corners" on page 296, to prepare the corners of your quilt.

1. Cut ruffling strips on the straight grain of the fabric. For knife pleats, cut enough strips so that when joined, the ruffle will measure twice the distance around the edge of your quilt. For box pleats, it should measure three times that distance. Cut the strips twice the desired finished width, plus ½" for the two seam allowances. For example, if you want pleats that are 1½" wide, cut a strip that is 3½" wide, which allows 1½" for the front half of the ruffle, 1½" for the back half, and two ¼"-wide seam allowances.

2. Piece binding strips together to make a strip long enough to pleat and fit around your quilt. Join the short ends to form a continuous loop.

3. Fold the crosswise loop of ruffling in half. Use a pencil or water-erasable marker to make marks 1" apart along the cut edge of the strip for pleats 1" wide. For narrower pleats, space marks ½" or ¾" apart.

4. Make knife pleats or box pleats, following the directions in the box on page 305.

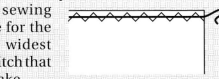

Fold

GATHERING A RUFFLE
Method One: Machine Basting
1. Machine baste ⅛" and ⅜" from the raw edges. Loosen the tension if possible.
2. Pull up on the bobbin thread to gather (while praying that it doesn't break).

Method Two: Heavy Thread
1. Set the sewing machine for the longest, widest zigzag stitch that it will make.

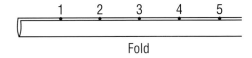

2. Lay a piece of heavy thread or crochet cotton ⅛" from the raw edge of ruffle. Zigzag over the thread, being careful not to stitch into it.
3. To gather, draw up on the heavy thread.

To make knife pleats:

a. Fold mark 1 forward to match mark 2, creating a pleat. Pin.

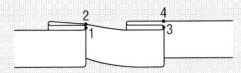

b. Fold mark 3 to mark 4. Pin.

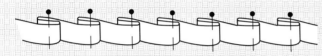

c. Continue folding pleats and pinning in this manner until you have pleated the entire strip. Machine baste pleats in place if desired.

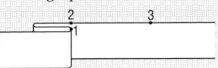

To make box pleats:

a. Fold mark 2 back to match mark 1.

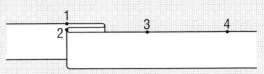

b. Fold mark 3 forward to match mark 4, making a box pleat.

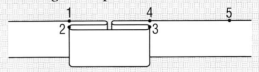

c. Continue folding one pleat back, then one pleat forward, until entire strip is pleated.

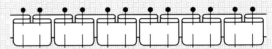

4. Pin the pleated ruffle to quilt top with raw edges even, easing them a little around the curved corners. Stitch ¼" from the raw edges. To finish your quilt, refer to the directions on page 299.

GLOSSARY OF STITCHES

Hand Stitches

If you do not wish to use the sewing machine, you can use hand stitches to sew the front and back of the quilt together, to sew binding strips together, to make covered cording, and to sew the binding to your quilt.

Running Stitch

Use the running stitch to sew layers of fabric together. Thread a hand sewing needle with a single strand of thread about 18" long and tie a knot in one end. Use a quilting needle or a longer one if you prefer. Take two or three short stitches at a time, sewing in and out through the layers of fabric to join them. Every 2" or so, take a small backstitch to strengthen the running stitches.

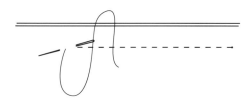

End stitches by sewing two small back-stitches, bringing the needle through the loop to secure your thread.

Quilting Stitches

Quilting stitches are short running stitches used to sew the front, batting, and backing of your quilt together. For complete directions on hand quilting, see "Loving Stitches," beginning on page 225.

Basting Stitches

Use basting stitches to hold layers of fabric together while you sew the final seam. They are usually removed after the seam has been sewn. Basting stitches are long running stitches, stitched with the "ins" and "outs" approximately 1" apart.

They are usually stitched one or two stitches at a time. To make it easy to remove basting stitches later, do not backstitch.

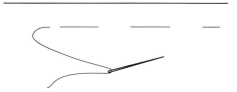

Finishing Stitches

Choose either the blind stitch (sometimes called the appliqué stitch) or the slip stitch to finish attaching the binding to the back of the quilt or to sew the front and back edges of a quilt together when it is not bound.

Machine Stitches

When you are constructing your quilt, sewing the front and back together, or applying binding or special edge finishes, set the stitch length on your machine for 10 to 12 stitches per inch. This size stitch is very secure, and your seam ripper will fit under it easily if you should need to use it.

When machine piecing a quilt, sewing binding strips together to make a long strip, or making continuous binding (pages 286–89), set the stitch length on your machine at 12 to 15 stitches per inch. These smaller stitches will hold the pieces together more securely.

When machine basting, set the stitch length at 6 stitches per inch. Use machine basting to sew the outer edges of the quilt layers together, when preparing a string of prairie points (pages 301–2), for gathering ruffles (page 304) and basting folds in pleats (page 305), or when making covered cording (pages 299–301). These longer stitches hold the fabric layers together but are easy to remove after the permanent stitching is completed.

ADDING A SLEEVE

If you plan to hang your quilt on the wall, add a hanging sleeve to the back.

1. Cut a strip of fabric 6"–8" wide and ½" shorter than the finished width of the quilt.
2. Turn under ¼" at each end. Press. Turn under again and stitch. Fold strip in half lengthwise with wrong sides together and long edges even. Stitch ¼" from the raw edge.

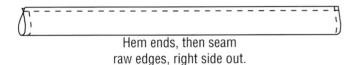

Hem ends, then seam
raw edges, right side out.

3. Press the seam open, centering it on the "tube" you have created.

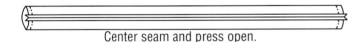

Center seam and press open.

4. Position the tube just below the inner edge of the binding with the seam against the quilt backing. Blindstitch the top edge of the tube to the quilt, being careful that your stitches do not go through to the front of the quilt.

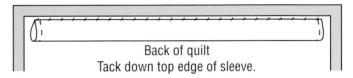

Back of quilt
Tack down top edge of sleeve.

5. Scoot the tube up a little before blindstitching the bottom edge in place. This adds a little give to the sleeve so the hanging rod doesn't put too much strain on the quilt.

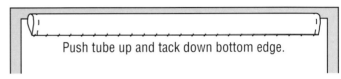

Push tube up and tack down bottom edge.

6. Insert a hanging rod through the sleeve and hang on two nails in the wall.

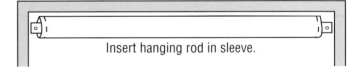

Insert hanging rod in sleeve.

SHARING YOUR HAPPY ENDING

You've finished your quilt by sewing the last 3" of binding securely, and you can't wait to take it upstairs and fling it on the bed to admire your finished masterpiece. But wait! Take a few moments to share some information with the future. Sign your newest work of heart with your name and other information you would like to remember. Record the date, celebrate the occasion, and dedicate it to someone special. Your quilt is now a part of history and you want to remember its story. Don't you wish your grandmother had done this with her quilts?

There are several ways to sign your quilt. You can use a thin-line permanent marker to write the information in a corner on the back of the quilt. You can write with a pencil or water-erasable pen, then embroider or quilt your inscription. You can also create a separate "designer" label to sew to the quilt back as shown below.

This information will bring back special memories after you have finished ten more quilts. Your family and friends will cherish your special "signed" gifts. It will help historians of the future remember you and help ensure a "happy ending" for your quilt as shown below.

Happy Endings
GALLERY

Finishing Your Quilt without Binding

Left: *Quilted corner*
Puffy edges
Rounded corner
Below: *Wide imitation*
binding
Appliquéd border

Finishing Your Quilt with Backing
Right: *Overlapped corner*
Mitered corner

Finishing Your Quilt with Binding
Below, clockwise from upper right:
Rounded corner
Folded mitered corner
Overlapped corner
Mitered corner

Finishing Your Quilt with Binding

Above: *Corded binding*

Special print binding

Striped binding cut on the diagonal

Striped binding cut on the straight grain

Below: *Rainbow binding*

Scalloped edges

Finishing Your Quilt with Special Techniques
Above: *Pleats*
   Covered Cording
   Prairie points
Below: *Pre-gathered ruffles*
   Fabric ruffles
   Eyelet lace

INDEX

CONTRIBUTORS

Mimi Dietrich

Mimi Dietrich is an award-winning quilter and the author of three "best sellers," *Happy Endings*, *Handmade Quilts*, and *Baltimore Bouquets*. She is a popular quilting teacher, whose workshops inspire students to share her enthusiasm and love for stitching.

Mimi lives with her husband and two sons in Catonsville, Maryland. She has written articles for national quilt magazines and is one of the "Founding Mothers" of the Village Quilters in Catonsville. She is also a member of the Baltimore Heritage Quilters' Guild.

Joan Hanson

Joan Whitelaw Hanson's infatuation with fabric began as a child when she spent many happy hours making clothes and quilts for her dolls. Joan taught home economics classes, and more recently has taught quilting in several quilt shops in the Seattle, Washington, area. Her first best-selling book, *Calendar Quilts*, was based on a class for which she designed twelve different quilts. She used a variety of quilt settings in this book. Her second book, *Sensational Settings*, carried this idea a step further, providing quiltmakers with a step-by-step method for planning quilt settings.

Joan lives in Seattle with her husband and two sons. Her love for fabric continues, as she tries to juggle kitchen, laundry, and carpooling duties with time for quiltmaking.

Jeana Kimball

Jeana Kimball has had an enduring fascination with all kinds of needlework, but it was the design freedom and personal expression quiltmaking offered that drew her to the study of quilts and ultimately to appliqué design. She has inspired and taught us all through her four books written for That Patchwork Place: *Reflections of Baltimore*; *Red and Green: An Appliqué Tradition*; *Appliqué Borders: An Added Grace*; and *Loving Stitches: A Guide to Fine Hand Quilting*.

Jeana lives in Salt Lake City, Utah, with her husband and teenage son and daughter. She is a well-known teacher and lecturer, with national and international audiences.

Donna Lynn Thomas

Donna Thomas made her first quilt—a gift for her husband-to-be—while she was a student at Penn State in 1975. She taught her first quilting class in 1982 and has been teaching ever since. She earned her National Quilting Association certification in 1988. After four years teaching and writing in Germany, Donna has returned to the States, still marveling at the universal warmth and sharing that seem to be typical of quilters.

Donna is the author of *Small Talk*, a book on miniature quiltmaking, plus the classic best sellers, *Shortcuts: A Concise Guide to Rotary Cutting*, and *A Perfect Match: A Guide to Precise Machine Piecing*. She lives in Kansas with her husband and two sons.

Roxanne Carter

Roxanne Carter is a prolific quiltmaker and quilting teacher. She has been sewing since the age of five, but it was quiltmaking that really sparked her creativity. The classes Roxanne teaches in Seattle-area shops are filled with students eager to learn her "tricks of the trade." Her quilts hang on the walls and grace the beds of her lovely home in Mukilteo, Washington. Roxanne's first book, *Shortcuts Sampler*, was written for That Patchwork Place.

Roxanne and husband Rob have a son, daughter, and two wonderful grandchildren.

Roxi Eppler

Roxi Eppler credits her artistic talent to her mother, who taught her to sew at the age of eight. After a brief flirtation with painting in the mid-1980s, Roxi "threw in the brush" and went back to her sewing machine. For the next two years, her wardrobe suffered as quilts became more important than clothes. Then she was inspired by a wonderful quilted garment worn by a fellow teacher at a seminar. Life has never been the same!

Roxi has designed for the Fairfield Fashion Show and has won several awards for her work. Roxi teaches classes locally and nationally. Her favorite quiltmaking technique, Smoothstitch™ Appliqué, is featured in all of the books she has written for That Patchwork Place. To pursue her love of quilting, Roxi's "real job" as a hair stylist has been cut back, so to speak.

That Patchwork Place Publications and Products

BOOKS

All the Blocks Are Geese by Mary Sue Suit
Angle Antics by Mary Hickey
Animas Quilts by Jackie Robinson
Appliqué Borders: An Added Grace by Jeana Kimball
Appliquilt™: Whimsical One-Step Appliqué by Tonee White
Baltimore Bouquets by Mimi Dietrich
Basket Garden by Mary Hickey
Biblical Blocks by Rosemary Makhan
Blockbuster Quilts by Margaret J. Miller
Calendar Quilts by Joan Hanson
Cathedral Window: A Fresh Look by Nancy J. Martin
Corners in the Cabin by Paulette Peters
Country Medallion Sampler by Carol Doak
Country Threads by Connie Tesene and Mary Tendall
Easy Machine Paper Piecing by Carol Doak
Even More by Trudie Hughes
Fantasy Flowers: Pieced Flowers for Quilters
    by Doreen Cronkite Burbank
Feathered Star Sampler by Marsha McCloskey
Fit To Be Tied by Judy Hopkins
Five- and Seven-Patch Blocks & Quilts for the ScrapSaver™
    by Judy Hopkins
Four-Patch Blocks & Quilts for the ScrapSaver™
    by Judy Hopkins
Fun with Fat Quarters by Nancy J. Martin
Go Wild with Quilts: 14 North American Birds and Animals
    by Margaret Rolfe
Handmade Quilts by Mimi Dietrich
Happy Endings—Finishing the Edges of Your Quilt
    by Mimi Dietrich
Holiday Happenings by Christal Carter
Home for Christmas by Nancy J. Martin and Sharon Stanley
In The Beginning by Sharon Evans Yenter
Jacket Jazz by Judy Murrah
Lessons in Machine Piecing by Marsha McCloskey
Little By Little: Quilts in Miniature by Mary Hickey
Little Quilts by Alice Berg, Sylvia Johnson, and
    Mary Ellen Von Holt
Lively Little Logs by Donna McConnell
Loving Stitches: A Guide to Fine Hand Quilting
    by Jeana Kimball
More Template-Free™ Quiltmaking by Trudie Hughes
Nifty Ninepatches by Carolann M. Palmer
Nine-Patch Blocks & Quilts for the ScrapSaver™
    by Judy Hopkins
Not Just Quilts by Jo Parrott
On to Square Two by Marsha McCloskey
Osage County Quilt Factory by Virginia Robertson
Painless Borders by Sally Schneider
A Perfect Match: A Guide to Precise Machine Piecing
    by Donna Lynn Thomas

Picture Perfect Patchwork by Naomi Norman
Piecemakers® Country Store by the Piecemakers
Pineapple Passion by Nancy Smith and Lynda Milligan
A Pioneer Doll and Her Quilts by Mary Hickey
Pioneer Storybook Quilts by Mary Hickey
*Quick & Easy Quiltmaking: 26 Projects Featuring Speedy
    Cutting and Piecing Methods* by Mary Hickey,
    Nancy J. Martin, Marsha McCloskey & Sara Nephew
*The Quilters' Companion: Everything You Need to Know to
    Make Beautiful Quilts* compiled by That Patchwork Place
Quilts for All Seasons: Year-Round Log Cabin Designs
    by Christal Carter
Quilts for Baby: Easy as A, B, C by Ursula Reikes
Quilts for Kids by Carolann M. Palmer
Quilts from Nature by Joan Colvin
Quilts to Share by Janet Kime
Red and Green: An Appliqué Tradition by Jeana Kimball
Red Wagon Originals by Gerry Kimmel and Linda Brannock
Rotary Riot: 40 Fast & Fabulous Quilts by Judy Hopkins
    and Nancy J. Martin
Rotary Roundup: 40 More Fast & Fabulous Quilts by Judy
    Hopkins and Nancy J. Martin
Round About Quilts by J. Michelle Watts
Samplings from the Sea by Rosemary Makhan
Scrap Happy by Sally Schneider
*Sensational Settings: Over 80 Ways to Arrange Your Quilt
    Blocks* by Joan Hanson
Sewing on the Line: Fast and Easy Foundation Piecing
    by Lesly-Claire Greenberg
Shortcuts: A Concise Guide to Rotary Cutting
    by Donna Lynn Thomas (metric version available)
Small Talk by Donna Lynn Thomas
Smoothstitch™ Quilts: Easy Machine Appliqué
    by Roxi Eppler
The Stitchin' Post by Jean Wells and Lawry Thorn
Strips That Sizzle by Margaret J. Miller
Tea Party Time: Romantic Quilts and Tasty Tidbits
    by Nancy J. Martin
Template-Free™ Quiltmaking by Trudie Hughes
Template-Free™ Quilts and Borders by Trudie Hughes
Template-Free® Stars by Jo Parrott
Watercolor Quilts by Pat Maixner Magaret and
    Donna Ingram Slusser
Women and Their Quilts by Nancyann Johanson Twelker

TOOLS

6" Bias Square®   Rotary Mate™
8" Bias Square®   Rotary Rule™
Metric Bias Square®   Ruby Beholder™
BiRangle™   ScrapSaver™
Pineapple Rule

VIDEO

Shortcuts to America's Best-Loved Quilts

Many titles are available at your local quilt shop. For more information, send $2 for a color catalog to That Patchwork Place, Inc., PO Box 118, Bothell WA 98041-0118 USA.

☎ Call 1-800-426-3126 for the name and location of the quilt shop nearest you.